THE MAN
IN THE
GLASS HOUSE

Also by Mark Lamster

Master of Shadows

Spalding's World Tour

Architecture & Film

THE MAN
IN THE
GLASS HOUSE

Philip Johnson,
Architect of the Modern Century

Mark Lamster

Little, Brown and Company
New York Boston London

Little, Brown and Company
Hachette Book Group
1290 Avenue of the Americas, New York, NY 10104
littlebrown.com

First Edition: November 2018

Little, Brown and Company is a division of Hachette Book Group, Inc. The Little, Brown name and logo are trademarks of Hachette Book Group, Inc.

The Hachette Speakers Bureau provides a wide range of authors for speaking events. To find out more, go to hachettespeakersbureau.com or call (866) 376-6591.

This publication was made possible by support from the Graham Foundation for Advanced Studies in the Fine Arts.

ISBN 978-0-316-12643-4
Library of Congress Control Number: 2018949012

10 9 8 7 6 5 4 3 2 1

LSC-C

Printed in the United States of America

For
John Manley
&
Robert Melik Finkle

I can't stand truth. It gets so boring, you know, like social responsibility.

—Philip Johnson

Contents

(Esto / Ezra Stoller)

Prologue

You cannot not know history."

Philip Johnson issued that famous maxim in 1959, and though he was talking about architectural tradition, he could just as well have been speaking about his own rich life, which was then barely past its halfway point. That life began in 1906 and ended in 2005, and he spent just about all of the ninety-eight years in between stirring up trouble.

There is hardly a city in America that is not graced—or fouled—by a building with Johnson's name on it, and often more than one. He craved attention, and made himself into a genuine celebrity. He was the architect of the imagination, a familiar face in his owl-frame glasses, a debonair, self-deprecating wit with a quip for every occasion.

His story, however, is much more than one of a charismatic man and his uneven architecture. Johnson lived the American century, and his story mirrored the nation's epic trajectory in that time. It opened with the highest aspirations and ambitions, embracing the possibilities of a modern world, yet concluded by abetting the accumulation of vast power and influence by a select few. His story, like the American story, was one of darkness as much as light; a story of inequity and bigotry, of the perils of cynicism, of human weakness and venality, of rampant corporatism, of the collapse of wealth and authority into the hands of a plutocratic class. Philip Johnson began his career proselytizing the public in the name of modern design. He finished it building for Donald Trump.

We cannot not know Philip Johnson's history because it is our history—like it or not. His dozens of works range in quality from the nadir of grim opportunism to the apex of civic and architectural achievement, but either way they shape our skylines, our streetscapes, and our daily lives.

Johnson's buildings are ubiquitous, but his influence far exceeds their mere presence. He was a shaper not just of individual structures or even of cities, but of American culture. When his interest first turned to architecture as a young man in the 1920s, modernism was an esoteric movement confined mostly to industry, social progressivism, and the occasional luxury residence. By the time of his death, the modern, with its sharp forms and sharp materials, was the defining language of the American city, the vernacular of business, and the default aesthetic of the avant-garde and the cultural aristocracy. He was not fully responsible for that shift, but he played an instrumental part in it.

His career began not as an architect but as a curator and a critic. Johnson was the founding director of the architecture department of the Museum of Modern Art, and one of its most important patrons. His gifts of painting and sculpture—works by Jasper Johns, Paul Klee, Roy Lichtenstein, Mark Rothko, Oskar Schlemmer, Andy Warhol—define that institution and its narrative of twentieth-century art.

But it was in architecture and design that Johnson exerted greatest influence. His landmark exhibitions established the way design is presented and understood; that both everyday objects and grand works of architecture are worthy of veneration. More critically, he used his platform at the museum to promote a controversial vision of what modern architecture could and should be—a modernity that was about form and style rather than the values that good design could promote: affordable, healthy, and environmentally sensitive building and planning that edified the private and public realms. When he tired of modernism he ushered in its rejoinder, postmodernism, and when he saw that as a dead end he reframed the field once again.

Johnson craved the attention that came with these reversals. He had a Barnumesque gift for publicity, and as with Barnum the principal beneficiary of his mythmaking was himself. Johnson, more than anyone, was responsible for the celebrity-driven practice—"starchitecture"—that came to dominate the profession at the end of the twentieth century and the beginning of the twenty-first. Through it all, he was a kingmaker, promoting the architects he favored and casting those he disdained into the wilderness.

He was controversial because he was happy to reverse himself, to lean in to his own hypocrisy, to occupy multiple positions even if they were diametrically opposed. Johnson was a historicist who championed the new, an elitist who was a populist, a genius without originality, a gossip who was an intellectual, an opportunist who was a utopian, a man of endless generosity who could be casually, crushingly cruel. For nearly a century, he had inhabited all of these oppositions, and countless others, concentrating in himself all of the contradictions and paradoxes of America and the century in which he lived. Not coincidentally, he was among the most loved and loathed figures in American culture. Many, somehow, loved and loathed him at once. Such was his strange charisma.

Johnson played to the image that he made of himself, especially in his later years: an avuncular, self-deprecating figure in a well-tailored suit. It was a long-practiced act that shielded him from criticism, suggesting that he was a harmless old wit, blameless for past transgressions. There were many of those, and not just sins of architecture. What he wished most to expunge from memory were his prodigal years in the 1930s when he launched himself as a virulently anti-Semitic fascist political leader, a would-be American Hitler, and an American agent of Nazi Germany.

He did what he could to redeem himself for those sins. He had always had Jewish friends, and they remained true to him. He promoted Jewish architects, built a synagogue without fee, and designed a nuclear reactor for the Israeli state. Did he expiate himself? The very question suggests Johnson's greatest gift, his unmatched capacity to occupy two poles at once.

Johnson's contradictions were embodied in the estate he built for himself in the verdant Connecticut suburb of New Canaan, and above all in the Glass House that was its centerpiece. It will always be the work that defines him: a simple rectangular box enclosed by glass, a modernist's platonic ideal of a home.

It was a tourist attraction and pilgrimage site for architects from the moment he moved into it, in 1949. Public curiosity became such a problem in its first year that he posted a sign along the road warding off intruders:

THIS HOUSE IS NOW OCCUPIED
PLEASE RESPECT THE PRIVACY OF THE OWNER

But in smaller type, that same sign promised hours when the house would be open for all to come and look. Was not the building of a glass house the ultimate demand for attention, to be seen? Indeed, his generosity in welcoming those many visitors was almost as legendary as the house itself. He loved to show it off, to give tours of its precisely landscaped compound, which he had embellished over the years with a series of buildings and follies, creating a private universe of his own, a pristine space removed from the cares and worries of the world. That had always been his dream, from long before he became an architect. "If I had all the money in the world I would just build continuously, and keep on experimenting," he wrote to his mother in 1930, more than a decade before he made architecture his profession.

The house, like the life he performed from it, was a work of provocation. He was a gay man with a fascist history living in a glass house, and he liked nothing better than to throw stones. He got away with it, usually. He liked to have other stone throwers he could play with, influential figures he could challenge and be challenged by intellectually. On any given day a visitor to the Glass House might encounter John Cage or Jackie O, Andy Warhol or Merce Cunningham, Jasper Johns or Robert Hughes, Frank Gehry or Isaiah Berlin. It was a place where one could speak seriously, where members of the intelligentsia mingled and mixed in sybaritic ease. As the legendary Yale architectural historian Vincent Scully put it, the house became "the most sustained cultural salon that the United States has ever seen."

Did Johnson actually live in the Glass House? People always asked. It was hard to believe he could, because it seemed more like an architectural manifesto than a place you could rightly call home. But he did live in it, at least in the early years. Even on those winter evenings when its thin glass walls made it almost insufferably cold; even on those summer afternoons when the sun's rays beat into it, trapping the heat indoors. Whatever one thought of him or his experiment in modern living, he had the audacity and fortitude to remain committed to it and until the very end.

Johnson's decline had been slow, the initial blow coming with open-heart surgery just after his ninetieth birthday. It was more than a year before he was back at his office on the thirty-ninth floor of the Seagram Building. It was through Johnson that Ludwig Mies van der Rohe, his architectural idol, secured that commission, and they designed it together, with Johnson as junior partner. His return was an event worthy of celebration, noted in *The New Yorker*'s Talk of the Town, but his participation in the life of the office was more ceremonial than active. He soon gave up his prime table downstairs in the Four Seasons, the power cafeteria he had created, in favor of bag lunches with an ever-diminishing circle of friends. He still liked to gossip, but those few initiates granted access found that their once-joyful sessions with him now had a melancholy air, and that his prodigious, steel-trap memory was beginning to fail. "The last time I saw him he didn't know who I was," said one prominent architect, who had been a frequent companion for lunch. "He didn't recognize me." Johnson's last appearance in the office came on a morose day in August of 2003. "I don't know where I am, and I never want to come back here again," he told John Manley, the gifted architect who had been his right hand for more than fifty years. His private nurse carried him out with the assistance of a draftsman.

David Whitney, his partner of forty-odd years, tried to insulate him from the world he had once courted, keeping even his close friends at bay, much to their chagrin. While he was still somewhat nimble, Johnson "hiked" the grounds of his New Canaan estate using a pair of trekking poles. They looked sporty enough so he did not think of them as canes. The idea of a walker was thoroughly abhorrent to him. Even in middle age, the thought of incapacitation was so terrifying that he simply wrote out of his life friends who became invalids.

A tai chi trainer came to the house a few times a week. Johnson practiced that meditative discipline indoors, in front of the Glass House's cylindrical red-brick hearth, the central anchor of the house. It was into that fiery maw that he had, years earlier, thrown the scrapbooks from his wayward years in the 1930s as a friend to the Nazis. Now, the area before the fireplace was the site of his daily exercise, a routine of light weights and stretching, often performed while leaning against the sliding doors of a wooden cabinet, which he burnished with his gentle buffing.

His body, however, was failing. He had a pacemaker and a replaced aortic valve. For years, he had worn specially made trifocal eyeglasses, modeled on those of the great Swiss-born architect Le Corbusier, but now even his eyesight was deteriorating. Increasingly deaf, he wore hearing aids in both ears. He had false teeth and barely ate; when he did, his Four Seasons diet of champagne and foie gras was replaced with consommé and toast. His drug regimen read like the catalog of a pharmaceutical supplier: Aricept, aspirin, colace, Diomax, Florinef, Lisinopril, Norvasc, Plavix, Prilosec, Proscar, Reglan, and Zocor, not to mention half a dozen vitamin supplements.

It was clear, in the frigid opening month of 2005, that after so long and so rich a life, his final days were upon him. He had never been a religious man, though he had acted the part when evangelical clients demanded it. He made no such pretense now. Johnson, who so loved the spectacle of society, ordered there be no great public ceremony upon his death, and that his ashes be committed to the fertile earth of his estate. He orchestrated his short remaining time with the same will to which he subjected his environment. His last days were a controlled aesthetic exercise. It was beauty, architectural and natural, that he worshipped, and he did so in an immaculate temple of his own design. He had his bed moved to the space in front of the fireplace that he loved so well, positioned so that he faced out toward his carefully manufactured landscape.

Johnson spent his last morning on the phone with Whitney, who had developed, by awful coincidence, his own terminal illness, lung cancer, now in an advanced stage. Knowing that he too would not survive the year, and wanting to make his own farewells to friends and relatives in California, Whitney had left Johnson for Big Sur, where the two had a vacation home, a playful shingled villa with stunning views and an observation tower shaped like a wobbly chess rook.

They had spoken the evening before, an emotional conversation, each at times breaking down, both knowing that the end was before them. It was okay, Whitney told Johnson; he could let go.

The next evening, as the clock approached ten, Johnson's attendants left him for a few moments, and a gentle snow began to fall through the New Canaan woods. Johnson had always thought the Glass House was most magical that way; the falling snow created the illusion that you were rising on what he called a "celestial elevator."

When his attendants returned, he was gone.

THE MAN
IN THE
GLASS HOUSE

The Johnsons of Cleveland: Philip, Louise, Theo, and Jeannette. (Getty Research Institute, Los Angeles)

CHAPTER 1

The Master's Joy

A sense of the fundamental decencies is parceled out unequally at birth.

—The Great Gatsby, 1925

On the morning of July 7, 1906, the *New York Times* led with coverage of the murder that had dominated the headlines for weeks. The victim was society architect Stanford White, shot dead on the roof of Madison Square Garden by the deranged husband of his showgirl mistress. Journalistic catnip, the story had all the ingredients required of a sensation: fame, wealth, sex, madness, beauty, and betrayal.

For the next ninety-eight years, those themes would define the life of the man who was in many respects White's heir, and who made his first appearance in this world that very afternoon.

Philip Cortelyou Johnson was not born in New York, the city where he would rise to fame, but in the Midwest, in the comfort of his family's substantial Cleveland home. If he did not arrive with a silver spoon in his mouth, one was surely close at hand. His father, Homer Hosea Johnson, was an established corporate attorney, a specialist in trust law in an era of great trusts, and at forty-four already a pillar of the community. His mother, the former Louise Pope, was the product of a distinguished line of Quaker industrialists, a dour matron with a sense of propriety as ample as her bosom, which was quite ample indeed. Their home at 2171 Overlook Road was a grand Tudor pile, with twin gabled wings facing over a broad lawn, and an expansive yard with a splashing fountain in the back. It was not quite a mansion like some of the neighboring properties, but it was of more than respectable scale for a growing family of quality and

3

aspiration. Johnson had developed it himself, along with several other properties in Cleveland Heights, an exclusive bedroom community that sat up on a brow overlooking a bustling metropolis on the rise.

These were promising days for Cleveland, an industrial metropolis just coming into its own. Old-timers could remember when the city was little more than a marshy lakeside outpost on the fringes of the national frontier. Within a generation, Cleveland had grown into something of a wonder, a small town transformed by iron foundries and steelworks, oil refineries, automotive plants, and myriad other factories. Proximity to the vast mineral wealth of the West, and a convenient situation at the nexus of rail and water transportation networks, made it appealing to business, "The Greatest Location in the Nation," according to civic boosters. Lured by jobs created on a grand scale, immigrants from Germany, Ireland, Bohemia, Italy, Poland, and elsewhere soon made it the fifth most populous city in the country. "The smoke of prosperity," according to one notable early historian, billowed from a thousand smokestacks. Most prosperous of all was John D. Rockefeller, the richest man in the world, who founded his Standard Oil empire along the muddy banks of the Cuyahoga.

The Cleveland of Rockefeller and the other barons of that age would not be a begrimed and sordid place. Daniel H. Burnham, the famous Chicago architect who made no small plans, gave the place a City Beautiful makeover. His vision transformed Cleveland into a showplace of grand avenues, monumental public buildings, and stone palaces. Overlook Road, the generously scaled, tree-lined thoroughfare on which the Johnsons made their home, was itself modeled on Euclid Avenue, Cleveland's "millionaires' row," then lined with the mansions of the city's ascendant aristocracy.

The Johnsons were comfortable operating in that society, even if their resources were of a more modest order. Homer, anyway, considered himself something of a gentleman. He traced his American roots back to one Jacques Cortelyou, a 1652 arrival in the New World, the source of his son's unusual middle name. He wore the signet ring of his father's clan, the Townsends, who maintained a seventeenth-century manor house, Raynham Hall, in the

English countryside. Homer eventually gave such a ring to his son, Philip, who thought it "pretty chutzpahish" to affect such airs.

Philip knew the less-than-glorious facts of the family history. Homer's grandfather, Hosea Johnson, was no aristocrat. The son of a millworker, he had been abandoned by his mother and raised by an aunt in western Massachusetts. In 1815 he came to Ohio, where he purchased land from a family in the rural town of New London. It was in the area known as the Firelands, large tracts of Ohio's Western Reserve set aside for those burned out of their homes by the British during the Revolutionary War.

Hosea worked that hardscrabble lot, making from it a living for himself and his family. In time, he passed it along to Homer's enterprising parents, Alfred and Philothea, who ran the farm and operated the local community bank. Homer himself was an only child, born in 1862 in New London, when Abraham Lincoln was president and the states were at war. The Johnsons were staunch abolitionists. They also believed in education, and were determined that Homer would not be a "dirt farmer" like his forefathers. When it was time for him to go off to college, he was instructed to clear a forested plot of the family farm and sell off the timber to meet his tuition. He went away to Amherst for two years, but returned to Ohio to be with his school sweetheart, Nettie Whitcomb. They graduated together from coeducational Oberlin in 1885.

Oberlin was more than just a place for rekindling that relationship. If the school today has a reputation as a bastion of far-left idealism, its progressivism was then congruent with the beliefs of Midwestern Republicanism, and it was understood to be a desirable institution for Ohio's bourgeois elite. Homer, handsome and popular, traveled easily in that society, a fraternity man—Phi Delta—with an eye to the horizon. "To hell with the past," he would say. "If you engage in a quarrel between the past and the present, your future is a failure." (His son, in his postmodern years, would have done well to heed that advice.) He earned his degree in classics, but one of his closest friends was Charles M. Hall, an ambitious young chemistry student who would, with Johnson's help, achieve extraordinary wealth.

Upon graduation, Johnson left to study law at Harvard, while Nettie moved west to Nebraska with her family. Long-distance relationships were difficult then as now, but theirs continued, in epistolary fashion. "Oh Darling I want you so much," he wrote to her. "You're the sweetest old girl I ever saw and I want to look at you right now." Homer got that wish the following spring, when she moved in with him at his Massachusetts boarding house. The couple was so ardent in their affections that their rather proper landlady refused to allow them back in the fall, as they were setting a poor example for her children. The couple returned to Ohio and married in 1888, but their storybook romance was abruptly and tragically foreshortened. Nettie became pregnant almost at once, but the child died soon after birth, and she did not last much longer herself. Within a year, she was dead from tuberculosis.

That double blow hit hard, but it focused Homer's attention elsewhere, specifically on his budding career as a Cleveland attorney. Homer Johnson was a man of easy charm, with the open, trustworthy face of a country parson and the gift of gab. Spencer Tracy could have played him in a film. That he radiated a sense of benevolent propriety attracted him to Cleveland's business leaders, who came to rely on the good counsel of his young firm, established in the year of his return from Harvard with M. B. Johnson (no relation), an Oberlin classmate.

Homer's friend Charles M. Hall became the firm's most important client. In a woodshed off his kitchen, Hall had developed a process to extract aluminum from bauxite. With Homer's encouragement and legal advice, he went on to capitalize on this invention as a primary shareholder of the Pittsburgh Reduction Company, which would change its name to the Aluminum Company of America, and later adopt the acronym that remains in force: Alcoa.

A free-spending young widower with a pleasant smile, a healthy bank account, and a way with words, Homer had no trouble finding companionship. He married again in June of 1896, to Elizabeth Gertrude Beggs, but the union was even shorter-lived than his first. Just two months after their wedding, while still on their honeymoon, Elizabeth died of pneumonia. Homer returned to Cleveland, crushed once more. But when he began to recover, he could at least take heart in the fact that he was not without prospects.

Louise Pope was not like Nettie or Elizabeth; she wasn't a charming looker, vivacious and gamine, the kind of girl who excited a man's passions. She would never receive love letters from Homer like the ones he'd sent to Nettie, flush with the desires of youth. Louise was no great romantic. She was stout and serious and proper, with a schoolmarm's demeanor — perfectly understandable, as she was just that. Seven years Homer's junior, she was born into a formidable clan, the Popes, a family of energetic Quakers from Maine by way of Maryland. Her grandfather, Alton Pope, built a textile business in a Quaker village outside Baltimore. With the onset of the Civil War, he decamped for the safety of Cleveland. Louise was the middle of five children born to Alton's eldest son, Edward, and his wife, the former Mary Elizabeth Riley, an Irishborn Canadian immigrant. Louise grew up in a fine house with a maid on fashionable Euclid Avenue, and for college was sent off to Wellesley, where she studied art history and sang in the glee club. (She was an alto.) She graduated in 1891, but continued her study of art history for a year after, returning to Cleveland following a European tour. She was especially inclined to the transformative late Gothic painting of Italy: Duccio, Masaccio, and — her favorite — Simone Martini.

While Homer's future seemed secure in the first years after his return from law school, the horizon was less assured for Louise. Her father, Edward, was not so facile a capitalist as either his father or his younger brother Alfred, who started out in the family textile concern, then made a fortune in iron and built himself an appropriately imposing Romanesque home on Euclid. Edward, meanwhile, floundered. He became dependent on his younger brother's largesse, and was forced to give up his own Euclid Avenue address for one considerably less grand. In place of servants there were boarders.

Louise's prospects were likewise shrinking; a life spent teaching math and hosting teas for the ladies of the Cleveland Wellesley Club (she was president) in her father's diminished house seemed to be in the offing. Meanwhile, her first cousin Theodate, Alfred's daughter, was inventing herself as an architect, though she'd never even attended college. Far worse, Louise had fallen for a handsome lawyer with a Harvard degree and a reputation as something of a prize among the eligible gentlemen of Cleveland society. That, of course, was Homer Johnson. Alas, he did not reciprocate her feelings. The two had known each other through social circles for years, and according to family lore he had long been aware of her feelings for him. Even then, he waited five years after the death of Elizabeth Beggs before finally taking Louise Pope to the altar, in October of 1901. It was a small affair, "near relatives and a few very intimate friends," Louise wrote to a cousin. By that time she was thirty-two and he was thirty-nine, and the match was something closer to a corporate merger than a romance.

The house they established was, predictably, a well-equipped but stern place. Now that she had means, Louise was quick to hire a full staff of her own. Two maids and a cook could soon be found dusting the furniture and preparing hearty meals at her Tudor manor, with a chauffeur minding a carriage house down the block. Keeping up with the Popes was clearly a priority. In 1901, the same year she and Homer were married, Louise's first cousin Theodate unveiled Hill-Stead, a riff on Mount Vernon that she designed for her parents in the Connecticut woods. (She got some help with the details from blue-chip New York architects McKim, Mead & White.)

Louise no doubt considered the idiosyncratic neocolonial house wildly gauche. To demonstrate her superior and more contemporary taste, she had her own home expanded. Frank Lloyd Wright was considered for the work, but she settled on J. Milton Dyer, a leading Cleveland architect who had studied at the École des Beaux Arts in Paris. The master bedroom, left to interior designer Louis Rorimer, was one of the most stylish spaces in Cleveland. Inspired by archaeologist Howard Carter's recent discovery of the tomb of Thutmose IV, Rorimer's design took the Art Nouveau and inflected it with an Egyptian theme of abstracted lotus buds, papyrus scrolls, pylons, and sunbursts—all carried out in the finest materials.

It was a showplace, but not too many people got to see it. Excepting the occasional gathering of Wellesley alumnae, the house was quiet, and the visitors few. Louise had a propensity for migraines and did not particularly care for company. Homer was more sociable, but he was also a strict prohibitionist, and this made an invitation to the Johnson home something less than an appealing proposition among his peers from the Union Club, the most selective of Cleveland institutions. He spent the preponderance of his leisure hours there, hobnobbing with the city's civic leaders. "Keep peace in the home at all costs," was one of his precepts. Often enough, his principal means for maintaining it was by not being there. The only regular guests were the family dentist and the local Unitarian minister.

As it was, the Johnson family expanded rapidly. Already in middle age, both Homer and Louise understood that if they were going to have children, as every respectable family must, there was little time to lose, even if neither was especially interested in or even suited to parenthood. A first child, Jeannette, was born in 1902 on the day they celebrated their first anniversary. A second, Alfred, came a year later, in 1903. Records suggest the couple lost another child either to miscarriage or stillbirth before Philip's arrival in the summer of 1906. A final child, Theodate, was born a year after Philip, in the summer of 1907.

There are no remaining photographs of the four happy siblings together. Alfred, who was bright and towheaded, died just two weeks shy of his fifth birthday, a victim of mastoiditis, an ear infection that is now easily treated with antibiotics. Philip was young enough at the time that, as an adult, he could not remember his death, or his brother at all. But the same was not true for his parents or his older sister. However distant Homer and Louise might have been as parents, the loss of their first-born son was a deep trauma, and it exacerbated Louise's already forbidding nature. Jeannette, too, was forever changed. She had doted on Alfred, and his loss transformed her into a hardened child, at once protective and domineering with her siblings. Philip and Theo, just a year separated in age, grew close, and came to resent their interfering older sister. "She was matriarchal not maternal," he would recall. "She'd always tattle on us. She was a little apart."

Homer Johnson at Townsend Farm. (Getty Research Institute, Los Angeles)

For the most part, it was not Louise or Jeannette, her self-appointed lieutenant, doing the mothering, but a series of European governesses, first of Swedish and then German origin. Philip could be forgiven if he came to see himself as a prop in his parents' kabuki act of haut-bourgeois respectability. An obedient son, he was happy, or at least amenable, when asked to play his part in the family drama. And so he became a walking doll, photographed in a succession of dresses (at the tail end of acceptability for boys), Lord Fauntleroy outfits, knickerbockers, and sailor suits as ordered by his mother. The clothes changed, but he always wore the same affectless expression. He had his father's round and fleshy face, but he was not inclined to smile. Even at age four, kitted out in an Indian chief's headdress, he evinced no emotion, but simply stared at the camera with a kind of blank self-possession.

Johnson was happiest while at play with his younger and more adventurous sister, Theo, whose gregariousness balanced his diffidence.

A joyless Johnson in native costume, at Townsend Farm. (Getty Research Institute, Los Angeles)

Their most pleasant hours were spent together at Townsend Farm, the New London acreage where Homer Johnson was raised, which he had assumed from his family and transformed into a gentleman's farm of more than three thousand acres. The family made the fifty-mile drive from Cleveland whenever they could, and almost always on weekends.

It was an alluring place. After decades of work in the fields, Homer's grandfather, Hosea Johnson, had saved enough to build a house up on a rise over his property. It was a home of prideful backwoods aspiration, a squat Greek Revival box of two stories, with four white columns out front supporting a pediment of overly grand proportion. The local carpenter who put it together, justifiably pleased with his efforts, celebrated the new home in verse:

She stands on a hill
And is plain to be seen.
What shall we call her?
We'll call her the queen.

Louise, inevitably, expanded the place with an extra wing and a porch in the back, though she always appreciated its down-home, American charm. As a matter of principle, Homer ordered that the field that had given its wood for his college education remain forever fallow.

For Philip and his sisters, Townsend Farm was a landscaped idyll of rolling meadows, apple orchards, decorative ponds, and tended woodlands. They kept to themselves, precluded by their parents from mixing with the local farm kids who ran around in overalls and bare feet. Philip had a dog named Brush and a chestnut horse named Snip on which he learned to ride, though he was never much of an equestrian. The area around the manor had the manicured look of a golf course, but Townsend Farm was in fact a working concern run by tenant farmers, with roaming cattle, lamb and pig pens, and sweeping fields of corn and wheat that

"The Queen," the house at Townsend Farm built by Johnson's great grandfather. (Getty Research Institute, Los Angeles)

towered over the heads of Philip and his sisters. At the age of five, Philip watched a gang of hired men in broad-brimmed hats and dungarees raise the wooden beams of a new tool barn by hand. It was his first exposure to the act of building.

Back in Cleveland, things were not nearly so relaxed for young Philip. He lived a sheltered and enclosed life, trapped in his room, a Rorimer showpiece of lacquered chinoiserie furnishings that was hardly suitable for a boy. Philip was just one more beautiful object on display. His native sense of isolation only increased after it came time for him to begin school. Louise started him off in kindergarten at the Laurel School, the lone boy in a class for girls. A year later he was switched to an all-boys school, where he fared poorly both socially and academically. Finally Louise enrolled him, along with Theo, in a public school in Shaker Heights. Each morning, the Johnson siblings were deposited there by limousine, an embarrassing situation that they tried to remedy by having themselves dropped off several blocks away, so they could walk in like everyone else.

Louise's protectiveness was exacerbated by the recurrent problems with mastoiditis that troubled both Philip and Theo. While on the family's spring holiday to the Blenheim Hotel in Atlantic City in 1911, Philip came down with his first case of the disease that had killed his brother.

By his own account, Philip was a loner at school. He ate his lunch by himself, and was reluctant to participate in sports and other group activities. The remoteness that had always been a part of his character, however, was metastasizing into a debilitating emotional affliction that would follow him throughout his early life: the son of Cleveland's famously silver-tongued lawyer stuttered. Homer's attempted remedy to this condition — a glass of water thrown in his son's face — proved ineffective. That incident was notable for the physicality of its abuse, which was unusual. More typically, Homer was some combination of distant and disapproving. That left Philip, who looked at him as an idol, pining for his rarely offered approval.

Homer's tough love did not help cure Philip of his diffidence. Nor did it shake him of the effeminate nature that Homer noted and that Philip did not yet fully understand. That he didn't know who he was manifested itself in his behavior. At school, he seemed congenitally incapable of completing assignments in a timely manner, despite his evident aptitude. Prolonged absences due to health and travel only increased his sense of isolation. Though the illness would not be diagnosed for years, Johnson was a victim of bipolar disorder.

Johnson's difficulties were compounded by the fact that he was not spending the entire school year in Cleveland. Beginning in 1915, the family decamped for the winter months to Pinehurst, a seasonal resort community in central North Carolina. Homer chose it for its golf program, then under the direction of Donald Ross, whose legend as a course designer and teaching pro was already substantial. Homer purchased a two-story shingle-style house, Rosemary Cottage, within walking distance of the clubhouse.

The "Cottage" wasn't really a cottage, but then everything at Pinehurst was something of a conceit, planned by the preeminent landscape architect Frederick Law Olmsted—the design visionary of Central Park—on the model of the traditional New England village. Always civic-minded, Homer and Louise established themselves as leading members of the community. Homer cofounded the Pinehurst Forum, a weekly discussion group for matters of political consequence. Louise, believing there was no adequate educational facility appropriate for her children, took the measure that might be expected of a woman of means who demanded her way in all things: she founded her own school. To helm it, she imported Mae Chapman, the principal of the Shaker Heights school in which Philip and Theo were enrolled the rest of the year. Chapman was a disciplinarian—a "bitch," Johnson recalled—but he kept his complaints to himself.

Louise was at turns smothering and detached. In those hours when the children were not at school, they were educated at home. "I was a pure mama's boy," Philip would recall. "I had no inkling that there was any knowledge in the world worth knowing except what she could tell me." Louise was particularly happy to lecture the family on art history, lantern-slide orations that would drone on interminably. Even Homer could not stop her once she built up a head of steam. "Just one more point," she'd protest, and forty minutes later she'd still be pontificating about some forgotten masterpiece at the Uffizi. For subjects in which she was not expert—botany, biology, Greek—she hired tutors. Homer, when he could, escaped to the links or the clubhouse.

The Johnsons spent the postwar summer of 1919 not at Pinehurst or Townsend Farm but in Europe. Louise, Jeannette, Theo, and Philip sailed in luxury on the Cunard Line's steamer *Aquitania,* just decommissioned from wartime service, and made a brief stopover in London before continuing to Paris, where they were reunited with Homer. Since March, he had been there as a member of the American delegation to the postwar peace deliberations. That he was tapped for such duty was a mark of his stature and connections, and also his interest in international affairs.

Homer's position came through Newton D. Baker, the Secretary of War, a former mayor of Cleveland and member of the Union Club. Knowing Homer was trustworthy, Baker appointed him to the four-man United States Liquidation Commission, which was charged with settling American accounts in postwar Europe. This was no minor appointment. The other commissioners included Henry F. Hollis, a former U.S. Senator from New Hampshire, and Charles Dawes, who would be elected vice president in 1924 on a ticket with Calvin Coolidge. Johnson liked to kid about this service—"I became the world's biggest mule dealer" — but the quips belied the scale of his responsibility. Together, he and his co-commissioners recovered some $893 million in American assets.

Homer's obligations to the commission were nearing a conclusion when the rest of the family arrived in Paris in July. The children, now in their teens, were pretty much left to their own devices. Philip, given his first taste of independence, learned the map to the Paris Metro by heart, and explored the city in all its breadth. Among his favorite activities was to ride out to the Parc des Buttes-Chaumont, a masterpiece of the Haussmann era, in the far reaches of the 19th arrondissement. He was initially attracted by its curious name, then discovered its romantic belvederes and ponds, waterfalls and toy pavilions. It could not help capturing the imagination of a dreamy boy on his own for the first time; this was what the family's New London estate could be, in the hands of a great designer. The experience would stay with him over the years, to be drawn on as he imagined the landscape he shaped for himself at his New Canaan estate.

While the Johnsons' experience of the cleanup of the Great War lacked nothing for comfort, they did venture out to see the carnage wrought in battle, scenes that offered a brutal contrast to the picturesque charms of Haussmann's grand avenues and romantic parks. Traveling in Homer's Army-issued Cadillac, they toured the bombed-out cities of Fismes and Reims. In Verdun, they spent a night exposed to the elements at the legendary Coq Hardi hotel, which had lost its windows during bombardment. The next day Homer was given a tour of the trenches and battlefields, then still restricted from the general public, though the bodies had been removed. Philip saw those ghostly killing fields, where more than three hundred thousand men lost their lives, from the safety and comfort of a chauffeured luxury sedan; the cataclysm of war seemed like nothing more than a curious spectacle offered up for his consumption.

The younger Johnson took little from that visit to the theater of battle. The side trip was just "sightseeing" that "meant nothing" to him, he would later recall. It would not be the last time he would take such a blinkered and touristic view of war's devastation.

After this trip, Homer once again separated from the family, engaged on yet another diplomatic mission, this time a fact-finding inquiry into atrocities committed against Jews in Poland in the months following the war's official conclusion. News of pogroms, reported in the Western press, threatened Poland's status as an ally at a time when it was seen as a bulwark against Soviet bolshevism. The three-man commission, led by the Jewish financier Henry Morgenthau, was to tour Poland, determine what actually happened, and make a report, ostensibly with a recommendation for future action that would preserve Poland's relationship with the West.

While Homer was traveling through Eastern Europe, the rest of the family made their way through the Jura to Geneva. Wherever they went, they encamped in style, Homer's position granting enough ration credits to insulate them from the austerity faced by local populations. The Johnson children were enrolled in school for the month of August to study and to refine their French. Afterward, they returned to the French capital through the château country of the Loire. The trip included a stop at Chartres for a visit to the great cathedral, which in later years Johnson would describe as a defining moment in his education. At once majestic and brooding, sublime and remote, the Gothic pile appealed directly to his adolescent personality, though his adult claims that his mother dragged him out of the place in tears of architectural exaltation seem dubious.

The family reunited in Paris. Philip, naturally gifted at languages, was especially pleased when his mastery of French proved so superior to Homer's that he was pressed into service as personal translator with his father's physician. As it was, Homer had larger problems than his difficulty communicating with Parisian medical professionals. After three months of travel through Poland, countless interviews, and audiences with any number of local officials, Morgenthau and his fellow commissioners could not reach an agreement on what they had seen, and chose to issue separate reports. The first, submitted by Morgenthau, meticulously documented atrocities committed in the cities of Częstochowa, Kielce, Lemberg, Lida, Minsk, Pinsk, and Vilna. These included the murder of 175 Jews and the ransacking of thousands of homes and businesses. Morgenthau concluded that these atrocities were conducted largely with the participation or tacit authorization of Polish governmental or military figures, and were the "result of a widespread anti-Semitic prejudice aggravated by the belief that the Jewish inhabitants were politically hostile to the Polish State."

This did not suit Johnson and the third member of the commission, U.S. Army general Edgar Jadwin. Their report, issued independently about a month later, whitewashed the atrocities, claiming—in contradiction of Morgenthau's findings—that "none of these excesses were instigated or approved by any responsible government authority, civil or military." Moreover, they determined that the "Polish nation is disposed to religious tolerance" and all but blamed the victims for their sorry situation, finding that "the history and the attitude of the Jews, complicated by abnormal economic and political conditions produced by the war, have fed the flame of anti-Semitism at a critical moment."

The report exemplified the casual anti-Semitism endemic in the United States generally, and in American political culture in particular. Beyond their very assimilated decorator Louis Rorimer (family name: Rohrheimer), the Johnsons had little meaningful interaction with Jews. Homer was perhaps even more biased against Catholics. His attitude toward blacks was paternalistic—he was a regular contributor to black colleges—a family tradition dating to their service in the Underground Railroad and in the Union Army during the Civil War. It was only natural that Philip, always a dutiful son, absorbed his father's prejudices.

The Johnson-Jadwin assessment of Polish affairs was most happily received. It was, of course, precisely what the American political establishment wanted to hear: that there was no need to antagonize an important and unstable ally over a few minor attacks on Jews, for which they were themselves to blame. Robert Lansing, the Secretary of State, delivered the Wilson administration's thanks for the "able and conscientious manner" in which Johnson had completed his service. Back in Pinehurst, he was given a hearty welcome at the annual banquet to begin the spring season, and in his remarks warned Americans to keep an eye on Europe while lamenting the difficulty of doing so, given the "corruption of sources of news and the coloring of press dispatches, which is a great evil and a great menace." In the coming years, it would be his own son doing that coloring.

As it was, beginning in 1920 Philip Johnson's dispatches were posted from Tarrytown, New York, where he was enrolled in the Hackley School, an elite college-preparatory academy for boys. Johnson, in his first year, was an odd fit. At fourteen, he was younger than most of his classmates, and even then he was small for his age. "Phil" was also something of a neat-freak. His obsessive behavior might have been seen as an emotional red flag, but at the time his constant picking-up after his roommate became a hall joke. (It is difficult not to view his need to exercise control over his environment, a trait he shared with his fastidious mother, as predictive of his future profession.)

The emphasis placed by headmaster Walter B. Gage on the benefits of athletic competition was also a problem. The football players were the school's chosen, but as the editors of the Hackley *Annual* gently put it, Johnson was "the intellectual type, rather than the athletic." The closest he got to the playing field was as manager of the track squad. In the afternoons, he could instead be found studying at the counter of the Tarrytown drugstore with a "full house" ice-cream soda. He didn't attend school dances, and the other boys picked up on his general air of reticence. In class pictures, he could always be found on the periphery, an outsider bearing his characteristic impassive gaze.

Academically he had few problems. Louise's relentless tutoring had placed him ahead of his grade in biology, Latin, and Greek, which was his favorite. His best subject was ancient history, his only weakness physiology. That he thrived most in a world of dead languages and lost civilizations was indicative of his social isolation. He was "the master's joy," according to his junior yearbook, the boy who "invariably has his lesson prepared and can recite it about ten percent faster and better than any other member of the class."

Success in the classroom bred self-assurance, if not arrogance. The stutter that plagued him resolved itself, and when it did his personality blossomed. He did, in fact, have his father's native gift for words, and also his interest in political affairs. In his junior year he came into his own, cofounding The Curia, a debate club dedicated to training its members in extemporaneous speech and to arousing "interest in current problems of the world and the school." Among its members was Alan Blackburn, a precocious, black-haired sophomore who had arrived midyear. The two became friends, and in the coming years would apply the skills honed in that club in ways their classmates would scarcely believe.

An emboldened Johnson became class secretary and editor of the yearbook as a senior, but his primary extracurricular activities were devoted to the arts, music in particular. He played piano in the Mandolin Club,

19

which covered the classical catalog and dance-hall numbers (there was, in fact, no mandolin player), and sang tenor in the Choir and Glee Club. He had a good, clear voice, and was just skilled enough at the piano to think he might have a future in it. He joined the Drama Club as well, and though he was no great thespian, he happily appeared in drag as an old lady, a character he played two years running. In another production, he appeared in blackface.

He had no romantic life, whatever. To the extent that he was beginning to recognize that he was gay, he repressed it. The only girl he had ever dated was Louise Rorimer, the daughter of his parents' interior designer, back in Cleveland. They shared a cosmopolitan bent and an interest in the arts, but that was the extent of their chemistry.

Johnson found a male role model in the person of Frank Bogues, the school drama teacher, whose benevolent presence earned him the affectionate nickname "Daddy." That name was particularly appropriate in the case of Johnson, as Bogues became the first in a series of older men to whom Johnson would attach himself. The two developed a mentor-protégé relationship that lasted well beyond Johnson's years at the school. They would often stay up talking deep into the night in Bogues's room. On weekends, Johnson took advantage of Tarrytown's proximity to New York and its cultural opportunities.

Johnson's immediate future, by then, was secure. By arrangement, the top two students at Hackley were automatically accepted into Harvard, and the only question was whether Johnson would be first or second in his class. (He finished second, to his aggravation.) Walter Gage, in an evaluation of Johnson for Harvard, sketched him as "a boy of sound character, well developed habits of study — brilliant mind," and "thoroughly reliable." His coeditors on the Hackley *Annual* had his personality pegged with somewhat greater precision. In that yearbook's final pages he appears in caricature wearing a pinstripe suit and owl-frame glasses, a uniform that would become familiar in the years to come. "Rhapsody of Words" was the title of his biographical sketch. Johnson, the editors wrote, "has very high ideals, but at times is rather careless in carrying them out." They could hardly have been more accurate.

CHAPTER 2

From Saul to Paul

The only thing I lack just now is, strange to say, self-confidence.
—Philip Johnson, 1927

Packing off to college is a trying rite of passage for even the most grounded of young adults. For Philip Johnson, still shy and insecure despite his maturation at boarding school, the anxiety was acute, and a long and lonely train ride from Cleveland to Boston did nothing to alleviate his apprehension. In Cambridge, he made his way to his quarters for the year: a three-bedroom apartment in Standish Hall, one of Harvard's red-brick freshman dormitories, to be shared with two other Hackley alums, Frank Couch and Carleton Smith. It was not quite so elegant as his digs back in Cleveland, but he had his own room, there was a study with a fireplace and a view of the Charles River, and—this being Harvard—maid service.

At the age of seventeen, he was truly independent for the first time, a state of affairs that left him feeling not so much liberated as deeply unsettled. The unfamiliar was scary, of course, and Harvard could be especially intimidating. Here was a new place with new people, many as bright and as cosmopolitan as he was himself.

This, however, did not account fully for his sense of unease. If it was just a bit of nervousness in his new surroundings, he would have gotten over it—like every other college freshman—after a brief period of adjustment. But there was a greater existential malaise that seemed to afflict him. Heretofore it had been left to his domineering parents to choose his path in life. To the present moment, he had scarcely made a decision of consequence for himself. Now, the most important of all, the task of personal definition, was his alone. Given his natural diffidence, so much freedom was altogether stultifying. "What a hopeless amount of things there are to know and be," he wrote to his mother.

Johnson's discomfiture was noted almost immediately, and prompted the Harvard College dean, Chester N. Greenough, to send a concerned inquiry about Johnson's personality to his parents. "My son is of a nervous, intense disposition and not inclined to have much patience if things do not go right," Homer Johnson wrote in reply. "I think he will learn by experience as some of the rest of us have had to, but he may be under the necessity of getting some hard knocks in order to learn." He worried, also, about his son's poor nutrition. "He has eaten so hastily and perhaps liberally a diet of milk and meat with very little fruit and vegetables that he has been considerably troubled with constipation," wrote Johnson *père*, proving himself the most unlikely of helicopter parents *avant la lettre*.

Homer delivered that assessment after a period of close observation during which he had come to know Philip on an intimate level as never before. Over the previous summer, the two had taken a father-son trip west by train to San Francisco. It was the most time they had ever spent together in such close proximity, and although there were a few highlights—a donkey ride through the Grand Canyon, a visit to the towering forests of Muir Woods—it was for the most part an uneasy experience for both men. No doubt it was undertaken as an opportunity for Homer to impart a sense of mental and physical toughness to his delicate son, though the nature of Philip's sexuality remained unstated. Louise, by contrast, had long since recognized that her son was gay, and treated him with sympathy, though she did not necessarily approve. (In later years, there were rumors within the Johnson family that Louise herself was gay.)

A reform of Philip's diet was one of the principal motivations for the journey, which included a side trip to Michigan's Battle Creek Sanitarium, a fashionable destination for health-conscious Americans of means. Under the direction of wellness guru John Harvey Kellogg—inventor, with his cereal-magnate brother, of toasted cornflakes—Battle Creek had achieved renown for its cures. The "Battle Creek System" entailed the examination of the blood and feces, followed by a series of natural remedies designed to achieve a healthy state, with emphasis on exercise and a controlled diet—drugs were not employed. The system appeared to be scientifically rigorous and rational, though today many of its treatments would fall into the category of pseudoscience. Homer, as fastidious about nutrition as he was about liquor, believed that his son's poor eating habits contributed to his emotional difficulties, a diagnosis in keeping with Kellogg's teachings. The Battle Creek System, with its emphasis on grains, laxative fruits and vegetables, and cleansing enemas of Bulgarian yogurt, offered a solution.

At Harvard, Johnson's problem was not so much what he ate but how he ate it—by himself. Whether at the Standish dining hall or the Georgian Cafeteria on Dunster Street where he was a regular, Johnson typically ate with his nose in a book. When not in class, he spent most of his time studying alone, though he devoted Friday evenings to the Boston Symphony. He made a handful of friends, but his primary act of sociability was to join the Glee Club. Otherwise, he was lonely. "I was an outsider, and I felt it at the time," he remembered.

Although he took some pride in his sophistication and social élan, Johnson was often his own worst enemy. He and Carleton Smith, his suitemate, liked to walk about campus speaking in French, an affectation that did nothing to endear them to their classmates. The would-be sophisticate was also something of a pedant. In a persnickety letter to the editor of the *Harvard Crimson,* for instance, he objected to a fellow student's use of the term "pacifist" as a descriptor when used only to describe conscientious objectors. He argued instead that a typical soldier might be opposed to war, but still fight given a higher commitment to the state and its laws, which he must obey "as he would his parents." That an individual might voluntarily disobey his parents still seemed anathema to him. It was, nevertheless, a well-crafted argument that demonstrated his rhetorical acumen, and hinted at an incipient authoritarian political bent. It was also the kind of letter that ensured one sat alone in the dining hall.

That he was gay exacerbated his problems. Harvard, in 1923, was not a congenial place for a homosexual man, though until recently it had harbored a raucous gay community. Prohibition had fostered a speak-easy culture in which the illegal was tacitly condoned, and the sense of sexual liberation that had flowered in Jazz Age New York had spread to more conservative Boston. At Harvard, the epicenter of this decadence was Perkins Hall, the dormitory of a congressman's son, Ernest Roberts, famous for his "bitch parties" with men in drag and flowing liquor. That all changed, dramatically, in 1920, following the suicide of a member of Roberts's circle. Harvard president Abbott Lawrence Lowell, a severe stick of a man who was the embodiment of Brahmin privilege and pro-priety, was in no way willing to accept homosexuals at Harvard. He formed a secret court to investigate the matter, then orchestrated a purge of the fourteen men it found "guilty," expelling them not just from cam-pus, but from the city of Cambridge—such was his power. Johnson was probably aware of what had transpired, but even if not, its effect on gay life at Harvard was deadening, driving it underground and imbuing it with a sense of threat and shame.

Lowell's intolerance and chauvinism informed campus life in other ways. He kept black men out of the freshman dorms (despite vociferous opposition) and attempted to sever the university's connection with women's college Radcliffe (without success). Lowell, a member of the Immigration Restriction League, harbored the same prejudice against Catholics as did Johnson's father. (In 1927, while Johnson was enrolled at the school, he led a commission that refused clemency for the anar-chists Sacco and Vanzetti.) Above all, Lowell made it a personal impera-tive to reduce the Jewish student population at Harvard, which had risen to 21.5 percent in the year before Johnson's arrival. The massive Jewish immigration to America had resulted in an influx of applications from high-achieving students who could not be rejected on the basis of aca-demic merit. Faced with this "Jewish problem," Lowell proposed what was effectively a quota system to resolve it.

That system directly contravened the school's egalitarian charter and was rejected by a divided Board of Overseers after considerable debate.

Louis Brandeis, the Jewish Supreme Court Justice and a graduate of Harvard Law, accused Lowell of being "blinded with privilege." Undeterred, Lowell instituted a series of "reformed" admissions policies that achieved the desired result. Applicants were now also judged on "character and fitness," and asked to supply a photograph (the better to distinguish "Semitic" features). Geographic distribution also became a criterion, as a means of reducing the number of urban students from the East—most prominently, New York Jews. By the time Johnson graduated, Harvard's Jewish population had been cut in half. This only mirrored the wider antipathy to minorities and immigrants in the United States. The restrictive 1924 Immigration Act cut the number of immigrants by 95 percent, and would have catastrophic consequences for Jews hoping to escape Nazi terror in the following decades.

Even Johnson thought Lowell "very narrow and behind the times," a relic from the previous century. His objections, however, were primarily directed at Lowell's emphasis on coursework and examinations. Johnson preferred the English model of guided independent study. Socially he and Lowell were not so far apart, and Johnson's own sense of privilege was about to become more acute.

Homer, in the winter of 1924, made an unexpected decision: each of his three children would be given their cut of his considerable estate. His justification was that it would not be of much use to receive an inheritance late in life, as by that time one should have already made one's own way. Giving his children capital when they were still young, on the other hand, might help them create something for themselves. "A son should take chances," he told Philip.

Philip's sisters, Jeannette and Theo, received the most stable assets in the family portfolio, primarily real estate Homer had acquired in and around Cleveland. Philip got the more volatile stocks he had amassed over the years, the most valuable being a block of shares in the Aluminum Company of America, which had come to him through his long association with Charles M. Hall. "Son, this is all you're going to get, so help me god you can go and spend it all next year," Homer warned.

Though for anyone else it would have been a fantasy come true, what

Johnson probably needed least at that moment was to become a man of independent means. If he had previously been inclined to float along aimlessly as he discovered himself, at least there was some imperative to find a direction. Now, unencumbered, he cruised through the fall semester, a lackadaisical performance that filtered back to his old headmaster at Hackley, Walter Gage, who informed Dean Greenough that he should be doing better. (The source, presumably, was Daddy Bogues, Johnson's old mentor, with whom he remained close.) Whatever the inspiration, Johnson's grades shortly improved. When he finished his freshman year he came out with four B's and a lone D, in chemistry. It was a solid if not spectacular showing, good enough for the dean's list—at the time, Harvard's "gentleman's grade" was a C. As a reward his parents sent him on a package tour through Western Europe, of which there is little record.

Back in Cambridge for the fall semester, Johnson continued his lonely existence, moving into a private apartment by himself on the second floor of a brick building at 369 Harvard Street, a few blocks from Harvard Yard. He lived alone not so much because he wanted to, but because he could find nobody who would agree to live with him. He was kept company by a reproduction *Madonna and Child* by his mother's favorite painter, Simone Martini, the subject matter and his constant stream of letters suggesting her still-outsize role in his life. The stifling attitudes toward homosexuality, meanwhile, exerted ever-greater stress on his fragile constitution, a situation aggravated when he developed a hard crush on a freshman student unaware of his interest. He took classes in the history of ancient art, English literature, and European history, but reported persistent trouble concentrating on his work. During these undiagnosed bouts of depression he could accomplish nothing at all.

The following semester his emotional difficulties were eclipsed by a more pressing physical illness. The ear pain he had suffered as a child returned, a relapse of mastoiditis. This time surgery was necessary to drain the ear of fluid. In late March he petitioned for a leave of absence, which was granted, and his mother took him back to Cleveland for the procedure. He convalesced at the family farm in New London, where he had always been most comfortably at home. The recovery was made easier by the presence of his sister Theo and, in particular, her friend Talita Jova, who joined the Johnsons at Townsend Farm. Though he was primarily interested in men, he was sexually ambitious and lonely, and Jova was attractive and attracted. The romance was short, but Johnson, as was his nature, developed strong feelings for her in the time they were together.

The affair was either interrupted or concluded at the end of July, when Johnson departed for the rest of the summer on a trip west to Yellowstone National Park. Having recovered from his surgery, he could now avail himself of the salutary effects of the outdoors. "There is delight in the hardy life of the open," Theodore Roosevelt advised American youth, and Johnson was to be sent out to experience it. As with all things orchestrated by his mother, there was an educational component as well: he would travel with a naturalist who would tutor him on ecological matters, and the two would join an expedition sponsored by the Forestry Service to map the park's endangered elk population.

The journey west took several days, with stopovers in Chicago and Denver. From his train window, he found the open plains and small towns of the Midwest unremarkable. What he did find inspiring was the majestic landscape of the West. The passage into Jackson Hole, carpeted in wildflowers of countless variety—fields of yellow goldenrod, purple lupine, pink fireweed, indigo larkspur, and white columbine—was one of the more stupendous visions of his young life. For a week he went on nature walks, absorbing the sheer grandeur of it all, which more than compensated for the rudimentary canvas-roofed shelter of the base camp. In the evenings, the camaraderie of the campfire suited him, pushing him to "think of greater things than ever before."

Yellowstone, then, was not the tourist destination it is today, and its future was very much in question. Upon arrival, Johnson found himself thrust into a debate over the stewardship of the park, with camps at odds over economic exploitation and preservation, and locals resistant to any outside authority at all. Johnson came down on the side of the

Philip Johnson, would-be park ranger. (Getty Research Institute, Los Angeles)

preservationists. "The ideal of a National Park to preserve for the people natural beauties and conditions is naturally the one to be encouraged rather than the economic ones," he wrote.

His sense of the park's natural beauty was less admiring when he was caught out on a pack trip with night approaching, a storm bearing down, and his small hiking group separated from the main body of the expedition. "I wish I was any place but here," he wrote. The situation was dangerous—though perhaps not quite so dramatic as he imagined. Johnson, always so carefully sheltered, became more terrified as the day wore on. At rest stops he comforted himself by composing a letter to his parents on toilet paper. "If I get out all right I shall laugh but I am not laughing now. I feel the calmness and solemnity of the near end of everything and my brain is working like a steam engine." Soon enough he was channeling Jack London, and the letter had transformed into a personal journal. "Thinking and writing of my mother and family makes me feel now that we may get out all right," he wrote. Talita, also, was on his mind, and he wondered if she thought of him. Above all, he found his predicament absurd. "The thought of my, of Philip C Johnson's being in a dangerous place by his own doing is funny. But the situation is not humorous. My only hope is that a snow storm does not come up, for in that case we should never get out.... Father's face haunts me, saying 'what's the use of taking unnecessary chances?' I love everyone, especially my family. God bless them." At the evening's campfire, he was once again philosophical. "I'd rather be a coward and keep my neck whole than be brave and lose it.... The paths of glory lead but to the grave."

The next day, having been "rescued" by the other half of their party, Johnson looked back at his diary with embarrassment. As it was, he was not afraid to sign up for another five-day trip, this time with a guide named Ike Powell, who a prejudiced Johnson worried would rob them and leave them for dead. "The guide is a Jew and bent for doing us," he wrote. That didn't happen, and the vacation culminated with a visit to Old Faithful. "By moonlight on a frosty night, it is a ghost that rises tall and dreadful in the white light," he wrote.

The trip west renewed him. Back at Harvard for the fall semester, he moved out of his lonely apartment and into Claverly Hall, one of the school's "Gold Coast" dormitories along Mount Auburn Street, the choice residence for the most privileged of Harvard's students. There was a pool and private squash courts—Johnson played every day, though he wasn't particularly good—and both maid and butler service. He bought a freesia plant for his room—he always liked to have nature indoors. Best of all, he had found a roommate, Peter August Escher, a handsome scion of a Swiss banking family who was willing to tolerate (barely) Johnson's obsessive straightening.

As might be expected, given his financial independence, Johnson began to indulge himself. He spent lavishly—on books, clothes, theater, a fancy car—and started to expand his circle of friends beyond Escher, treating those who interested him to theater tickets and expensive dinners—a sense of grand generosity that would stay with him throughout his life. Sometimes he was too generous. A friend crashed Johnson's brand new Peerless roadster, presumably while driving drunk (Johnson kept a case of gin in the rumble seat), then refused to ask his parents to foot the sizable repair bill for fear they would withdraw him from school. Meanwhile, Johnson signed check after check until he was given a stern talking-to by his father, who had noted with alarm that he had drawn some $25,000 from his accounts in a single year—a princely sum considering Harvard tuition was in the neighborhood of $250.

What's more, the prospect of choosing a profession and working for a living no longer appealed to him, at least at the moment. "I can see perfectly the value in it, and want to spend some time doing it before I am much older," he wrote to his mother. For the coming summer, he proposed not employment but a trip to Europe with Daddy Bogues, his boarding school mentor. The two tested themselves as traveling companions, in October, on a weekend tour of Connecticut, with Johnson at the wheel, a trip that proved a revelation. Johnson described himself as so taken by the beauty of the area in which he would some day build his estate that he was "out of words." They moved on to meet his mother's architect cousin, Theodate Pope, at Avon Old Farms, the boys' boarding school she was designing in Middlebury. "It is the purest mess you ever saw," he wrote to his sister Jeannette. "It is built out of red stone and in no particular architecture that I could discover. Inside it is dark as a pocket. You can scarcely read a book in broad daylight. Daddy and I had a good talk with her and both pronounced her thoroughly cracked." It was his first recorded work of architectural criticism, and typically biting.

Architecture, for the moment, was not a subject he understood as a potential career option. If anything, music appealed to him most. He had a good ear and a ready understanding of classical composition, but the primary attraction was the powerful emotional impact music had on

30

him, a physical release from the prison of his own mind. Predictably, he expressed a "violent" love for opera, Wagner in particular. "It was a gory thing and I saw red blood in my eyes," he wrote of one performance at Symphony Hall. "I had thoroughly convinced myself that I had slaughtered the whole world and that god and I were rejoicing in it."

That same sense of exaltation would eventually draw him to architecture, but in the interim he set out to improve his technique at the piano. In furtherance of this goal, he hired a private tutor and purchased a new Mason & Hamlin baby grand for two thousand dollars, the largest check he'd ever signed. Homer, of course, was skeptical. In that very first letter to Dean Greenough he had advised that the instrument was a good outlet for his son's "excess steam," but that it should be dropped at once if there were evidence of its encroaching on his studies.

Johnson's grades were suffering, but it was not so much his piano lessons as his own poor attitude that was to blame. Believing he was smarter than his peers, he resented students who achieved higher grades yet was simply too lazy to do the work necessary to make up the difference between mediocrity and excellence. He could "get the point" of a course without the extra labor required to get an A, and even then still wind up on the dean's list, so why push himself? The condescension he directed at his Harvard classmates was brutal. "Their mentality is so inferior," he wrote to his mother, "that all I can get is a sort of amusement that is really wasting time." He described the students in his introductory course on ethics as "absolutely lacking in any curiosity at all."

Among the most apathetic of his classmates was his own roommate, Peter Escher, who closed the fall semester with failing marks and was forced to withdraw from school. Johnson replaced him in the suite with John Bethel, whom he described as "an innocuous person," but one with "a great capacity for neatness and cleanliness"—the most critical of virtues. Johnson's emotional volatility, meanwhile, was becoming more acute. His moods began to swing dangerously from periods of transcendence and productive energy—"excess steam," as his father called it—to extended stretches of distracted focus and withering self-recrimination. "Everybody seems to know so much and to be able to think so logically except me," he wrote in one bleak moment. "I have spent all my life in broadening, as it is called, in other words finding out all things I don't know." In February, he confided to his sister Theo, now a student at Wellesley, that he might indulge himself in a "convenient nervous breakdown" and a recuperative trip to Pinehurst.

Just as Escher was exiting his life, a new figure and a new subject were fortuitously entering it to fill in the gap and ground him intellectually. The man was Raphael Demos, the instructor of his philosophy course on ethics, a rather unkempt Greek native with a kindly disposition and a thick accent. In a matter of weeks, he became what Johnson called his "fairy godmother." Johnson was a willing protégé. "Just now he is concentrating in Demos, next year in something else," quipped Demos, who quickly pegged Johnson's peripatetic nature. If there was something more between them, neither admitted it.

Demos tutored Johnson in classical philosophy, with emphasis on Aristotle and Plato. Johnson could read Plato in the original Greek, and was especially attracted to the philosopher's ideas on human ambition and the necessity of a vital life. "Plato once said that from small men you could expect nothing," he wrote to his mother. "The great moving men might be bad or might be good but at least they were positive personalities."

This squared with the ideas of Hermann Graf Keyserling, a German baron whose travel writing and philosophical musings had captured Johnson's imagination. Aristocratic, worldly, and erudite, Keyserling appealed to Johnson's sense of romantic possibility, as did his Platonic ideas. "Think how much we judge a man by his actions." Johnson wrote to his mother, channeling the German. "As if a thief were any worse a man than a Puritan who obeys the conventions just because of his inhibitions. Certainly the thief is better in that he does not even try to live up to any ideals."

One imagines that Louise and Homer Johnson were alarmed by their son's apparent lack of "ideals," not to mention his general air of condescension and sub-optimal academic performance. At least, it appeared, he had regained some of his energy. "I am learning an astounding amount every day," he wrote. "I never progressed so fast in all my life, vistas are

opening out all around." That he was at an "up" point in one of his neu-
rological cycles was clearly a factor in this rejuvenation, but so was his
entry, through Demos, into the circle of Albert North Whitehead, recently
arrived from England to take command of Harvard's Philosophy Department. With pince-nez glasses and an enormous bald cranium, Whitehead was the very paragon of donnish authority. Among the several
achievements that girded his substantial reputation was the landmark
Principia Mathematica, a three-volume philosophical framework for
mathematics on which he had collaborated with his protégé, Bertrand
Russell.

That Johnson was neither prepared nor inclined to discuss the tenets
of Newtonian physics or the intricacies of Whitehead's exceedingly esoteric philosophy did not preclude him from joining the regular salon at
the Whitehead residence. He knew how to be sociable, and though he
was out of his depth with the man of the house, Mrs. Whitehead took
kindly to him, giving him a copy of *War and Peace,* which he chose not
to read. (Too long.)

It was on one of those evenings that Johnson met Francesca Copley
Greene, "Bunny" to her friends, a bright and exceptionally beautiful
Radcliffe student from one of Boston's grandest families. The two
became fast friends, and suddenly Johnson had a surrogate family. The
salon at the Greenes' Cambridge house was more informal and artistic
than that of the Whiteheads, and tolerant of homosexuality. The paterfamilias, Henry Copley Greene, known as Harry, was a man of musty
charm, an author of sophisticated if turgid historical dramas. His
wife, Rosalind, had a similarly empathetic nature and was a lifelong
confidant of the essayist May Sarton, who would write openly about lesbian relationships.

Johnson's bond with the Greenes grew stronger as the semester ended
and he set off on his planned trip to England with Daddy Bogues. He
sailed for Europe in late June, traveling with the Greenes, who were
headed for Cherbourg and a summer on the Continent. (Bogues made
the crossing separately.) Philip and Francesca spent an indolent crossing
alternately reading *Anna Karenina* aloud to each other and playing deck

tennis — a sport now all but forgotten. For Johnson, it was a blessing to have a companion on the trip, and he was unhappy to lose her when the ship made its first stop in France. The next day he arrived in London, and if he was lonely he had much to keep him occupied in the week before the arrival of Bogues. His first order of business was the purchase of a car, a Morris Cowley, which cost him £180. From there it was off to Savile Row, where he outfitted himself as a proper English dandy, with all the accoutrements: cane, top hat, gloves, and a bespoke raincoat. He liked English tailoring, and indeed English men in general. "They look so much better than our men," he wrote his mother. "I am doing my best not to succumb at all."

When Bogues arrived, the two began their tour proper, with Johnson behind the wheel of the car he had taken to calling "Little Saffron." Their first stop was Canterbury; they arrived on Johnson's birthday, forgotten in the excitement of the journey. It was not long, however, before Bogues began to frustrate his younger traveling companion. That he could not read a map to save his life was an inconvenience. His greater crime was a general lack of curiosity about things architectural, a subject that was rapidly developing into a Johnson obsession. To Johnson's dismay, Bogues was more interested in the occupants of buildings than in the buildings themselves. Worse, he had "postcarditis." Johnson learned to turn this to his advantage; when Bogues dawdled over a card rack, Johnson ducked off to the nearest cathedral or monument. The only trick was to avoid his compatriots when he got there, or at least the tour-group set. If Johnson had little regard for his Harvard peers, his attitude toward the hoi polloi was snobbish in the extreme. "It is not that I mind Americans per se," he wrote. "But I hate the kind that comes from Kankakee and can't tell the difference between the nave and the transept."

Despite these obstacles, the trip allowed Johnson to immerse himself in architecture as never before. He indulged in the visceral pleasures of that exploration and discovery, but also found himself drawn to the peculiar history of buildings and the technical challenges of their construction. His tastes, in their immaturity, were both idiosyncratic and passionately held. The cathedral at Salisbury, with its towering spire so familiar from the paintings of John Constable, was a disappointment to him—too pretty and tranquil in its perfectly composed setting. Stonehenge he compared unfavorably to a decayed military barracks.

It took a special kind of aesthete to write off Salisbury as too beautiful and Stonehenge as too decrepit, but that was Johnson. What seemed to inspire him most were the robust forms of the Norman Romanesque, which could be at once graceful and muscular. Winchester Cathedral was a particular favorite; he spent most of a day exploring its towering vaults. The two travelers also made time for a visit to Winchester College, one of the venerable cornerstones of the English system of education and a model for their own Hackley. They seemed less interested in the academics or even the physical plant, however, than in a rather predatory review of the students themselves, finding them varying in appearance from "rotten" to "most attractive."

The trip culminated with a meeting with Theodate Pope, his mother's architect cousin, who was in England on her own architectural tour. "I am convinced that she is crazy now," he reported to his mother of her familial rival. "I thought she knew something about architecture, but when it gets beyond the phase of raving over some English Cotswold villages, she doesn't seem interested."

Back at Harvard in the fall, Johnson settled in for his junior year, putting his architectural interests aside. He switched his concentration (the Harvard equivalent of a major) from classics to philosophy, and embarked on a challenging class schedule with advanced courses in Aristotelian and Kantian philosophy, physics, and psychology. With the support of Demos, he did well enough to once again earn a place on the dean's list in both the fall and spring terms. His moods continued to be erratic, but at least now he had the Greenes to lend social and emotional support. He also had a sympathetic roommate in Alan Blackburn, his old friend from the Hackley Curia, now matriculated at Harvard. "I have no convictions, concepts, beliefs at all," he informed his mother. "It is necessary for me to be at this stage a thorough eclectic."

Once again he traveled to Europe for the summer, but this time the trip was for academics rather than pleasure, and to Germany rather than

England. The purpose was to refine his German language skills in preparation for an academic career in classical philosophy. The impetus for this had no doubt come from Homer Johnson, who was concerned about his son's lack of direction, and had used his connections to arrange an interview for him with Louis Lord, of the Oberlin Classics Department. Johnson, meanwhile, had landed on academic probation for having failed to meet his language requirement. (After protest by his mother, the probation was rescinded.)

Now he chose to work on his proficiency in Heidelberg, the picturesque university town on the Neckar that was the epicenter of German intellectual liberalism. He boarded with a local family whose members couldn't speak English—the better to practice his German—and befriended a boy from Oxford. The two traveled in the area together, getting a small taste of the freedoms of Germany in the Weimar years.

Johnson, who had professed an interest in American politics, would later claim to have paid little heed to the state of affairs in Germany at the time, which seems highly implausible. National Socialism, though still nascent, was something more than a fringe movement in the summer of 1927. The Nazis held the first of their Nuremberg rallies in mid-August, a massive spectacle of parades, flags, and nationalist speechifying under the direction of Adolf Hitler. The three-day event took place within easy driving distance of staid Heidelberg. Attendance at its torchlit Saturday night ceremony reached fifty thousand. Even if Johnson was not there, he could hardly have been unaware of it, and on such matters he was never short of an opinion. Certainly, the Italian fascist leader had caught his attention. A photo album from that same summer, with snapshots presumably taken before his departure for Europe, shows Johnson in a cape, jodhpurs, and jackboots at the family farm in New London. The caption reads, "Mussolini?"

In Cambridge for the fall semester of what was effectively his senior year, he threw himself again into philosophy, but Demos was no longer there to serve as his tutor. In place of Aristotle and Plato, Nietzsche became the central figure of his thinking, a defining shift of allegiances. He read *Thus Spake Zarathustra* and was attracted to Nietzsche's sense of elitism. "Surpass, ye higher men, the petty virtues, the petty policies, the grains-of-sand-regards, the swarming of ants, the miserable ease, the 'happiness of the greatest number!'," wrote Nietzsche. That kind of language appealed to Johnson, a perennially melancholic aesthete who imagined himself an intellectual *übermensch,* a man above the "mob."

But not everyone thought so, or at least not entirely. Johnson had a destabilizing conversation with Whitehead, who gently made it clear that Johnson's future was not going to be in philosophy, or at least not in Whitehead's brand of scientific metaphysical inquiry. Johnson was bright, but in well over his head when it came to fantastically complex logical systems. "I never could understand it," he would remember. He was more interested in teasing out the implications of Nietzschean ethics, and the coming of a new society of elite supermen. Whitehead, plenty comfortable with his own elite status, was uninterested in such matters. He informed Johnson that he gave only As and Bs to his students (in fact, not true), and that Johnson was going to get a B—not failing, but a condemnation nonetheless. Whitehead suggested he take a year in law school.

The rejection plunged him into a profound depression and left him wondering what he might do for the future. Law school? The teaching job at Oberlin? "I get mixeder up all the time," he wrote to his mother. By December he was all but incapacitated, incapable of work and spending more and more time in the supportive environment of the Greenes, who advised that he seek professional help. Through their assistance, he found Dr. Donald J. MacPherson, a psychopathologist on the faculty of Harvard's Brigham Hospital—Johnson called him a "nerve specialist"—with a sympathetic demeanor. The doctor diagnosed an "acute stage of cyclothemic reaction"—the trough in a cycle of manic depression—and advised the Harvard dean of students that Johnson should be withdrawn from the school for two to three months, at a minimum. He assured Johnson that in time he would heal, that his emotional sickness was no different from a broken leg or a case of the measles. On December 13, Johnson filed his formal petition for a leave of absence, writing with almost comic understatement, "I have had a slight nervous breakdown and should like to rest."

MacPherson also picked up on Johnson's homosexuality, presuming the stress from his repression and fear of parental disapproval were intensifying his emotional difficulties. MacPherson gently explained that homosexuality should in no way preclude Johnson from leading a happy, fulfilled, and successful life. He offered Shakespeare and Tchaikovsky as examples of gay men of extraordinary achievement. If his history wasn't quite accurate, Johnson appreciated the thought behind it.

There was a mixed reaction within the Johnson family to Johnson's leave and now-open admission of homosexuality. His mother had known of her son's sexual preference for some time and treated him with great empathy. His sister Theo understood, as well. Jeannette, however, was more like her father, who was most assuredly not pleased. "Why are you like that?" he demanded while Johnson was trying to recover. "Why don't you buck up?"

To escape his father's disapproving presence, Johnson decamped to the family's winter cottage in Pinehurst, where he read crime novels for distraction (Dashiell Hammett was his favorite) between bouts of weeping and occasional calls to MacPherson for support. Homer's lack of sympathy was perhaps accentuated by his own problems, for he was under punishing stress at the time, having been implicated in a scandal that threatened to destroy his career and that suggested the timing of his financial gift to his son had not been entirely altruistic.

His precarious position was the result of actions he'd taken as executor of the estate of his college friend Charles M. Hall, who had died prematurely at fifty-one in 1914. The position left Johnson in control of an enormous block of stock in the Aluminum Company of America, its reported value in the neighborhood of $30 million at the time of Hall's death. Light, tensile, and strong, aluminum was ideally suited to a new century charged by speed and consumption. The Aluminum Company, backed by Hall's patents, monopolized the American market in the metal. In 1912, the Justice Department began proceedings against it for violations of the Sherman Antitrust Act; the government would spend much of the next four decades trying to break it apart. Oberlin, alma mater of both Hall and Johnson, was one of the principal beneficiaries of this extraordinary fortune, which Hall had devoted, with all the paternalistic chauvinism of the age, to the education of the "three races" of the world—white, black, and Asian. Oberlin was chosen as the "white" beneficiary. The others were Berea College, a racially integrated school in Kentucky, and the American Missionary Association.

In January of 1924, after nearly a quarter century of service, Homer Johnson had retired from the Oberlin Board of Trustees. This was also the moment when he distributed his stock in the Aluminum Company to his son. Legally he could no longer represent the school as a trustee, serve as the executor of the Hall estate, and remain a stockholder in the Aluminum Company—those obligations were coming into serious conflict. The problem lay in the person of Arthur Vining Davis, Hall's former partner and now the chief executive of the company. Davis believed his position was threatened by the industrialist Andrew Mellon, who was himself a significant stockholder in the company. As a solution, Davis arrived at a plan to bolster his own position and "freeze out" Mellon through the purchase of the Hall estate stock. This was to be done at what was considered a fair price, but through a syndicate that would shield Davis's identity in order to keep Mellon in the dark. Johnson backed the plan despite what he admitted were its "doubtful ethics," with the proviso that the trustees of the three beneficiary institutions grant their consent. They did.

Those institutions, however, began to have misgivings when they saw what happened to the stock they had sold to Davis and his syndicate at $5 per share; after a month it was selling at $34. A year later it was selling at $65, and a year after that, in 1927, at $125. (It peaked in 1929 at $197.75.) Though it had never been Davis's intention to defraud the beneficiaries, the trustees of those institutions began to think they had been badly sold. And knowing Davis's true and arguably fraudulent intention— to block Mellon—they had leverage when they set their lawyers on Davis and Johnson for gross breach of trust.

Johnson, at least, could claim he had no personal stake in the matter— he had very smartly transferred his stock in the company to his son. But mostly he was fortunate that the Oberlin trustees had little interest in a public fight that would have exposed their own negligence and placed them in the awkward position of litigating against the estate of the school's most distinguished benefactor. The case was settled out of court, with Johnson freed of responsibility. That resolution, however, did not come until 1930. In the intervening years, Homer Johnson was left in mental purgatory to worry over his financial and professional future.

Should it be any surprise, then, that there were tensions within the Johnson family when Philip left Harvard in December of 1927? It is not hard to imagine Homer's perspective. Here was his disappointing son, sitting in tears in the family winter home as he became richer and richer with every passing day—a millionaire well before his twenty-fifth birthday—all at the potential expense of everything he had ever built.

There was at least some good family news: Philip's older sister, Jeannette, had become engaged to marry, and her fiancé, John Bourne Dempsey,

Philip of Arabia. Johnson adopted the native garb on the family trip down the Nile in 1928. (Getty Research Institute, Los Angeles)

a distinguished and socially dexterous Cleveland attorney educated at Yale, met with unanimous approval. This made for a fine excuse to take one last grand tour of Europe as a family, and if it broke Philip out of his depressive funk, all the better. It also had the salutary effect of separating father from son, at least for a while: Homer, engaged in his own affairs in Cleveland, would meet up with the rest of the clan in Europe in time for his daughter's nuptials, set for the beginning of July in Paris.

The tour, beginning in January, took the Family Johnson on a route around the Mediterranean, beginning at Gibraltar and moving on to Algiers and then Cairo. There was not a monument, mosque, or museum that the Johnsons failed to visit in the Egyptian capital, and when they had fully exhausted its treasures they departed on "The Cruise of the 'Lotus,'" billed as the "supreme" tour of the Nile, with stops at Thebes, Luxor, Aswan, Abu Simbel, and points in between. Johnson, by this time, had taken to dressing in full Arab mufti, including head scarf, as if he were T. E. Lawrence. (The local guides, meanwhile, wore American-style collegiate sweatshirts with "Farajallah Tours" embroidered in block letters on the front.) Philip of Arabia had also grown himself a mustache, albeit a thin one. For a future architect with a romantic sense of grandeur, the trip among so many Ozymandian ruins only amplified his native taste for the monumental.

That was not the case for the next stop on the tour: Athens. For the better part of his life, Johnson would look back on his first visit of the Parthenon as a transformative experience, one that moved him to tears. The truth, however, was altogether different. Homer had arrived to join the family in Greece, and given the difficulty of their relationship, his presence was destabilizing. Snapshots taken at the Acropolis show a profoundly unhappy group: father in a dark overcoat, son brooding in a trenchcoat with the brim of a fedora pulled down over his eyes. With his mustache starting to grow in, he now had the look of a petulant movie villain, a costume that suited him no better than the Arab dress he had taken on in Cairo. Homer and Louise did not need Dr. MacPherson to see in their son a self-loathing young man lurching about in search of an identity.

An unhappy Johnson hides under a fedora at the Athenian Acropolis. (Getty Research Institute, Los Angeles)

The trip continued on, uncomfortably and inexorably, moving through the Peloponnese, Sicily, Monte Carlo, and finally to Paris. Jeannette's wedding ceremony, at the Ritz, was attended by a handful of society friends who had crossed the Atlantic for the occasion, along with the American ambassador. She wore an elegant white gown by the French designer Paul Poiret. Her brother would surely have approved, but he was not present. Homer and Louise, exasperated by his brooding and worried that his depressing attitude would ruin the wedding, had sent him home to straighten himself out.

Desolated and now alone, Johnson, either of his own volition or (more likely) on orders from his father, returned for another course of treatment at Battle Creek. The designated therapy for his condition — "neurasthenia" — entailed cold baths, Swedish massage, and a diet designed to reduce toxins in the alimentary canal. Kellogg was also radically opposed to homosexual behavior—he believed in abstinence, and considered even masturbation a dangerous vice—and it may well have been Homer's intention to "cure" his son through Kellogg's system, which promised the rehabilitation of the mind through the rehabilitation of the body. If it could not be corrected, homosexuality might at least be suppressed with plenty of exercise and a proper diet.

Battle Creek was a pleasant place to stay, a far cry from the modern medical facility, its main building graced with a brand-new fifteen-story tower. The architecture was generously proportioned in the Classical manner, and crafted to Kellogg's exacting standards: floors of tile for easy cleaning, broad corridors to accommodate strolling patients, and a powerful ventilation system—fresh air being a vital component of his program. The building was a metaphor for the body and a tool for improving it; efficient, sterile circulation was essential. Through the lobby was a greenhouse, the "Palm Garden," where patients could mill about and "enjoy the tropical scene." Perhaps it was in that heated environment that Johnson noticed a handsome actor from Kansas City, a young man of similar age. After the two finished their treatment they drove off in Johnson's Peerless roadster for a romantic tour of New York's picturesque Finger Lakes, Kellogg's retrograde abstinence theories be damned.

Johnson returned to Harvard in the fall, a twenty-two-year-old with senior standing beginning his sixth collegiate year. Having been rejected by Whitehead and with zero interest in law school, he had resigned himself to the teaching job at Oberlin. He changed his concentration back to classics from philosophy, and enrolled in a pair of classes in Greek, along with one each in music and fine arts. For a semester he muddled through, once again dependent on the kindness of the Greenes and the protective supervision of Dr. MacPherson. But as the new year approached, he regressed. Feeling overwhelmed, he dropped his class in art history. In April he was advised by MacPherson to take no more than one class at a time—this being the most he could manage "without a return of further symptoms." MacPherson's directive was passed along to the Harvard administration, which was generous enough to grant Johnson that special privilege, and also a leave of absence for the coming fall semester. His coursework, anyway, was all but complete—he needed just one final class to qualify for graduation.

Freed from the pressure of a full academic schedule, Johnson could explore his own interests, and at an opportune moment. Architecture, the subject to which he had recently been drawn, now seemed to be opening itself up to him. There was a certain appeal to the idea of practicing it professionally, but he was not enthusiastic about the prospect of architecture school. The beaux arts model of architectural education placed considerable demand on one's artistic ability, and Johnson was not confident in his own hand. Moreover, he had come to believe that this pedagogical model—a relic of the French *ancien régime*—was past its sell-by date, an obsolete system of training inappropriate to a modern world of speed and astonishing technological progress. If practice was out, however, there was another possibility: he could *study* architecture.

That this might be a viable option may well have occurred to him, if only subconsciously, upon reading the lead feature in the February 1928 issue of *The Arts,* a highbrow magazine to which his academic-minded mother had subscribed him. The author was a recent Harvard graduate named Henry-Russell Hitchcock, now teaching at Wesleyan—they were not yet acquainted, though the name may have been familiar—and its subject was the architecture of the Dutch modernist J. J. P. Oud. This was radical work, crisp in its unadorned lines, pointing toward a new aesthetic born of industry but no less handsome for it. Johnson was captivated by Oud's work, and also by Hitchcock's authoritative essay, which opened with a call to arms for modern design. "Architecture should be devoid of elements introduced for the sake of ornament alone: to the engineering solution of a building nothing should be added," Hitchcock began. He equated the nascent modern school to earlier periods of architectural achievement: the Greeks with their temples, the French builders of the Gothic cathedral. The bold photographs and uncompromising text stood out unmistakably from the rather staid pages of the magazine.

Johnson would later claim that reading the article engendered a "Saul to Paul" conversion, when he at once and declaratively set his future on a course toward modern architecture. Like his claims about the Parthenon, that seems doubtful, but it surely suggested there was a place in the world for an energetic young scholar of modern architecture, an attainable and appealing alternative to a career as a designer.

There was nothing quite like Oud's Hook of Holland in Boston in 1928, but there were a few enterprising students looking to introduce modern art and design to Harvard. Their leader was Lincoln Kirstein, an imperious son of Boston privilege with an intense, roving mind. Like Johnson, he was gay and attractive, but in a severe, aquiline way; he could be described, with some justification, as "smoldering," the cliché in this instance being altogether apt. Kirstein always seemed on the verge of some kind of eruption, his ire often directed at those he considered lesser mortals. He, too, had a distant and disapproving father of high social standing: Louis Kirstein—philanthropist, defender of Jewish causes, adviser to presidents—had made a fortune as a department store executive, building Filene's Basement into a discount empire. If Lincoln felt somehow tainted by the family's rag-trade wealth, he made up for it with frigid intellectual hauteur. Unlike the preternaturally diffident Johnson, Lincoln Kirstein never questioned his own genius. "Whatever situation I put myself in—given enough time—I feel sure my innate sense and past experience will pull me through," he wrote. At the time, he was just a freshman.

Johnson knew Kirstein only informally, if at all. They may have met in the circle of Alfred North Whitehead, and they could commiserate about their difficulties in absorbing the professor's logical systems. Despite his self-assurance, Kirstein did even worse in Whitehead's class than Johnson. (He got a D-minus.) Kirstein, however, was several years behind Johnson, and ran with a fast crowd with whom Johnson, who had spent so much time on leave, was unfamiliar. For all that, Johnson was aware of *Hound & Horn*, the so-called little magazine Kirstein had launched in the fall of 1927 with his freshman roommate, Varian Fry. Their ambition was to publish avant-garde poetry and literature, their two great models being Ezra Pound and T. S. Eliot.

A year later, Kirstein, who harbored vague ideas about a future as a painter, set out to do for the visual arts what *Hound & Horn* was doing for literature; specifically, he wanted to create a space for modern art in notoriously conservative Cambridge. The idea may well have come from Alfred H. Barr, a magnetic young professor of art history at Wellesley. The son of a minister, Barr was already developing a reputation as a relentless proselytizer for the new.

Barr became a mentor to Kirstein, suggesting possible exhibitions and otherwise tutoring him on new directions in art. On a practical level, he provided Kirstein with entrée to Paul J. Sachs, the man who had the knowledge and resources that would allow them to realize their idea for a space for contemporary arts. Short of stature and not prone to suffer fools, Sachs had left a career as an investment banker in the family firm—his father was a founding partner of Goldman Sachs—for a position as assistant director at Harvard's Fogg Art Museum. Beginning in 1922, he also taught a class, Fine Arts 15A, known to students simply as the "museum course." This was a first-of-its-kind seminar that covered every subject a museum professional might need to know, from curating to exhibition design to financial development.

Sachs was, indisputably, expert in these matters. Legend had it that he got himself to sleep each night by making precise mental inventories of European museums, room by room. He had seen them all, and had a print collection of his own that could rival many an institution's. With his wealth and connections, Sachs was a power broker par excellence, a fact that sometimes irritated his academic colleagues but made him attractive to students—especially favored pupils who came to think of him as "Uncle Paul." In the coming years, his protégés would occupy the directorships of nearly every major American collection.

Barr, Kirstein, and Sachs would together shape the future of American modernism, and at the same time exercise great influence over the life of Philip Johnson. But they first met without him over dinner at Sachs's Victorian mansion, Shady Hill, to launch the Harvard Society of Contemporary Art. Its inaugural show, in a gallery over the Harvard Co-op, opened in February of 1929 and featured works by an eclectic group including

Charles Demuth, Edward Hopper, Georgia O'Keeffe, and John Marin. If there were none of Barr's favored Cézannes or Picassos, the artists included at least represented some movement toward the modern. More definitively avant-garde was the setting itself: walls draped in ecru with silver panels on the ceilings and metal-top display tables. For America, let alone conservative Boston, it was something altogether new.

It is hard to believe that Johnson did not see such a noteworthy exhibition, but there is no record of its contents or its unusual installation capturing his imagination. In May, however, the society mounted something that did: an exhibition of R. Buckminster Fuller's Dymaxion House. Of course, it grabbed everyone's attention. The idea of a modern house even along the lines of Frank Lloyd Wright was considered radical at the time, and especially at conservative Harvard, but here was something truly fantastic: a hexagonal home of translucent walls slung by cable rigging from a central mast. Suspended above ground, it appeared like a futuristic fever dream of a tree house, and Fuller promised a world populated by them. Indeed, his guarantees seemed more outlandish than the building looked: it would, Fuller claimed, be constructed in twenty-four hours; protect against floods, fires, and "marauders"; and eliminate forever the ills of drudgery, exploitation, politics, and selfishness. Quite a house. If nothing else, it was a brilliant *coup de théâtre,* landing stories in the international press and a photo of a severe-looking Fuller next to his model in the *Boston Globe.*

Johnson had special reason to be interested; aluminum would be the principal material with which this modern marvel was to be constructed, and it did not escape him that the metal was the basis of his growing fortune. Which is not to say that he approved of the house, however much it was in his personal interest to do so; he was too much of an aesthete to approve of Fuller's techno-futurist dream. "I disliked it very much," he would later recall. He was, however, impressed by the spectacle, a lesson he would later apply in his own exhibitions.

Just as Fuller's Dymaxion House was commandeering attention on Massachusetts Avenue, Barr was delivering a well-publicized series of five lectures on modern art and architecture at Wellesley's Farnsworth

Art Museum. Tall and gawky, with metal-frame glasses that gave him a kind of nerdy charm, Barr had already developed something of a cult following among Wellesley coeds. Entry into his popular course on modern art required that students submit to a quiz in which they were asked to describe the importance of fifty masters of "modern artistic expression," a list that included the likes of George Gershwin, Jean Cocteau, Frank Lloyd Wright, Saks Fifth Avenue, and New York's 1916 zoning law. Not shy to publicity, he had the test published in *Vanity Fair* in 1927. There was, to be sure, no other class like it, anywhere — the term "modern" then generally indicating art since the Renaissance.

Johnson was always vague about precisely who tipped him off to Barr's lecture series. Either it was his sister Theo, then completing her senior year at Wellesley, or his mother, who was president of the school's alumni association. (Theo seems the more likely candidate.) What Johnson witnessed was a bravura oratorical performance. During his first three talks, Barr delivered a scientific history and theory of modern art. His fourth lecture was on the Bauhaus, the innovative design academy in Dessau, Germany founded by the patrician architect Walter Gropius; the fifth on the avant-garde of Moscow.

Barr spoke on these subjects with great energy and conviction, and also a firsthand knowledge that few Americans could match. He had spent months traveling through Europe in 1927 and 1928, the trip financed by a personal grant from Sachs, who had instructed him to concentrate his energies on art since the late-nineteenth century, a field in need of scholarship and which he could have to himself. The trip was a revelation: traveling with his roommate, Jere Abbott — another Sachs protégé — Barr toured the Bauhaus and interviewed its masters, then moved to Moscow where he met and befriended the director Sergei Eisenstein, among other members of the Russian avant-garde.

It was Barr's great genius to coalesce the many disparate threads of what he had seen into a comprehensible and unified narrative. He was offering, however, something more than a review of recent artistic developments, more even than an intellectual framework on which one might classify them. Above all, he beckoned with the allure of the new, an exclusive knowledge to which few others were privy. That was a narcotic Johnson could never refuse.

According to Johnson, Barr's lecture series was yet another decisive moment in his life. As he liked to tell it, he approached Barr after one of the talks—which one he never indicated—and the two developed an immediate rapport. Johnson, in all his innocence, wondered whether the time might be right to launch a modern art museum. "I'm starting one in the fall," replied Barr. "Why not include architecture?" answered Johnson. And with that, an impressed Barr offered the position as architectural curator to Johnson.

That episode, appealing as it sounds, was a product of Johnson's imagination, a fiction of dramatic convenience. Although the Museum of Modern Art would indeed open its doors to the public in the coming fall—and the lecture series all but formulated its future program—Barr had not yet been approached to be its founding director; that would not come until June, and he would not have the job formally until the end of July. In fact, Barr recalled Johnson introducing himself at the opening, on May 2, of a small design exhibition, *Modern European Posters and Contemporary Typography,* at Wellesley. The show was curated by Barr, and it consisted entirely of posters and a few small works of graphic design that he had acquired on his recent trip through Europe. The show, perhaps the first of its kind in America, included several Bauhaus exhibition posters by Herbert Bayer, a striking cubist composition by E. McKnight Kauffer, stylized railway and steamship posters by A. M. Cassandre, and the extraordinary constructivist collage poster for Eisenstein's film *October* created by Vladimir and Georgii Stenberg—identified by Barr as the "brothers Sterenberg."

It is not hard to imagine the two men talking among these works, Johnson asking about their origin and making characteristically perceptive observations, Barr responding with his thoughts about their design and with stories of his efforts to acquire them—the entire lot cost a sum total of $125. It is instructive to recall how young both men were, and how close in age. Though Barr was already an associate professor, he was just twenty-seven; Johnson, still an undergraduate, was twenty-two. Barr was clearly the academic authority, but Johnson was well-traveled himself and no intellectual slouch. Their enthusiasm for the new was shared. That they did, in fact, have an immediate and easy rapport is the one matter on which all parties agree.

They met again at a reception following the performance of *Antony and Cleopatra* by Wellesley's Shakespeare club—Theo was the female lead—and once more at her commencement, in mid-June. There was no firm offer of a position at the would-be museum. Johnson, in fact, was already planning a trip abroad for the coming semester—he had notified Harvard of his intention to take a leave of absence in April, before he had even met Barr. He proposed to return to Germany, where he would continue the study of German in preparation for his modern language examination, a requirement for graduation.

Now, his budding relationship with Barr intensified his desire to explore the radical new modernism of Europe. Barr, for his part, hoped that he would be in a position to bring Johnson into the as-yet-unnamed museum in some capacity, an invitation he would similarly extend to Lincoln Kirstein. To assist him on his travels, Barr gave Johnson an architectural itinerary of notable works.

And with that, Johnson was off.

CHAPTER 3

A Man of Style

I certainly have swallowed this modern faith of the architects hook, line and sinker, but that makes it all the more fun.
—*Philip Johnson, 1929*

He felt better. The realization that architecture could be his calling freed something within him, replacing his natural diffidence with a sense of direction and purpose. His bouts of relentless energy were no longer offset by corresponding troughs of lugubrious mental atrophy. He could now justify his vision of himself as a Nietzschean *übermensch,* a man above the crowd, a prophet leading the way toward a new aesthetic Jerusalem.

He saw everything through the filter of architecture and design, and nothing escaped his jaundiced eye. At times this tendency verged on the ridiculous. "What I like about the Black Forest is that it is neither black nor a forest," he wrote. Johnson's intellectual transformation, meanwhile, was mirrored by a physical one: he shaved off the fuzzy brush of a mustache he had grown in Egypt the previous summer. "I shall never conceal myself again," he informed his mother, a pledge that seemed to be about more than just facial hair.

Johnson departed for Europe in late August, traveling on the *Bremen,* the most advanced ocean liner in the world, then on its maiden voyage east across the Atlantic. Over the three days it was docked in Brooklyn and open to the public for tours, it was a significant attraction, drawing some 75,000 curious visitors. Johnson thought it "beautiful" and well appointed. But if it was modern, it was not quite modern enough, at least not according to Johnson the critic, now recasting himself as an authority on contemporary design. "My final judgment of the decoration is not so favorable," he wrote, after some consideration. "There are too many unfunctional decorations and too little use of solid color, and too much convention in chairs." That was not all. The food was awful and there were too many Jews and they "talked English brokenly."

Johnson's uncompromising rejection of decorative ornamentation characterized his early thinking about architecture. It was, clearly, thinking derived from his discussions with Barr and his reading of Hitchcock's essays, and it betrayed the dogmatic immaturity of youth. But soon after his arrival in Germany, he found someone who shared these ideas: John McAndrew, a Harvard graduate (class of '24) from Chicago, who had completed his coursework in the architecture school and had only to finish his thesis to earn his degree.

They met standing in front of a van Gogh at the Mannheim Kunsthalle. Johnson noticed him, a handsome man in an ill-made suit, and introduced himself with a disparaging remark, the exact nature of which was soon forgotten, about the Dutch painter. McAndrew smiled and replied with a witty remark of his own. The attraction was mutual. On the drive back to Heidelberg, where both were staying, they found they had much in common. He "hates the people I hate," Johnson reported. Likewise, McAndrew was "crazy about modern architecture." In fact, they had been converted to this religion by the same man. Barr, always on the lookout for disciples, had similarly adopted McAndrew the previous year.

From then on, the two men traveled together in Johnson's Packard roadster, lovers and pilgrims in search of the modern. They drove along the Rhine, where the architecture they found was predominantly Gothic and Romanesque—periods that Johnson, a self-professed modernist prig, now found largely anathema. He didn't care for the buildings, and when they crossed the border to visit Strasbourg, he didn't much care for the people, either. "I am convinced the French are awful," he wrote. He preferred Germans, and also their diet: hearty bread, soups with sausage, beans cooked with onions. Homer Johnson, so concerned with his son's intestinal health, would have been appalled.

The first revelations came in Stuttgart. On instructions from Barr, the two visited the Weissenhofsiedlung, a showcase housing project at which they could compare the works of the great European modernists, among them Oud, Le Corbusier, Walter Gropius, and Mies van der Rohe. There were twenty-one buildings in all, each a whitewashed block with a flat roof and punctured ribbon windows. It was a marvel of modern severity, a demonstration of what a working-class modern community could be, and with no "unfunctional decorations" to raise Johnson's ire.

Indeed, it was what he had hoped to see, the modern philosophy about which he had read made manifest in three dimensions. Evaluating the individual contributions, he declared Oud a "kindred spirit," Le Corbusier "all function," and Gropius "the greatest of them all." Those impressions would be recalibrated over time, and he entirely neglected Mies, the presiding force of the project, who would soon displace Gropius as his idol. It was a galvanizing experience, and Johnson fully threw himself into it, boldly knocking on doors and asking residents for tours of their homes.

"One good sign has already developed," he reported. "I like the work by the best architects best. I mean that the ones that Barr and those people said were the greatest are head and shoulders above the rest of the mob." Indeed, they had inspired him beyond expectation. He now wanted to build, and in his hubris imagined himself walking among modernism's great masters as an equal. "If I could build a house over there, or rather a string of apartments, that [sic] everyone would be crazy about them."

In the meantime, he needed a rest. So much driving and the stress of communicating in a foreign language day after day exhausted him—at least that's what he told his mother. More likely he just needed a break from the relationship with McAndrew, which had developed quickly. Also, there was someone else. And so he slipped off to Geneva, accompanied by a young Dutchman, his name lost to history. The two stayed at the luxurious Beau Rivage, and Johnson spent much of the time sitting naked on his balcony admiring the view.

Afterward, he traveled to London. A toothache had bothered him since his final days on the *Bremen,* and by September it required action he was not prepared to entrust to a German dentist. It was also a fine excuse for a fortnight of shopping and theater in the English capital. One afternoon during his stay he ran into Noël Coward—they had met on his previous London trip—who was in the midst of the hit run of *Bitter Sweet,* an operetta with a gay subtext. Coward was particularly glad to see that Johnson's offending mustache had been removed. "I am prepared for quite an evening," Johnson wrote before a night at the theater. If he was not formally out of the closet, he was at least living up to his pledge that he would no longer "conceal" himself. He treated himself to a return to Germany by air—his first flight and nearly his last. The sartorially inclined young gentleman had filled a steamer trunk with expensive new fashions from Savile Row, and the added weight nearly doomed the plane.

In September, Johnson and McAndrew reunited and set off again, this time for Holland, their goal being an audience with Oud, which they did not achieve. He was away recuperating from his own bout of nervous exhaustion. They visited his work, though, with Johnson finding his Hook of Holland housing project—about which Hitchcock had written so effusively—to be "the Parthenon of modern Europe." They continued north to Hilversum to see the work of W. M. Dudok, another modernist pioneer, and then back to Germany—through Amsterdam, Düsseldorf, Essen, Hanover, and finally Berlin, which was to become their new base of operations. Johnson duly sent Barr a letter apprising him of their discoveries.

McAndrew, knowledgeable and sexually appealing, was an ideal travel companion, the senior member of their partnership. He knew modern architecture more roundly than Johnson, but had fewer opinions, or at least less strident ones. The two decided to collaborate on a book project, an illustrated guide to modern architecture, with photographs and brief descriptions of the newest buildings. Given their relative inexperience, they wisely chose to keep the analysis to a minimum, instead commissioning short statements of principle from key figures in the movement. That they were more interested in how this architecture looked than in how the buildings functioned or the new way of living they embodied was reflected in their willingness to "sacrifice the best buildings if they don't photograph well."

Johnson assimilated what he saw with characteristic rapidity. They visited the suburban Berlin home of architect Erich Mendelsohn, known for his expressionist Einstein Tower observatory in Potsdam. His house, still under construction, was a more doctrinaire form of modernism, boxy where the tower was fluid, with planes of glass opening out onto lakes and a forest of pine, with trim of travertine. "I have always thought he had good taste, but this gives him restraint as well," Johnson informed Barr. Mendelsohn had become "international" — Johnson's first use of the term to describe the new modern style.

It was not just the modern that Johnson and McAndrew appreciated. If the Gothic was out of favor, the Baroque was not. Johnson and McAndrew traveled to Potsdam, the German royal retreat, to explore the resplendent palace of Sanssouci. One could hardly imagine an architecture in more flagrant opposition to the dogmatically restrained modernism they preferred: nary a surface of that rococo palace lacked ornamentation. Still, Johnson was "properly thrilled." The sheer lavishness appealed to his native sense of grandiosity and indeed his attraction to extremes of all kinds — to anything that could provide some kind of relief from the timidity and diffidence that had afflicted him since he was a boy.

Extravagance endeared him to Berlin, then in the later stages of its Weimar-era cultural decadence. The city had a unique, doomed energy, a grotesque amalgamation of the glamorous and the sordid. Christopher Isherwood, whose *Berlin Stories* define that moment, noted that it was a scene best appreciated by an expatriate, someone immune to the more sinister and pervasive realities of desperation, fear, and malevolent extremism that characterized it. "Only a very young and very frivolous foreigner," he wrote, "could have lived in such a place and found it amusing." Johnson fit that description, and he had the added benefit of great wealth. Berlin, like the bombed-out towns he had seen with his family after the Great War, was a spectacle for him, one he could experience while remaining insulated from its privations. But he was hardly the passive camera, shutter open wide, described by Isherwood, though he was at times thoughtless. He indulged himself in the city's offerings, elevated and profane, without remorse. "The only thing I am studying intensively is how to have a good time in Berlin," Johnson informed his mother, assuring her that one "does not need much study before perfection is reached."

He moved from the hotel he had shared with McAndrew to a pension on the fashionable Kurfürstendamm, a street alive with cosmopolitan energy at all hours, day and night. The tree-lined boulevard was the central artery of Berlin's cultural life, its Champs-Élysées. Johnson spent hour after hour sitting at its busy cafés, nursing drinks and admiring passersby, achieving a sense of cosmopolitan contentedness that he had not known before.

There were few evenings that he could not be found at the opera, symphony, or theater. In the afternoons he visited art galleries and museums, and went to the movies—in one memorable day, he sat through six films. His tastes were fairly conservative, at least at first. In his letters there is no mention of the avant-garde theater of Berthold Brecht or the music of Kurt Weill or Paul Hindemith, and he was disparaging of the new German cinema. With the traditional visual arts he was somewhat more adventurous. The stark physical and emotional brutality of painters Oskar Kokoschka, Max Beckmann, and Emil Nolde drew his attention, though he did not appreciate them at first. He nevertheless became a habitué of the gallery of Alfred Flechtheim, Berlin's preeminent impresario of avant-garde culture. Flechtheim cut a striking figure about the city, preceded wherever he went by his magnificent Jewish nose, so formidable an appendage that it was cast in bronze by the sculptor Rudolf Belling. It was at Flechtheim's gallery that Johnson first came to know the work of Paul Klee. Johnson also became an avid consumer of *Der Querschnitt*, the pioneering arts journal founded by Flechtheim and dedicated to new literature, painting, and photography—a diversity suggested by the title, which translated to "The Cross Section."

In Weimar Berlin, Johnson commissioned a portrait from the Jewish photographer Helmar Lerski. (Getty Research Institute, Los Angeles)

As a patron, Johnson was adventurous, if particular, in his tastes. He sat for a portrait by the stylish Jewish photographer Helmar Lerski, who lit his subjects dramatically in natural light and shot them in cinematic close-up. It took him several days before he was satisfied with the setup for Johnson's portrait, but the result was particularly powerful. Johnson sat in three-quarter profile, the brim of a sharply raked fedora just peeking down at the right temple. He looked as solid as a Greek statue, and just as beautiful.

Johnson knew it, and took advantage. There was, of course, more to Berlin than high culture. Berlin's doomed libertinism was exhilarating, especially to a young gay man from buttoned-up, Prohibition-era America. Berlin did not so much have a nightlife as a full-fledged "pleasure industry." Its tolerance attracted a gay population estimated at three hundred thousand. By night, the Kurfürstendamm was a veritable runway of strutting gentlemen and "line boys." Cocaine was cheaper than liquor. Johnson threw himself into the city's libidinous café culture, spending nights in clubs such as the Alexander-Palast and the Zauberflöte, which catered to gay men of means. The more respectable places had cabarets and dance floors ringed by balconies running up floor after floor. It was a layout, perhaps not coincidentally, that would become a regular feature of his own architecture.

In October he traveled to Prague, which proved a marked and unpleasant contrast. He found the Czech capital dirty and lacking in grandeur, its public art in poor taste. He did not care for the language, either: "awful." Worst of all were the Czechs themselves: "stupid people, with their too broad mouths and blank expressions; Bohunks, I calls em. [sic]" He couldn't wait to return to Berlin; it was like coming home.

That same month, Johnson, traveling with McAndrew, made his first pilgrimage to the Bauhaus, the trade school for the arts founded by Gropius in 1919. The intent was to teach all of the art and design disciplines in one fully integrated school, with instruction by "masters" who could prepare students to meet the physical and artistic demands of the modern world, and do so using modern methods.

The school was in tumult at the time. Facing budget cuts and dissension among the faculty, Gropius had resigned his position in 1928. He was replaced by the Swiss architect Hannes Meyer, an ardent communist and proponent of functionalist design. "All things in this world are a product of the formula: function times economy," wrote Meyer. His dogmatic tenure was rocky from the outset, and his politics exacerbated tensions with local officials, already under pressure from right-wing nationalists. Several notable faculty members departed, among them the young architect Marcel Breuer, whose bent-tube chairs had already captured Johnson's attention.*

The Bauhaus itself, more than its pedagogical program, made the

---

* The graphic artist Herbert Bayer also departed. Johnson had seen his work in Barr's Wellesley exhibition.

greatest impression on Johnson. The complex was Gropius's master-work: a pinwheeling composition of buildings with a glass-walled work-shop, dormitory, offices, and classrooms connected by bridges. "It has a majesty and simplicity which are unequaled," Johnson informed Barr. This elegance was not just superficial. It had a "beauty of plan," Johnson explained, the emphasis indicating a depth of architectural comprehension that moved beyond the purely visual. (Barr, of course, had seen the place with his own eyes, so this bit of intellectual showboating was hardly necessary.) Back in Berlin, Johnson met Gropius himself, visiting him in the fanciful Gothic apartment building near Leipziger Platz where he had his home and office. It was, perhaps, not where one would expect to find the leader of the modern movement, but Johnson was charmed. Gropius, he wrote, was "a utopian who sees things in a big way, and has the magnetism to draw people after him, never contented with a thing accomplished, always fighting for a new idea."

Berlin's gay nightclubs were not especially famous for engendering lasting relationships, but on an evening in October, Johnson found someone who would replace McAndrew in his affections, and who would play a significant role in his life over the coming years. That man was Jan Ruhtenberg, a striking Scandinavian ten years his senior. Ruhtenberg had sharp features, slicked-back blond hair, and a well-cut suit that complimented his athletic frame. Like Johnson, he was beautiful, but in a Teutonic way. His given name was Alexander Gustaf Jan von Ruhtenberg, and his family had been titled by the Queen of Sweden in 1672. He was born in Riga, schooled in St. Petersburg, and had studied art history at the University of Leipzig. At the moment, Ruhtenberg was clerking in the Berlin office of the furniture manufacturer Deutsche Werkstätten, but his ambitions were in architecture, and he had already taken on some minor design commissions, never mind his absent professional qualifications. He was charming and courtly, and it seemed to Johnson he knew everyone in Berlin—architects, artists, actors, musicians. He also had a wife and three children.

Ruhtenberg and Johnson became inseparable almost at once, their affair an open secret. Ruhtenberg's artist wife, Hanna von Helmsing, had already come to terms with her husband's sexuality; the two lived together in a segregated apartment, and conducted largely separate lives, united only by a commitment to their children. Though Johnson would show no affinity for kids in his later years, he developed an attachment to the Ruhtenberg children, who adored him right back. "Onkel Philip" was happy to bounce Jan Thiel, the eldest, on a knee, or engineer elaborate train crashes with the model railroad he purchased for them.

Johnson with Jan Ruhtenberg (center) and his wife, Hanna von Helmsing. (Getty Research Institute, Los Angeles)

That Ruhtenberg was so well connected made him an ideal replacement, as Johnson discovered when the two visited the Bauhaus just a few weeks after his first trip there with McAndrew. He had since moved on to Paris, their book project ostensibly dead. With McAndrew, Johnson had been led around by an American student. This time, thanks to Ruhtenberg, they were treated with deference, given an audience with the expatriate American Lyonel Feininger, who taught printmaking, and the honor of a pre-theater dinner at the home of Wassily Kandinsky. Johnson, however, was unimpressed with the host. "Kandinsky is a little fool who is completely dominated by his swell Russian Grande Dame of a wife," he wrote Barr. "He has millions of his sometimes painful abstractions sitting around the house and thinks he is still the leader of a new movement. It is sometimes pathetic sometimes amusing."

Paul Klee, on the other hand, had "the simplicity of a great man, without hide bound theories, or illusions as to his greatness." Johnson was charmed enough to purchase a drawing from him, a delicate composition of inked lines in geometrical patterns that suggested an abstracted cathedral. (The title was *Sacred Islands*.) To Johnson, its lines recalled a sectioned onion. McAndrew had seen a similar piece on their previous trip and hadn't cared for it, but now Johnson bought it anyway, for a mere 600 marks (about $75), an expense that still made him feel somewhat guilty.* It was his first art purchase, but several more followed in Berlin: an etching by Picasso, a drawing by Aristide Maillol (a gift for his dear friend Francesca Greene), and several works by Ruhtenberg's wife, Hanna.

Johnson, by this time, had begun to indulge his architectural ambitions. He had seen the possibilities of modernism and wanted the freedom to experiment on his own. That he considered this a possibility despite his lack of formal training and work experience is a testament to his audacity, and also his wealth. For someone of lesser means, the thought would have been pure folly. But Johnson had a willing client, or at least a client willing to humor him: his mother. Louise Pope Johnson, a progressive in the arts who liked to be one step ahead of the neighboring Joneses, wanted to remodel her Pinehurst living room, and at the same time renovate a nearby investment property, a neocolonial bungalow previously owned by the town postmaster, R. A. Barrett. It is probable that Johnson discussed these commissions with her before his departure on the *Bremen*, but it was during his stay in Germany that he began work in earnest, taking first McAndrew and then Ruhtenberg on

---

* It is now in the collection of the Museum of Modern Art, a gift from Johnson.

as his collaborators. What he lacked in education and experience they could provide, even if neither was a licensed professional.

The plans Johnson developed with McAndrew for the Barrett house were ambitious in scope and radical in design: among their ideas, they proposed to eliminate a bedroom and a parlor, shifting the traditional layout of the house toward a more modern open plan. Equally dramatic was the interior, which was unapologetically cribbed from Oud's Hook houses, with gray carpet, canary-yellow curtains, a bright red door, and blue trim—a symphony of primary colors and shining chrome. This would have been the first De Stijl interior in the United States. "It sounds rather ugly," he told his mother, but he would be willing to stake his reputation on it, "if I had one."

As he would throughout his career, Johnson took an exceedingly broad view of the notion of architectural authorship, pushing even the traditional bounds of a profession in which the principal of a firm takes credit for the work of his subordinates. Johnson was not particularly concerned that his ideas were unoriginal, nor even that they were his at all. He claimed that he could "hardly disentangle" his own thoughts from McAndrew's, so close had been their collaboration. Johnson was not above outright theft, either. He considered hiring a prominent "interior decorator" to draw up a design for the Johnson living room—so that he would "get lots of new ideas, and the plans too." He also went to Marcel Breuer for a consultation. Not surprisingly, Breuer thought he should have the commission for himself. The idea of hiring Breuer in fact appealed to Johnson, even if it meant losing the job. He liked being an impresario, and there were several farmhouses on the Johnson family properties in New London that he had his eye on. "What I want to experiment with is simple houses," he wrote to his mother, and also to design some "simple furniture."

Wrapped up in his architectural fantasies, insulated by his wealth, and swept up by a new relationship and the exciting world of Weimar Berlin, Johnson was all but oblivious to the greater events of the fall of 1929. He noted the premature death of Gustav Stresemann, the German foreign minister and force of political stability, less for its political ramifications than for the somber funeral decorations throughout the city. He seemed only vaguely perturbed by the news of a run on Wall Street. "I heard something disquieting about a new bottom or something," he wrote of the Black Friday crash. "I hope it isn't true." He begged his mother not to put the kibosh on the designs he had created for her "because of the Stock Exchange or something."

In fact, the troubles of Wall Street did not preclude Louise Pope Johnson from going ahead with the renovation of her living room—with a design by Louis Rorimer. His art deco aesthetic was modern enough for her, though it seems that as a concession to her ambitious son she had Rorimer adopt some of his ideas. And so the Pinehurst living room had gray carpet, a blue sofa, yellow pillows, and lots of aluminum trim. Johnson didn't get the bright red door he wanted, but the curtains—an arresting drapery of flaming vermilion—were awfully close.

Throughout the fall Johnson had been corresponding with Barr, and otherwise keeping track of his developments through his mother. "I would rather be connected with that Museum and with Barr than with anything I could think of," he informed Louise in the beginning of November, just a few weeks before the museum opened its doors for the first time. "I will have to hump myself and learn something in a hurry though." He had done just that, his detail-filled letters back to Barr indicating the breadth of his travels and knowledge. He was beginning to think in terms of exhibitions, too, purchasing a few modern lighting fixtures at the Bauhaus with the intention of using them for a show on the school. They were in his trunks when he arrived in New York from Europe just two days before Christmas.

It was astonishing how rapidly the Museum of Modern Art had come into being. In retrospect, there was clearly a void that needed filling. European modernism had made its grand debut on American shores in 1913 with the Armory Show, at which Marcel Duchamp's *Nude Descending a Staircase* was the most provocative attraction. But in the decades since there had emerged no formal home for the modern in the recalcitrant and snobbish American museum world. Duchamp, in collaboration with Katherine Dreier, had founded the Société Anonyme as a kind of roving collection, but it was rather ad hoc and without a permanent residence. For the most part, the modern was the province of private galleries.

How to fill this vacuum? The idea for the Museum of Modern Art was born in the fall of 1928 in, of all places, Cairo. Johnson had been there just a few months earlier, touring the city in his Lawrence of Arabia rig. He had fortunately moved along before the arrival of Abby Aldrich Rockefeller and Lillie P. Bliss, for it seems unlikely they would have been amused by his getup. Rockefeller, the wife of John D. Rockefeller Jr., notably lacked a sense of humor. The two women had met by chance in Cairo, and it was there that they touched on the idea of an institutional home for the kind of progressive art in which they were both interested. On the return voyage, Rockefeller recruited a third society matron to the cause, Mary Quinn Sullivan.

Their first order of business was finding an executive to run their museum, and they quickly landed on A. Conger Goodyear, who must have seemed created by the gods for the purpose. Educated at Yale, Goodyear had executive experience as an Army colonel during World War I and then with his family's lumber business. More recently, he had directed Buffalo's Albright Gallery, where he had shown courage in his willingness to promote modern art. Indeed, he had been pushed off the museum's board over his purchase of a Picasso—*La Toilette*, of 1906—then considered too avant-garde and risqué for local tastes.

Goodyear brought in a distinguished team of advisers to the Museum of Modern Art, among them Harvard's renowned museum authority, Paul J. Sachs. He, in turn, recruited Barr as the museum's director and guiding curatorial spirit. Johnson was privy to almost none of this. By the time Barr accepted the appointment, Johnson had long since departed on his annual tour of Europe.

After a frantic few months of preparation, the Museum of Modern Art (MoMA) opened on November 8, 1929 with a show of paintings by Cézanne, Gauguin, Seurat, and van Gogh. It could hardly have chosen a less auspicious moment, with the stock market still in free fall. Its home was not particularly inspiring, either: a converted office space on the twelfth floor of the Heckscher Building, an ornate commercial tower on the southwest corner of Fifty-seventh Street and Fifth Avenue. Curiosity, however, was a powerful draw for a public still largely unfamiliar with the modern. From the start there were lines down the block, and the Heckscher's other tenants were furious over endless wait times for elevators.

Johnson missed that first exhibition but arrived in New York in time for the next, a survey of American painting. That show, which opened in December of 1930, was not particularly exciting, but the energy flowing out of the small office Barr had established in the back of the gallery was infectious. Among the cast of characters was Jere Abbott, who gave up a position running the arts department at Wesleyan to serve as his friend's chief deputy, and Cary Ross, a man Friday from Tennessee who left medical school at Johns Hopkins for a life in the arts. Ross was an especially romantic figure, handsome and independently wealthy: he often told stories of his days hobnobbing in Paris with the likes of Hemingway and the Fitzgeralds. Another fixture was Margaret Fitzmaurice-Scolari—"Daisy" to her friends—a young art historian who had been teaching Italian at Vassar when the museum opened. She had come down to see the inaugural exhibition and was introduced to Barr by a mutual friend. They became an item almost immediately, and married over the following summer, barely six months later. Barr, who curated all things, loved the woman but did not care for her name. He thought *Daisy* was no better than *Margaret*, however, so he promptly lopped off the last three letters of *Margaret*. Henceforth she was known as *Marga*.

"It was a fantastic atmosphere," she recalled. "You felt an unbelievable vibration. It sort of centered around Alfred but, nevertheless, everybody was adding their contributions, reminding one another of things and saying, 'We could do this.' 'We could do that.' It was absolutely electric." It was a hothouse, and not just in the figurative sense: Barr had the windows boarded over to maximize the gallery's limited wall space, thereby eliminating all natural ventilation. To escape the heat, the team gathered at a Chinese restaurant just around the corner or at the bachelors' pad Barr shared with Jere Abbott before he and Marga moved in together.

Johnson, just returned from Europe, was one of several figures orbiting the core group; when visiting the city, he kept a room at the Biltmore Hotel. Among the others were architecture historian Henry-Russell Hitchcock—though Johnson would not become close with him until the summer—and New York gallerist J. B. Neumann. Johnson insinuated himself into this gang, his easy rapport with Barr picking up right where it had left off. It was a peripatetic existence, however. Johnson, who still had one semester left at Harvard before his graduation, spent the early part of the term shuttling back and forth between Cambridge and New York.

Johnson became officially associated with the museum for the first time in April, not as a curator but as a member of the newly formed Junior Advisory Committee, a group of younger trustees-in-waiting that Barr hoped would back his more progressive ideas (such as holding exhibitions of modern architecture) and also support the museum financially. The first chairman was George Howe, a socially dexterous Philadelphia architect, but he was soon displaced by Nelson Rockefeller, very clearly being groomed as his mother's heir. George Gershwin served for a time, his presence lending a celebrity cachet to the proceedings, which were typically well lubricated by drink. Lincoln Kirstein and Eddie Warburg, both due to graduate from Harvard with Johnson in June, were also inaugural members. They would all become close friends, though not immediately. Kirstein, always a severe judge of character, summed up Johnson quickly, and he was not impressed. Johnson, he found, was overly pushy and lacking in seriousness, "a rather silly, gossipy, enthusiastic person."

There was truth in that assessment, though it was not widely shared among the other initiates of Barr's circle. Johnson was popular and seemed to fit right in with the group. That he was wealthy and boyishly handsome did not hurt his cause. The Barr circle, too, was a fraternity of sympathetic gay men who understood their homosexuality not as a personal defect. Abbott, Hitchcock, Kirstein, Ross, and Warburg were all gay. That was part of New York's attraction—it was a city where one could live, if not entirely out in the open, more freely than in conservative places such as Boston or Cleveland. "For the nation's bachelors, this city is the Mecca," a *New York Times* magazine story declared in September of 1928. "New York appeals to the nation's bachelors because it is a city where the young man can lead his life with the least interruption," the *Times* wrote, and one did not have to read too closely between the lines to understand the meaning. Better yet, the paper wrote, it was a city of opportunity for anyone "preparing for fame and fortune in the arts." That surely described Johnson.

Though he was commuting from Cambridge, Johnson managed to find a partner of his own within the Barr circle, someone who was in many ways his doppelgänger. Like Johnson himself, Cary Ross was the product of a second-tier American city (Knoxville), and he held an Ivy League degree (from Yale). He was also, like Johnson, independently wealthy, directionless, handsome, and prone to mental instability. Above all, he possessed those elixirs Johnson found so utterly irresistible: style and taste. The living room of his apartment, on East Fifty-first Street, was furnished with chairs designed by Le Corbusier with his collaborators Pierre Jeanneret and Charlotte Perriand: a steel-frame sling-back (known as model LC1) and his now-iconic reclining chaise longue, also steel-frame and with a swoopy, body-hugging curve. That chair today is ubiquitous as a design statement in modern interiors, but Ross probably had the only one in the United States at the time. He also had a bent-tube end table by Bauhausler Marcel Breuer, and in the bedroom a pair of Le Corbusier beds with matching Picasso prints hanging above. For Johnson, so busily remaking himself as an authority on modern design, it was the ideal New York crash pad.

Was it a fling or a relationship? For all their similarities, on that they could not agree. Ross was not interested in an exclusive arrangement. Johnson, who had left Ruhtenberg with his wife back in Berlin, wanted something more formal. The emotional burden of this situation fell on Johnson just as he was coming under the pressure of satisfying his final requirements for graduation from Harvard, after seven years of struggle. He had successfully petitioned to have his last semester's course load reduced to a single class, but he would still have to stand for his final examinations, in Greek and German. Marga Barr, who had a calming, maternal presence, visited him in Cambridge in April. She found him studying frantically, and despondent over the state of his relationship with Ross. The situation had thrown him into another funk, prompting a new round of consultations with Dr. MacPherson. Shortly thereafter, possibly on Marga's advice—or secretly under pressure from Barr himself—Ross traveled to Cambridge to formally cut things off, or at least come to some kind of mutual understanding.

In the aftermath, Johnson wrote Marga a heartfelt letter describing his predicament. "You are the only one who knows about Cary and me, and to whom I can talk now," he told her. "As you know, the only reason it came about was because he is good-looking and identified with that group down there in my emotional life. Well it seems now that it was merely a passing whim with him, and he was too weak to tell me, and let me go on thinking more. He came up the other day, and naturally I soon found out where the land lay, and am now in a species of hell which I heartily dislike."

In fact, that was not the end of the affair. Johnson managed to pass his exams, but he did not bother to hang around Cambridge for his own graduation ceremony; most of his own classmates and friends were long since gone. Instead he sailed for Europe, where he would meet up with the Barr gang, which had reassembled in Paris. When Johnson arrived on the French coast, Ross was standing on the pier waiting for him. They spent the night together in Cherbourg, enjoying the local cuisine if not the uncomfortable accommodations at their second-rate hotel—they were in France, but there were no Le Corbusier beds to be had. The next day they drove together to Paris, establishing themselves in greater comfort at the Élysées Palace hotel. Johnson, as usual, had taken a car along with him on the transatlantic journey, a Cord convertible with rolling fenders and an elongated hood that seemed to reach straight into the future.

It was a bright moment. The Barrs, Alfred and Marga, had married in a small Paris ceremony a few days before Johnson's arrival. Revolving around them was a coterie that included Hitchcock, the Neumanns, composers Randall Thompson and Virgil Thomson, and the Hollywood film producer George Kates. Johnson busied himself visiting exhibition after exhibition, and with tours of the latest architecture. He drove out to see Le Corbusier's houses in the Paris suburbs, the Villa Savoye and the Villa Stein, which he considered artistic achievements if rather arbitrary in design and utterly impractical. His interview with the architect himself did not go well, setting a tone for a bitter relationship that would last for decades. "He is an objectionable man but unquestionably a genius," Johnson noted.

Johnson's itinerary was still in flux when he arrived in Paris, though a reunion with Ruhtenberg in Berlin was always in mind. The Barrs would also be traveling to Germany, visiting artists and galleries in preparation for the coming MoMA* exhibition season. They would be accompanied, at least part of the time, by Ross and the Neumanns. Neumann, described by Johnson as "an Austrian Jew art dealer who is one of the most charming people I have ever met," wondered whether Johnson might join his art gallery as a dealer, and also offered him a position as correspondent for the German art magazine *Die Form,* to which he was connected.

Johnson declined these overtures because his primary interest was modern architecture, and he had found another mentor to attach himself to, the very man whose writing had supposedly inspired him to turn to that field in the first place: Henry-Russell Hitchcock. Presumably, the two were deputized by Barr to at least begin thinking about a museum exhibition on the new architecture. Because nothing was guaranteed on that score (Barr had yet to put the idea to the board), the two decided they would collaborate on a book. Johnson, of course, had already conceived such a project the previous year, with McAndrew, and he was happy to see the idea rejuvenated with a more esteemed coauthor.

---

* The acronym MoMA did not come into official use until 1966, but it is used here for convenience.

Hitchcock, in turn, wanted to rewrite and expand his own book, *Modern Architecture: Romanticism and Reintegration,* this due in no small part to Barr's criticism of it. In a generally positive review in *Hound & Horn,* Barr had complained that the book was both "too erudite for the ordinary reader" and rather timid in its advocacy of the new. It also needed better pictures.

The two men could not have made a more unlikely pair—it's a shame that Kates, the film producer, did not see the possibilities of this architectural Laurel and Hardy before him, a scenario ripe for slapstick. Whereas Johnson was impeccable in appearance and comportment—the very picture of an urbane swell—Hitchcock was a lumpy bear of a man with a scraggly red beard, notoriously unkempt and ill-mannered, with a penchant for rambling (if brilliant) disquisitions on all manner of subjects. Johnson was at first in awe of him, but gradually began to find his intellectual footing, though he considered it a moral victory if he could get a word in edgewise once Hitchcock launched into one of his lectures. (His mother's rambling lantern-slide orations must have come to mind.) Overall, though, he was excited simply to be working with Hitchcock, a man he had admired for so long.

From the beginning, it was agreed that Hitchcock would take the primary authorial role, with Johnson working in more of a bureaucratic and editorial capacity. But he was hardly a pushover. Johnson had already seen more of the new modern architecture in person than Hitchcock, and as it was his car and his money bankrolling the expedition, he was by no means a silent partner. "I find that if I contradict loudly and positively enough that he begins to think something is wrong with his ideas after all and we come to an agreement," wrote Johnson. The longer they stayed together, the more comfortable Johnson became in expressing himself. Intellectually, it turned out, they were an almost perfect complement, each covering the other's weaknesses: Hitchcock had the authority and breadth of knowledge Johnson lacked; Johnson could break Hitchcock of his academicism, and was a natural evangelist. And so they began work on the defining book that would make the persuasive argument Barr wanted, *The International Style,* though for the moment they were still thinking that it would be published in German.

Where better to begin their pilgrim's progress than at the office of J. J. P. Oud, the Dutch architect who had first brought Johnson and Hitchcock together, in print if not in person? They were accompanied on this first leg of their journey by a young member of Le Corbusier's studio, whom Johnson found no more agreeable than his employer. They left him in Belgium, a nation Johnson found "dirty and disagreeable." Antwerp, in particular, was "overcrowded with Flemish idiots." Typically, he managed to suspend his prejudices when introduced to someone he considered interesting. In Brussels, Johnson and Hitchcock were hosted for dinner at the home of architect Henry van de Velde, pioneer of the art nouveau. Johnson judged him "the most charming man in the world."

Van de Velde was displaced in Johnson's affections by Oud from virtually the moment they met. The two, in fact, seemed to form a bond almost immediately after Johnson and Hitchcock arrived at Oud's Rotterdam office. Like Johnson, he had only recently emerged from a nervous breakdown. As a younger man, he had also been a strident polemicist, a founding editor of the influential journal *De Stijl* and a close friend of the artists Theo van Doesburg and Piet Mondrian. Oud's more disputatious days were behind him, though. Indeed, it was his moderate nature that had alienated him from his former *De Stijl* colleagues, who questioned his devotion to their project to create a pure architecture of color and plane. Conversely, he cared too much about aesthetics to be embraced by the more doctrinaire functionalist wing of the modern movement—those who saw no room for the art in architecture.

Oud became a kind of informal adviser and mentor to Johnson and Hitchcock, proposing architects and buildings for them to visit. He knew everyone there was to know and was on good terms even with those whom he ideologically opposed. Johnson was so enthralled with him that he got the idea that Oud might build something on the family property back in Pinehurst, now that Homer had warned him off the idea of building himself. He wrote to his mother with the suggestion, telling her "I would have perfect confidence in him."

A few weeks later, before any mention of the house project, he tried to capitalize on his newfound relationship with Oud. A brazen Johnson asked Oud to travel to Paris on his behalf to purchase a painting by Mondrian, one of Oud's old friends. Johnson had sent Oud a copy of Hitchcock's book, and he presumably considered this some kind of lopsided quid pro quo. Specifically, Johnson hoped Oud could acquire a painting from the artist that was "not too expensive." Oud declined, though he was kind enough to forward Johnson's inquiry to Mondrian, with instructions that the artist make the selection himself. "I think you can leave it to him to choose it for you," he wrote Johnson.* Johnson was not entirely trusting, however, and had Hitchcock pick it up for him on his return to the States through Paris. In the end, Johnson got just the bargain he wanted, a square composition with red and blue fields. But he was right not to trust Mondrian: he paid 2,000 francs for the picture, which had gone unsold during an exhibition in Zürich the previous year at a price of 1,300. The Dutch painter was no doubt happy to unload it, as it was in lousy condition—so bad that when Johnson turned it over to the museum as a gift, in 1941, it was accepted only on the condition that the artist come in and restore it.

From the Hague, Johnson and Hitchcock drove across the German border to Hanover and Hamburg, whence they took a plane to Sweden for a short visit to the Stockholm Exhibition of 1930. The fair, to promote Swedish design and manufacturing, featured dramatic pavilions of glass and steel by the architects Gunnar Asplund and Sigurd Lewerentz. Johnson and Hitchcock admired the exhibition, especially the temporary Paradise Café—it would go in their book. Johnson was less enthusiastic about Denmark, a country he thought should be "prohibited by law." But it was Denmark that might have done well to restrict access to

---

* The painting, *Composition no. II with Red and Blue* (1925), remains in the MoMA collection.

Johnson. Speeding through a small town near Copenhagen with the Cord's top down, Johnson spotted a young woman stepping out to cross the street. As traffic was rare, she did not check to see the American roadster gunning toward her at forty-five miles per hour. Johnson slammed on the brakes and swerved toward a rock pile, but he hit the woman anyway, knocking her to the ground. She was dazed, according to Johnson, and fled the scene in embarrassment. Meanwhile, Johnson's radiator overheated and the car would not restart until it was given a push down the road by locals. "It was not the least my fault," Johnson claimed, "but it was a scare and made an unhappy evening." A reasonable lesson to take from the incident—presuming Johnson's recollection was honest—would have been to ease up on the accelerator. Johnson, however, liked to go fast.

Eventually they reunited with Barr, Neumann, and Ross, who had been traveling together through Germany. It made for an awkward party. Ross, who had previously had a relationship—or at least a dalliance—with Hitchcock, was now depressed at the state of his relationship with Johnson, which was all but over. In a turnabout, it was now he who seemed vacant and unhappy. Johnson, meanwhile, had his own relationship problem. Though there had never been anything between them romatically, Hitchcock's constant presence was wearing heavily on him. That he was "somewhat uncouth" may have seemed charming when they were beginning their travels, a mark of Hitchcock's eccentric genius, but by the time they arrived in Berlin, Johnson had grown tired of his traveling companion and offered a litany of complaints about his behavior: Hitchcock was deaf and smacked his lips when he ate. He was short-tempered with waiters and officials. He left his clothes lying around the floor of their room. He didn't bathe often. (In the words of their mutual friend Lincoln Kirstein, he smelled like "dried wine and cockroaches.") He was a depressive, and his foul moods affected all those around him. His German was embarrassing, but he liked to use it anyway, and loudly, because he was so hard of hearing. He did, at least, have the good sense to leave important matters to the more fluent Johnson.

There was relief in Berlin, and it came in the person of Jan Ruhtenberg. The two, having not seen each other for a year, ran off to a cottage loaned to the Ruhtenbergs in Wannsee, the lakeside retreat on the outskirts of the city, where they could relax and enjoy the beach. Back in Berlin, Johnson moved in with the Ruhtenbergs, and Jan designed handsome modern stationery for him with their address on Achenbachstrasse. He needed it. His days were spent hustling materials for "the book," which took up an ever-increasing portion of his time and mental space—he was now dreaming nightly about architecture—though it was still without a publisher. In their naïveté, Johnson and Hitchcock presumed they would find one in Berlin, but those prospects were unrealistic, given the grim state of the German publishing industry and the fact that they were writing in English. Undeterred, Johnson hired a secretary to assist with his correspondence.

The book, also, commanded more travel. The short break was enough to steady him for another journey with Hitchcock, this time a tour south through the Rhine and down into Zürich, where Oud had arranged a meeting with architectural historian Sigfried Giedion, the preeminent European propagandist for the new. This was to be a great meeting of the minds, and also something of a confrontation of architectural philosophies, for Giedion broadly represented the functionalist camp—architecture as a mechanistic practice—whereas Hitchcock and Johnson were more interested in aesthetics—modernism as a style. The visit was nevertheless cordial, and they toured the city together looking at new works. "The things he liked we didn't," noted Johnson. Their travels, he thought, gave them a far greater knowledge of the field than Giedion—an advantage that would show in their book, once published.

When Hitchcock had to return to Paris and then the United States, he was replaced at Johnson's side by Ruhtenberg. They continued west from Switzerland into Austria and then Czechoslovakia, which Johnson liked no better now than he had a year earlier. Once again, his actions behind the wheel of the big Cord convertible proved deeply troubling. Speeding down another country road, he noticed in the corner of his eye a girl on a bicycle slowly approaching on an intersecting street. In the oncoming lane was a man driving a motorcycle with a sidecar carrying another man and a child. Johnson did not brake, nor did the motorcyclist, both presuming the girl on the bicycle would stop. She didn't. "All I saw was the girl flying through the air after being tossed by the motorcycle," said Johnson. Ruhtenberg was so traumatized that he refused to get out of the car. Johnson did, helping to lift the motorcycle off its driver, who was not severely injured. He carried him into the back seat of the Cord. Moments later, an ambulance coincidentally drove past, and its paramedics took over the scene. Johnson immediately got back in his car and sped away. He never checked on the girl.

The trip into Czechoslovakia was not without its recompenses, the primary one being a visit to the city of Brno, a pilgrimage station for anyone serious about the new architecture. There the two met Otto Eisler, a Jewish architect ten years Johnson's senior, who had worked under Gropius in Dessau and was among the leaders of the modern movement in the region. In short order Johnson and Eisler developed a bond, never mind the latter's religion, beginning what would be a sadly truncated relationship. Eisler toured the visitors through his new work and other modern landmarks in the city, many built by his family construction firm for the city's large and prosperous Jewish population.

The great revelation of Brno came on their visit to one of those houses: Mies van der Rohe's Tugendhat house. This was the *ne plus ultra* of modern domestic architecture, the height of restrained elegance. The clients were a Jewish family of considerable means and progressive ideals, and they had asked Mies to create a home that would conform to a modern lifestyle. He gave them a masterpiece. The house sat on the brow of a hill, with wide planes of glass overlooking the city. Its materials were the most precious available: a dividing wall of onyx, a hemispherical screen of macassar ebony, stairs of Italian travertine, chrome columns. Mies outfitted it with furnishings from his own studio — including the specially created "Brno" chairs, covered in white pigskin — arranged in composed settings.

These features gave the house a sense of ample luxury, but equally remarkable was its plan. While the private spaces of the Tugendhats and their servants were removed from the public in the conventional manner, the living room, dining room, and library flowed openly from one to another, all while maintaining their individual integrity. One contemporary critic compared the house's rhythm to music, an apt metaphor. Years later, Johnson would adapt many of its elements when designing his own Glass House.

Mies, by then, had already come to occupy a large space in Johnson's life. Before leaving New York for the summer in Europe, Johnson had taken a lease on a one-bedroom apartment in the Southgate, an apartment complex on East Fifty-second Street. This was about as design-forward a building as could be found in the city, a new development in restrained art-deco style designed by Emery Roth, an architect known chiefly for his luxury apartment towers along Central Park: the Beresford, the San Remo, and the El Dorado. The neighborhood was in the midst of rapid gentrification from a seedy haven of tenements into an exclusive enclave, Sutton Place. The Barrs had agreed to take the apartment directly above Johnson's, and the Neumanns also planned to move into the complex, making it something of a community. Johnson harbored the idea of designing the apartment for himself, and had even left instructions that it be stripped of base moldings and door frames so all of its surfaces would be flush. Once in Berlin, he started to work on it with Ruhtenberg.

That plan changed after Johnson had the opportunity to visit a few of Mies's Berlin interiors. It occurred to Johnson that it would be a coup to have the German take over his apartment in New York. "I think it would be the cheapest possible kind of publicity for my style," he wrote to his mother. There would be no other interior like it in the United States, though it wouldn't come cheap. The Barrs would gladly have had such a design, but they could not afford it. In another letter, Johnson warned that it would indeed be "rather expensive," but that it was nevertheless critical for him professionally to have a "show apartment."

Johnson presented this idea to Mies at his office near the Tiergarten, showing him the apartment plan he had already started working on in collaboration with Ruhtenberg. Mies was "polite but distant." He seemed more receptive when he discovered that Johnson and Ruhtenberg were on their way to the Bauhaus, to which he had recently been named director, and that he could hitch a ride with them in Johnson's Cord. It turned out Mies was happy for the commission, given the state of the German economy, and also impressed with the initial plan that Johnson and Ruhtenberg had developed. Johnson was, of course, thrilled. Although he still liked Oud better as a person, he decided Mies was the single greatest man he had ever met. "He keeps his distance and impersonality at all times," he wrote, "only letting down graciously once in a while, thus honoring you as the nod of a god would."

Johnson rushed to conclude arrangements for the apartment in the few days he had left in Berlin. While the job would be overseen by Mies, the project would largely be managed by his frequent collaborator and mistress Lilly Reich, whose authority as a designer of furniture and interior spaces Johnson duly appreciated. Ruhtenberg would also play a significant role, acting as his agent in Berlin while Johnson was back in New York. (Within the year, Ruhtenberg would develop this into an apprentice position in the Mies atelier.) Before Johnson's departure, the Mies office presented him an itemized estimate of the job cost: 10,240 reichsmarks, of which 2,000 were the architect's fee (the latter figure roughly corresponded to a year's blue-collar salary). Johnson left funds to cover the bill, or most of it, in an account to be administered by Ruhtenberg.

He had tied things up neatly for himself, and his future now seemed assured. He would have the show apartment he wanted, a personal and professional triumph. He was satisfied, too, with the progress he had made on the book — what was left could be accomplished just as easily in New York. When completed, it too would be a formidable achievement. His relationship with Ruhtenberg had been joyful and mutually beneficial. He could be forgiven for thinking the last few months a whirlwind, his focus so intently centered on architecture and his own personal growth that he was almost oblivious to other developments in the world.

If he had taken note of the rising National Socialist movement in Germany, he did not mention it in his surviving correspondence, though there were hints that he had been touched by its virulence: there were his derisive comments about Czechs and also a complaint about the resort of Baden-Baden, which he found "not as pleasant as it should have been" because it seemed to him there were no other gentiles. Perhaps he felt the same way on September 17, standing once more on the long, low deck of the *Bremen,* as Germany faded gradually from his sight, if not his mind.

CHAPTER 4

Show Time

After all what I want most to do is be influential, and if there is a method why not learn it.

—Philip Johnson, 1931

On a fall evening not long after his return, Johnson stood in a patrician New York drawing room with the Museum of Modern Art's board of trustees seated before him. They were an imposing lot, a mix of society fixtures and captains of industry, and they were all looking to him with that combination of curiosity and skepticism characteristic of privilege. Most imposing of all was Abby Aldrich Rockefeller, who held regal authority over the proceedings. She was the board's treasurer, but that title hardly described the nearly divine authority she wielded over the museum in 1930.

Johnson had come before the trustees, at Alfred Barr's request, to sell their planned exhibition of modern architecture. Barr expected his debonair protégé would charm with his wit and impress with his zeal for the subject that had been his veritable obsession over the past year. Johnson, he thought, would be a natural before the board. He was a product of the rarefied social world of the trustees, and he could speak to them in a suave but assured manner that would give them confidence.

But Johnson began fumbling the moment he was introduced. He had not prepared sufficiently, presuming that he could speak extemporaneously and that his knowledge and enthusiasm would carry the day. Instead he labored on, and as he did so he heard the sighs of board members who found their patience sorely tested. When he finished, there was silence. Then William T. Aldrich, Mrs. Rockefeller's priggish architect brother, a classicist of the old school, leaned over to advise her of his opinion: "It's a lot of nonsense, my dear."

That might have been the end of it, and architectural culture might have progressed differently over the next century, but Abby Aldrich Rockefeller kept her own counsel and was not put off by her younger brother. She had faith in Barr, whom she had hand-selected to run the museum, and there was enough grist in Johnson's presentation, however poorly delivered, to warrant her tacit approval. "Now, ladies and gentlemen," she said, "I know you're not interested in this, but it just may be that when this report is put into writing you might find it interesting." It wasn't a full-on endorsement, but it was close, and there was no one in the room with the temerity to gainsay her. Johnson, though humiliated, walked out with a chance—and the conviction that he would not squander it.

Johnson should have been prepared for an unreceptive audience. When the museum's founding matrons were steaming back from Cairo in the fall of 1928, they hadn't thought of presenting architecture shows at their would-be institution, even if it was the "mother art." The museum was to be a place for painting and sculpture of the kind they collected themselves, and that other museums, specifically the Metropolitan, would not accept. That reluctance was an affront to their taste and their stature. Theirs was an altruistic mission, but not one completely devoid of vanity; for the most part the trustees displayed their pictures in conservative drawing rooms with the kind of period furnishings found in *Town & Country*. Architectural exhibitions were the purview of professional organizations and world's-fair committees. Putting buildings in museums just wasn't done. For those interested in architecture, New York offered a perfect solution: just walk outside and look up.

In time Johnson would make his own contributions to that famous skyline; indeed, he would become the most prominent skyscraper architect in the world. For the moment, however, he deemed skyscrapers a menace, a product of "American megalomania." It was not just their height that offended him, though he worried that they would block out light and create cities of unappealing density. His principal objections were more esoteric, driven by his increasingly dogmatic yet still somewhat confused ideas about what a new architecture should be. Though critics had proclaimed the emergence of a new "skyscraper style" in America, Johnson saw no such thing, only a motley assortment of tall buildings—engineering marvels, perhaps, but with no consistent aesthetic signature. He ridiculed the decorative flourishes of America's great towers—the projecting eagles of the Chrysler Building, the spire of the Empire State Building—even as those very elements endeared them to the public, and would be aped by himself years later.

For the moment, he wanted none of it. As far as he was concerned, Mies van der Rohe had theorized what a truly modern skyscraper might be: a crystalline tower with a steel skeleton visible through its translucent glass skin. That was the future.

What he flubbed in person before the MoMA board, he managed to convey on paper in sharp, confident prose, his thoughts condensed and neatly organized into three hastily typewritten pages. "There is today both here in America and abroad a marked activity in architecture," he began. "Technical advances, new methods and fresh thoughts are solving contemporary building problems in a manner that can truly be called modern." The challenge was that the public was unaware of this movement, and that the American scene was characterized instead by "a chaos of conflicting and very often unintelligent building." The show would remedy this problem, giving Americans the intellectual tools necessary to understand the new architecture. To do this it would focus on the work of a group of nine exemplary modern architects. There would also be a section on industrial building and mass housing, and an international competition for young architects. He even had a date picked out for the opening: February 1, 1932.

Johnson's hubris was evident throughout this proposal. He promised "no little benefit will accrue to the museum in sponsoring the exhibition." It would be a publicity coup, he claimed, that would draw a hitherto-untapped audience of homeowners, educators, and businessmen to the museum. He proposed a supervisory committee to oversee the show, and had the audacity to place Mrs. Rockefeller's name on it. Also named to this committee was a man who had heretofore expressed scant interest in modern architecture: Homer Johnson. Though he was not necessarily enamored of his son's field of endeavor, Homer could at least be pleased that his son was engaged productively and establishing himself in the upper reaches of New York society.

Johnson recruited his father to be both guarantor and rainmaker, for an architectural exhibition was an inherently costly proposition. The show required architectural models, photography, and a suitably forward installation design — a commission he proposed for no less an eminence than Mies. Added to these expenditures were the costs of administering his planned competition and printing a catalog. (Never mind that the same material would be covered in the book on which he was collaborating with Hitchcock.) To defray costs, and also to spread the modernist gospel, Johnson proposed offering the exhibition to other venues after the run at the museum was complete, and indeed it would become the museum's first traveling exhibition.* It also helped that Johnson offered his curatorial services to the museum at no charge, as well as those of an "executive secretary," a position gladly accepted by Alan Blackburn, his schoolboy friend from Hackley and Harvard. Johnson also offered a personal "business headquarters" (his apartment) because there was no space for him in the museum's one-room office in the Heckscher Building.

That first proposal, which landed on Goodyear's desk at the beginning of December, established the essential contours of the show, which would be freighted with the ungainly title *Modern Architecture: International Exhibition*. There were, however, several significant modifications, the most obvious being the scrapping of Johnson's proposed architectural competition. That would have been a costly administrative burden, and the inexperienced Johnson already had enough on his hands. Raising funds was his chief obstacle, a problem he had himself worsened by promising to find corporate underwriting and to steer clear of the museum's usual benefactors. (He worried, justifiably, that the trustees would reject his exhibition lest it cannibalize the museum's other fundraising efforts.)

---

* It visited twelve additional American museums, as well as the Bullocks Wiltshire department store in Los Angeles.

Mrs. Rockefeller declined not only to join his advisory committee but even to meet him again in person until the trustees had given their consent. In her place, Goodyear recruited board member Stephen Clark, a shrewd collector who was heir to the Singer sewing machine fortune.

To assist in fundraising, Johnson put together a pamphlet to be sent to potential donors. Five hundred copies of "Built to Live In" were printed, its title conveying a sense of reassurance that the "modern style," contrary to popular perception, could be accessible, humane, even luxurious. Johnson's text opened with a primer on modern architecture, tracing its roots to the technological innovations of the nineteenth century. In the modern future, load-bearing walls of brick and stone would be replaced by steel columns and curtains of glass. Homes, offices, and even cities would be planned according to functional logic, though not without consideration of aesthetics. A local bank would no longer look like a Greek temple; it would assume a form determined by its program and materials of construction. But this architecture would not be purely functional — Johnson now abhorred those purely functional architects who renounced any aesthetic impulse as a bourgeois conceit. Johnson's new architecture could both embrace functional logic and achieve beauty. "While the architect accepts the machine age, he also transcends it," he wrote. "The modern architect builds to reveal beauty of construction, plan, and materials."

Johnson's curatorial inexperience was nowhere more apparent than in the selection of the nine practitioners and firms he planned to feature as exponents of the new modernism, a group that would be supplemented by works from lesser figures. Among the headliners, four would come from Europe — the quartet of Gropius, Le Corbusier, Oud, and Mies — and the remaining five were all to be American. This was a curious decision given Johnson's general disdain for American building, and even more curious when one examined whom exactly he chose. This motley cast comprised Norman Bel Geddes, the industrial designer known for streamlining; the brothers Monroe and Irwin Bowman, who ran a virtually unknown architectural practice in Chicago; Raymond Hood, chief architect of Rockefeller Center; the Philadelphia firm of Howe & Lescaze (George Howe being familiar from the museum's Junior Committee); and Frank Lloyd Wright, the gray eminence of American modernism.

As a group, the Americans had no coherence. Bel Geddes, hardly an architect at all, was quickly dropped. The Bowmans were chosen because they had proposed an aluminum-clad apartment building in Chicago, and this appealed to Johnson given his personal interest in that metal and his plan to approach Alcoa as an underwriter. Hood was considered "modernistic" and thus unsuitable, but a necessary evil given his close relationship with the Rockefeller family. (Goodyear made sure of his inclusion.) Only Howe & Lescaze had any track record designing in Johnson's preferred idiom. Their thirty-six-story Philadelphia Savings Fund Society (PSFS) building, then under construction, was the first skyscraper that might truly be described as of the International Style. Finally there was Wright, chosen rather cynically as a figurehead because the idea of a major exhibition on modern architecture without him would have been unfathomable, not to mention weaker at the box office. "He has nothing to say to the International Group," Johnson wrote to the critic Lewis Mumford, whom Johnson had enlisted to help curate the housing portion of the show. "Wright was a great pioneer but he is a romantic and has nothing more to do with architecture today." Mumford disagreed, and would be thrust uncomfortably between the two when their relationship began to combust and Wright threatened to pull out altogether.

During that recruitment process, Johnson had other matters to deal with, the most urgent being the design and fabrication of his own living quarters. Most of the Mies-Reich furniture was not yet in commercial production and had to be custom-made in Germany. Johnson, in the midst of planning the architectural exhibition, left the installation to Alfred Clauss, a German-born architect who had worked in Mies's office on the Barcelona Pavilion of 1929, the architect's signature statement of modern elegance and planning. After emigrating to the United States, Clauss had joined the firm of Howe & Lescaze; he soon went into a partnership with another young associate there, George Daub.

When the apartment was complete, it was just the showpiece Johnson had envisioned, a swanky bachelor's pad he could model as an example of "his style," designed by the man he considered its foremost practitioner. Johnson would later claim that Mies, with few other commissions in that difficult economic moment, worked on it "as if it were six skyscrapers," a far stretch even by Johnson's somewhat lax standards for verity, and especially so insofar as much of the work was in fact done by Lilly Reich.

The Johnson apartment on East 49th Street in 1934, with furnishings by Mies and Lilly Reich. (© The Museum of Modern Art / Licensed by SCALA / Art Resource, NY)

Authorship aside, the place was undeniably dramatic. The living room was designed for entertaining, with a grand piano at one end and a pair of Mies's signature Barcelona chairs and a Mies daybed (actually designed by Reich) artfully composed on the far side of the room. The walls were white, with a floor-to-ceiling drape of blue silk along the window wall, closing off the space, and a rug of straw matting—unheard of for such an opulent setting. As Johnson began to design for himself in the coming years, the room would become a model—in particular the way Mies articulated space with precise arrangements of furniture and flat planes of color. Even Kirstein thought it the acme of "luxe and utility," though he could not help commenting that the straw rugs attracted dirt and that the Barcelona chairs, though "wonderful" in themselves, were too big for the room.

Otherwise, the apartment was sparse. The dining room was unadorned but for a circular glass table surrounded by four of Mies's MR chairs; little accommodation was made for the kitchen, which Johnson did not use. The bedroom was small, with a single twin bed, a simple black cabinet, and a round glass bedside table with a Bauhaus-school table lamp for reading. Johnson's study got the most elaborate treatment: a slab of a desk covered in brown leather and supported by four chrome legs, with the Brno chair Mies had designed for the Tugendhat house that Johnson so admired. There was a bracketed shelving system for books along one wall, with chromed supports. That furniture is today famous the world over, and accessible if somewhat pricey, but at the time it was unusual and hand-fabricated. Of all the pieces, the desk would stay with him the rest of his life (it remains in the Glass House); on its pliant surface he would do most of his architectural composition.

That was for the future. For the moment the desk was used primarily for his efforts on behalf of the architectural exhibition and his campaign to spread the modernist gospel. While the writing of the book that would come to be *The International Style* was left in the hands of Hitchcock, Johnson took to the popular press with a series of increasingly provocative reviews. His first appearance in a major national publication came in the March 1931 issue of *The New Republic* in the form of a distinctly ungenerous review of *The New World Architecture,* a survey authored by the distinguished theater and art critic Sheldon Cheney. Calling Cheney's analysis "shopworn," Johnson harped, "we seek vainly in his book for a discussion of just what constitutes modern architectural style." Johnson, in fact, had hoped to use his review as a vessel for just such a discussion, but the *New Republic* editors declined to print his harangue. He managed to do a bit better in a review of Joseph Urban's new building for the New School for Social Research in the journal *Arts,* also appearing in March of 1931. Here he was no less condescending—"Urban's admiration for the

New Style is more complete than his understanding"—but he was granted space to enumerate the three principles of that new idiom: a plan derived from function; an absence of applied ornament; the achievement of beauty through proportion and design.

Johnson soon managed to put his definition before the public in the most visible manner possible. The occasion was the annual exhibition of the Architectural League of New York, ordinarily a sleepy clunker of a show, but this time conceived with grander aspirations to honor its fiftieth anniversary. It was, nevertheless, presented in uninspired fashion at the Grand Central Palace, a dank exposition hall on Lexington Avenue between Forty-sixth and Forty-seventh streets. The proceedings represented the breadth of the field, which meant the propensity of exhibited works were traditional in character. "Columns and gables, gables and columns," griped one critic. There were various entries that could be described as "moderne" or "modernistic"—the Empire State Building won the show's Gold Medal—and even a few that could be counted in Johnson's approved style, notably a model of Howe & Lescaze's PSFS tower. But the rejection of a handful of modern submissions offered ripe opportunity for publicity.

That came in the form of a rival exhibition. Put together in little more than a week, *Rejected Architects* opened on the afternoon of April 21 in a storefront across the street from Carnegie Hall, just ten blocks north of the Architectural League's show. Naturally, it was catnip to the press, all the more so as the upstarts hired a man with a sandwich-board advertisement for their exhibition to walk back and forth in front of the Grand Central Palace, to the immense consternation of the league. "Young Architects Stage Rival Show," read a *New York Times* headline, "Call Seniors Reactionary."

The sandwich board was Alfred Barr's idea, and the storefront came courtesy of one of his art-world connections. Johnson played the role of impresario, authoring (and presumably paying for) an accompanying pamphlet. "In 1931 a Salon des Refusés is still useful," he wrote, comparing the participants to "such rebels as Manet and the Impressionists." The kind of architecture favored by this group of young bucks was made plain on the pamphlet cover, which pictured a drawing of a starkly modern country house clearly modeled after Mies's Tugendhat house. The architects of this home were, not accidentally, Mies's erstwhile protégé Alfred Clauss and his partner George Daub. Especially noteworthy was the site for this would-be project: Pinehurst, North Carolina.

Johnson nowhere disclosed that his parents were the clients for this proposed home, to say nothing of the fact that he had spoken of the job with Oud on his trip to Europe the previous summer. The project, in any case, would never pass beyond the model stage, nor would the other house that Clauss & Daub presented in the exhibition. That one had been designed some time earlier for the aviator Charles Lindbergh, but on a purely speculative basis. This led to some trouble when a laudatory story about the two projects appeared in *House Beautiful* under Johnson's byline. Lindbergh, a traditionalist in architecture and fiercely protective of his privacy, had his actual architects, Delano & Aldrich, deliver a stern cease-and-desist order precluding further use of his name. Johnson did manage to land at least one legitimate client for Clauss & Daub, however: the Standard Oil Company of Ohio, one of Homer's clients. The commission was for a series of gas stations in Cleveland. At least two were built, and Johnson put one of them in the exhibition at the museum.

For Johnson, taking a rather literal ownership stake in this movement was important, for the truth was that the intellectual ringleader of the *refusés* was not him but Clauss, the man who had installed his apartment. Clauss had initiated the *refusés* movement before Johnson was even involved, bringing together an impromptu group, most of whom either came out of the office of Howe & Lescaze (a breeding ground for young moderns) or were otherwise based in Philadelphia. In the *Times*'s coverage of the show, Johnson is nowhere mentioned, whereas Clauss is described as the group's "guiding spirit." Indeed, the pamphlet lists Clauss & Daub's New York office—not Johnson or the museum—as the party to which further inquiries should be directed.

Rejected Architects, whatever its origin, was a gauntlet thrown down before the profession, and one that raised the stakes for Johnson's more ambitiously planned exhibition at the museum. By this time he had begun to crystallize his own thinking about what an exhibition should be, his ideas shaped by Barr and explored in the boozy meetings of the Junior Advisory Committee. He was emboldened enough to share his developing philosophy with Mary Quinn Sullivan, one of the founding "Three Ladies" of the museum. "Exhibitions should have a definite purpose," Johnson explained, meaning they should make some polemical argument, as would his architectural show. He also advocated for the expansion of the museum's educational outreach through lectures, an augmented publishing program, development of the museum's fledgling library, and increased advertising—still considered somewhat crass in the genteel museum world. Most seriously of all, he emphasized the broadening of the museum's curatorial program to other arts, in particular architecture and photography.

Johnson retained the essence of that curatorial philosophy throughout his lifetime association with the museum, much of it served in a position of influence from which he could impose it on others. He was already confident enough to offer his ideas to Lincoln Kirstein, who was busy organizing a groundbreaking exhibition on the Bauhaus for the Harvard Society of Contemporary Art, then still in operation in Cambridge. Kirstein accepted his assistance but still found Johnson an irritating lightweight. "His inferiority renders his enthusiasm personally aggressive and his learning a bludgeon," Kirstein wrote in his diary. "In short I can't stand him." Johnson, however, was too useful to ignore. He not only lent the exhibition his Klee, *Sacred Islands,* and a scarf of rayon silk (designed by Bauhaus textile master Gunta Stolzl), but essentially wrote portions of the brief catalog.

Johnson had more trouble when it came to his own architectural show. Having a strong point of view was second nature for him, but actually mounting an exhibition with so many moving parts was another matter. His first order of business was confirming the participation of his featured architects. Bel Geddes, jettisoned almost immediately, was replaced by Richard Neutra, an Austrian-born Jew who had worked with Frank Lloyd Wright before establishing himself permanently in Los Angeles. Logic should have dictated that the addition of Neutra be accompanied by that of Rudolph Schindler, another Austrian émigré based in Los Angeles; their work was similar in nature and they had once been close friends. Johnson, however, did not see it that way; when Schindler indelicately asked to be included, he was impolitely rebuffed. A correspondence continued over the coming year and became increasingly hostile, culminating with a blasting missive from Schindler that read all the more harshly for being in the all-caps of a telegram:

I am not a stylist, not a functionalist, nor any other sloganist. Each of my buildings deals with a different architectural problem, the existence of which has been entirely forgotten in this period of rational mechanization. The question of whether a house is really a house is more important to me, than the fact that it is made of steel, glass, putty, or hot air.

Schindler would not be the only one to attack the curators as style-obsessed aesthetes. Johnson, for his part, later regretted his decision to exclude Schindler, but at the time he seemed to enjoy wielding his king-making power. Besides Schindler, he turned away numerous other prominent candidates, foremost among them Buckminster Fuller, whom he considered a techno-charlatan. Those deemed worthy, however, were subjected to Johnson's extravagant hauteur. One would think, for instance, that Raymond Hood, the distinguished eminence responsible for the Rockefeller family's signature architectural project, might warrant considerable deference from a junior and still-probationary curator at the museum they controlled. But Johnson was undaunted. After tossing Hood the backhanded compliment that his recently completed McGraw-Hill Building was "much better than any picture of it," he had the audacity to add, "the motif at the top strikes me as unnecessarily decorative." This from a twenty-five-year-old with a résumé no thicker than one of his favored planes of glass.

There was one architect who would not stand for Johnson's upstart arrogance, a man whose grandiose sense of self was unsurpassed and in full flower: Frank Lloyd Wright, then just months away from the publication of his own autobiography. Johnson considered Wright a superannuated figure with "nothing to say" about modern architecture, but he understood that a show on the subject without him was well nigh impossible, and so Johnson initiated a campaign of obsequious letter writing, abetted by Mumford, to persuade the great man to participate, which he agreed to do—albeit grudgingly. The relationship between the two did not commence auspiciously: Johnson first promised to visit Wright on a trip to Chicago, then failed to appear. Thereafter Johnson irritated with a request that Wright submit images of his completed work for review—an inconvenient and expensive task in those days, and one that Wright considered well beneath his dignity. (The demand was intended primarily for the lesser-known architects in the show, as was a biographical questionnaire asking them to provide details of their education, travel, and "racial background.") For Wright, who loved the spotlight and was ever in need of work to support his personal extravagance, the promise of so much publicity was impossible to refuse, even as Johnson specifically warned him that many of the selected architects would "probably not meet with your approval." For the moment, Wright was in.

Having squared away his most pressing obligations at home, Johnson sailed for the Continent at the end of May. From a home base in Berlin, he would spend the summer of 1931 securing the participation of the European invitees to his exhibition. On the way he stopped first at the Hague to recruit Oud to the cause. He came offering the carrot that he had previously only hinted at: the Pinehurst commission for his mother, despite the fact that Clauss & Daub had already exhibited plans and a model of this project for the *Rejected Architects* show. Oud represented a major upgrade, though it was clear that even his project was unlikely to get built. The only question was whether the Dutchman—a perfectionist who worked slowly and, like Johnson, was prone to debilitating bouts of depression—could complete a model in time for the show. "I cannot take the risk of overwork[ing] myself again for a thing that may have value only for an exhibition," he would write. Johnson was typically relentless, however, continually brushing aside the gentlemanly Oud's anxieties about the deadline. Over the course of the summer and fall, the architect's fastidiousness would prove a constant nuisance.

In Berlin, Johnson once again moved into the Ruhtenberg home on

Achenbachstrasse, but there was no awkward ménage this time, as Hanna, Jan's wife, had left for a summer on the Wannsee with the children. The affair resumed where it had left off, but Ruhtenberg was busy day and night working in the Mies office and on his own projects, leaving Johnson time alone. One evening he ran into Julien Levy, a dealer in modern art and photography who was familiar from New York. Like Johnson, he was striking in appearance, though with sharp features, and he too had followed the path from Harvard—where he took Sachs's museum course—to Barr's New York circle. Johnson had already come to profit from that relationship: Levy's developer father had arranged for the loaned storefront in which the *Rejected Architects* show was held. Johnson now reciprocated that act of generosity, chaperoning Levy on evening explorations of Berlin's pleasure factories. Years later, Levy could vividly recall these debauched nights. "The grotesque decadence I was to discover over and over again in Berlin those few short weeks," he wrote, "could only be compared, one might suppose, to Paris during the last days of Louis XVI." Levy, who would become the dealer of Salvador Dalí, Marcel Duchamp, and Frida Kahlo, was not easily shocked.

During the days, Johnson collected materials for the exhibition and completed his share of the work on *The International Style*. He once again complained of "torpor," and briefly checked himself into a hospital. His work, in truth, was not especially demanding, not least because he had hired an efficient German secretary to take care of his bureaucratic drudgery. Johnson's primary responsibility was to round up illustrations for the book and write the accompanying captions. (The intellectual heavy lifting was left to Hitchcock.) The process did not endear him to the architects he so admired. Mies stopped answering his calls, as did Otto Haesler, a linchpin of the exhibition's "housing" section. Even Oud, whom he considered a close friend, was intransigent, threatening to withhold his model until he was absolutely satisfied with it. "I shall only send it to the exhibition if it is just as good as I like it," he wrote Johnson in mid-August.

The signal event of Johnson's summer was the Berlin Building Exhibition, a bellwether international fair held on the city fairgrounds. The centerpiece was a series of model homes designed by prominent architects under the banner "THE DWELLING OF OUR TIME." This was ideal bait for Johnson, and on August 9 he published a long review of the exhibition in the *New York Times*, his first appearance in the paper of record. "That the city of Berlin should hold such an ambitious exposition at all when its inhabitants are daily expecting complete bankruptcy is a wonder," he wrote. "That the city should at the same time pick its best modern architect to direct the architectural section is a second wonder." That architect was Mies van der Rohe, and Johnson was quick to lavish praise on him without any disclosure of their relationship. (Neither did he appear conflicted in noting that, "of the younger men, Jan Ruhtenberg is the most gifted and original.")

Mies's contribution to the exhibition was more than curatorial. Beyond choosing the participants and overseeing the installation of their work, he was responsible, with Lilly Reich, for one of the show's signature model dwellings. It was a cross between the now legendary Barcelona Pavilion, produced for the 1929 World's Fair, and the house for the Tugendhat family. With glass walls facing a private garden, and interior spaces divided by interlocking planes of rich woods, plaster, and blue silk, it was a defiantly modern statement, and unapologetic in its austere opulence — this was no workers' housing. "The Mies home is admittedly luxurious." Johnson told *Times* readers. "For this reason, Mies is disliked by many architects and critics, especially the Communists."

That analysis indicated Johnson was more closely attuned to the German political climate than he generally let on in his letters home. His emergent political allegiances became clear when he asserted that Mies's unhindered control over the proceedings demonstrated that "submission to an artistic dictator is better than an anarchy of selfish personal opinion" and that "America, which can make changes so quickly, must also one day wake up." Taken at face value, this was another jab at the curatorial dog's breakfast that was the Architectural League's annual exhibition at the Grand Central Palace. But his choice of loaded terminology was not accidental. By the summer of 1931 Hitler was a figure who could no longer be ignored, even if his National Socialist party was still a minority at the polls. Earlier in the year the Führer had very publicly established himself in Berlin's Kaiserhof Hotel, and the city itself was practically in open warfare between his SA storm troopers and Bolshevik street fighters. Johnson's language, if nothing else, foreshadowed his own dark efforts to "wake" America politically in the coming years.

Architecture was of interest to the Nazis, not least because Hitler fashioned himself as an authority on the subject. Johnson hoped that the Nazis would come around to the monumental power and abstract beauty of the Miesian aesthetic, and in that wish he would always be disappointed. Though Hitler had yet to make public any specific grievances against modern architecture, Nazi party organs had begun to describe it as a tainted product of foreigners and Jews. It mattered not that this attack was entirely disingenuous (Mies and Gropius, for instance, were neither foreign nor Jewish); the Nazis simply pointed toward Berlin's most conspicuous examples of modern design, a handful of Jewish-owned department stores, to justify themselves.

The most prominent of these was the rising Columbus Building on Potsdamer Platz, a building designed by Erich Mendelsohn, who was Jewish and credited its steel-frame construction to his study of American commercial architecture. It is not entirely coincidental that Mendelsohn, too, had fallen from Johnson's favor. His taste for the architect had begun to deteriorate the previous summer, when Mendelsohn was hesitant to turn over photographs Johnson had requested for his book. Johnson suggested, in private, that he and Hitchcock might retaliate by trashing the architect in print, despite their admiration for his work. But now, in a letter to Hitchcock, he simply wrote Mendelsohn off as a mediocrity who "doesn't know the first thing" about the new style. Mendelsohn's Jewishness was never the explicit justification for Johnson's distaste, but one can sense how his feelings might have been colored from a remark in a letter to Barr regarding Johnson's plans to leave it to Barr to recruit the Tugendhat family to the cause of the exhibition. "You don't seem to mind Jews," he wrote, excusing himself from the efforts.

Johnson's rising interest in fascist politics was abetted by his new-found friendship with Helen Appleton Read, a Wellesley graduate and

New York sophisticate who was the art critic of the *Brooklyn Eagle* and a regular columnist for *Vogue*. Condé Nast's fashion magazine suited her, as she was relentlessly urbane and *au courant* in all things, politics included. She had been an early and enthusiastic proponent of the Museum of Modern Art, which is how Johnson got to know her. Read had a special affinity for German culture, and counted among her friends Ernst "Putzi" Hanfstaengl, a Harvard-educated publishing scion who had ingratiated himself with Hitler. The Führer enjoyed Hanfstaengl's counsel and company (he was good with a tune on the piano) and relied on him as a liaison to the foreign press corps, who generally considered Hanfstaengl a buffoon. In the coming years, Read and Johnson would travel together through fully Nazified Germany. Like Johnson, she praised Mies's contributions to the Building Exhibition, telling *Vogue*'s readers that it was ideally suited to "the Utopian race of the future."

Johnson wrote a lengthier review of the Berlin exhibition for the professional journal *T-Square,* edited by the architect George Howe. Johnson would himself become an investor in (and editor of) the journal, rechristened *Shelter*. Of particular interest is his attention to the criticism of Mies's glass-walled model house. "Americans always ask two questions about living in such a house: 'What about privacy in a glass house?' 'How can it be heated in winter or kept cool in summer?'" Johnson dismissed these concerns, just as he would later on when he built his own glass house, and otherwise took Mies's work as a model for his own.

In that review, Johnson credited Lilly Reich for her striking installation design, a mode of display that she had been pioneering for more than a decade.* Reich favored precise and systematic compositions offset by crisp typography and the bold use of color. For the exhibition's display of wood veneers, she tacked square-cut boards against flat partitions, aligning them neatly on a grid. Enormous raw timber beams were stacked in rows on the floor, dramatically exposed for review. The impression was one of modern objectivity, as opposed to Victorian

---

* This was not entirely true. In 1922 Reich helped curate a show on German industrial design at the Newark Museum, in New Jersey.

fussiness. "This type of display has not yet reached America," Johnson wrote of the presentation. He would make sure that would change, though he wouldn't always be so generous in assigning credit.

There was much to be done when Johnson returned to New York in September. Because there was still no room for him in the museum's office, he rented a temporary space for himself and his deputy, Alan Blackburn, in a commercial building in Long Island City. There he worked on the catalog for the show and put the finishing touches on *The International Style,* which would be published by W. W. Norton & Company. Hitchcock was forever behind with his responsibilities. "You know very well that you have spent insufficient time in rewriting," wrote a "horrified" Johnson.

Curating the exhibition was his primary responsibility. The housing section was especially challenging, not least because it interested him so little. Johnson was moved by aesthetics, not the travails of working men and women—especially if they were Catholic or Jewish—a condition foreign to his experience. Still, the subject had long been a preoccupation within the modern movement, and some concession to the problem seemed obligatory, with unemployment at 24 percent and Hooverville shantytowns springing up across the country. Hoover himself set the wheels in motion for a housing conference in Washington that would bring together leaders from across disciplines—banking, construction, architecture—to develop strategies and programs to ameliorate the problem. Johnson, however, declined to go. "I rather doubt the value of that conference," he wrote.

Johnson was also forced to resolve the embarrassing situation of the Bowman Brothers, the young Chicago builders of aluminum apartments. Johnson, in placing them alongside such figures as Wright, Mies, Le Corbusier, and Gropius, had not realized just how inexperienced they were. Specifically, they had built exactly nothing besides their own office interiors. Their all-metal apartment building, which had been scheduled to rise in October of 1930, was still just a paper project. "I hardly dare to make an exhibition of an architectural firm that has built nothing," he wrote them, in September. Still, he was reluctant to bounce them from the show, especially given the aluminum connection. Also, they had offered him an opportunity to invest in a corporation they were organizing to build prefabricated housing. With that he decided a model of a new apartment project would be enough to secure their presence.

Less easily resolved was the status of the ever-imperious Frank Lloyd Wright. Johnson had spent much of the summer lamenting the status of Wright's conjectural "House on the Mesa," a compound of horizontal slabs stepped around a rectangular reflecting pool, which Wright, in his hubris, called a "lake." Although it exhibited some characteristics of Johnson and Hitchcock's International Style—mainly, a flat roof and planar construction—it was, like all of Wright's architecture, entirely sui generis. Indeed, so distant was Wright from their ideal that Hitchcock and Johnson did not even include him in *The International Style*. This presented a certain existential problem to Johnson in his curatorial capacity, however, as the entire purpose of the show was to present a united front. Conversely, Wright himself, with his Olympian ego, was not inclined to be lumped together with the other internationalists. He was a nation of one.

All parties were happy enough to bury their heads in the sand in respect to these issues until, less than a month before the exhibition's scheduled opening, Wright abruptly cabled Johnson with the news that he was withdrawing from the show. "My way has been too long and too lonely to make a belated bow to my people as a modern architect in company with a self advertising amateur and a high powered salesman," he wrote. "No bitterness and sorry but kindly and finally drop me out of your promotion." Presumably Johnson was the "amateur" and Hitchcock the "salesman," but you couldn't be absolutely sure. As was par with Wright, the tone was damning, florid, and self-aggrandizing, the meaning not quite clear, like something badly translated from the Italian. His derisive characterization of the show as a "promotion," however, was accurate, and he would double down on it in the future, repeatedly describing it as "propaganda." It took the special pleading of Mumford and Hitchcock to convince Wright to return to the fold, but even then he was reluctant.

The curators' propagandistic aspirations were laid bare in Barr's hyperbolic preface to *The International Style*. Writing with missionary zeal, he proclaimed the book to be of "extraordinary, perhaps epoch-making, importance." With the museum's concurrent exhibition, it would demonstrate "beyond any reasonable doubt" that "there exists today a modern style as original, as consistent, as logical, and as widely distributed as any in the past."

The months and weeks leading up to the exhibition opening, on February 9, 1932, were frenetic and full of tension, with the inexperienced Johnson assisted only by Blackburn, his equally inexperienced aide-de-camp. Johnson could hardly count on Barr, whose attentions were elsewhere, first on a landmark Matisse exhibition, which opened in November, and then on a Diego Rivera show. The latter closed on January 27, 1932, leaving all of two days for the galleries to be cleared out and for Johnson to install a preview of his architecture show for a select group of high rollers, dignitaries, and young architects.

That timeline was bitterly difficult for Johnson, who was deeply

A model of Le Corbusier's Villa Savoy at the Modern Architecture *exhibition of 1932.* (© The Museum of Modern Art / Licensed by SCALA / Art Resource, NY)

anxious about the launch. Two days to install the show? It was a herculean task, and one he could not even hope to complete. On the evening of the preview, Johnson stood uneasily off to the side, his discomfort noted by friends and relieved only by the fact that attendance was sparse. Over the next ten days, he managed to put the show in order: the models were placed on pedestals and dramatically spotlighted from above, the photographs and text panels, all of uniform height, set neatly in a ribbon that wrapped through the galleries. The mode of presentation, new for the United States, was plainly cribbed from Mies and Reich.

His design was overshadowed, understandably, by the exhibits themselves. Here were the great figures of modernism, collected and displayed in America for the first time. There was a section on housing, and another illustrating the spread of the International Style around the globe, the whole culminating in a final gallery featuring models of homes for the gentry: the Pinehurst house for his parents by Oud, Le Corbusier's Villa Savoye, Mies's Tugendhat House, and Wright's House on a Mesa. Public buildings and mass housing schemes were given peripheral treatment. Gropius and his Bauhaus model were relegated to a preliminary gallery, along with the Bowmans. Mumford's essay on housing was dumped into the back of the catalog. The emphasis was given to the promulgation of an aspirational domestic style.

The public response to this clarion call was measured curiosity. Total attendance during the show's six-week run was roughly thirty-three thousand, a respectable if unspectacular showing.

There was one individual who was, at least for the opening, notably absent: Philip Johnson. The immense strain placed on him during the installation, coupled with his fears of critical reaction, had prompted another nervous breakdown. Exhausted, or perhaps just seeking a place to hide, he had checked himself into the Alice Fuller Leroy Sanitarium, a private hospital on the Upper East Side that catered to the well-heeled. It was there, on the morning after the opening, that he received a telegram offering "hearty congratulations" from Mrs. Rockefeller herself. "We all feel very proud and grateful for what you have done," she wrote. "It is a splendid show and I am sure will have far reaching effect."

That was true, and it was nice to have her confidence, but Johnson was equally concerned with the press notices, which were mixed. "Here we have, beautifully and rather convincingly illustrated, what has come to be known as the International Style," wrote critic Edward Alden Jewell in the *Times*. A more detailed and less effusive treatment was given in the paper's Sunday magazine by H. I. Brock. Granting that the show was "an arresting spectacle," he nonetheless blistered the "insistent monotony" of international modernism, in which every building looks like every other. "A church and a factory are easy to confuse," he wrote, derisively. The reviews generally broke down along partisan lines, with traditionalists opposed and progressives more receptive. Johnson, however, was displeased with all of the notices, writing somewhat naively that no one took his ideas quite seriously enough—that reviewers generally quoted from the catalog and left it at that. "I can safely say there was not one real critical review of the Exhibition," he carped in a letter to Oud.

There was one critic who was not inclined to let him off lightly. After reading Brock's essay in the *Times* (and perhaps scanning the catalog), Frank Lloyd Wright dashed off another of his bitter missives, this time with the demand that "every trace" of his name be removed from the exhibition when it traveled to its additionally scheduled venues. Being especially sensitive to the notion that he was yesterday's news, Wright was not happy to come off as some kind of idiosyncratic historical pioneer. It didn't help that Hitchcock's catalog essay, which identified Wright as "one of the great architects of all time," placed him in a pantheon with such figures as Emerson, Melville, and Whitman—none of whom had drawn breath in well more than three decades.

Beyond ego, Wright simply rejected Johnson's way of thinking about architecture. For Wright, the idea of a style achieved by following a set of predetermined aesthetic principles was abhorrent. He saw architecture as something wholly different—an expression of individual artistic genius tailored to the exigencies of contemporary life and the natural environment. "Why, I ask you, should I, who have dedicated my lifetime to an ideal of organic architecture, trail along with this attempt to steal the hide and horns of that ideal and make the animal come alive by beating the tom-tom," he wrote. "I not only feel out of character but out of sympathy with the whole endeavor. I belie my whole cause by coming with you, as I suspected I would when, suspiciously, I first withdrew. Now my worst suspicions are confirmed."

Johnson responded to this affront by return mail. "I regret very much that our era of ballyhoo disturbs you so," he began. Dropping the sardonic tone, he begged Wright to come and see the show for himself before making any rash decisions. Johnson had a talent for charming his way out of trouble, and hoped he could convince the older man to see reason once he'd had a chance to cool down. The House on the Mesa, Johnson assured him, was "extraordinarily beautiful." But Johnson was disabused of such notions when Wright's next missive arrived, and he was subjected to the full force of the master's condescension. "Good God, my boy — your letter is humiliating," it began, and it got only more hysterical from there.

Wright did, however, offer a means beyond this self-imposed impasse. If the museum would consent to print and distribute a statement by Wright, he would not withdraw. For convenience, this "somewhat ungracious" note, titled "Of Thee I Sing," was enclosed. Its preamble left no doubt as to Wright's position — he was "totally in disagreement with the premises of the propaganda." The International Style, in its supposed erasure of the individual will, he deemed "communistic" and antithetical to American democracy. What's more, the "self-selected group of formalizers" — that is, the curators — were "superficial and ignorant" aesthetes, not to mention vainglorious, impecunious, and impotent.

Demonstrating the lack of backbone of which he was accused, Johnson acceded to Wright's demand, though not without asking the master to cut down his screed, which came in at well over a thousand words. Wright refused, and it was probably just as well. The piece, typical of Wright in its hyperbolic extravagance, was just the type of thing that an innocent reader would pick up and summarily put down as too Baroque and too nebulous to take seriously.

It was progress, at least, that there was someone willing to treat Johnson's ideas with some degree of sophistication — however harshly. And in this Wright was not entirely alone. The April issue of *Shelter*, the monthly architectural magazine in which Johnson was now both an investor and an associate editor, was largely devoted to the show—another instance of Johnson deputizing his wallet in support of his career. Although Johnson himself did not contribute, there were pieces by Hitchcock, Mumford, Hood, Neutra, and several others, including a fantastically vituperative piece by Arthur T. North, who deemed the International Style a "fantastic abnormality" that would only "engage the intelligentsia until something worse comes on the scene." Johnson even had Wright agree to include "Of Thee I Sing" in the issue, though he stripped it of its rude preamble. This was a clever act of intellectual jujitsu, for the cumulative effect of so many other pieces effectively neutered Wright's turgid sermon. Further evening the score was a tandem book review by George Howe of Wright's *An Autobiography* and Hitchcock and Johnson's *The International Style*. To read the former was "to have an experience," wrote a diplomatic Howe, while the latter was "an admirable and scholarly work"—though Howe did find the captions (Johnson's chief authorial contribution) excessively judgmental.

Wright's reaction to the publication of *Shelter* was another spewing of invective. He accused Johnson of "pirating" a photograph of the House on the Mesa model to accompany his essay, and of removing its preamble without his permission. Nor was Wright especially impressed with the other contributors to the publication, even North, whom he colorfully described as "a horse's ass not clever enough even to choose a good horse." The metaphors grew uglier when it came to Johnson and his associates. "Philip, my King, a strange undignified crowd you are, all pissing through the same quill or pissing on each other. I am heartily ashamed to be caught with my flap open in the circumstances."

Even this, amazingly, drew an obsequious response from Johnson. "I have appreciated your efforts to remain friends despite the many misunderstandings which I sincerely regret," he wrote, though Wright had patently made no such efforts. "I feel as strongly as ever that I have a great deal to learn." In the next paragraph Johnson invited himself to visit Wright in Taliesin.

Hitchcock was not so forgiving. "I must say that at last I am convinced that there is no further reason for attempting to remain on working terms with you," he wrote. "I regret now that we have ever begun to know you personally." But as it turned out, even he could not completely renounce Wright. In the fall the two made that pilgrimage to Taliesin and the three buried the hatchet—at least temporarily. (Meanwhile the museum's white-shoe counsel, Sullivan & Donovan, had advised there was no cause for worry about Wright's threatened litigation.)

Wright, however, was correct to fear that the exhibition, despite the tepid initial reaction, would have significant long-term ramifications. Though Johnson and Hitchcock had not scored a massive public victory, their proselytizing, especially within the profession, framed the way architecture was to be understood, and it was a frame that did not allow for a particularly broad perspective. It removed from the conversation not just Wright's individualism but any notion of regional identity, and (Mumford's efforts notwithstanding) all but eliminated any concern for progressive social values. What was left was an aesthetic, and they had even given it a name: the International Style. The handy term was such a useful catchall that it is often still used, wrongly, as a synonym for all modern architecture.

The religion of the modern had a new evangelist, and henceforth Johnson would have an institutional platform to disseminate its gospel. On July 3 the museum introduced him to the public as the chairman of its newly established Department of Architecture. It was a reward for Johnson's work, and it marked another stage in Barr's ambition to build a center that would promote modernity across disciplines. Johnson— the "brilliant young authority," according to the *Times*—would produce one major exhibition every few years and curate a gallery devoted to architecture in the museum's new quarters, a converted five-story townhouse owned by the Rockefellers on Fifty-third Street. Everyone had the good taste to skip over the small fact that Johnson was still not being paid. For that matter, he was picking up the tab for the entire department.

He could afford do that—to work for free when so many others couldn't find work at all. The Depression had but a small impact on Johnson's lifestyle; if there was somewhat less money to count on, it was still enough to live grandly, especially when other people could be purchased so cheaply. And buy them he did.

Johnson, dressed to the nines. He was beautiful and he knew it. (Getty Research Institute, Los Angeles)

CHAPTER 5

The Maestro

We must learn once more to feel as a nation and act as a nation if we want to stand up before the world.

—Adolf Hitler, 1932

Even in the grip of the Depression, there was no talk of destitution at the Upper East Side townhouse of Kirk and Constance Askew. The seemingly effortless sophistication that Fred Astaire and Ginger Rogers would bring to the screen was already being performed in real life by the Askews in 1932. "You *happened* at the Askews," Johnson said of evenings spent in the couple's presence. Paul Bowles, an occasional guest, claimed it was "the only salon in New York worthy of the name." Initiates were welcome to swing by any day of the week. Tea was served at five, cocktails at six, dinner at seven-thirty. On Sundays there were large parties—"at-homes," the Askews called them—formal affairs at which New York's cultural illuminati drank martinis of bootlegged gin, provided in quantity by the hosts, while making conversation in a large drawing room with Victorian décor and modern paintings.

Kirk Askew, a slight man of wooden mien, was raised in a middle-class family in Kansas City, and came to know the art world's in-crowd at Harvard, where he took Paul Sachs's museum course. After graduation, he landed a job with the blue-chip London art dealers Durlacher Brothers, and soon thereafter the firm's New York gallery, selling Old Masters to the Park Avenue set and the institutions they patronized. The clients bought Baroque, but he established the gallery's back office as an informal clubhouse for young modernists. "He collected people in hopes that some of their distinction might rub off," said Johnson. His wife, Constance, a divorcée eight years Kirk's senior, was among the most glamorous women in the city—a stunning blonde born to debutante balls and summers abroad. The composer Virgil Thomson compared her to Greta Garbo.

At the Askew salon, one might engage on the latest developments in music with Aaron Copland, theater with Gilbert Seldes, literature with E. E. Cummings, or painting with Pierre Matisse, the artist's gallerist son. Muriel Draper, the grande dame of New York's high bohemian set, was a frequent guest. (Her own townhouse a few blocks away was another regular gathering point for the arts crowd.) Political discussions were allowed but not encouraged—the Askews' was not the place to pontificate about Hoovervilles and bread lines. Kirk's practice was to circulate, facilitating conversation while shifting overflow to an adjacent cork-lined study. John Houseman, another regular, described him as a "smiling, relentless, and faintly malicious" host, and his demeanor set the tone for events. Constance, by contrast, moored herself to a sofa, drawing friends in by personal gravitation.

Among the guests who used the Askews' townhouse as a sort of drop-in hotel was A. Everett "Chick" Austin, a Barnumesque dynamo who was director of the Wadsworth Atheneum in Hartford. He had landed there in 1927, another Sachs protégé from Harvard, and injected new life into the place with his great energy and taste for modernism. Architecture was a special fascination. His home, which he designed, was one of the most curious in Hartford; from the outside it appeared to be a grand Palladian villa, but inside it had the dimensions of a railroad car, and several of its rooms were appointed in Gropius-inspired Bauhaus style. Henry-Russell Hitchcock may well have helped him put together his office at the Atheneum, and Austin's aspirations did not stop there: he wanted the museum to build an addition in the International Style. (His father-in-law was a trustee, which helped.) When Johnson and Austin met at the Askews' salon, they found they had an immediate rapport, one propelled by their shared zeal for the new.

They were also both gay men—or, more accurately in the case of Austin (who was married), bisexual. In that they were not alone. Much of the artistic society, male and female, that gathered at the Askews' was gay. They were drawn to a world of culture in which they could express themselves more openly — if not completely openly — and live among those of shared values. To be gay was its own form of modernity: at once a statement of sexual progressivism and a flouting of traditional standards of behavior. Johnson, Austin, and so many others of their circle had come to New York precisely because it was a place where they could live more freely. "New York is the greatest stag city in the country," the *Times* had declared in 1928. That remained true in the early 1930s, though the Depression-plagued city had grown meaner and less tolerant, with homosexual life driven more deeply into a shadow world.

The Askew affairs ran until midnight, at which time the festivities would typically continue elsewhere, perhaps at Michel's, a local speakeasy, or up in Harlem. The Cotton Club, where Cab Calloway entertained a whites-only crowd, was a favorite choice. But there were other clubs and parties, some more discreet, where gay life could be lived more openly, and the races mixed. Beyond the scrutinizing eyes of the establishment, in a zone inhabited by the city's black underclass, you could get away with more, especially at night, and especially if you had the right connections. Carl Van Vechten, an Askew salon regular considered the white bard of the Harlem renaissance, was a guide to the territory. "We knew that Harlem was the only place there was any freedom," Johnson would recall. He would often cab it uptown with Hitchcock and Kirstein; when Austin was in the city, they would pile into his convertible for the ride.

It was on one such evening, in late March, that the group went up for a party at the home of Leonie Steiner, an Englishwoman who lived with a black actress and two young black boarders who were available, for a price. Johnson was immediately smitten by one of the young men, a fledgling cabaret singer with a sweet voice, lithe frame, and delicate features. Jimmie Lesley Daniels was only eighteen, but he'd been in the city for more than two years trying to earn a living as a singer. Born in Laredo, Texas, in 1908 he had appeared briefly on Broadway in a 1930 Katharine Cornell vehicle, *The Dishonored Lady*. But other stage parts were not forthcoming, and without money or education, he was forced to rely on his body. Johnson spent the night with him and thereafter wanted exclusive possession.

Johnson paramour Jimmie Daniels, photographed by Carl Van Vechten. (Carl Van Vechten Trust)

Daniels was something irresistible to Johnson, and not just because he was pretty and had a pleasant voice. He was another act of transgression—perhaps the ultimate act of transgression—but one that he could pretend was something more: a love affair and an act of modernity at once. Johnson, in his later years, would refer to Daniels as "the first Mrs. Johnson," which, aside from being untrue—Daniels was not his first serious relationship—suggested a domestic tranquility that rarely existed between the two men. Theirs was hardly a partnership of equals. After their first night together, Johnson immediately set Daniels up in a Harlem apartment of his own. Henceforth he expected Daniels to be available to him—and was displeased when he wasn't. In mid-April, a month after their first meeting, Kirstein recorded just such an incident in his diary. Johnson, he wrote, had been "in a pet because his nigger boyfriend Jimmy [sic] Daniels had not called him up." Later on that same evening, when Johnson caught up with Daniels at a party, he instructed him to curtail his drinking or "he wouldn't be any good in bed later on."

Johnson, in retrospect, admitted he had not treated Daniels fairly. "I was naughty," he recalled. "I had rather an upper-lower class feeling about him. I didn't realize it at the time, but it must have galled him. Everything that I was doing that was interesting he wouldn't be included." But even when Johnson tried to be good, it wasn't easy. A gay couple of mixed race in Harlem was already pushing the bounds of public accept-ability. In the more conservative precincts Johnson inhabited, it was entirely beyond the pale. "I tried to have him downtown," he recalled. "It didn't work out so well. They'd say, 'I'm sorry we're full tonight'—a totally empty dining room." It was a shame, because Daniels was by all rights bright, and a gifted vocalist and muse. George Platt Lynes photo-graphed him, as did Van Vechten. Richmond Barthé sculpted his bust in bronze. And it was upon listening to Daniels's "impeccable enunciation" as he sang "I Got the World on a String" one evening at a Harlem club that Virgil Thomson decided that his opera *Four Saints in Three Acts* should have an all-black cast. Hitchcock, who was with him that night, suggested he "sleep on it."

Johnson was not a particularly faithful or considerate partner. Not long after dispensing with Daniels, Johnson began an affair with a gifted student of classical music who had found his way into the Askew salon: John Cage. He was six years younger than Johnson, and though his groundbreaking work as a composer lay in the future, he was quite evi-dently a powerful intellect. Their romance was brief, however. Cage cut it off after Johnson neglected to invite him to a society party: he was not willing to be treated as Johnson's plaything.

Johnson found others to fill that role. He later claimed that he could not live without at least one sexual experience a day, and that did not include self-gratification. He would often go to the movies with the Barrs or Alan Blackburn (the deputy he had known since his Hackley days and who shared some of his more authoritarian political views), only to duck out in the middle of the show for a paid liaison. The Barrs forgave him these disappearances, understanding the difficulty of life for a gay man in a homophobic society. His theater of choice was the Cameo, on Forty-second, a first-run house specializing in the avant-garde Russian films that Barr admired.

Things didn't always work out as Johnson planned. On one such evening, he picked up a fifteen-year-old boy — "his specialty," according to Kirstein — and led him through the labyrinthine hallways of his chosen house of assignation, Broadway's enormous Times Square Hotel. "Rest Assured" was the hotel's mantra, but that was very bad advice: Johnson took his pants down, and when he looked up he understood he was not going home satisfied. It was a blackmail job. How would he like to be busted as a pederast? Of course he was terrified. What would Homer and Louise think? Or Mrs. Rockefeller? An arrest would ruin him. It wouldn't help the museum, either, to see its golden boy scandalized. The reactionaries who considered modernism the perversion of a decadent class would have a field day — the city was already in the midst of a prolonged crackdown on gay life. Naturally, he paid up. It wasn't much money, anyway.

All the high jinks covered for the fact that Johnson was often unhappy and restless, still prone to manic emotional swings. When he wasn't with the in-crowd at the Askews' or finding his pleasures in Harlem or elsewhere, New York was "dull and disagreeable." In his down moments, it didn't matter that he was young and handsome and wealthy, a tastemaker proclaimed as something close to a genius in the *New York Times*. He worried that the praise wasn't quite deserved, that he couldn't live up to his own hype. Hadn't the effort to do so landed him in Alice Fuller Leroy's hospital for the broken and moneyed? The rarefied crowd at the Askews' could make even a Nobel laureate insecure.

In June, just three months after the closing of the groundbreaking *Modern Architecture* show, Johnson and Hitchcock traveled to Chicago to prepare for their next exhibition, a history of Chicago School architecture that would open after the new year, in February of 1933. At face value it was a curious subject as a follow-up to its controversial predecessor; a scholarly look back rather than another dogmatic argument about the present or future. The title they chose, *Early Modern Architecture:*

Chicago 1890-1910, betrayed the academic nature of the production, which would focus on the work of H. H. Richardson, Louis Sullivan, and Frank Lloyd Wright. As with their previous collaboration, Hitchcock would do the intellectual heavy lifting, and it would be left to Johnson to enliven what he produced for public consumption—to take what was academic and make it polemic. "We don't want people to merely look at this show," he wrote. "We want them to study it and carry away with them a conception of what went into the making of the greatest epoch in our American architecture." That hyperbole was characteristic of Johnson, a manifestation of his philosophy that all exhibitions should make an argument. And here there was a strong argument to make: that those early Chicago architects had invented the skyscraper, and that their steel-framed buildings were the first to eschew revivalism and promote an indigenous American style. What's more, the purity of that style, honest and direct, stood in contrast to the "Skyscraper Style" of the present day as epitomized by the Chrysler and Empire State buildings, with their flourishes that Johnson found so detestable.

One might presume that the two curators would have thought better than to make Wright one of the principal subjects of the show. Only a few weeks earlier, Hitchcock had informed Wright, in no uncertain terms, that he regretted ever meeting him. Everyone, however, seemed willing to forget the recent unpleasantness in the pursuit of future glory; Johnson and Hitchcock's trip west occasioned a visit to Wright at Taliesin, at which time they patched up their grievances, at least temporarily. Johnson had some additional good news. He had been selected as director of the American exhibit at the upcoming Triennial architectural exhibition in Milan, and he could think of no better way to advertise the nation's architectural flair than by featuring Wright. Happy for the honor and presuming it would entail free passage to Europe (it didn't), Wright obliged.

Johnson left for the Continent himself in midsummer, traveling not alone but with his mother, his younger sister, Theo, and the family chauffeur. In Berlin, he reunited with Ruhtenberg, who crossed the Baltic from Stockholm, where he had moved after separating from his wife.

Johnson and Ruhtenberg's time together was short, however, for Johnson's passions took him in other directions. The extent of Hitchcock's expertise had begun to weigh ominously on him; on their recent scouting trip to Chicago, it had seemed Hitchcock could divine the history of any building they approached merely by glance, his analyses often correcting the written record. This represented a perhaps-impossible standard, but Johnson once again began to think that he should have a historical subject on which he could be the defining authority. The figure he landed on was Ludwig Persius, a German architect who was a protégé of Karl Friedrich Schinkel. It was a curious choice. Every subject is at some level a reflection of its author, and Johnson had chosen to celebrate the work of a follower, an epigone who would forever live in the shadow of his mentor.

Johnson had a German instrument maker custom-build a portable camera designed specifically for shooting architecture. It was a handsome little box with a lid of wooden strips that retracted like a rolltop desk. Johnson's interest in Persius required several trips to Potsdam, the Prussian royal retreat. These were pleasurable outings on which his family and Ruhtenberg tagged along. Even Johnson's mother came. Traveling in the big car, they attracted gawkers—limousines were so rare in Depression-racked Germany that many presumed the chief passenger was Hitler, traveling incognito. Louise typically remained in the car while Philip had James, the chauffeur, carry his photographic equipment and set up his tripod to best advantage. The setting was beautiful; Potsdam was a little arcadia, and Persius's works were scattered, like moldering baubles, among the royal estates of Schloss Glienicke and Sanssouci. The project lifted Johnson's flagging spirits until he met with Paul Ortwin Rave, a Schinkel scholar, who dismissed it as the work of a dilettante. A serious study of Persius required more than "a fancy camera." That hurt, the insult feeding his insecurity and incipient sense of resentment. It was like reliving Whitehead's dismissal all over again.

Rejection of aesthetic ambition had also fueled the rise of Adolf Hitler, who had begun to capture Johnson's attention. While in Berlin, Johnson reconnected with the critic Helen Appleton Read, who had returned to Germany for the year on a fellowship to study contemporary German art. But that subject took a back seat to her attraction to the Nazis and their charismatic Führer. In her, Johnson had someone with whom he could discuss his growing interest in (and admiration of) fascist politics, a subject that was off-limits with his mother and sister and the more liberal Ruhtenberg.

These conversations came at a destabilized and dangerous political moment. While Johnson was touring palaces in a chauffeur-driven limousine, Berlin was under martial law and Germany itself perilously close to civil war. That the Republic was in grave and perhaps irreparable danger was clear, but just what would replace it was not. It was by no means certain that Hitler would manage to attain the powers that he desired; Hindenburg, the aged president, was still the most popular figure in the country, and the Junker military class he represented held the erstwhile Austrian corporal in disdain.

While ruthlessly maneuvering behind closed doors, Hitler relied on elaborately staged public spectacles to galvanize supporters and sow fear in those who might oppose him. These had been a part of the Nazis' propagandistic program from the earliest days of the movement, and they could be counted on for martial music, seas of swastika flags, and phalanxes of uniformed men and women moving, singing, and saluting in unison. The pageantry was imperial in nature, suggesting Hitler as a new Germanic Caesar, but also Wagnerian in its staging and visceral tenor.

Johnson had a proclivity for this kind of performance; just a few years earlier, while at Harvard, he walked out of Boston's Symphony Hall enthralled by Wagnerian bloodlust. "I had thoroughly convinced myself that I had slaughtered the whole world and that god and I were rejoicing in it," he wrote to his mother.

Johnson got his first taste of the man who would make that sordid fantasy real on the first day of October 1932 at a massive Hitler youth rally in Potsdam. The trip was arranged by Read through Putzi

Hanfstaengl, who made it a special point to bring in members of the American press. (Several reporters were charged for interviews with Hitler, a neat little moneymaking scheme.) The event was organized by Hitler Youth leader Baldur von Schirach, a charismatic twenty-five-year-old with whom Johnson had much in common. Unlike so many Nazi thugs, he was educated and of artistic temperament, an author of (uninspired) poetry. He also had an American background: his maternal grandfather served in the Union Army and was part of the honor guard at Lincoln's funeral. Like Johnson, he was a zealot for a cause that he believed was charged with morality. For Johnson it was modernism, for von Schirach fascism. But Johnson was leaning toward the latter, too.

Attendance at the rally was greater than anyone anticipated. Some eighty thousand boys and girls descended on a tent city thrown up on a Potsdam airfield, with field kitchens dispensing meals of bockwurst and bread. Many of them had hiked for days to get there. In the evening there was a torchlight procession to Potsdam stadium, which was packed beyond capacity. Songs filled the air, and swastika flags bedecked with garlands waved in celebration. From a dais, Schirach introduced Hitler, who was at his most electric. "We must learn once more to feel as a nation and act as a nation if we want to stand up before the world," he told the assembled throng. "Through our movement a new and strong generation is growing up that has a new courage and does not surrender."

The speech appealed to the insecurities of youth, calling on the assembled to overcome a great moral calamity and join in a grand collective mission. Energized by what he described as the "febrile excitement" of the rally, Johnson devoured it. Hitler was "a spellbinder." The vicious anti-Semitism that laced the remarks only reinforced the prejudices inherited from his father. That so many of his friends and so many of the artists and architects he admired were Jewish didn't matter; he compartmentalized those feelings. Later he would rather unconvincingly justify his attraction to the Nazis in sexual terms, as a kind of homoerotic fascination with the Nazi aesthetic: all those chiseled blond men in jackboots and pressed uniforms. It was easier to whitewash sexual desire than the egregious social and political ideas that truly captivated him.

Following the excitement of Potsdam, Johnson traveled to Rome to reconnect with the Barrs. Alfred's presence there was not entirely voluntary, and not merely because he did not like sharing a roof with his Italian mother-in-law. He was burned out. That he had built MoMA from nothing in such short order, and that he had established it so quickly as a mainstay of New York City's cultural diet, was an accomplishment of extraordinary artistic vision and diplomatic skill. Yet the effort drained him. He was a brilliant curator but a poor bureaucrat, a micromanager and a perfectionist. Engineering the museum's move to its new home on Fifty-third Street was an immense burden, and when it finally opened there, in May, he was saddled with an equally onerous political headache. The inaugural exhibition in that renovated Rockefeller townhouse was a mural show, curated by Kirstein, with work that was unabashedly radical in its politics. One mural depicted John D. Rockefeller Sr., J. P. Morgan,

Johnson and Alfred Barr find a moment of levity at Lake Maggiore in 1933. (© The Museum of Modern Art / Licensed by SCALA / Art Resource, NY)

Herbert Hoover, and Henry Ford cavorting behind bags of money with Al Capone, while their gun-toting forces stood over a jailed union leader. For Barr, the stress of managing the fallout, on top of the move, was debilitating. His nights were sleepless and he developed a mysterious vision problem. Doctors could find no other cause but stress. Hence his appearance in Rome, on a year's leave of absence from the museum, at half pay.

The reunion with Johnson was supposed to help lift Barr's spirits, and there were moments when it did make for a pleasant diversion. With Marga, they traveled through picturesque Tuscany together — Arezzo, Cortona, Orvieto. But the inescapable subject in Europe in the summer of 1932 was the rise of fascism. The Barrs did what they could to gently reform Johnson's thinking, without success. Instead, they traveled with him to see the philosophy to which he was attracted given chilling architectural form at the Exhibition of the Fascist Revolution, opened by Mussolini at the end of October. An enormous blood-red gate guarded by three equally enormous metal pylons capped with ax blades guarded the entry to the show. That dramatic design, along with the propagandistic displays inside, had been created by Italy's leading modern architects.

Johnson returned home in November; he sailed from Cherbourg, but not before spending a few days in Paris. There he ran into the composer Virgil Thomson, who was anxious to return to the United States to organize a staging of his opera *Four Saints,* with a libretto by Gertrude Stein. Thomson had already enlisted the Barrs, Hitchcock, and Chick Austin as financial backers. Now Johnson stepped in. When Thomson informed him he was so broke he could not afford passage back to New York, Johnson spotted him the two-hundred-dollar fare for a round-trip ticket.

In New York, Johnson's apartment would be Thomson's home in the city, at least for a while. He turned out to be a difficult houseguest, with an acid tongue and a gruff manner. "It was like living with Oscar Wilde," Johnson remembered. He might have put up with it, but his new, German-born butler, Rudolph Voisemeier, was not so forgiving. After one condescending remark too many, Voisemeier threatened to quit unless the composer was put out on the street. Johnson obliged, and Thomson was shuffled off to a spare bedroom at the Askews'.

A few months later, in April, Thomson was back at the Johnson residence, and flying high on champagne. The occasion was a "musical evening" cleverly arranged by Johnson both as a showcase for Thomson, who was still looking to fund his opera, and Johnson's younger sister, Theo, now graduated from Wellesley and hoping to launch a career as a classical vocalist. Johnson invited the bigwigs from the Museum of Modern Art board, and most everyone attended, including the museum's grand matron, Abby Aldrich Rockefeller.

The evening culminated with Theo, in a leopard-print jacket, singing Thomson's *Five Phrases from the Song of Solomon,* with Thomson accompanying on percussion. It could have been a complete disaster for everyone had Theo lacked ability. But she had the musical talent (or at least the discipline) her brother did not: a supple soprano voice and a sense of musicianship nurtured by conservatory training. When she finished the piece, there was enthusiasm enough for an encore. Thomson was especially taken with her, and they would remain close throughout their lives. In 1940 he proposed marriage. "I can't marry you and you know why," was her response. She did not want to be in one of his "queer marriages." He responded by sneaking naked into her bedroom while she was in the bath. She threw him out, and they didn't speak for six weeks.

Johnson was so pleased with the evening that he wiped out Thomson's debt. It demonstrated his International Style in action, showing that it was not some socialist aesthetic for the working classes, but *the* new style for a discerning tastemaker of social standing. And it was an advertisement not only for Johnson's style but for his services, for he was now living in an apartment that he had designed himself. He had moved into the place, in a small building on Forty-ninth Street between Second and Third avenues, not long after his return from Europe.

Johnson had imagined himself as an architect for some time, but even his mother had not seen fit to hire him. His only client thus far was Mrs. Ray Slater Blakeman, a society figure who hired him to decorate a small bedroom in her Park Avenue residence. When it came to his own first New

York apartment, he put aside his design ambitions in favor of Mies—a coup too good to pass up. The Barrs had him design a tubular chair (really a copy of Mies's MR chair) and a standing floor lamp for their apartment, but only because they could not afford Bauhaus originals. Now Johnson could have things both ways: he could design an apartment for himself in Miesian style, but with the safety net of his authentic Mies and Reich furnishings.

He proved a faithful and capable disciple. He stripped the walls and painted them a flat white, then covered the floors with jute matting. Floor-to-ceiling drapes in blue and beige screened the window walls, giving the apartment a sleek, boxy geometry. "Here is the apartment of a bachelor, expressing his comforts in a direct and logical fashion," opined the home design magazine *Arts & Decoration* in a feature with photographs by Berenice Abbott. There was just one plant for color—a rubber tree in the living room, lit by exposed-filament bulbs, the kind that now suggest vintage artifice but were then exemplars of stark modernist clarity.

The most conspicuous addition to the home was a large painting in the living room with wooden, pastel-hued figures posed on the central stairway of the Bauhaus, in Dassau. It had an air of elegy about it; Oskar Schlemmer had painted it in August as a response to the shuttering of the school by Nazi authorities. This was, perhaps, an odd choice of subject matter for Johnson, given his growing admiration for the Nazis and their Führer, but at the time he believed, however naively, that National Socialism might still be reconciled with modernism. He outlined this position in an essay, "Architecture in the Third Reich," that Lincoln Kirstein published in the October 1933 issue of *Hound & Horn*. Johnson conceded that the Bauhaus was "irretrievably" tarnished by its association with Communism, but suggested Mies was an apolitical figure who could "satisfy the new craving for monumentality" while proving that "the new Germany is not bent on destroying all the modern arts which have been built up in recent years." Hitler's racist and menacing rhetoric, that he might be bent on destroying more than just modern art, was left unmentioned.

Johnson, by this time, was fully aware of Hitler's ruthlessness. In the summer of 1933 Johnson had returned to Europe to visit the Milan

Triennale for which he had selected work by Frank Lloyd Wright, and to continue his investigations into the architecture of the Third Reich. In Germany, however, few were talking about architecture. In March, Hitler had returned to Potsdam for the formal inauguration of his dictatorship. His authority was further consolidated in the height of summer during the Night of the Long Knives, Hitler's murderous purge of all those who might challenge his authority. Chief among them was Ernst Röhm, leader of the Sturmabteilung (Storm Detachment, or Brown Shirts), whose well-known homosexuality had been tolerated. Henceforth, there would be no leniency for homosexuals.

Johnson's blinkered political ideas, which Alfred Barr had tried to reform more gently in the past, became the subject of bitter dispute on a trip taken along with Marga to Lake Maggiore. What might have been a pleasant diversion was marked by acrimony over Hitler's seizure of power and Johnson's continued fascination with the dictator's Nazi party. Barr had no illusions about Nazi barbarism, and wrote several essays on the subject, though he had trouble getting them published.

It was Barr, in fact, who was responsible for Johnson's purchase of the Schlemmer painting, which he found in the storeroom of a Stuttgart museum a week after the Nazis' victory at the polls in March of 1933. Barr was in Stuttgart then, receiving treatment for his own nervous disorder, but the atmosphere, with Hitler's shock troops parading in victory, was not particularly conducive to recovery. The painting had been featured in a Schlemmer career retrospective at the time of the election. A week after it, the local Nazi paper pilloried Schlemmer's work as "half-baked rubbish" that "might as well be left on the junk heap." That was enough to close down the show. As a foreigner, Barr managed to finagle permission to see it in its dismantled state, and immediately thereafter cabled Johnson back in New York, asking him to buy the painting "just to spite the sons of bitches."

The idea, from the outset, was that Johnson was buying the painting for the museum. But Barr didn't have the acquisition budget to make such a purchase on a whim, nor could he do it without board approval. Johnson was a convenient way around this problem, a deep pocket Barr could rely on when he found something he just had to have. The previous summer, Johnson had paid for Otto Dix's comically satirical portrait of the German laryngologist Wilhelm (later William) Mayer-Hermann. The gift was announced with great fanfare to the press as "the first important modern German painting to be acquired by a New York museum."

The Dix portrait went straight to the museum, but the Schlemmer did not. When Barr telegraphed Johnson about the painting, Johnson responded with a telegram to the artist in which he offered 12,000 reichsmarks for it, sight unseen. Schlemmer accepted what was an apparently generous offer. The two also agreed that Johnson would purchase a second large canvas from the Stuttgart show, *The Race.* It was similar in theme to *Bauhaus Stairway,* with wooden figures moving through a glass-enclosed architectural space, but with arms extended in a manner that at once suggested athletic exertion, dance, and a Nazi salute. Johnson offered Barr his choice of the pair, on the assumption that he could sell the other to Chick Austin for the Wadsworth Atheneum. He eventually did that, but he held onto both paintings for several years, not turning them over until it was politically expedient for him to do so. Meanwhile, he shorted Schlemmer on the payment, wiring him only 1,200 reichsmarks. Decades later this became a matter of legal contention. Johnson claimed that the initial figure was merely a typo.

Chick Austin was more than just a safe harbor for paintings Johnson might want to flip. He was Johnson's first serious client. The new Avery Memorial Wing that Austin commissioned for the Atheneum was set to be a showplace of modern design, the first such museum building in the United States. The architects were local, but for the interior Austin wanted authentic International Style furnishings, and that's where Johnson came in. To supplement pieces by Mies, Breuer, and Le Corbusier, Austin commissioned numerous items to be designed by Johnson: tubular steel chairs, silk curtains, sofas, a bureau. All of it was either inspired by or cribbed directly from Mies and Reich, but Johnson did show a certain flair in his design for a two-sided gallery bench, a leather-topped slab with a padded-tube backrest held above its midsection by a metal arm.

The work was not entirely his own. Still lacking formal training, Johnson needed someone with technical experience to help him execute his ideas. He had just the person in mind, too: in August of 1933 he summoned Jan Ruhtenberg from Stockholm, where he had moved to take advantage of family connections that secured him several small architectural commissions. But the promise of greater things in America was irresistible. When Ruhtenberg arrived in November, he and Johnson rushed to complete the work for the Avery Memorial, which was to open with a Picasso retrospective—the first in the United States—on February 6, 1934. Just two days later the Atheneum was to host the grand premiere of Thomson's *Four Saints in Three Acts,* complete with its all-black cast. This was to be the social event of the season. The entire Barr set turned out in black tie—nearly everyone in the group had some role in the production. Johnson sat in the second row, in front of Hitchcock, who had designed the program. Also in attendance: Paul Sachs, the Barrs, Carl Van Vechten, Muriel Draper, Alexander Calder, Salvador Dali, and Frederick Ashton. Buckminster Fuller made a splash by arriving in his Dymaxion car, a three-wheeled aluminum cocoon, with Isamu Noguchi and the socialite Clare Boothe. Jimmie Daniels, who had supposedly inspired the production, was not invited.

Capitalizing on this excitement, Johnson kept shaking his connections for work to keep himself and Ruhtenberg busy. An interior for an Upper East Side physician's office would have been his first commercial job, had it not fallen through. He was severely disappointed when Abby Aldrich Rockefeller passed him over for the commission to design a private gallery on the top floor of the Rockefeller townhouse on Fifty-fourth Street. "I wanted that job badly," Johnson wrote Barr, not least because it would have established him as the designer of choice among the smart set. She was not interested in hiring an amateur, however, and instead selected Donald Deskey. Johnson held out hope that her son, Nelson, would hire him for his new apartment, but was again disappointed. That job went to Wallace K. Harrison, who would become something of a nemesis, and Johnson's chief competition for Rockefeller family patronage. Harrison, by marrying into the family, would always have an advantage in that department.

One of Johnson's connections did come through, however. In the spring of 1933 Eddie Warburg, scion of the Jewish banking dynasty, was still living with his parents in their palatial Fifth Avenue mansion.* Cherubic and sprightly, Warburg had developed a reputation as a libertine and a dilettante among the Barr circle, which was rather unfair. At the museum he acted as a kind of minister without portfolio; he was especially active in establishing the museum's film department. He was also instrumental in Lincoln Kirstein's efforts to establish a ballet company in New York with the choreographer George Balanchine. Warburg had always had a daring sense of style; at the age of twenty-one he had purchased Picasso's *Blue Boy* for a significant sum, an acquisition his parents considered so bold that they refused to let him show it alongside their Old Masters. Instead, he converted a top-floor squash court into a private gallery.

Warburg became Johnson's first true client. Johnson found an apartment for him in a fourth-floor walkup on Beekman Place, just a few blocks from his own and from the Barrs. It was small, just a studio, but it had two windows that looked out on the East River, which made it appealing. Johnson knocked them out and put a broad picture window in their place to capitalize on the view. The rest of the apartment he stripped down to its bones. When he was done, the apartment was transformed into a statement of nearly clinical modern gravity, with whitewashed walls and an exposed radiator. The floor was linoleum, shiny and efficient, but the whole was not without luxury. A dividing wall of macassar ebony and space-defining floor-to-ceiling silk curtains brought a sense of material richness, borrowed directly from Mies. Johnson designed much of the furniture, which was decidedly foursquare, as was his thinking. In the living room, two squared-off club chairs faced a squared-off sofa over a rectangular coffee table in black lacquer. "The discipline was so violent," Warburg recalled. "If you moved an object an inch it threw everything off kilter." There was so little sound baffling that a dropped spoon sounded like a gunshot. Another problem surfaced when a dubious Felix Warburg climbed the four stories to inspect his son's new digs. He sat himself at his son's desk to make a phone call, and when he leaned forward his tubular chair slipped out from under him, slamming his chin

---

* The mansion is now home to the Jewish Museum.

into the desk. Eddie was mortified, but his father had a sense of humor. "That's what I like about modern art," he said. "It's so functional." (Johnson blamed the chair, a Mies design that had a tendency to instability before its manufacture was taken over by the Knoll company.)

The incident was quickly forgotten; the treatment Johnson received for the design was generally flattering. *House & Garden* featured the apartment in 1935, granting tacit approval to its "restful simplicity and bright airiness." If that wasn't quite the ringing endorsement of Abby Aldrich Rockefeller, it carried enough weight to propel a burgeoning career, and testified to the growing acceptance of the International Style as a suitable aesthetic for Americans of taste.

Johnson parlayed that work into a shared commission for a house, a job he would write out of his biography in the future. The client was Simeon B. Chapin, a Chicago financier who had befriended Philip's father on the Pinehurst links. Chapin was looking to build a small vacation home on the dunes of Myrtle Beach, in South Carolina. Homer suggested Chapin speak with his son. But Johnson did not immediately recommend himself for the job. Instead he brokered a deal between Chapin and William T. Priestley, a young architect just returned from the Bauhaus, where he had studied under Mies. Why not adapt Priestley's thesis project, a two-story Miesian block, for Chapin? All parties agreed that this was a fine idea, and in July of 1933 Johnson mounted a small exhibition at the museum devoted to the house. The act of generosity was typical of Johnson, in that he got something out of it beyond the pure pleasure of altruism.

Johnson's benefit did not stop with the exhibition. Johnson and Ruhtenberg eventually took over the job of reworking the house from Priestley. In November Johnson wrote to his Dutch friend Oud about the transformation of the project. "I am not sure whether it is a compliment to you," he wrote, "but I discover that all my trys at designing my house come out looking much more like yours than like Mies'." That was true; the house, which sat dramatically facing the water on a dune, had a boxlike aspect that recalled Oud's residential work. The walls were white, and it had broad windows facing the sea, with a wide terrace on the second story. Just how much of that was a product of Johnson's will is hard to say. Of the three architects involved in the project, Ruhtenberg was the only one who ended up taking credit for it on his résumé. He was also the only architect among them with enough experience to build something in three dimensions. Whoever was responsible for its execution, it was among the earliest freestanding International Style homes in the United States.

Johnson did not import Ruhtenberg only to help him with his architectural commissions. Johnson was overburdened by work at the museum, in particular the plans he and Barr had hatched to mount a major industrial design exhibition as a follow-up to the *Modern Architecture* show. The trustees, however, were not enthused. "A big show was decidedly frowned upon," Nelson Rockefeller informed Johnson after a board meeting in January of 1933. Architecture had been a push in the first place; industrial design, considered a lesser art, and one even more distant from the museum's core mission, was a tougher sell yet. But there was good news in Rockefeller's brief missive. If Johnson could adjust his expectations, the trustees would be receptive to a "small, carefully selected show," something to introduce the subject and test the waters before committing fully.

Johnson made that case with *Objects: 1900 and Today*, a jewel of a show that reassured the trustees and advertised his curatorial flair. It opened in April of 1933 and cleverly juxtaposed the highly decorative objects of the Art Nouveau with contemporary pieces in the Bauhaus aesthetic—the opposition being an inherent argument for the new. With no budget to speak of, and no collection to fall back on, he was forced to borrow creatively. Many of the modern works were taken from his own apartment. A set of Rosenthal spoons came from the collection of Mrs. Rockefeller. He sent his sister Jeannette rummaging through the family's Cleveland home in search of Tiffany lamps and the brackets from his mother's dresser. The provenance of these items lent the show a distinct Oedipal flavor, which put Johnson in a somewhat delicate position: he could hardly be seen as disparaging the traditional taste of the museum's chief patron while at the same time campaigning for expanded powers. He finessed his way out of this difficulty by celebrating both the old and the new. This was just the kind of flexible and catholic thinking that would characterize his later architectural career, and it worked. Mrs. Rockefeller and her fellow trustees were sufficiently pleased to authorize the larger exhibition Johnson and Barr had wanted from the outset. She did, however, give him a dressing-down for failing to keep her spoons polished.

That major show was *Machine Art,* a sensation from the moment it opened on March 7, 1934. Here were things nobody had considered putting in an art museum before: beakers, a cash register, a circular saw, a Dictaphone, perfume bottles, pans, springs of all sizes, a toaster oven, a waffle maker, a telescope, a vacuum, and even a dentist's X-ray machine. In front of the museum Johnson installed a large display case holding an aluminum aircraft propeller. The show boasted signature pieces by notable designers—a tubular chair by Marcel Breuer, bowls by Walter Dorwin Teague and Russel Wright—but they were not privileged over anonymously manufactured industrial items. All told, it was to be understood as the death knell for the decorative, the picturesque, and the handmade. "The craft spirit does not fit in an age geared to mechanical technique," Johnson wrote in the accompanying catalog.

For all its celebration of the machine, this was not to be a show of purely utilitarian objects. The museum, in its communications, took pains to stress that the items selected for the show were chosen because of their exceptional form—because they were *beautiful.* The catalog, with a dramatic photograph of a ball-bearing assembly on its cover, opened with a quotation from Plato's *Philebus* that inspired the aesthetic philosophy behind the show: "By beauty of shapes I do not mean, as most people would suppose, the beauty of living figures or of pictures, but, to make my point clear, I mean straight lines and circles, and shapes, plane or solid, made from them by lathe, ruler and square. These are not, like other things, beautiful relatively, but always and absolutely."

Johnson had by now developed concrete ideas about how to display the "always and absolutely" beautiful objects of industry so that those not predisposed to do so might consider them similarly. He set a faucet in isolation on a pedestal, as if it were a Greek statue. Other pieces he lined up on custom-designed walnut tables and on shelves of black and white

Carrera marble. Larger items were arrayed neatly on plinths along the floor. The show took up three floors of the museum, with rooms divided by pastel-colored canvas screens, and by spur walls of aluminum, steel, and laminate. Everything appeared in a diffuse, even glow thanks to a dropped ceiling of muslin fabric that concealed overhead lighting.

In America, no one had seen anything quite like it. Industrial design shows at the few museums that held them were generally small affairs. At the Metropolitan, things were treated more grandly, set in opulent period rooms that were the polar opposite of what Johnson brought to the Museum of Modern Art. His inspiration was quite clearly the installation design of Mies and Lilly Reich, in particular her work at the Berlin Building Exhibition. Based on their examples, Johnson was able to create something more refined, an original and fully immersive environment that the museum proudly trumpeted to the press. "For the first time, the Museum is giving as much attention to the installation as to the Exhibition itself," a press release advertised.

The 1934 Machine Art *show at the Museum of Modern Art put industrial design on a pedestal.* (© The Museum of Modern Art / Licensed by SCALA / Art Resource, NY)

It had taken months of tireless work to put it all together. Beginning in the fall of 1933, Johnson traveled and wrote to corporate officers unused to requests from fashionable New York museums, begging and cajoling them to lend their wares to his very unconventional show. He used his family connection to Alcoa chief Arthur Vining Davis to secure loans from that company and its various subsidiaries, and he hit up Nelson Rockefeller to lean on his family interests to produce objects for the show. The Rockefeller name, in other cases, had a way of liberating items from suspicious donors. To design the catalog he enlisted Josef Albers, a former Bauhaus master extricated from Nazi Germany, with the financial backing of Eddie Warburg and Mrs. Rockefeller, on his suggestion. A young Ruth Bernhard, also a German émigrée, took the striking photographs that appeared in the catalog.

His most critical collaborator was Jan Ruhtenberg. Exactly where Johnson's design ideas ended and Ruhtenberg's began is impossible to know, but logic suggests a significant portion of the design, and certainly the details of its execution, should be attributed to Ruhtenberg, who had the formal design training Johnson did not. A museum press release, however, did not credit Ruhtenberg, and stated all fabrication was done by museum staff. This was contradicted by a staged photograph taken during the installation, with Ruhtenberg standing on a ladder working on the drop ceiling while a pointing Johnson offers direction from below. The only formal acknowledgment of his work was in the catalog, where he was credited for "his assistance in designing the installation."

That this show might be a bonanza for the press did not escape the museum's recently hired publicity director, Sarah Newmeyer. To help promote a show that needed little additional assistance, she enlisted a panel of experts including aviator Amelia Earhart, philosopher John Dewey, and Labor Secretary Frances Perkins to award prizes to the three most beautiful objects in the show. The ensuing photograph of Earhart holding a large spring made by the American Steel & Wire Company proved invaluable. Dewey, the father of pragmatism, added intellectual weight to the show's philosophical pretensions. "I think it somewhat extraordinary that modern machine production for industrial purposes should illustrate as well as it does the statement of Plato regarding the abstract beauty of geometric forms," he said. "I hope that all those who are skeptical about the aesthetic possibilities of machine production will see the Exhibition."

They came in droves, a little skepticism about the proceedings making it only more appealing. A carpet sweeper as art, and not just art but a work of Platonic beauty? Even within the museum the show was treated with mild condescension—someone gave it the derisive nickname "Pots and Pans," which stuck. Cartoonists at the *New Yorker* couldn't resist it. "I'm sorry, sir, but we ain't been able to turn a wheel since our differential bearing went on view at the Museum of Modern Art," said a factory worker in drawing by Alan Dunn. In another, the rotund and self-satisfied proprietor of Acme Faucet proclaims to a factotum, "Recognition at last! The Museum of Modern Art wants to give me a one-man show."

The jokes belied the museum's serious effort to brazenly confront the public, and to convert doubters into believers. Visitors were given a survey card and asked to choose what they considered the show's most alluring object. What they liked best they could purchase for themselves: the catalog, which Johnson described as "a practical guide to the buying public," listed the retail price of all household items, many of them inexpensive. The message was clear: this new art of the machine was not just for the museum, but accessible to every American family.

Given its polarizing nature, the reception of *Machine Art* was mixed, with more conservative-minded reviewers critical of the museum for degrading itself with so many quotidian objects and for the hubris of its references to Platonic philosophy. But reviewers of all stripes were nearly unanimous and unequivocal in their admiration for Johnson, and for his (and Ruhtenberg's) installation. Lewis Mumford, no easy mark, claimed Johnson's design was in itself the show's "very best example of Machine Art." Henry McBride made a similar argument in the New York *Sun*. "The only art in the present show is that contributed by Philip Johnson," he wrote, and then described Johnson as "our best showman and possibly the world's best. I'll say the world's best until proof to the contrary is submitted." The *Times*, doubling down on the accolades given Johnson after the *Modern Architecture* show, pronounced him an "exhibition maestro."

The museum's trustees were justifiably elated by this response. "I do not think that the Museum of Modern Art has ever put on a more beautifully arranged or interesting exhibition and the trustees as a group are extremely proud of the work you have done and most indebted to you personally," Nelson Rockefeller wrote. "You have a right to be well satisfied with the results of your labors."

That assessment, and the other plaudits, were wholly warranted. Though overshadowed in history books by the *Modern Architecture* exhibition, *Machine Art* stands among the most influential shows of the twentieth century. It redefined which materials might and might not be suitable for display in the context of an art museum, and dramatically elevated the status of industrial design. It also established the standard for how design objects should be exhibited—with all the prestige of fine art—which after more than eight decades remains the dominant mode of display. In some ways the effect was paradoxical. Though the intention was to celebrate the anonymously designed product of the machine, it inspired a class of celebrity designers to make objects ever more idiosyncratic and lacking in function—an outcome that Johnson endorsed fully.

Remarkably still in his twenties, Johnson was once again a boy king in New York. He had the support of the museum's trustees and the confidence of its director. The press adored him, and he had a budding reputation as a designer in his own right. He had even secured a place for himself in the canon of design history. In his personal life, he had a circle of distinguished friends who respected him, kept him entertained, and pushed him intellectually. His parents, who had worried over his lack of direction, now believed in him. In the depths of the Depression, he had the financial security that most Americans could only imagine. Anyone else rationally examining their station in life and finding it thus would surely have been "well satisfied." But Philip Johnson was not satisfied. In fact, he had been feeling restless and constrained for some time.

With the world coming apart, architecture just seemed too small, too parochial. He wanted a bigger stage on which to enact his radical ideas. And so the man who had everything threw it all away.

Johnson pictured in a cape at Townsend Farm. The caption in the family album reads, "Mussolini." (Getty Research Institute, Los Angeles)

CHAPTER 6

The Gold Dust Twins

The tragedy of youth today is idleness.

—Philip Johnson, 1934

The news of Philip Johnson's mission of career and social suicide appeared on the front page of the *New York Herald Tribune* a week before Christmas in 1934. "Two Quit Modern Art Museum for Sur-Realist Political Venture," read the headline. Johnson and his schoolboy chum turned aide-de-camp, Alan Blackburn, had resigned their positions to launch a political movement. "The Need Is for One Party" was their slogan, and their National Party would be it. They admitted no platform aside from vague assertions about the need for populist agitation, though they did have designs for a uniform and a symbol. Their shirts would be gray, and their flag would boast not a swastika but a "flying wedge." (Think *Star Trek*, but at an angle.) Their first order of business was a road trip to Louisiana to study the ways of Huey Long, the demagogic senator who had transformed his state into his personal empire.

The story was a plant, and the source was Johnson, who had become expert at manipulating the media in the promotion of his provocative museum exhibitions. It was an editor's dream, the true story of a pair of misguided swells embarking on an adventure to reinvent American society by catering to the impulses of the masses. A writer could play it straight or for laughs, but either way it was irresistible. Johnson correctly figured that the *Times* would run something on the dry side. The *Herald Tribune* would afford the more colorful treatment Johnson desired, and he had a contact there: Joseph Alsop, a junior reporter with a Harvard

131

degree who had covered the *Machine Art* show. Johnson got a bit more than he bargained for. Alsop, who would make a name for himself covering the trial of Bruno Hauptmann (and go on to a storied career as a Washington insider), had a veteran's instinct to step aside and let his subjects embarrass themselves—which they did in spectacular fashion.

Alsop found the pair in Johnson's museum office, which was littered with art books and catalogs from firearms manufacturers. The two considered the choice of appropriate weaponry a more urgent matter for their party than the writing of its platform. Blackburn was in favor of large pistols; Johnson preferred the submachine gun, it being the acme of modern technological prowess. Were they really thinking of armed insurrection? When Alsop pressed the two for some explanation of their beliefs, the Harvard graduates pontificated about the need for an emotional rallying of the American spirit. "We dislike intellectualism," Blackburn said. "As soon as a thing's put into words it means something else. Intellectuals don't have the third dimension. You don't just put a lot of professors together and stir them around in a cauldron and get something wonderful. There's got to be more than that."

Johnson picked up on this theme. "All you need is faith, courage and loyalty," he said. "If you have them, you'll get things done. That's the terrible thing today, why the Dillinger and Capone gangs are the only groups that have got courage and loyalty from their adherents. Beyond that nothing is needed, not even consistency. The only necessary consistency is consistency of feeling." Admittedly, their ideas seemed half-baked. "We're adventurers with an intellectual overlay, so we're almost articulate but not quite articulate," said Johnson.

If Dillinger and Capone, America's most notorious gangsters, were unlikely political models, the disparagement of "intellectualism" was especially rich coming from a pair of Harvard-trained museum administrators. Was Johnson, seen most recently calling upon Plato to describe the beauty of a waffle maker, renouncing his every belief? Alsop didn't say, but he did reveal that the two had been brewing their adventure for months.

In April, Johnson had hosted the first in a series of political meetings at his new apartment—he had moved yet again, to a duplex on Forty-ninth

Street that he was now sharing with his sister Theo. It had a large, double-height living room that was perfect for them both; she could practice her singing at his grand piano, and he had more space for his political meetings. Sixteen people came to the first of these events; the most recent, in spring, drew more than one hundred. Reluctant to admit their names, Blackburn told the *Times* that their followers represented a "cross-section of the people you might meet in New York in a day, from taxi drivers to brokers." Included among the group was Johnson's German butler, Rudolph Voisemeier, and his personal secretary, Ruth Merrill, whom he had hired in 1933 to assist with both his private and his museum work. She was there not as a member of the group but to take notes and keep a list of those who came to these events, a list Johnson instructed should be kept absolutely confidential. According to testimony later given to the FBI by several participants, the meetings were virulently anti-Semitic.

Johnson and Blackburn did not confine their efforts to his tony apartment. In an effort to get in touch with the concerns of the common man, Alsop reported, Johnson and Blackburn spent the summer on an 8,000-mile cross-country expedition. Driving in Johnson's car, the two traveled from New York to San Francisco and back, with stops "every two hours" so the principals might "converse with the populace." The trip only confirmed in their minds the necessity of their political efforts. "People don't feel the New Deal has got anywhere," Blackburn told Alsop. That was not entirely accurate, but it was undeniable that Franklin Delano Roosevelt had failed to miraculously lift the United States from the Depression in his first hundred days, and that the incipient and imperfect programs of the New Deal had left him open to attack from demagogues of all persuasions. He was assailed as a tool of Wall Street, a wealth-redistributing Communist, a do-nothing imbecile, and just about everything in between. Political pretenders multiplied like malevolent rabbits, men of varying allegiances and abilities, each with an army of uniformed acolytes: gray shirts, silver shirts, khaki shirts, black shirts. For the would-be firebrand, it was a golden moment. The field was open.

Seeds of the Blackburn-Johnson political collaboration could be traced back to their schoolboy days at Hackley, where they were members of The

Curia, the debate society for students with an "interest in current problems of the world." Now it was Blackburn who took credit for the idea of forming a new party, advertising himself as its leader, with Johnson as a "co-founder." This represented a distinct reversal of their relationship; heretofore Blackburn had been subservient to Johnson, who was a year older and had brought Blackburn into the museum orbit as his personal aide. An efficient bureaucrat, Blackburn made a useful place for himself in the museum administration, operating under A. Conger Goodyear as its day-to-day finance manager.

Johnson was generally more of an enthusiastic follower than an initiator, and his subservient position, at least at the beginning of the venture, fit his personality. But he knew that, as he was financing their activities — Blackburn had no private income — he could take possession of their movement at any moment. Furthermore, he was the only one of the two who could offer anything close to the charismatic leadership they found so wanting in the American political firmament. Johnson, handsome and dexterous, at least had some record of engendering public enthusiasm. Blackburn, by contrast, was a middle manager, barely five feet tall, with compressed features and a shifty expression that made every photograph look like a mug shot.

Questions inevitably arose as to whether the Johnson-Blackburn relationship was more than Platonic. Johnson, in later years, denied that they were anything but friends, but he could well have been protecting Blackburn, who later married. Ione Ulrich, who worked with the pair at the museum, told the FBI that Johnson was "a sexual pervert" and Blackburn "his victim." That analysis may have been simple homophobia, but in any case she didn't take either of them seriously as political operators. "He is not the vicious type who is a danger to the community," she said of Johnson. He was simply "a fanatic for social reform."

That zeal was propelled by a man who had become Johnson's unlikely intellectual guru and political Svengali. His name was Lawrence Dennis, and though he is now largely forgotten, he was one of the more compelling figures of the febrile years of the Depression. An imposing man with a thrusting jaw, mail-slot eyes, and an orator's gift for language, Dennis fashioned himself as an intellectual lightning rod with the 1932 publication of the provocatively titled book *Is Capitalism Doomed?* Dense but eminently quotable, it described an America brought to economic crisis through a misplaced faith in an amoral business class indifferent to the national welfare. "Business needs to receive orders not give them," he wrote. The problem, as he saw it, was that there was no suitably inspiring authority to deliver those orders. America was without "adequate spiritual leadership," and absent a profound shift in direction would inevitably give way to "some system of economic dictatorship." That kind of talk made Dennis a fixture in the parlors of New York society, his presence sure to enliven any gathering with the frisson of political engagement. Johnson met him at one such event; being congenitally attracted to zealous, charismatic men and susceptible to a nationalist worldview, he was immediately taken.

Dennis's warnings about "the needs of the race for both biological survival and spiritual growth" elided a secret that few could have imagined: he was a black man passing as white. Born in Atlanta to a black mother and a white father, he received his first taste of public attention as a globetrotting child evangelist at the turn of the century. At home the bigotry of the Jim Crow era ate at him, and he found a way to escape it—his skin was light enough for him to pull off the deception. His feat of self-invention began at the elite Phillips Exeter academy and continued at Harvard, from which he graduated in 1920. He joined the Foreign Service—another establishment bastion—and distinguished himself as a savvy operator in the revolutionary backwaters of Latin America. Before there was a CIA to manage American covert affairs, Dennis was an American fixer with a portfolio that would have suited a Graham Greene character. As a chargé d'affaires in Honduras, he engineered the removal of strongman Tiburcio Carías Andino in favor of a president more acceptable to the United Fruit Company, and followed up that success by engineering the ouster of the president of Nicaragua.

Dennis was disturbed by the American interventionism he facilitated, but proud of his achievements and furious when passed over for promotion. The issue of race was unspoken; unwilling to broach it, he blamed his stalled career on his status as an outsider within the old-boy network of the service. He resigned in a flurry of bitter press, complaining to the *Washington Post* of incompetence, extravagance, and high-handed dealing in an agency in which only the privileged could advance. He moved on to the Peruvian desk of J. & W. Seligman, a Wall Street investment bank with interests in South America. This didn't last either; in the prelapsarian years before the Crash of 1929, the firm's mandarins did not appreciate his Cassandra calls about a forthcoming economic collapse. After being fired, Dennis responded with a series of articles lacerating Wall Street in *The New Republic*. On Black Monday he looked like a prophet.

Among the conceits of *Is Capitalism Doomed?* was the author's professed lack of resolution as to its titular question. Was capitalism doomed? Dennis wouldn't say, at least not in print. In person, he was less equivocal. By the time Johnson latched on to him, Dennis was already honing the arguments that would animate his next book, *The Coming American Fascism,* which left no question as to the true nature of his thinking. "The international bankers and American liberals of internationalist leanings are leading this country straight towards communism," he wrote. The anti-Semitism of the attack was veiled — "banker" and "liberal" could easily be read as code words for "Jew," though with plausible deniability. The only reasonable alternative — indeed, the inevitable alternative — was fascism, and the best option was to map out what a "desirable" form of it would entail: an American variant to what Hitler and Mussolini brought to their respective nations. Freedoms would be curtailed, along with due process of law. Women? They "could not leave the kitchen without detriment to the community and themselves."

Johnson's personal resentments dovetailed neatly with those harbored by Dennis, which helps explain his intellectual attraction. As a gay man, Johnson was also "passing" in the establishment world; like Dennis, he had invented himself as a propagandist of a new ideology that might reshape a modern society that had accepted him but from which he nonetheless was an outsider. Heretofore that activity had been confined to the aesthetic world of the museum. Dennis presented an opportunity that was much broader, and thus more desirable. He also appealed to Johnson's sense of entitlement, for he argued that the nation's new leaders should be drawn from a financial and intellectual elite caste best suited to represent the public. That call spoke directly to Johnson, a man of wealth who was prone to see the world in Nietzschean terms.

There was also something deeply Oedipal in Johnson's embrace of Dennis, in that Dennis's political philosophy stood as a wholesale rejection of the Republican values Homer Johnson held dear, even if father and son shared some of the same racial prejudices. Certainly Homer would have been appalled at Dennis's vilification of the business class, of which he was an active and enthusiastic champion. Equally abhorrent were Dennis's ideas about foreign policy. "Cooperation to keep the peace is impossible," Dennis wrote. Nations were simply too self-interested to attain this goal as a group, and the results were inevitably calamitous. The great example of perfidy undertaken in this pursuit was the treaty obligations imposed at Versailles. Homer Johnson, of course, had been a member of the American delegation in Paris. His reaction to his son's political transformation was silence; his son had become a disgrace, and he couldn't bear to tell him. His mother pretended nothing had changed.

More vocal was the response from Johnson's friends and colleagues. Barr was appalled but tolerant of his protégé and continued trying to win Johnson back via rational argument. Lincoln Kirstein was less forgiving. He learned of the Gray Shirt movement not long after the first meeting was held, and his reaction was laced with bitter condescension. "I felt like immediate assassination but I probably can count on him to destroy his own possibilities," he wrote in his diary. A few weeks later, he angrily confronted Johnson on a street corner. In a heated conversation, Johnson tried to assure Kirstein that he was not an anti-Semite, and that his nascent organization was "merely a group of young men interested in 'direct action' in politics, who believed in a totalitarian state and leadership instead of democracy." Kirstein responded that while he had "no great fear of Phil Johnson," he could not ignore the specter of anti-Semitism. Johnson protested again that his aims were not anti-Semitic. "Not yet," Kirstein replied.

Henry-Russell Hitchcock also had been aware of Johnson's political ambitions, and similarly found them revolting. "Of course you and I know that this has been coming to a head for over a year and that it is far better that it should at last have broken," he wrote in a heartfelt letter to Lewis Mumford the day after Alsop's story appeared in the *Herald Tribune*. Beyond personal upset, he worried that Johnson's activities would stain his own work and set back the cause of modern architecture. "I hope that this outrageous development which is possibly more painful in its implications to me than to people who have been less closely associated with Philip than myself, will not too completely throw a shadow on the architectural work of the Museum of Modern Art."

That concern was valid, but it had been somewhat mitigated over the preceding months as Johnson gradually removed himself from the museum. In October, a final major exhibition was mounted under his aegis, though his input was minimal. The subject was slum housing, which should have been of keen interest to someone so concerned with the plight of the everyman. But it had never captured Johnson's imagination. Although he was nominally its director, Johnson ceded most of the work to G. Lyman Paine Jr., an architect with the New York City Housing Authority. He did, however, make one significant contribution: the design of a model apartment executed on a practical budget. It had all of his signature moves: an austere aesthetic of space-defining curtains along with simple, clustered seating arrangements. The furniture, including a tubular chair, was available through Macy's.

Johnson's design, which was uncredited, was cleverly contrasted with a three-room tenement salvaged from a building slated for demolition, complete with the hanging laundry, dirty dishes, and mismatched furniture of its most recent occupants—the museum even added cockroaches, supplied by a sailor stationed at Guantánamo. The juxtaposition was a clever bit of curatorial savvy. But it also suggested Johnson's superficial attitude toward the problems architecture might address. When it came to the substantive economic and policy questions that might actually alleviate the housing crisis, Johnson had nothing to say; his voice was conspicuously absent from the show's provocative catalog, *America*

Can't Have Housing, which featured essays by leading thinkers in the field, among them Walter Gropius and Lewis Mumford. The entire endeavor, at some level, seemed antithetical to his efforts to decouple modernism from its association with socialist workers' housing and make it an acceptable style for the American aristocracy.

Not everyone at the museum shared Hitchcock's concern about the potential stain of Johnson's departure. Its irascible president, A. Conger Goodyear, accepted Johnson's resignation with regret, noting his "extraordinary gift of museum showmanship" and "integrity of taste." In fact, Goodyear was tickled enough by Johnson's Gray Shirt movement to count himself a member. He never had a problem thumbing his nose at the establishment; that sensibility was what drew him to the Museum of Modern Art. He was especially pleased at the idea of the road trip to Baton Rouge; the Goodyear family had lumber interests in Louisiana, and he had a favorable opinion of Huey Long.

The idea that Long might serve as a model for Johnson and Blackburn was born of Dennis. "It will take a man like Long to lead the masses," he said. "I think Long's smarter than Hitler, but he needs a good brain trust....He needs a Goebbels." Johnson and Blackburn departed for Louisiana with the pretension that they might fill this intellectual void, and at the same time learn the ins and outs of building a political machine from a master of the craft.

Secretly, Johnson had grander ambitions. He was not interested in just being a member of Long's "brain trust." When interviewed in 1942, Johnson's former secretary Ruth Merrill told the FBI that Johnson believed "the fate of the country" rested on his shoulders, and that "he wanted to be the 'Hitler' in the United States." His desire to join Long as an adviser was a means to that end. "By joining with Huey Long he could eventually depose Huey Long from control of the country and gain control of it for himself," Merrill told the FBI. Whether that meant assassination or a bloodless coup was unstated.

On December 22 Johnson and Blackburn departed New York for Baton Rouge so that they might put their secret plan into action. They drove the enormous land yacht that was Johnson's Packard 12 convertible to poverty-stricken Louisiana, where Long had built an empire on the promise of making every man a king. In the trunk were two suitcases, a Bible, and a selection of works by Machiavelli, Nietzsche, Plutarch, and Shakespeare. In retrospect the endeavor has an air of satirical fiction, or perhaps a psychologist's case study in what we now call cognitive dissonance.

To the people of Louisiana, however, it was assuredly unfunny. They were hurting in ways that are hard to grasp today, even with the economic troubles that face blue-collar Americans. There was no escape from paucity. Americans didn't have enough food. Electricity was by no means universal. Maybe a house had a telephone, but even a short call was a luxury. The extent of rural poverty was astonishing; projects like James Agee's *Let Us Now Praise Famous Men* and Dorothea Lange's photographic study of migrant workers illustrated the grim subsistence that defined life for so many Americans.

It was a time for tragedy, but Johnson and Blackburn seemed like characters out of a farce, and Long was pure caricature. The seventh of nine children, he was born in the Louisiana backwoods and learned to stump as a traveling salesman pitching shortening and patent medicines. He perfected that craft well enough to put himself through law school, and made a losing bid for governor in 1924. Four years later he won that office, and in short order consolidated virtually all power within the state unto himself.

Drawling, charismatic, and menacing, Long championed the little man and set their ire on the entrenched business interests that had dominated the state since Reconstruction. It wasn't all talk. He delivered for his constituents, bringing roads and schools and hospitals to a state beset by poverty. He delivered for himself, too — his corruption was as boundless as his energy, and enforced with all the state's perverted muscle. "I used to get things done by saying please," he said. "Now I dynamite 'em out of my path."

With Hitler and Mussolini rising in Europe, that kind of demagoguery was nothing short of terrifying. In his 1935 novel, *It Can't Happen Here,* Upton Sinclair took Long as the model for Buzz Windrip, a Southern populist turned American dictator. The obvious moral: it *can* happen here. (Long would likewise serve as the prototype for Willie Stark, the rabble-rousing protagonist of Robert Penn Warren's 1946 classic, *All the King's Men*.) By the time Johnson and Blackburn motored into Louisiana, the *New Orleans Times Picayune* was openly referring to Long as a dictator. In point of fact he was a United States Senator, having relinquished his governorship (though none of his power) to a handpicked successor, O. K. Allen, who accepted puppet status. A detail of thuggish guards protected Long wherever he traveled, and only a handful of yes-men were granted access to the man they called the "Kingfish."*

Visitors, including the two tourists from New York, were turned away. Outside New York, reports of their intentions had received considerable notice—not all of it the kind they hoped for. One Ohio paper accidentally landed on the truth when it suggested the pair had assassination on their minds: "Quit Art to Knife Huey Long," read the headline, with the story below erroneously reporting that the two planned to "build up a private anti-Long political party" and to go "scalping" for the senator. Those rumors, combined with their glib talk about guns in the *Herald Tribune* and their association with the pet museum of the Rockefellers—regular subjects of Long's vitriol—resulted in a most suspicious welcome by Long's henchmen.

In any case, they had little to offer. Long didn't even need Johnson's architectural guidance. The week the two arrived in Baton Rouge, Long announced a plan to redesign the city on the beaux arts model of Washington D.C., with the street in front of the state capitol widened into a grand thoroughfare befitting his imperial self-image.

Johnson and Blackburn did not give up quite so easily; to return to New York so quickly would have made them not just pariahs but laughingstocks (to the extent that they weren't already). So they remained in Louisiana, exploring Long's public works projects and the sundry other products of his Share Our Wealth campaign. They also received a lesson in his bare-knuckle political tactics, for the state was on the verge of

---

* The name was borrowed from a character on the *Amos 'n' Andy* radio program.

141

insurrection. The fuse igniting an already volatile situation was a five-cent-per-barrel tax on oil refined in Louisiana that Long had instituted in the waning days of December, just as Johnson and Blackburn were setting off on their journey. His primary target was Standard Oil—a Rockefeller company—which stood to lose $1.5 million a year and responded with an immediate round of layoffs. Outraged workers blamed the Kingfish and organized in protest under the reformist banner of the Square Deal Association, joining an ever-growing chorus of Long dissenters. Resistance was especially strong in Baton Rouge and New Orleans, prompting fights between warring factions in front of court buildings and other public facilities. At the end of January, Long's police uncovered an assassination plot, and a Baton Rouge deputy sheriff admitted under oath that he had repeatedly tried to kill the senator. Long, in response, imposed martial law. To Johnson, it must have felt like Berlin in 1932.

With a new session of Congress beckoning at the beginning of February, Long departed his own capital for Washington. Walking out of the lobby of his Baton Rouge hotel to the car that would deliver him to the train station, he was flanked by phalanxes of state militiamen armed with Tommy guns and tear gas. Following along on that trip, not quite a part of the senator's entourage but hoping they might be, were Johnson and Blackburn. By this time Long's henchmen had determined the two New Yorkers were harmless. Johnson left the big Packard in Louisiana, presuming they would be back anon.

The two tourists finally got to meet the tousle-haired Kingfish in Washington. The hallowed event took place at the Broadmoor, the Connecticut Avenue hotel that was Long's base of operations in the capital. He received the two in pajamas, as was his wont (he preferred purple silk), and the conversation was brief. Long had to give a speech the next evening; Johnson offered to provide material. Over the next day he scoured *Bartlett's* for quotations about wealth and passed them to Long's designated secretary.

Long used the material, but by this time it was dawning on Johnson that the one thing Long did not need was help with oration, his greatest gift. Johnson, however, had an idea about how Long might spread his message, one that predicted the future of media campaigns in its application of advanced technology. He had recently discovered the Visomatic, a portable projector of still images that simultaneously played a phonographic record. Though rudimentary in concept, it could place a candidate in the home of a prospective voter as television does today, building the kind of personal intimacy that is the goal of every politician. Johnson understood its transformative potential — here was modern industrial design in action — and finagled coverage of it in the *Washington Post*. "Suppose Einstein, or Huey Long, or some other great man is speaking from the picture," he told the paper, "once he's seen on the Visomatic machine and heard there, too, people will understand him more. The appeal is tremendous." Unfortunately, he did not have images and recordings of Long to demonstrate its utility. Instead, his example was an advertisement for a popular brand of extra-smooth peanut butter.

The Visomatic, rather than a triumph, proved to be Johnson's undoing. Long did not think the contraption would be of great value, certainly not great enough to offset the damage the two comical Ivy Leaguers with their newfangled device and velvety peanut butter might do to his man-of-the-people image. That the *Post* headline referred to them as his "tutors" surely sealed matters — as if he were in need of instruction from a pair of Harvard sophisticates. They issued a statement that they were "admirers only," but it was too late; they had to go. Johnson's dream of riding Long's coattails to the White House only to knock him off and claim power for himself was fully put to rest. Earle Christenberry, Long's chief retainer, delivered the facts of their political inconsequence in no uncertain terms. "How many votes have you got?" he asked. "You come back with a million votes, or a hundred thousand votes, and you can see Huey any time. But you ain't got nothin'."

It was a bruising kiss-off, but it left them with a window of opportunity. Long's ambitions extended well beyond Louisiana, and he was in the midst of building a national Share Our Wealth organization that would allow him to challenge Roosevelt in the 1936 presidential election. Christenberry suggested Johnson and Blackburn take up that cause in

Johnson's home state of Ohio—rural territory where Long's message might be well received. With nothing waiting for them in New York but the cold shoulder of society, the two would-be politicos had no better option.

In New London, the pair took up residence in an old clapboard house on North Main Street that had been the home of Johnson's grandmother. They stayed there courtesy of Homer Johnson, who in no way supported their political activities. New London then was a picture-postcard farming town of whitewashed homes and leafy yards where everyone knew everyone else's business. Presumably, Homer hoped a return to its quaint Midwestern atmosphere might restore his prodigal son's wayward values; at the very least, the remote location would reduce his ability to embarrass himself and the family.

That line of thinking would prove to be grossly mistaken.

Upon arrival, Johnson's first order of business was a renovation of his grandmother's house, which sat in the center of town. The principal change entailed knocking out a large section of the front wall of the house and installing in its place a floor-to-ceiling plate-glass window looking out on the street—"the largest piece of glass anyone had ever seen in Ohio." Here was a premonition of the Glass House for which Johnson would become famous in the years to come, one that read as a declaration of modernity, an announcement that a new force had come to town. A big glass window was not just for looking out; it was equally an invitation to look in by an occupant who wanted to be seen.*

Johnson and Blackburn quickly drew the suspicion of the town's respectable citizens. Who were these bachelor interlopers, men of means from the big city, living together in a house with an unusual design of their own making? Johnson and Blackburn worked diligently to ingratiate themselves with their new neighbors. They threw a rollicking party for the younger set at the local high school, with live music and dancing and a fully stocked bar; Blackburn found himself a girlfriend, Janette

---

* Homer was pleased with at least this portion of his son's work. He spent his last days in the house and died there in 1960 at the age of 97.

Emerson, whom he would eventually marry. All seemed to be going smoothly until Johnson came down with rheumatic fever and returned to New York for treatment. He spent a month recuperating at Roosevelt Hospital. It was a bleak time; physical illness had again struck him at a moment of emotional vulnerability. He had few visitors besides his mentors Alfred Barr, who never gave up on him, and Lawrence Dennis, who had no reason to.

Johnson was visiting his parents in Cleveland when his plans were again altered by events beyond his control. On the evening of September 8, 1935, Huey Long met the fate he himself had predicted: one of his many political enemies shot him at the state capitol building in Baton Rouge. He died two days later. Johnson and Blackburn hurried to Louisiana for the funeral rites, but they were late in coming and missed the spectacle, which drew some two hundred thousand mourners. That was the end of Long, but not of his mission, or theirs.

Back in Ohio, Johnson and Blackburn embarked on a grassroots campaign to build a constituency for their would-be National Party, cobbling ideas from the various populist movements that had achieved traction with the American public. In addition to the Share Our Wealth campaign, now under the direction of the charismatic fundamentalist preacher Gerald L. K. Smith, their platform incorporated the ideas of Francis Everett Townsend, a California physician moved by the lack of a social safety net for the elderly. Townsend's proposed remedy to this crisis was a two-hundred-dollar monthly pension for retirees, the presumption being that, in addition to its essential humanity, this subsidy would encourage retirement, opening up jobs for the young and unemployed, thereby stimulating the economy out of the Depression. Serious economists dismissed Townsend (Roosevelt had his own concurrent plan for Social Security), but with clever promotion and the sympathetic doctor as a figurehead, a Townsend Movement achieved a sizable national following.

Johnson and Blackburn took the doctor's message across Ohio, traveling from town to town, speaking to audiences large and small, often with Johnson's Visomatic machine deployed to add a bit of sound and fury. In December, seven hundred people came out to a high school in Sandusky to hear the two neophyte politicians. "The tragedy of youth today is idleness," Johnson told them, by way of endorsing Townsend's pension plan. Blackburn stuck to the Share Our Wealth script, advocating a redistribution of capital. America, he told a rapt audience, had come to a point where five hundred millionaires made more money than two million farmers.

Wealth redistribution was a curious platform for Johnson, whose personal fortune then stood in the neighborhood of half a million dollars—an enormous sum in those Depression years. His father was even wealthier, a "multi-millionaire" according to the local press, and among the largest property holders in Huron County. For all his talk, Johnson never actually considered sharing his wealth in any real or significant way. But he was burdened by it. Later in life, he attributed his political adventure to a general feeling of "guilt for being rich" and a warped sense of *noblesse oblige*. That his wealth came to him through no effort of his own exaggerated his feelings of shame and inadequacy. "Museums were not a proper way for a person of responsibility to behave in this serious time," he said. He wanted to be a man of the people—or, more accurately, their champion.

In November of 1935, two months after Long's assassination, Johnson latched onto the issue that would establish his proletarian bona fides: the price of a bottle of milk. The dairy farmers of rural Ohio, Johnson discovered, were paid but one cent for every ten-cent quart of milk sold in Cleveland and Cincinnati and Toledo. Where were the other nine cents going? So began Johnson's campaign against the "Milk Racket." Passing himself off as a "dairy farmer" (the 1,800-acre Johnson family farm did produce milk), Johnson endorsed a state bill to set price standards and began agitating for a strike among small producers. By December he had gained enough traction to take to the airwaves, beaming his message to the public on WHK in Cleveland and WAIU in Columbus. "I demand a peaceful settlement of this problem," he told milk-drinking Ohioans. "If the farmer does not get his just dues, then I shall certainly urge a 100 percent strike."

As 1935 slipped into 1936, Johnson raised the volume of his campaign.

In the first week of January he was back on the radio, pontificating about "cheating" milk dealers and the "procrastinating" state senate. He mortified his father by decking out his Packard roadster with SHARE OUR WEALTH banners and parking it in front of the Union Club. Homer held back his frustration, but his friends didn't. "I hope you're not coming around to stir up a strike in my plant, young man," admonished the president of the White Motor Company, one of Homer's biggest clients. Anonymous letters arrived at the Main Street house begging Johnson to end his campaign. "If you want to hurt your father still more than you already have, just keep up with this." Johnson felt threatened enough to call in the Federal Bureau of Investigation when an official at the local bank, one Anson Gear, began leaning on him. In his statement of defense, Gear countered that Johnson was trying "to dominate the policies of this town without the consent or approval of anyone, other than himself, and in such a manner that it has become very distasteful to the businessmen of this vicinity." The FBI took no action.

Johnson liked being an outlaw, just as he had when he had opened the *Rejected Architects* show. If his activities were distasteful to the entrenched business interests in the vicinity, he found common cause and strong support among the local dairy farmers, who extolled him as something of a hero. That had been the goal all along—to galvanize a constituency that might be a springboard for a greater political career. Johnson kept up the milk activism for another month, but the strike threat had already served its true purpose. He had been frank about his grander desires in an interview the previous December, telling the *Cleveland Herald* of his intention to run for the Ohio legislature as representative of Huron County.

He formally declared his candidacy in March, running as a Democrat. He had first gone to the GOP—historically the Johnson family party of choice—only to be rebuffed. The Ohio Democrats were happy to have a figure of rising popularity with deep pockets in their camp. In the following months he threw himself into community affairs; he was elected first vice president of the local Rotary Club and won the presidency of the New London Park Board, a position from which he could apply his aesthetic ideas on a civic scale for the first time. These were necessary steps for any aspiring pol, and Johnson carried them off with his best charm. On primary day in May, he scored a decisive 40-2 victory and was poised for a November landslide.

Instead, he walked away from the race. During the campaign he had come to realize that he was ill-suited for the niceties of electoral politics: kissing babies and hobnobbing with the hoi polloi. Worse still was the prospect of victory and the responsibility of serving the people in the state capital. Rabble-rousing for a milk strike was one thing; negotiating the regulatory fine points of a milk-control board was a lot less interesting. He was too ambitious and too impatient to serve as a backbencher in Columbus, sitting through interminable legislative sessions. That was "boring," and boredom was one thing Philip Johnson would not suffer.

Not coincidentally a better opportunity had presented itself in the name of Father Charles E. Coughlin, the Roman Catholic radio priest whose weekly audience stood at some ten million listeners, making him the biggest draw on air. Born in Canada and ordained in Toronto, Coughlin began broadcasting in 1926, delivering a weekly program from the Shrine of the Little Flower in the Detroit suburb of Royal Oak. In his first years he was a moderating presence on air—he attacked the Ku Klux Klan, which retaliated with a cross burning—but with the onset of the Depression he became more assertive. His sympathies, always, were with the common man, his principal targets the "plutocrats" and financiers of Wall Street and beyond. Like his Louisiana ally Huey Long, whose water he gladly carried, Coughlin had a pleasant, boyish face that contorted like putty when he got himself into a good lather. By 1934 his message, beamed out across America on CBS, was popular enough that he drew some eighty thousand letters a week. Contributions were such that he was able to remake his church in grand art deco style. Standing next to its sanctuary was Coughlin's Charity Crucifixion tower, an immense limestone-and-granite spike with a 28-foot-tall relief of Christ chiseled on its side—a cross the KKK could not burn. Coughlin broadcast from his office at the very top of the 104-foot tower, his trusty Great Dane Pal invariably at his feet.

Coughlin was an ardent and enthusiastic supporter of Roosevelt in his 1933 campaign for election, and he remained a staunch advocate during the early days of the Roosevelt presidency. But that enthusiasm soured and became ever more bitter as the Depression persisted past Roosevelt's first hundred days. His principal objections were economic, if not entirely rational. "He gave indiscriminate support to nearly every available monetary nostrum without regard to logic or consistency," wrote historian Arthur Schlesinger Jr. "For Coughlin economics was a minor branch of rhetoric." In mid-1935 he broke formally with Roosevelt and established the National Union for Social Justice (NUSJ), a political action organization. For Johnson it represented a more expedient path to national prominence than a term in the Ohio legislature.

Johnson's formal engagement with the NUSJ began in January of 1935, when he and Blackburn spoke before a local affiliate of the group. There Johnson demonstrated his ability to conflate the various wedge issues that were Coughlin's bread and butter. The "bankers of the nation" were behind the Birth Control League of America, he told the assembled. Abortion was anathema to Coughlin, but it had never been of concern to Johnson, whose own lifestyle would hardly have been above reproach in the eyes of the radio priest. But since when was he afraid of a little hypocrisy in the service of his notoriety? By February he and Blackburn were NUSJ district managers for Huron County.

When Johnson won the Democratic primary in May, his allegiance to the party was a formality; his true loyalty was now with Coughlin and the NUSJ. He was not alone, either. Fifteen Coughlin disciples scored primary victories in Ohio. Proximity to his Royal Oak headquarters helped: Toledo was barely 75 miles from the Shrine of the Little Flower. New London was barely twice that far, a distance Johnson and Blackburn covered one day in the early spring. Coughlin was happy to meet them, and to find a place for them in his organization. And why not? Johnson could now fulfill Christenberry's injunction to come bearing votes, and if the number was not a million or a hundred thousand, he had demonstrated an ample capacity for activism and organization — and a considerable purse. Coughlin put the two to work on the house organ, *Social Justice,* and they rented a place together in nearby Birmingham, a large Tudor house on a pretty suburban lot. It wasn't long before one of Coughlin's blue-collar acolytes referred to Johnson and Blackburn as the Gold Dust Twins. The name stuck.

Coughlin needed two capable deputies at that moment because he was engineering the debut of a full-fledged third party for the fall election, one that would corral the nation's disaffected under a single populist umbrella. His Union party would combine the forces of the Share Our Wealth organization, the Townsend Movement, and Coughlin's own vast army of listeners. Coughlin would be the leader of this upstart party, but he required a figurehead to lead its presidential ticket; his political activism was already ruffling feathers in the Catholic hierarchy; a bid for office was out of the question. Johnson, acting in an advisory capacity and having no allegiance to the Catholic church, suggested Coughlin "pull a Luther" and go off on his own, an idea that was summarily rejected. Instead, Coughlin enlisted William Lemke, an anodyne Republican congressman from North Dakota whose politics and personality were compatible. In May, when Coughlin introduced him to the public at a rally in Cleveland's Memorial Stadium, Johnson was on the dais.

Lacking charisma and political dexterity, Lemke was a dud as a presidential candidate. When he spent a night at the New London house on a swing through Ohio, he struck Johnson as both slow-witted and unpleasant—"an asshole." Still, Johnson donated $5,000 to the campaign, a sum that represented something close to 40 percent of his annual income. That kind of contribution insured his status as an adviser to Coughlin. This was precisely the role he had envisaged for himself a year earlier, when Lawrence Dennis advised that Huey Long needed a "brain trust" and a "Goebbels." Long was gone now, and if Johnson harbored dreams of deposing Coughlin they were unspoken. It didn't matter, anyway: Coughlin was receptive enough to let Johnson fully apply the lessons he had learned as an observer of the Nazi propaganda machine.

With Lemke incapable of rousing the party faithful, the burden fell squarely on the shoulders of Coughlin. This effort reached its apex in early September, when Coughlin was scheduled to address a mass rally at a fairground on Chicago's north side. Johnson was dispatched early to stage the event, which he modeled on the Hitler Youth rally he had witnessed in Potsdam in the fall of 1932, taking inspiration also from the works of Italian fascism he had visited in and around Rome.

Johnson had a clear idea of how his grandstand for Coughlin might appear, but there was just one problem: he had no ability to execute his vision, and there was no Jan Ruhtenberg or Alfred Clauss at his side to do it for him. Blackburn was of no use—he was a pencil pusher, but of the wrong variety. He needed a young architect who would lend his services, ideally without a fee. Given the nature of Coughlin's politics and the progressive bent of most young moderns, the prospects did not look good. But Johnson had someone in mind who could hardly refuse him.

That man was Fred Keck, who had a small office in Chicago that he ran in partnership with his younger brother. Keck's relationship with Johnson had not begun in the most auspicious manner; Johnson had rejected Keck's request to be included in MoMA's inaugural 1932 *Modern Architecture* show. Keck didn't yet have the résumé to justify that kind of exposure, but Johnson had been impressed with him, and in 1933 he turned to Keck to help organize a small show at the museum, *Work of Young Architects in the Midwest*. It opened in April of 1933, timed to take advantage of the publicity attendant upon Chicago's Century of Progress exposition. Keck's work was prominently featured, a validation for which he was profoundly grateful.

Keck was therefore uncomfortable saying no when Johnson called for assistance. The prospect appalled him, however. A World War I veteran who rarely spoke of his service, he had little sympathy for Coughlin's bravado or his politics; he was a Roosevelt Democrat and his wife was Jewish. On the day Johnson arranged to come into his office, he made himself conveniently absent. Undeterred, Johnson blew in that morning and sidled up to the first associate he saw. "We were never introduced," he said to Robert Bruce Tague, who was but a year out of architecture school. Johnson feigned some interest in the house Tague was working on, and got down to business. "He described exactly what he wanted drawn, like dictating a letter," said Tague.

A Chicago newspaper illustration points to Father Coughlin on Johnson's fascistic white speaking platform in 1936. (Collection of the author)

On a field normally used for driving golf balls and racing midget cars, Johnson erected an enormous white wall, fifty feet wide and two stories tall, surmounted by a row of seven waving flags. In front of and attached to the wall was Coughlin's speaking platform, also all white. This rectangular block rose more than halfway up the wall, silhouetting Coughlin's lone figure against the blazingly bright backdrop. In front a pair of ramps—white as well—spanned the length of the platform, rising symmetrically to the dais at the center so Coughlin could receive a procession of dignitaries who would walk up one side and then down the other. From a distance it all looked like marble (though of course it was just drywall, hastily constructed) and made an impression of monumental authority, intellectual purity, and clarity of purpose. It was the language of the International Style conscripted into fascist service, an idea that would surely have been repugnant to the many progressive idealists who had done so much to inspire it.

*   *   *

When Coughlin took the stage on the afternoon of September 6, he stood before some eighty thousand spectators who had paid 50 cents each to hear his words. It was the largest crowd he had ever addressed in person and he got off to a rousing start, though he was upset with Johnson for having arranged a large police escort with sirens blaring; that did not fit his champion-of-the-little-guy message. Coughlin also preferred to supply his own theatrics, his arms gesticulating wildly and the pouf of hair above his brow bouncing in response. A microphone draped around his neck gave him freedom of movement and he paced back and forth, shaking his fist in the manner of demagogues everywhere. "We're through with the sham battle of politicians, and now we're on our own," Coughlin declared; he was for a presidential candidate who would "put patriotism first." That did not describe the present occupant of the office: "We all know for whom we're voting if we vote for Mr. Roosevelt—for the communists, the socialists, for the Russian lovers, the Mexican lovers, the kick-me-downers." He excoriated Roosevelt for his economic policy, and in particular for his fealty to the financial institutions of Wall Street. He closed with a call to arms: "Form your battalions, take up the shield of your defense, unsheathe the sword of your truth, and carry on in Illinois so that the Communists on the one hand cannot scourge us, and the modern capitalists on the other cannot plague us."

Coughlin's passionate delivery, despite Johnson's best efforts, went for the most part unheeded. The writing was on Johnson's very white wall even during that speech in Chicago. It was not a good omen when the flags snapping loudly in the wind above Coughlin's head had to be taken down midstream—a design flaw courtesy of Johnson. More to the point, Coughlin was forced to spend an undue amount of his speech denying reports that the Vatican was so displeased with his politicking that it was going to put an end to it. "That's a lie," he said. "If they had cracked down I wouldn't be here today." But they were growing unhappier by the day. Two weeks after his Chicago event, the archbishop of Cincinnati rebuked Coughlin for describing Roosevelt as "anti-God" and for threatening violence if Communists took control of the country.

Coughlin was unrepentant. On the evening of September 26 in Philadelphia, he once again mounted a platform (presumably Johnson's Chicago bandstand reassembled) and reiterated his claims.* But when Coughlin began his speech this time, the crowd numbered not one hundred thousand (as had been anticipated) or even eighty thousand (as in Chicago) but rather twenty thousand at most. The festivities began with a flag-waving welcome procession for Lemke. Then, when the Pledge of Allegiance was read over a loudspeaker, the entire mass stood to attention and thrust their arms upward and forward. As the reporter for the *Philadelphia Inquirer* noted, "it closely resembled the Nazi salute."

Coughlin's declarations that he would not be muzzled by the Vatican became moot on November 3, when he and his Union party were muzzled by the American public. Roosevelt's victory was one of the most lopsided in the history of American presidential politics; he won the electoral ballot 523 to 8 over Republican challenger Alf Landon while taking in more than 60 percent of the popular vote, an indisputable mandate. Lemke couldn't even deliver his home state and polled fewer than a million votes nationwide. Coughlin had hoped he might reach as many as nine million and carry thirteen states, though toward the end of the campaign he realized this was a pipe dream.

It was a crushing rebuke, and one that left Johnson and Blackburn with the realization that Lemke and Coughlin were a dead end. "We didn't want to be associated with a loser and a priest," Johnson remembered with characteristic indelicacy. It was not enough to be the brain trust. They still believed the nation required new leaders, but now they would serve their own cause.

---

* Before his speech he delivered a radio address to the nation from a facsimile of his office in the Shrine of the Little Flower erected adjacent to the platform.

CHAPTER 7

An American Führer

We seem to forget, also, that we live in a community of people to which we are bound by the ties of existence, to some of whom we owe allegiance and obedience, and to others of whom we owe leadership and instruction.

—*Philip Johnson, 1938*

How might one build a political movement in the wake of electoral disaster? Johnson and Blackburn returned to their base of operations in New London, understanding that the small Ohio town could not fulfill their aspirations. Johnson had tried his hand at local politics, and balked. Coughlin's prominence, however compromised, suggested an alternative path to power: radio. Johnson had demonstrated an affinity for the medium during his campaign on behalf of the state's dairy farmers. He understood the potential that broadcasting offered to the would-be provocateur. That his voice was thin and somewhat effeminate—to some it read as gay, a political liability—was a fact he would have to overcome.

Again Johnson's pocketbook proved decisive; he could sponsor his own broadcasts, paying for airtime that would ordinarily be unavailable to him. He found a willing station in WSPD of Toledo. His program, "Youth of the Nation," debuted at one o'clock on Sunday, November 8, a mere five days after Lemke's ignominious defeat, and ran for thirteen weeks, with abbreviated transcripts appearing in *Social Justice*. Blackburn shared the microphone, but the ideas were all Johnson's. "Young men have ambitions. You have ambitions. Has the day come when we cannot carry out our ambitions?" the two men asked. The words seemed an unconscious airing of their own fears. With Roosevelt's resounding victory, there was little room for maneuver, and they resorted to the proto-fascist boilerplate that had failed Coughlin. "Instead of politics we need patriotism," they proclaimed. "Instead of politicians we need leaders."

A week later they returned to the air to speak about the failure of their generation to live up to the example set by their parents. "We young men shall never fight in a war of independence. We shall never join in a conquest of new lands. We may never fight to save the Union of these United States. It is too late even to be among those who made America rich in material things," they announced. That bit of analysis proved especially inaccurate. It was their so-called Greatest Generation, after all, that would defend the nation from the very totalitarianism they advocated, then power its unparalleled postwar economic boom.

The commentary of those first episodes hedged toward the anodyne, but as the election slipped further from memory, Johnson and Blackburn became sharper in their language. By December they were retreading Long's populist calls for wealth redistribution, telling their listeners that "America cannot exist half in prosperity and half in penury." A week later they took after the Red Menace in language that seemed, once again, unintentionally self-descriptive. "Small groups of small men, willful, well-organized, thrive on a docile America, thinking it will never rouse itself to shake off these bonds," they warned. Communists were dangerous, and so were "the international bankers" who were "organized to sell out America." That Communists and capitalists were somehow in cahoots was patently ridiculous—the unspoken invocation of Jewish conspiracy was the unifying thread—but logic was not of principal concern to the aspiring demagogues. Their intellectual confusion manifested itself the following week, when they released a five-point program for American revival that called for: a central bank controlled by the federal government; guaranteed employment for all men; income sufficient for lifetime security; private property "subject to control of the people for the public good"; and a "second to none" national defense to guarantee peace. But they were against Communism.

The ideas were muddled, but they found an audience. In the second week of January, Johnson and Blackburn gathered their followers for the

first meeting of their Youth of the Nation action group. Shortly thereafter, having rechristened it the Young Nationalist Movement to Save
America from Communism, they staged an automotive rally, with thirty
cars carrying some two hundred passengers on the hour's drive from
Toledo to Freemont, Ohio, where they gathered on the steps of the Sandusky County Courthouse. Johnson led the motorcade in a new Lincoln
Zephyr, a mean-looking streamlined coupe outfitted with loudspeakers
from which he promoted the nationalist cause and warned of the dire
threat of the Red Menace. An honest accounting would have noted that
the Red threat was not quite so dire as Johnson and Blackburn suggested, at least internally. In the 1936 election, Earl Browder, running as
a Communist, and Norman Thomas, the Socialist candidate, combined
for fewer votes than even Lemke.

Rationality, however, was not a requirement to appeal to an immature audience harboring resentments against forces that seemed beyond
its control or understanding. Johnson and Blackburn's party, an alt-right
avant la lettre, was composed of hard-core reactionaries, pro-Nazi
German-American Bundists, Klansmen, and members of the Black
Legion, an Ohio-based secret society that took the Klan as its model.
(Legionnaires wore black hoods emblazoned with a scull and bones.)*
Johnson tried to convert this group into his own version of the SA, the
brown-shirted paramilitaries he knew from the streets of Berlin. Borrowing Nazi intimidation tactics, he had his group march on the Communist party headquarters in Toledo. The Communists responded by
cutting the radio station's power line during one of Johnson and Blackburn's programs.

Johnson catered to his acolytes, inviting them to dinners at his home in
New London and at Townsend Farm. But there was no escaping the fact
that he was leading a gang of dead-enders, and that the Young Nationalist campaign was destined to go nowhere. And it was becoming entirely

---

* The group was the subject of a moralizing Hollywood film, *Black Legion,* starring
Humphrey Bogart as a remorseful Legionnaire who kills his best friend, a dairy farmer.
"Those guys don't fool," he warns in one portentous scene.

his show, as Blackburn's attentions were increasingly directed to his fiancée, Janette Emerson. Soon enough Blackburn returned to New York, where he took a job at the New York Association for the Blind.

Johnson resolved this problem in classic patrician fashion—by removing himself from it. With the advent of summer, he left for his annual holiday abroad, a luxury of which he had not availed himself since his departure from the museum. His destination: Germany.

This was an unusual choice for an American tourist in 1937. Nazi xenophobia, bellicosity, terror, and austerity made Germany a less-than-appealing spot for casual sightseeing and carefree indulgence. But Johnson wasn't a typical vacationer. With Huey Long no longer around to model his political aspirations, a return to the epicenter of fascism was in order. In Berlin he befriended Werner Sombart, a distinguished academic economist whose writing gave intellectual cover to Nazi ideologues. The intermediary was almost certainly Karl F. Geiser, a retired political science professor from Oberlin and one of America's more respectable Hitler apologists. Geiser had spent much of the past two years in Germany translating Sombart's *Deutscher Sozialismus,* which he published in America under the more nondiscript title *A New Social Philosophy.*

Johnson met Sombart at a dinner in honor of the sixtieth birthday of Hjalmar Schacht, the financier who engineered the economic machine Hitler required to satisfy his grand ambitions. Sombart was the kind of thinker ideally suited to Johnson. Though he was an economist, his ideas were not based on the complex mathematical and quantitative analysis that drove high finance. That would have been beyond Johnson's reach, just as Whitehead's metaphysical logic was in his college days. Sombart's work was something different, a fusion of moral and economic philosophy with general questions of social science. How were economic theories (and theorists) conditioned by their histories? Could there be such a thing as a German economics? These were the kinds of intellectual inquiries that sparked Sombart's mind, and now Johnson's.

Inspired by Geiser, Johnson committed himself to translating Sombart's contribution to the book of essays published in Schacht's honor, despite his lack of any formal training in economics. Neither did he have much gift for the art of translation; he left the very first word of Sombart's title, *Weltanschauung,* in the original German, offering the weak excuse that "it has already become a familiar term." His full title— *Weltanschauung, Science and Economy*—didn't quite roll off the tongue either. Johnson's work on the essay would continue for nearly two years.

Meanwhile he found time for a reunion with Mies and Lilly Reich. Johnson treated the two to lavish dinners at Schlichter's, in happier days the restaurant of choice for the Berlin avant-garde, and ventured together with them to the port cities of Lübeck and Stettin (now Polish Szczecin) to look at Mies's favored works of Gothic architecture. These trips took the three within a few short miles of the Nazi concentration camp at Sachsenhausen. They were all well aware of its existence but studiously avoided discussing it.

There may have been something valedictory about those trips, at least for Mies. Johnson's hope that Mies might emerge as the architectural savior of the Nazi state, expressed in his 1933 article on the architecture of the Third Reich in *Hound & Horn,* had not come to fruition. Mies had tried, however. Apolitical and opportunistic, he took work where it could be found. In 1926 this meant a monument for the martyred Marxist revolutionaries Rosa Luxemburg and Karl Liebknecht; in 1934 a pavilion for the German delegation to the 1935 Brussels World's Fair, unequivocally a work of Nazi state propaganda. The pavilion was not executed, and the truth was that there was little other work at the office at Am Karlsbad 24. The Nazis had largely discredited modernist architecture, leaving it acceptable mainly for works of industry, where aesthetics were not at issue. Mies was forced to live on the decreasing royalties from his furniture designs. As the architectural historian Franz Schulze wrote in his biography of the architect, "wealthy, liberal clients"—among them, prominently, Jews—"were nowhere to be found."

And so while Germany was for Johnson a place of attractive energy, Mies had started to think about a permanent departure, though he told Johnson otherwise. "I'm still German, and I'm going to stay," he said, unconvincingly. Actually, he had already responded positively to an invitation to direct the architecture school at Chicago's Armour Institute of Technology (now the Illinois Institute of Technology). Other opportunities, all emanating from the United States, led Mies to temporarily set aside that offer. Among these was an apparent offer of the directorship at the architecture school at Harvard. Mies had been the front-runner for the position, but pulled out of consideration when he learned that he would be put up for the job against Walter Gropius, who would eventually take it. Mies considered even the thought that he should be in competition with Gropius insulting.

Johnson, who loved nothing so much as gossip, must have been delighted with Mies's stories, and above all with the sad tale of his discussions with Alfred Barr, who had approached Mies the previous year with the possibility of building a new home for the Museum of Modern Art on Fifty-third Street, an offer Barr was forced to rescind almost as soon as he floated it. The conservative museum trustees preferred an architect they could trust (and control), specifically Philip Goodwin, a society architect who had recently joined the board. As a consolation, Barr had arranged a private commission for Mies back in the States, a house in Jackson Hole, Wyoming, for Helen and Stanley Resor, whom he also knew through the museum's board. The commission brought Mies to Chicago in August, where he took the job at the Armour Institute.

Johnson also returned to the Midwest at the end of the summer, but he stopped along the way in London, hoping for an audience with Oswald Mosley, the aristocratic founder of the British Union of Fascists—a model for Johnson's American organization. He never got to Mosley, however, probably because the British fascist was overburdened with his own campaign, which left him besieged by protestors and cordoned by security. On July 4, a Mosley-led parade of three thousand British fascists was met in Trafalgar Square by an angry mob more than three times as large.

Johnson enjoyed intellectual combat and was not opposed to intimidation tactics, just so long as it was his party doing the intimidating. He did not have the fortitude for the minority position. By the end of August he was safely back in bucolic New London, where he helped organize the town's Labor Day celebration, which was altogether more peaceable. Featured activities included a hot-air balloon ascension, a Ferris wheel, and horse races. Best of all was a raffle for a brand-new 1937 Chevrolet sedan. Johnson donated it himself, making sure the local press duly noted his largesse.

New London was merely a pit stop. With Blackburn absent and the Young Nationalist cause stalled out, he returned to New York and reunited with Lawrence Dennis, whose campaign to establish himself as the leading intellectual force of American fascism continued.

Dennis had traveled to Europe in the summer of 1936 to fully explore the movement in its native environment. The trip began in Italy with an hour-long audience with Il Duce but focused on Nazi Germany. His visit there was facilitated by Ulrich von Gienanth, the propaganda attaché at the German embassy in Washington (but also an agent in the SD, the intelligence arm of the SS). Dennis's ambitions to meet with Goebbels, Göring, and Hitler went unfulfilled, but he was granted a private session, "one thinker to another," with Alfred Rosenberg, the chief theorist of the Nazi myth of Teutonic superiority. Rosenberg (who was most assuredly not Jewish) made it a special point to entertain influential foreigners, hosting monthly *Bierabends,* or happy hours, at which he could expound, in his heavy Latvian accent, on the ideas he'd put forward in *Myth of the Twentieth Century,* one of the principal texts of National Socialism.

Keeping his own racial background a secret, Dennis suggested Germany should "treat the Jews more or less as we treat the Negroes in America." A certain level of discrimination was acceptable, but Nazi extremism was "in conflict with American opinion." Getting no traction with Rosenberg, he sought a more public outlet for his ideas in a meeting with Ernst "Putzi" Hanfstaengl, Hitler's Harvard-educated confidant; Dennis thought Hanfstaengl could help him secure a German edition of *The Coming American Fascism.* Dennis was also given a taste of Nazi spectacle. The propaganda ministry arranged tickets to the Olympic Games in Berlin, then sent him on a lavish junket to the annual *Parteitag* congress in Nuremberg, where he watched Hitler speak to an assembled crowd of one hundred and twenty thousand. Afterward he was treated as a personal guest in Gienanth's baronial home.

In the fall of 1937, when Johnson reconnected with Dennis in New York, Dennis was not riding quite so high. The trip to Europe had been partly financed by a partner in the investment firm E. A. Pierce. Dennis had been hired at a hefty $500 a month to serve as an adviser to the firm, and he produced an economic treatise, *An Intermediate Deflation,* published by the company. The title could just as well have described his own status after he came off the company payroll. Into the breach stepped Johnson, with a stipend of $100 month. The money paid Dennis's bills and freed him to work on his next book, *The Dynamics of War and Revolution,* which he would self-publish in 1940 with financial assistance from Johnson and laundered funds from the Nazi state.

Their relationship renewed, Dennis happily served as Johnson's conduit to Gienanth. They met in Washington in the spring of 1938 as Johnson prepared to depart for Germany for the summer. Johnson hoped that the attaché might facilitate his journey and set him up with a pass to the *Parteitag* events in Nuremberg, as he had for Dennis. This was of special interest to Johnson; the previous summer's rally had been the Nazis' greatest masterstroke of visual propaganda to date. Albert Speer, Hitler's architect, translated the Nazi thirst for monumental national aggrandizement into three dimensions, lining the Nuremberg Zeppelinfeld with 130 searchlights, each shining nearly five miles into the air. The "Cathedral of Light" formed an open room that vanished into a glowing night sky, fusing architecture and ideology at an unprecedented scale. Johnson, naturally, wanted to see the next one, and Gienanth was happy to oblige.

For Gienanth, Johnson might as well have been sent from the heavens: here was a provocateur willing to abet the Nazi propaganda campaign at no charge. Johnson was then still at work on his translation of Sombart's *Weltanschauung, Science and Economy,* but that was just one of his several writing projects. At the time he was also writing his first work of

what might be generously termed economic philosophy, for the pro-
fascist journal *The Examiner.*

Titled "A Dying People," the piece was a Malthusian analysis of
American decline. Johnson argued that the United States, defined exclu-
sively as a nation of white Christians, was committing "race suicide."
Americans were not having enough children to sustain the country, and
the growing use of birth control (to which he was opposed) was merely a
symptom of a broader degeneracy of national values. "The philosophy of
individualism and materialism is eugenically bad," he wrote. "It leads us
only to the satisfying of the immediate physical desires of each individual, not to the satisfying of the imperatives of racial maintenance. And it
leads us to selfishness in time as well as in place.... We seem to forget,
also, that we live in a community of people to which we are bound by the
ties of existence, to some of whom we owe allegiance and obedience, and
to others of whom we owe leadership and instruction."

Coming from Johnson, the article pushed hypocrisy to some as-yet-
unexplored height of hypocritical absurdity, reflecting the sense of self-
loathing and inferiority that had debilitated him so often in the past. He
was, after all, a man of almost pathological individualism, materialism,
and hedonism, a man who was by the nature of his homosexuality bound
to be childless.

"A Dying People" was published over the summer of 1938, when
Johnson was traveling in Germany, where racial purity, a subjugation of
self to state, and dictatorial leadership were the national obsessions
Johnson felt they should be at home. Elsewhere in Europe, Germany was
now spreading those ideals by force. On March 12 Hitler had annexed
Austria, installing a puppet regime that brought the full specter of the
Nazi system to his native land. Czechoslovakia was clearly next on his
acquisition list, and the threat of a German invasion was imminent when
Hitler mounted Speer's stage at the Nuremberg *Parteitag* rally on September 12. Gienanth, good as his word, had secured Johnson a pass to
the event. As he had in the past, Johnson found himself "carried away"
by the Führer's magnetism. With the world gripped with anxiety

wondering whether he would plunge the German army into the Sudeten-land, Hitler delivered a venomous, ranting soliloquy, just barely backing away from war.

His threats were enough. By month's end, the allies would meet his demands, at Munich.

Europe's fraught state of affairs was the backdrop to a summer in which Johnson immersed himself in the workings of the Nazi state. He partici-pated in a program administered by the Vereinigung Carl Schurz, a pri-vate organization that disseminated Nazi propaganda to foreigners.* Under its auspices, Johnson visited Hitler Youth camps and reviewed the status of the national building program with government officials. He also initiated relationships with several prominent figures responsible for propagandizing Americans, among them Dr. K. O. Bertling, director of the state-subsidized America Institute (a friend of Dennis), and Hans-Heinrich Dieckhoff, the German ambassador to the United States.

Johnson's relationship with Dieckhoff, which began over lunch in Berlin, carried over when both men returned to the United States in the fall and continued until Dieckhoff was recalled to Berlin in November, following the atrocities of *Kristallnacht*. (The United States recalled its ambassador after the pogrom, and Germany responded tit for tat by bringing back Dieckhoff.) In 1942, when Johnson was questioned by the FBI about the tenor of his discussions with Dieckhoff, he described them as "purely social," his goal being merely to form "a judgment of the workings and theories of National Socialism."

Johnson, meanwhile, continued to see Nazi officials in New York and Washington, meetings he would likewise characterize as "purely social." He was now lunching not only with Gienanth but Heribert von Strempel, the political and press attaché of the German embassy. (Gienanth operated

---

* The American Carl Schurz Foundation split from its German counterpart in 1940. It was bankrolled in part by the Warburg family and spent a considerable portion of its funds aiding Jewish refugees from the Nazi state.

under the aegis of Goebbels's Propaganda Ministry; Strempel was his counterpart in Ribbentrop's Foreign Ministry.) In his 1942 interview with the
FBI, Johnson described their conversations as "all generalities—that is,
discussion of the United States and the world, and isolationism."

A more plausible scenario is that Johnson was exchanging information on the activities, politics, and membership of American fascist circles, and discussing the means by which the Germans might disseminate
their propaganda. According to records captured after the war, the Nazi
diplomats were specifically interested in obtaining mailing lists and
names of individuals who might be sympathetic to their cause. Johnson,
who had built a network of nationalist supporters in both Ohio and New
York, was in a position to deliver precisely that type of material. Indeed,
Johnson had been keeping confidential lists of would-be supporters since
April 1934, when he instructed his private secretary, Ruth Merrill, to
take names at the first fascist gathering at the duplex apartment he
shared in New York with his sister.

The means of disseminating fascist propaganda was, in fact, a preoccupation with Johnson, a subject he raised specifically in April of 1939
with Viola Heise Bodenschatz, the author of a series of self-published
pro-German pamphlets. "What interests me especially is, how do you
get distribution?" he wrote her. "That seems to me the key question of
those of us who would like to get some daylight into the ever darkening
atmosphere of contemporary America."

A German-American citizen born in Louisville, Bodenschatz had an
unusually strong tie to the Third Reich. Her husband, a German-born shoe
manufacturer, was the brother of Luftwaffe General Karl-Heinrich Bodenschatz, Hermann Göring's Chief of Staff and liaison officer to Hitler.
Just how Johnson had first met her is unclear—Dennis was the likely
connection—but they struck up a friendship and agreed to meet over the
following summer in Germany. In the meantime, Johnson pumped her for
information. "Do you look for war?" he asked. "I do not, but that may only
be because I am ignorant. I feel that England won't fight and that Hitler can
take what he wants when he wants to. But I would give a good deal to hear
from you before I jump into the cauldron maybe. What think?"

Johnson's Berlin contacts also included Friedrich "Fritz" Auhagen, who had lectured on German literature at Columbia University in the early 1930s, though his own academic training was in economics and the engineering of mines. When Johnson called on him in Berlin, at Dennis's recommendation, Auhagen was waiting to return to New York, where he would act as a freelance propaganda agent for the Nazis, his services financed through organizations controlled by the German state. According to records of the German embassy in Washington, Auhagen was paid to run a lecture bureau that would promote the Nazi political agenda while maintaining the appearance of independence and objectivity.

That organization was the American Fellowship Forum, which was born in New York on March 16, 1939, with Philip Johnson among its founding members. Its aim, according to Auhagen, was to foster "a new spirit of cooperation among Americans of all classes, races and creeds." At its first meeting, held in April at New York's Capitol Hotel, five hundred came out to hear Dennis speak. "The economic and political interests of the United States and Germany do not clash," Dennis told them. Skirting any discussion of Nazi barbarism, he suggested that the two nations could exist harmoniously, each as the presiding power in its own hemisphere. He also recapitulated the arguments on race suicide Johnson had presented in "A Dying People."

That Johnson essay, along with Dennis's inaugural address, was republished in the first issue of *Today's Challenge,* the American Fellowship Forum's quarterly journal, which was mailed out to the membership in June of 1939. Auhagen, in his efforts to cast the forum as an open-minded and respectable space for thoughtful dialog—indeed, a patriotic service to the American people—also recruited contributions from the political leaders of the isolationist movement, among them two U.S. Senators, William Borah of Idaho and Ernest Lundeen of Minnesota, and New York congressman Hamilton Fish, a longtime Roosevelt antagonist.

The final essay of that first issue—"Can the Jewish Problem Be Solved?"—was written by another Dennis contact Johnson met in Berlin during the summer of 1938: George Sylvester Viereck, a German-born

American citizen whose history of propagandizing for Germany dated to World War I. Though Viereck claimed revulsion at Nazi anti-Semitism, he saw no reason to combat it: his "solution" to the "Jewish problem" was to remove the Jews from the German state. An international committee could decide where they would go—perhaps a homeland on Madagascar. Viereck presented himself as a patriotic and moderate American offering independent insight. In fact he was a clandestine Nazi agent, or *V-Mann*,* who was paid several hundred thousand dollars by the German government to disseminate propaganda in the United States.

For the German authorities, this was an increasingly pressing concern; after Munich, the extent of Nazi ambition and brutality was ever more clear, intensifying the "great debate" between isolationists, who would keep the United States out of European affairs, and interventionists, clamoring for the financial and material support of the country's Western allies. (The idea of direct military engagement was not yet on the table.) Nazi propaganda efforts were therefore concentrated on keeping America neutral by lending support to the isolationist movement. In this effort the cartoonish American Nazi Party, which was toxic to patriotic Americans, was an embarrassing public relations problem. The class of philosopher-fascists represented by Dennis and Johnson was a lot more appealing to the Nazi diplomatic corps. They made no direct claims to Nazism, but were clearly interested in transforming the American political system into a form that would be sympathetic to German National Socialism.

They were also in a position to operate as a kind of think tank for the fascist cause, providing intellectual backbone to influential members of the isolationist movement—both those who merely wished to maintain America's independent posture and those who sympathized with the Nazi state outright. Dennis was absolutely frank that this should be their mode of operation. "I think our strategy should be to turn out something which could be read and used by men like Senator Reynolds, Bennett Clark, Vandenberg, Lindbergh, etc.," he wrote Johnson, as they were

---

* Short for *Vertrauensmann,* or secret agent.

planning the launch of a new publication Johnson would subsidize.* "Writing for a small influential public and having no organization of dumbbells to embarrass us, we might be able to go on right through a war, by observing a little caution and innuendo."

Dennis's reference to Charles Lindbergh was telling; in the coming months Dennis would become an informal adviser to him, and Lindbergh would become a contributor to *Today's Challenge*. The blue-eyed, blond-haired aviator, a genuine national icon who seemed the very model of Teutonic discipline and fortitude, was establishing himself as the face of the American isolationist movement. It is easy to forget just how widespread this sentiment was at the time. Johnson was hardly the only member of the architectural establishment associated with isolationist ideas; Frank Lloyd Wright, in particular, was adamant in his isolationist beliefs, and prone to anti-Semitic language.

The three Midwesterners had much in common, and Lindbergh and Johnson had strikingly similar backgrounds: both had a politically active father who practiced law and a schoolteacher mother. Lindbergh's political engagement, however, seemed a continuation of his father's isolationism. In 1936 Lindbergh visited Germany for the first time, ostensibly on a mission to inspect Göring's air force. The trip, during the Olympic Games, was a propaganda coup for the Nazis. Impressed by what he saw, Lindbergh returned in 1937, and in the days leading up to Munich he pushed hard for appeasement. Some historians argue that his effusive reports on German air power were decisive, or at least influential, in shaping Britain's misguided policy. Back again in Berlin in 1938, Lindbergh was personally presented with the Order of the German Eagle by Göring, an award that came with a personal message from Hitler.

While Johnson cloaked himself behind a veneer of respectable intellectualism, he was not only aware of but actively supported the more brutal representatives of the fascist cause in America. Though he would later deny it, he admitted to the FBI that he attended several American

---

* Dennis refers to the U.S. Senators Robert Reynolds (North Carolina), Bennett Clark (Missouri), Arthur Vandenberg (Michigan).

Nazi Party rallies at Madison Square Garden. (Lindbergh himself head-lined one such event, barely a month before Pearl Harbor, on October 30, 1941.) Johnson also became a financial benefactor of the Christian Mobilizers, a virulently anti-Semitic organization of street brawlers run by another Dennis protégé, Joseph E. McWilliams, a soap-box dema-gogue who built his following with attacks on Roosevelt, the "Jew Deal," and the "Jewspapers" that supported it.

Johnson also reconnected with Father Coughlin's National Union for Social Justice, which had become even more strident in the years since Johnson had worked directly with the radio priest. By the fall of 1938 Coughlin had become openly and bitterly anti-Semitic, going so far as to print the discredited "Protocols of the Elders of Zion" in *Social Justice*. Coughlin's radio program became so incendiary that it was canceled by its New York affiliate, WMCA; a heavy police presence was required to keep the peace around the Times Square street hawkers who sold *Social Justice*. But violence was not uncommon. When the police were not around, Coughlin's adherents provoked Jews into fights, responding in superior numbers and with weapons. In February of 1939 a young man named Irving Berger, returning home after a date, was stabbed on the subway platform at Grand Central by thugs who identified him as Jew-ish. A year later, in January of 1940, seventeen Coughlin adherents were arrested by the FBI in Brooklyn and charged with plotting to overthrow the government of the United States. Among their targets for bombing were the offices of the *Daily Worker* and the Cameo Theater, the Times Square movie house where Johnson and Barr enjoyed watching Russian films.

Johnson knew about the activities of the NUSJ in New York because he had been in contact with the organization through *Social Justice*'s New York editor, Humphrey Ireland. Indeed, he had offered himself up to Ireland and *Social Justice* (as well as *Today's Challenge* and the *Examiner*) as a no-fee foreign correspondent for the coming summer of 1939, when he would be traveling across Europe, with Nazi Germany serving as his base of operations.

Social Justice seemed an appealing venue for Johnson's writing, as his aspirations to become a publisher himself had failed. Through Dennis he had come to know Paul Palmer, a fellow traveler in fascist circles who was the editor and proprietor of *The American Mercury,* the literary magazine cofounded by H. L. Mencken. (Mencken held isolationist views of his own but was no longer associated with the magazine.) In 1936 Dennis had unsuccessfully tried to broker a sale of the magazine so that it might become a front for the Nazi government. Now Johnson wanted to purchase a controlling share from Palmer, to transform it into a mouthpiece for his own brand of fascist propaganda. Palmer declined, however, and sold the publication instead to the *Mercury*'s Jewish business manager. Johnson believed Palmer thought he was too capricious to run the magazine, which may or may not have been true. In any case, Johnson was indignant about the sale. "The Jews bought the paper and are ruining it naturally," he wrote to Viola Bodenschatz.

In fact, Palmer did want to go in on a publication with Johnson and Dennis; he just wanted to do so secretly and on a project that would be entirely new. Dennis made this explicit in a letter to Johnson. Palmer, he wrote, wanted "to preserve anonymity at least until the thing had got a respectable following.... We could write most of the first drafts, let him edit and tone them down, and then circulate them under any formula considered practical or expedient."

That collaboration never came to pass, but Johnson kept writing. Before departing for Europe, he completed a tendentious new essay for the *Examiner* on the philosophical foundations of Nazism. "*Mein Kampf* and the Business Man" was pegged to the release of a pair of new English translations of Hitler's rambling manifesto, which Johnson had evidently read with some care in the original German. "Hitler's German style may not be elegant, but it is always clear, which cannot be said of either translation," he wrote, by way of review. The ostensible aim of the piece was to clear up a general "misunderstanding" of Hitler, especially among the liberal intelligentsia, whose animus precluded a rational examination of the roots and implications of National Socialism. "A long tradition in political thinking lies behind *Mein Kampf*," Johnson explained. "The importance of the book, what makes it an extraordinary document, is that it presents the means—and successful means, as events have shown—for realizing these ideas in a particular, highly complex situation.... The problems that this situation presented were ones of action, and in meeting them Hitler has shown himself to be one of Goethe's 'doers.'"

Johnson didn't stop with Goethe. Hitler's nationalism and racism, he argued, could be traced all the way back to the Greeks, to Aristotle, Plato, and Heraclitus. The logic was tenuous, but that didn't matter. Hitler's genius, he argued, was not the "doctrinal purity" of his thought but his ability to "bring these ideas into the market place by uniting them with tremendous powers of moral and national feelings. He has had the realism to grasp the forces which move people to action, understanding that any system of ideas which does not comprehend these forces is as unreal as it is impotent."

The specific unreal and impotent system Johnson had in mind was liberal democracy, which he equated with plutocracy. "The values of Liberals are merely the values of business men, of money," he wrote. The anti-Semitism of this argument was unstated, but its broader implications were clear: America and its allies were fully controlled by amoral bankers, whose only interest was profit. "Hitler threatens, on all levels, the rule of the business man," Johnson wrote. That sounded good as academic theory, but in practice it was utter nonsense. Hitler had realized early on that seriously threatening the "business class" would be his undoing, and granted immense authority to German industry, eliminating unions and providing it with slave labor. Johnson further argued that business interests were categorically opposed to war, as any large conflict would necessarily preclude trade. That also proved inaccurate. Hitler, notably, counted Henry Ford, America's greatest industrialist and most notorious anti-Semite, as one of his great inspirations. In 1938 he awarded him the Order of the German Eagle. Ford's German subsidiary continued operating throughout the war.

Johnson left for his summer as a correspondent at the beginning of June, traveling on the *Europa* with his sister Theo and his new friend Viola Bodenschatz, who was on her way to visit family in Germany, as she did every year. Twenty years his senior, and with a vaguely patrician air and shared values, she represented a kind of ideal maternal figure. The two agreed to tour Poland and the Baltics in Johnson's Lincoln, which he brought with him, while apolitical Theo would presumably remain in Berlin.

But before embarking on his tour with Bodenschatz, Johnson visited England, to assess the situation there for his readers back home. In London he found a nation gripped by anxiety, but largely unprepared for war. "The present policy seems to consist mainly of scaring everyone, by advertising campaigns, into volunteering to do something in their spare time," he told the readers of *Today's Challenge*. The country was not on a proper war footing, he explained. Also, he didn't care for the baggy volunteer uniforms. Across the channel, he found France in a similar funk: worried for war but ill-prepared and factionalized. "They want *securité* not *gloire*," he wrote.

In his dispatch to *Social Justice*, Johnson was frank about the cause of France's problem. "Lack of leadership and direction in the State has let the one group get control who always gain power in a nation's time of weakness—the Jews." For Johnson, the "Jewish question" was only worsened by the torrent of refugees from the Third Reich. "Even I, a stranger in the city, could not help noticing how much German was being spoken, especially in the better restaurants," he wrote. "Such an influx naturally makes the French wonder, not only about these incoming Jews, but also about their co-religionists who live and work here and call themselves French." More than three decades after the Dreyfus affair, Johnson was still wondering whether a French Jew—or an American Jew, or a Jew of any nationality—was even a possibility.

From Paris, Johnson moved on to the lion's den, Berlin, settling into luxurious quarters at the Bristol Hotel, on Unter den Linden. Life in the war economy of the Third Reich was ascetic, he informed his readers, and subject to steep rationing. There was no soap, clothes were hard to come by, and there was nothing good to eat. "The food you can get is very boring, too much potato, too much bread, too much cabbage and turnips and no coffee, no cream, no milk, no eggs and hardly any butter, and very little meat," he wrote. Despite such hardships, however, the population seemed squarely behind the Führer. "Today the Germans are impervious to the moral admonishment that they ought not to conquer their neighbors," he wrote, accurately, though he didn't seem to be bothered by it. He compared German expansionism with the American doctrine of manifest destiny: "conquest is good or bad, depending on who does it, you yourself or somebody you don't like."

A dutiful correspondent, Johnson met repeatedly with Richard Sallet, Gienanth's predecessor in Washington and now a press attaché in the Foreign Affairs Ministry, and Werner Assendorf, a representative in the American wing of the Propaganda Ministry. Through Assendorf he was able to attend the propaganda-office press conferences led by Otto Dietrich, the Nazi press chief and Hitler confidant. He considered himself one of the few objective American journalists (if not the only one) on the scene. "Our American correspondents in Berlin," he wrote, "write anti-Nazi propaganda in their news stories.... [A]ll the reports we read on this side of the ocean are colored." Not surprisingly, he made few inroads with his fellow journalists.

Johnson did have time to visit with the economist Werner Sombart, however, and he had Viola Bodenschatz to accompany him on his reporting expedition into Poland and through the contested territories along the Baltic Sea. Karl Bodenschatz, Göring's chief deputy, arranged for their papers of passage, but not without offering a sharp confidential warning to his sister-in-law. War with Poland was "inevitable," he told her, and Hitler's demand for the Polish Corridor—the spit of land that separated the German mainland from the open city of Danzig and East Prussia—was merely a pretext for his grander ambitions. The Führer had every intention "to take all of Poland." Karl assured Viola, however, that any invasion would not come until mid-August at the earliest.

Bodenschatz chose not to disclose this information to Johnson, though it was hardly secret. William L. Shirer, one of the American correspondents who had little patience for Johnson, made that clear in a diary entry on August 10. "Any fool knows they don't give a damn about Danzig," he wrote. That much was "freely admitted in party circles."

Johnson, despite his self-professed objectivity, seemed blind to the reality before him. When he pressed Bodenschatz for inside information as to Göring's perspective on the Polish question, she parried. "Well, Philip, I believe that [Göring] has supported many of Hitler's aggressive policies in the past, but I am led to believe that he foresees the dangers of attack on Poland," she told him.

The pair crossed the border without incident, stopping first in Gdynia, a freshly minted port city constructed by the Poles. "Ugly," was Johnson's jaundiced verdict of this industrial center thrown up in miraculously short order. Just a few miles to the east was the open city of Danzig, nominally independent but with a significant Nazi presence and the object of Hitler's public campaign against Poland—effectively another Sudetenland. Johnson, like the German leader, saw no reason why the handsome Hanseatic trading city should not be formally given over to the Third Reich. "The longer I am here, the more I struggle to grasp once more what could possibly be the reason for Danzig's not being a part of Germany," Johnson wrote in *Social Justice*. "It is the most German city I have been in."

The pair's exploration of contested lands continued in Memel (now Klaipėda), a wedge-shaped region along the Baltic coast that separated German East Prussia from Lithuania. Bodenschatz was interested because she had authored a 1935 booklet, *Mournful Memel,* on its history and the sad state of its political affairs. It had been detached from Germany at Versailles, then annexed by Lithuania in the 1920s. Germany tacitly accepted that situation, but a German-speaking population under a foreign flag was obviously inimical to Hitler's worldview. Bodenschatz, not surprisingly, had supported Nazi demands for repatriation, which were met, at gunpoint, the previous March.

Johnson neglected to mention this side trip in his correspondence, because it was thoroughly overshadowed by the events that followed. Driving south through East Prussia, the odd couple crossed the Polish border, expecting to find a landscape not much different than the one they had left behind; Europe's borders, Johnson noted, were really "arbitrary lines" on a map. But what they encountered was a shock. "I thought at first that I must be in the region of some awful plague," he wrote. "The fields were nothing but stone, there were no trees, mere paths instead of roads. In the towns there were no shops, no automobiles, no pavements, and again no trees. There were not even any Poles to be seen in the streets, only Jews!"

Johnson, a speed demon behind the wheel, could not get his Lincoln above ten miles an hour on the unpaved roads that led south through crumbling villages and Jewish shtetls. Progress was slowed throughout by curious onlookers who ran alongside the car. Johnson could barely believe he was in Europe, and frankly did not count the population as European. Jews, he considered a stateless caste. Now, he told Bodenschatz, he could understand why Hitler considered the Poles a "subhuman Slavic racial type" and that German territorial expansion into Poland would be "legitimate."

Arrival in cosmopolitan Warsaw, a Baroque city of parks and palaces— "a Western capital in an Oriental setting"—did nothing to dissuade Johnson of his prejudices. They stayed in the Hotel Europejski, the lap of luxury on central Victory (now Piłsudski) Square, a building that would have been right at home in Paris's 1st arrondissement. Which is precisely what Johnson liked about it, and Warsaw. "Here, the upper class speaks French," he wrote. It was like they weren't Poles at all.

Such was not the case in the industrial capital of Łódź, the next stop on the itinerary: "a slum without a city attached to it." His opinion was no doubt colored by homes boarded up for the coming onslaught and painted with anti-German slogans; a sign reading "Down with Hitler" was not his preferred idea of architectural ornamentation. The fare at the local cinema, "Confessions of a Nazi Spy," wasn't appealing either.

The movie title was an ill omen. At the border station at Kępno, the two sat nervously in Johnson's car as Polish soldiers inspected their papers. It looked like they might get through unmolested, but just before their release the phone rang with orders from headquarters: detain the Americans and confiscate their papers. After a long delay, several officers arrived; the pair were driven back to the Polish intelligence office and separated. Johnson was strip-searched and then questioned. Did he think, just because he was a rich American, he could come to Poland to "cause trouble"? The interrogation lasted through the day and into the evening. At dinner the two detainees were fed a simple supper of cutlets, fried potatoes, and rye bread.

The experience was terrifying, but in his account of the event for *Social Justice* Johnson left the impression that it was his captors who were worried. "All the Polish officials showed great nervousness," he reported. "They should have let me go after seeing my American passport and my American car." In fact, their release was secured by the quick thinking of Bodenschatz, who offered to send one of the arresting officers a packet of American stamps upon learning he was a collector. When she recounted the incident to her brother-in-law, he coolly responded: "We may be paying this Polish official a visit before he has time to receive your stamps."

The inevitability of that onslaught, and the Poles' incapacity to defend themselves against it, was crystal clear to Johnson. Upon their release from the security office at Kępno, Johnson and Bodenschatz were given a brief tour of the local defensive works hastily being constructed in the border area, which consisted primarily of trenches and barbed-wire fencing. "Tell the Germans what you saw," his guide told him. "Tell them what a glorious spirit of patriotism burns in the breast of the Poles. We shall hold them! We shall fight them till we die." Johnson, in fact, followed this direction, but his German hosts only laughed. He knew they had cause, too, for he had seen the Wehrmacht's mechanized units waiting for action on the German side of the border. "The Poles are brave," he wrote, "but they are no match for the massive war machine that would be pitted against them."

With the knowledge, courtesy of his Bodenschatz connection, that the invasion was still a few weeks off, Johnson left Berlin on another road trip, traveling this time with his sister Theo south through occupied Czechoslovakia and Austria, then on to Hungary, where the two caught a plane to Istanbul. Though his attentions were generally removed from the field of architecture, on the drive south through Brno he telephoned Otto Eisler, the Jewish architect he had met in 1930 while touring that city with Henry-Russell Hitchcock. They had become fast friends then, with Johnson advertising him in a letter to Lewis Mumford as "the best architect in Czechoslovakia." The Eisler house, a clean modern box the architect designed for himself and his brother, went into the *International Style* book. Now, the voice on the other end of the line was practically unrecognizable: weak, weary, and deeply suspicious. "What do you want to see me for?" Eisler asked. "I just want to know how things are going," replied a chipper Johnson, seemingly oblivious to the brutalities of the Third Reich. "They're not going well," Eisler replied, but he agreed to the visit.

Johnson found Eisler at home and in bad shape. In April he had been arrested on the charge of disrespecting the Führer, and was held for six weeks at the notorious prison at Špilberk Castle. He was now required to present himself daily at Gestapo headquarters. "Obviously you don't know, but I've been in the hands of the Gestapo," Eisler told him. "I don't know how long I can talk to you."

Decades later, Johnson described the meeting as "one of the worst moments" of his life and protested that he had not realized Eisler was Jewish—highly unlikely, given their previous interaction. Confronted, in any case, with the handiwork of the Nazi regime, he sent off a letter to J. J. P. Oud, a mutual friend, in the hope that he might be able to arrange an exit visa with some kind of job offer. He made no effort, however, to intercede on Eisler's behalf with Karl Bodenschatz, who might easily have helped. According to his testimony at Nuremberg after the war, Bodenschatz was specifically in charge of handling such entreaties, and—bearing the imprimatur of Göring—they were often successful. "In all cases that I dealt with help could be given," he testified. Even after the war, Johnson made no effort to learn of Eisler's harrowing story of escape to Norway, capture (he was shot trying to cross into Sweden), and survival of Auschwitz.

Johnson was with Theo in Istanbul on August 23 when the news broke that Hitler and Stalin had signed their Nonaggression Pact, sealing Poland's fate. With war now an imminent certainty, Johnson returned to Berlin. The world was on the brink, and he wanted to be in the middle of it all. "I just felt excitement," he would recall years later, as if the stakes were no greater than a baseball pennant race. He had judgment enough to drop his sister off in Zurich along the way. From there she moved along to Paris, where she took an apartment in the same building as their mutual friend Virgil Thomson, and began volunteering for the Red Cross. It was a demanding job that took a toll on her vocal cords (there was a lot of shouting involved), but aiding refugees appealed to her in a way that neither her brother nor Thomson could understand. "She added nothing to her usefulness, merely lost her voice and a large part of her luggage," said Thomson.

While Theo was tending to the victims of Nazi oppression, her brother was a willing observer of the German extermination machine. Two weeks into the war, on September 18, Johnson joined the foreign press corps on a supervised junket to the front under the aegis of the Propaganda Ministry. The terrible cost of the war was apparent as soon as they crossed the border: the Polish war dead, men and horses, lay rotting along the roadside. The convoy stopped for the evening at Sopot, located on the Baltic between Gdynia and Danzig.

In the evening Johnson was assigned a room with William Shirer, the gimlet-eyed CBS correspondent who had pegged Johnson as a fascist. "None of us can stand the fellow and suspect he's spying on us for the Nazis," he wrote in his diary. "For the last hour in our room here he has been posing as anti-Nazi and trying to pump me for my attitude. I have given him no more than a few bored grunts."

Early the next morning the reporters were shaken from bed by the thunder of the German battleship *Schleswig-Holstein* shelling Gdynia. So rousted, they were brought to an observation post to watch the German military—infantry, navy, and air force working in unison—decimate the newly built port city that was the pride of Polish industry. The morning attack was focused on a school building, from which Polish soldiers fought valiantly against superior forces until they were annihilated by a bombing run, an operation carried out with brutal efficiency. That it was tragic was obvious. For most of the reporters it was also profoundly uncomfortable. "Grotesque the spectacle of us, with little danger to ourselves, standing there watching the killing as though it were a football game and we nicely placed in the grand-stand," wrote Shirer. The next day they were given privileged seats for a bitter speech by Hitler at the Danzig guildhall. "I, myself, am conscious of the greatness of this hour," said an imperious Führer, irritated that his troops were not yet in Warsaw. He stormed out trailing Himmler.

Like Shirer, Johnson used the word *spectacle* to describe the Nazi onslaught, but for him the connotation was altogether different. In a letter to Bodenschatz written after both had returned to the United States, he described what he saw in the days after the attack on Gdynia. "Do you remember Markow?" he wrote. "I went through that same square where we got gas and it was unrecognizable. The German green uniforms made the place look gay and happy. There were not many Jews to be seen. We saw Warsaw burn and Modlin being bombed. It was a stirring spectacle."

While Shirer and some of the other correspondents returned to Berlin after Hitler's speech, Johnson continued on with his inspection of the German campaign, which concluded, officially, on September 21. When he finally did return to Berlin, he did not linger. Berlin had run out of coffee, which was unpleasant, but more troubling was the threat of British attack from the air, now that the world war was officially on. At night the city he had once loved as a capital of libertinism and intellectual possibility closed itself up into a pitch-black void of fearful darkness. On October 6 he got in his Zephyr and headed south for the port of Genoa. Unlike so many desperate refugees, he had no problem arranging passage back to the United States.

Johnson summed up his observations of the German invasion of Poland in a final, tendentious piece for *Social Justice,* in which he targeted not the Nazis but his fellow American correspondents. "I find that America knows too much about the war—90 per cent of it wrong," he wrote. "Our 'neutral' press gives impressions only on one side of the war." He was prepared to correct the record. "You have been led to believe that the Germans have devastated Poland. 90 per cent false! Modlin, Mlava and the hamlet of Nowogrod I saw in ruins. But 99 percent of the towns I visited since the war are not only intact but full of Polish peasants and Jewish shop keepers. Fields everywhere were full of potato-digging Poles. Next year's rye fields are being plowed—in many cases by German soldiers with army horses. Fishermen continued to fish undisturbed on the Vistula, five miles from Warsaw."

Was Johnson a willing victim of the German propaganda machine or something far more sinister: the Nazi spy Shirer believed him to be? Ernest Pope, another American journalist who knew Johnson in Germany, corroborated Shirer's assessment. In a 1943 interview he told the FBI he suspected Johnson was an informant for the Gestapo. In the context of those suspicions, Johnson's repeated private meetings with Nazi officials, both at home and abroad, raise legitimate questions as to the precise nature of his activities. There is no evidence, however, that he violated American law. There was nothing illegal about Johnson speaking privately with Nazi officials in 1939. Those conversations would have become unlawful only had Johnson accepted financial remuneration from the German government—an act that would have made him an unregistered agent of a foreign power. It was on this charge that his friends Fritz Auhagen, Viola Bodenschatz, and Lawrence Dennis would be arrested in the wake of the Pearl Harbor attacks and America's entry into the war. But for Johnson money was never an issue: he was insulated by his own wealth. Indeed, he was the ideal vehicle for the Nazis, a man willing and able to finance their interests out of his own pocket.

This was precisely what his father had feared when, upon his return from Europe in the aftermath of the First World War, he warned his Pinehurst friends about the "corruption of sources of news and the coloring of press dispatches." Now it was his son who was leading the charge of misinformation, of fake news. Whether Shirer was accurate in his assessment of Johnson is perhaps unknowable, but in his diary entry of October 8, 1939, the newsman captured the world situation with succinct and tragic accuracy: "And now darkness. A new world. Black-out, bombs, slaughter, Nazism. Now the night and the shrieks and barbarism."

CHAPTER 8

Pops

My testimony is crisp and so obviously truthful, that all are for me.
—Philip Johnson, 1943

In the months after his return from Germany to the United States in September of 1939, Johnson embarked on a campaign of tendentious speech-making, offering himself up to audiences in Massachusetts, New York, Ohio, and Pennsylvania as an objective, eyewitness source on the latest developments in Europe. "Facts and Fiction in the Present War" and "Hitler's Germany—America's Future" were typical lecture titles. Americans, he warned, were being misled by the press, and would do well to embrace the inevitable fascist victory. "It is an unusual privilege and pleasure to hear his hard-hitting, penetrating debunking of propaganda," crowed an advertisement in the *Forum Observer,* the mouthpiece of Fritz Auhagen's American Fellowship Forum. In an effort to further this message, Johnson reunited with Lawrence Dennis, renting office space in New York with a plan to launch a new magazine that would be a platform for their ideas.

Johnson found a new address for himself as well. In early 1940 he and Theo moved into a small duplex apartment tucked behind a brownstone along the Third Avenue elevated subway line. To reach it you had to know it was there, because it was invisible from the street; access was through a narrow passage that took visitors past the brownstone. Johnson called it Hidden House. The lack of visibility made it an ideal clubhouse for Johnson's fascist society, a salon where they could meet beyond prying eyes. A Hollywood set designer could not have imagined a better villain's lair, right down to the icy modern decor.

That interior design was in much the same character as his previous apartments, with his Mies furniture arranged in rigid compositions, walls stripped of detailing, and rooms divided by floor-to-ceiling curtains. The concept was clearly Johnson's, but as in the past he was assisted in the execution by a trustworthy subordinate with professional qualifications. In this case that was Bruce Simmons, a society decorator with whom Johnson was friendly.

Professionally Simmons proved capable, but he was alarmed by Johnson's extensive library of fascist literature, and by the odd comings and goings of visitors speaking unidentifiable foreign languages. Was Johnson a spy? Simmons contacted the Federal Bureau of Investigation and became a confidential informant. By then Johnson's activities were hardly a secret to the Bureau. In September of 1940, when Simmons first alerted the agency, Johnson was already the subject of no fewer than five separate FBI case files. Just three months earlier, in June, J. Edgar Hoover himself had dispatched the special agent in charge of the Cleveland office to investigate Johnson's activities. Hoover's memo was flagged, "Philip Johnson: ESPIONAGE."

Johnson would later claim all innocence of such affairs: "It sounds as if I must have been hiding something; I simply wasn't," he said. The FBI never charged him for his activities, despite their suspicions and evidence of his collaboration with Nazi officials. Informants placed him in meetings with the German agents Ulrich von Gienanth and Heribert von Strempel as late as September 1940. Whatever his actual role, the cloistered apartment signaled another aspect of Johnson's psyche; a growing sense of anxiety that he had backed the wrong political horse, and a mortifying sense of his own ostracism from polite society. How could Johnson, who had argued tirelessly for an architecture of intellectual transparency, and who would eventually build a glass house for himself, read his own home as anything but a statement of shameful self-abnegation?

What Johnson was mainly doing in those months in Hidden House is largely a mystery. "Twiddling my thumbs and trying to figure out what to do with my life," Johnson would later claim. His disassociation with the Museum of Modern Art was especially troubling. In the years since he and Blackburn had summarily departed on their political adventure, he had watched the museum morph from a minor dependence of the Rockefeller family interests into one of the city's leading cultural institutions. The architectural department he had founded was now operating smoothly without him, despite his efforts to remain involved. In the early years of his political adventure, he had in fact kept some connection. He sent long letters of advice to Ernestine Fantl, his former secretary and assistant, who had assumed his curatorial duties by default and was at work on the difficult task of putting on a show on the temperamental Le Corbusier. (Stick to photos rather than his "badly constructed" models, Johnson suggested, and take a jaundiced view of his urban planning ideas—"the bunk.") Johnson also lent a curatorial hand to his longtime collaborator and mentor Henry-Russell Hitchcock on his landmark exhibition of the work of American architect H. H. Richardson.

But those shows were now years in the past, and lately he had had only minimal contact with the museum as it put on major exhibitions on Alvar Aalto, Frank Lloyd Wright's Fallingwater, and the Bauhaus—a show largely shaped by Bauhausler Herbert Bayer and by Walter Gropius, whose functionalism Johnson had come to disdain. The museum was also devoting increasing attention to industrial design, acting as a kind of popular tastemaker with shows such as *Useful Household Objects Under $5* and its slightly less spendthrift successor, *Useful Household Objects Under $10*. Johnson's *Machine Art* show had pioneered this direction for the museum, but these exhibitions were perhaps a bit too down-market and a bit too utilitarian for his tastes.

Most upsetting was the fact that, in 1937, the entire department was placed under the direction of John McAndrew, the young architect and acolyte of Alfred Barr's who had toured Europe with Johnson as something more than a friend in 1929, before Johnson had glommed onto Hitchcock. This news was a blow to Johnson's pride—Johnson had developed an aversion to McAndrew for reasons not quite clear, but probably owing to an ingrained sense of territorial jealousy. Now McAndrew was also taking a hand in the design of the museum's new building, which opened in 1939 with Philip L. Goodwin and Edward Durell Stone as architects. That burned. Johnson, who had used the museum to shape the direction of American architecture, had to watch from the sidelines as the museum established its own architectural identity in a building of which he did not approve.

Johnson had wanted that job to go to Mies, a desire shared by Barr but not the museum's board, which had rejected him in favor of Goodwin. Stone, who had impressed Nelson Rockefeller with his work on the design of Radio City Music Hall, was assigned as a junior partner, a young voice who could make sure the building was sufficiently modern. The design they arrived at, a rectangular box sheathed in white marble panels with a pair of floating window bands, made a stark contrast with the townhouses that surrounded it on Fifty-third Street. But Johnson hated it, thinking it a kind of modernism-lite, and he held a special place of disdain for the ocular cutouts—"cheeseholes," Johnson called them—that McAndrew had insisted they punch into a projecting canopy along the roofline. He would forever hold a grudge against Stone, who would become one of his chief competitors, even when Johnson was borrowing his ideas for future expansions of the museum.

Sequestered in Hidden House, Johnson was powerless as these events unfolded, a man without portfolio or direction, his influence at the museum all but gone. A return to that institution was for the moment out of the question, and a resumption of his side career as a café society interior designer untenable, given his recent history. He arrived at the idea of a retreat to the halls of academia, where he might reinvent himself for the future. Architecture school would remove him from the scene for a few years, and return him with a professional degree in the field that he had always loved, and hopefully with his past swept under the capacious rug of history.

Where he would go was not much of a question. Although Mies, whom he revered above all architects, was by then ensconced at the Armour Institute in Chicago, Johnson had no intention of following him there. He worried, with good reason, that he would entirely lose his identity in the shadow of the German master. (Mies, like Wright, had a reputation for breeding disciples rather than independent talents.) Yale and Princeton were also out; he was a Harvard man, and Harvard, in 1940, was the most progressive architecture school in the nation. Just arrived there was none other than Walter Gropius, the founder of the Bauhaus, who had come to America on the run from the Nazis. Gropius was charged with the transformation of graduate architectural education—he was the program director—moving it from the beaux arts model that had so turned off Johnson back in the 1920s to a modern course that would integrate the intellectual and aesthetic principles of the Bauhaus with the need to develop students who could assume positions of leadership in the world of American architectural practice. Johnson had soured on Gropius as an architect, but in the latter's educational capacity he figured they could at least coexist.

Harvard was happy to have its prodigal son back in the fold, despite his problems as an undergraduate and his more recent political infelicities. He had always been an exceptionally gifted student, and he was wealthy. The prospect of adding him to the architecture-school roster was particularly appealing to the school's dean, Joseph "Vi" Hudnut, who considered him a personal friend and viewed him as something like an additional faculty member. Johnson, after all, had quite literally written the book on modern architecture. *The International Style* was a standard text in the school's compulsory history class, from which Johnson was excused. The result was an occasionally uncomfortable relationship with his masters, and in particular Gropius. The pair would largely avoid each other in Johnson's years at the school, two sharks swimming uncomfortably in the same tank.

The question facing Johnson in the spring of 1940 was not so much whether Harvard would accept him, but if he, at the age of thirty-four, could swallow his pride and return to school with students who would be a decade his junior. Beyond that social problem was his acute sense of insecurity about his own abilities. Could he make it as an architect by himself? Johnson had worked as something of a professional designer for years, and he had always required a partner to help him carry out his visions. For that matter he had borrowed liberally from others, taking

185

their ideas for his own, sometimes with little to no mediation or dispersal of credit. That would no longer be possible. In school his performance would be naked, his talents revealed for what they were and were not. He was particularly concerned about his limited ability as a draftsman, a liability that would have sunk his chance at a successful career in a traditional beaux arts program.

A visit with the ex-Bauhausler Marcel Breuer, transplanted with Gropius to Harvard, convinced Johnson that he could hack it. Johnson had met Breuer, a bluff Hungarian known to all as "Lajko," (pronounced, Ly-ko) in Germany, and had celebrated him in his books and exhibitions as one of the leading proponents of international modernism. "Do you think I could be an architect?" a nervous Johnson asked him on a visit to Cambridge. Breuer told him to hold out his hands. "I don't see anything wrong," he said. "The fingers all work." With that, Johnson returned to school.

It was a dark time to enroll. In the fall of 1940, as Johnson moved into a two-story house with an Irish maid and a view of the Charles (no university housing for him), the Nazis were in Paris, the Battle of Britain was at its apex, and the atmosphere on campus was nervous and bleak. Johnson's activities, also, were catching up with him. An article in the September issue of *Harper's* magazine identified him as a pro-fascist flunky of Father Coughlin. (He was, however, misidentified as a scion of the Johnson & Johnson family, a fact the company's lawyers anxiously dispelled in a letter to the editor, copied to J. Edgar Hoover.) A month later, *Fortune* described him as a Nazi-sympathizing socialite.

Even before these revelations were made public, Johnson had begun the difficult project of rehabilitating his image. Reversing his isolationist position, he now advocated increased support for America's allies abroad and a war footing for its armed forces. Did this constitute a genuine change in his beliefs, a more cynical reading of the political landscape, or some combination of the two? The fact that FBI informants still had him meeting with Nazi officials in September of 1940 suggests a more jaundiced interpretation. But he also seemed eager to demonstrate his own patriotism. Over the summer he had applied to serve as an officer in the U.S. Naval Reserve. Just as he was beginning his first semester at Harvard, however, he learned that his application had been denied. A position was not available for "an individual of your particular qualifications," he was informed by mail. If he had any question as to the real reason for his rejection, he could find it in the bottom left corner of the letter: "Copy to: Dist. Intell. Office."

Blocked in his attempt to join the military, Johnson formed a Harvard chapter of the Committee to Defend America by Aiding the Allies, an organization created earlier in the year by progressive editor William Allen White to push for a more interventionist foreign policy. Operating out of an office in a charming Victorian a block from the architecture school, Johnson formed a committee of one. With the campus surprisingly apathetic, Johnson abandoned this effort for lack of interest, but not before he was visited by a second-year student who had come across one of his fliers in the architecture school. Landis Gores, thirteen years younger than Johnson but preternaturally erudite, had come to enlist but instead found himself engaged in a discussion of Socratic philosophy. Gores had just graduated from Princeton, where he had studied classics, counting among his inspirations Johnson's erstwhile mentor, Raphael Demos. Despite their age difference, with their shared backgrounds they found themselves "thoroughly kindred spirits," forming a relationship that would help each of them launch their professional careers.

Johnson made other friendships at Harvard, which was then producing something of a golden generation of architects that would include Edward Larrabee Barnes, Ulrich Franzen, Gores, John M. Johansen, Dan Kiley, I. M. Pei, Paul Rudolph, and Hugh Stubbins, all of whom would go on to storied careers. Johansen, a gifted visionary with his eye always on the future, became especially close to Johnson in his first year. John Barrington Bayley, a gay social butterfly who had bounced in and out of Harvard, was another of Johnson's confidants. Of all his new friends, none was more perspicacious than Carter Manny, a strait-laced Midwesterner who appreciated Johnson but could see him for what he was. Johnson, he wrote, was an "eccentric bird" and "too much an aristocrat architect, caring nothing for practicality or cost."

From the outset, it was clear that Johnson was not quite like his peers. He was as likely to spend an evening with the dean as he was at one of the group apartments shared by his fellow students. They could readily see that he had a broader knowledge of modern architecture than many of their teachers, who were only now adjusting to the new idiom after years of traditional training and practice. Fellow students regularly turned to Johnson for impromptu "crits" of their projects, and he was unafraid to speak up at end-of-term juries, which led to some hard feelings with the professoriat. Demonstrating his leadership status, he persuaded his fellow students to construct their models all of the same material so that they would have a pleasingly uniform appearance during final reviews. As for the task of actually constructing those models, he was less useful—he had to pay a fellow student to help him with his own.

Overall it was a successful first year. Johnson took five courses, achieving his highest grade (A) in, of all things, descriptive geometry—technical drawing. He did less well in statics (B) and construction (B-). A review of his notebooks from those years indicates a proficient and diligent student, exacting in his calculations and sketches. Although he was not a natural draftsman, he was more than competent technically, well capable of illustrating his ideas on paper. It helped that his Miesian designs tended toward rectilinear geometries rather than complex interlocking curves that required greater facility with the pen.

Of the projects Johnson produced in that first year, there was a kindergarten (perhaps the single typology he was least interested in or suited to), a restaurant, a beach pavilion, and a small house. The pavilion, which received plaudits even from Gropius, was a one-story brick block with a glazed beachfront side, clearly indebted to Mies. The house—which fused the Miesian aesthetic with elements Johnson borrowed from Le Corbusier's masonry-walled de Mandrot House—was carried off, according to Gores, "with assurance and sensible panache."

The success of his first year was undercut by the best-selling publication, in May, of Shirer's *Berlin Diary*, which pegged Johnson not just as a misguided American intellectual but as a potential Nazi agent.

188

Johnson's Harvard peers, by this time, were generally willing to give him a pass; Johnson's contrite openness about his long and ill-considered relationship with Father Coughlin and Lawrence Dennis was generally enough to convince his fellow students that he had reformed. But his candor was partial and strategic: Johnson admitted to his history with American fascists, but never broached his more troubling relationships with high-ranking Nazi officials.

With the beginning of the fall semester, he would again try to demonstrate his patriotic zeal and his remorse for past activities. In November he stopped by the office of Louis Kirstein, father of his friend Lincoln, to drop off a check for $100 as a donation to the United Jewish Philanthropies. At school he joined the newly formed Harvard Defense Group, acting as its Radio Coordinator. But his history caught up with him, and he was dismissed from the organization by Arthur Schlesinger Jr. (The two would become friends when Schlesinger served as an adviser to the Kennedy Administration.)

That winter, with the United States fully into the war, and many of his classmates in active service, Johnson tried again to join the war effort. This attempt appeared to be successful: his application was accepted by the Office of Facts and Figures, the propaganda agency that would morph into the Office of Strategic Services (OSS) and, in the postwar years, the CIA. That Johnson might now be charged with disseminating American war propaganda was absurd on its face, given that he was then under FBI investigation for acting in just that capacity for the Nazi government. But he never got the chance. Withdrawing from Harvard on February 10, he left for Washington, where he was granted an interview with the agency's director, William "Wild Bill" Donovan. America's wartime spymaster, however, had quickly learned enough about Johnson to know that his appointment would be impossible. As Johnson sat before him, he gently explained that he had wanted him for the program—Johnson's fluent German was a valuable skill—but that Shirer's book precluded any such commission, as a matter of propriety if not security. Two days later, a dejected Johnson reenrolled at Harvard. Meanwhile the prospect of his joining Donovan had set off alarm bells across the capital, with memos flashing back and forth between agencies, warning of his history.

Johnson was disappointed, but he could nurse his wounds in comfort. In Cambridge he had taken up residence for the year at the Hotel Continental, a five-story brick hotel in the English style. These were quarters far more luxurious than even his Brahmin classmates could reasonably afford, given student budgets and the more general privations of wartime. But Johnson had still grander aspirations on the housing front. Over the previous summer he had purchased a small plot on leafy Ash Street just off exclusive Brattle Street and around the corner from the Stoughton House, the celebrated 1882 mansion by H. H. Richardson. His real coup was to convince the school's administrators to allow him to build a house on this lot as his thesis project.

The design of the house occupied him for much of the year and in some ways became a group project among his fellow students. Johnson was never immune to borrowing a good idea, of course, and he understood it would be politically expedient for him to include his classmates in the design process, at least a little bit, so they might feel some ownership of it and not turn against him in jealousy. This proved to be an effective strategy. As Gores would later recall, Johnson's peers were "on the whole delighted, definitely impressed, understandably envious, but able to digest the matter with good humor and considerable downright witticism."

The house was to be Miesian in character, with Johnson's first plans inspired by the master's Barcelona Pavilion of 1929. But this created problems: on a small plot, the open plan would present the interiors to the street, and Johnson was not yet ready for the exposure, both literal and figurative, of a glass house. Instead he designed a simple structure with a glass front, but he enclosed his plot behind a nine-foot-tall plank fence, creating a small internal court that he paved with squares of bluestone set in sand. Bedroom, dining room, and living room looked out on this enclosed space, with kitchen and bathrooms tucked into a small service core.

The result would be a house that, just like Johnson's apartment in

New York, was hidden from view, walled off. The neighbors, quite predictably, were displeased. In a community defined by genteel colonials tucked sensitively behind bushes or picket fences, Johnson's aggressive, obscuring fence, pushed up to the lot line, was not only stylistic apostasy but an offense to decorum. There were ruffled feathers, and then a lawsuit, but in the end there were no ordinances precluding Johnson's design.

Work on the site began in April of 1942 with the laying of a concrete slab and proceeded swiftly. To manage construction (and to sign off on his documents), Johnson imported S. Clements Horsley from New York, a contracting architect he had come to know through the Museum of Modern Art. For one of the only times in his career, Johnson would advertise the project as a product of "prefabrication." The practice was actually more expensive than bespoke building, but saving money was not Johnson's goal. He had other reasons for choosing the method, first because it would speed up on-site fabrication (making it easier for him to

Invitations to Johnson's 1942 Ash Street House were a special privilege for his Harvard classmates. (Esto / Ezra Stoller)

supervise while in school) but mainly as a concession to the prevailing wisdom at Harvard. For Gropius, prefabrication had become something of a holy grail, an obligation of modernism in an era of mass housing shortages and wartime mobilization. Appeasing Gropius, the school's dean, was a necessity for Johnson, even if the entire prefabrication concept was at odds with his rarefied idea of domestic living.

Watching the rapid rise of the house became something of a ritual for Johnson's fellow students, who charted its progress with curiosity, taking it as a daily lesson in the practicalities of building. Johnson convinced the faculty to allow him to use it to satisfy his "practical experience in building" graduation requirement. When it was finally complete, in August, Johnson christened it with a grand party for his mother, Louise. "It is a good house for entertaining," he told her. Thereafter it became the latest of Johnson's salons, an invitation considered a rare privilege among Johnson's peers. Exclusive dinners were catered by Johnson's Portuguese butler and his maid. Among the regular invitees was I. M. Pei, who had transferred to Harvard from MIT, and his wife, Eileen. The aristocratic Pei had attracted Johnson's attention as a promising student even before he had made the switch, and the two would remain friendly competitors in the coming years. Most students, however, were not granted such intimacy, their experience instead limited to the larger garden parties he would throw as a matter of course; on one memorable evening, one of Johnson's slightly inebriated classmates accidentally crashed into one of the large window panes fronting the garden—still a novelty in a home setting—shattering it into a million pieces and cutting himself badly. A furious Johnson just walked away, muttering under his breath.

After his years of curatorial instigation, he understood that the house presented him with a plum opportunity for self-promotion, with the prefabrication angle being catnip to the press. *Town & Country* called the undertaking "highly successful." The *Boston Globe* gave "The Fence House" a full-page spread on a Sunday. The design, Johnson told the editors, could be reproduced on an assembly line, just like one of Ford's automobiles. (Not said: only then would it be cost-effective.) The *Christian Science Monitor* pictured him on the phone in his glass-fronted living room, a contemporary man of action, ready for any challenge. The only sour note came from *Architectural Forum,* which noted, with some accuracy, that it was more apartment than house, and that it "would be almost totally unlivable" for the average American family. Of course Johnson did not have, and frankly had no interest in, the average American family.

Mies, for his part, was unimpressed. Johnson showed him the plans just after the war, hoping he might deign to visit, but the master refused. Years later, Johnson had an acute memory of the courtly condescension of Mies's heavily accented rejection: "When ve do this kind of court house, ve don't put quite so many columns in."

The response of the Harvard faculty was mixed. Johnson's special privileges, his propensity to speak as an equal authority during juries, and his general air of hauteur did not sit well with various members of the professoriat. Moreover, the very presence of the Ash Street house seemed an act of lèse-majesté, particularly as several members of the faculty, but especially Gropius and Breuer, had recently built houses of their own — in the less expensive suburbs, far from campus — to which students were regularly invited.

Johnson wrote effusively about these houses in a year-in-architecture essay for a 1941 annual almanac. For reasons unclear the piece went unpublished, but it showed Johnson at his most self-serving, praising a series of his friends and in particular the school in which he was enrolled along with its influential faculty members. "In the East, the influence of the Harvard Architectural School has continued to grow," he wrote. "The best houses in this strongly European tradition are the ones by Gropius and Breuer." Beyond that bias, the essay demonstrated Johnson's broad vision of his field, with attention paid to a rising school of California modernism and to the formidable infrastructural works of Robert Moses, the Tennessee Valley Authority, and the WPA. Especially perceptive was his realization that, in the rapid preparation for war, the entire architectural profession would be forced to reinvent itself lest its imperatives be absorbed by civil and military engineers capable of orchestrating immense building projects in short order.

Johnson's professed admiration of the Breuer house, a composition of boxy volumes and local stone, was real. Breuer was among the few faculty members for whom Johnson had genuine respect, and he eagerly sought his approval throughout his time in school. But he didn't much care for Gropius's house, which he considered an awkward work of ungracious functionalism, too close to workers' housing for comfort. (To get from the front door to the living room, you had to walk through Gropius's office.) Gropius, he would quip savagely, was "the Warren G. Harding of architecture."

The courtly Gropius, for his part, was privately dismissive of Johnson. It is unclear to what extent Johnson's fascist history contributed to Gropius's feelings, though it seems to have only confirmed his evaluation of Johnson as a decadent and misguided reactionary. Johnson's unapologetic allegiance to Mies was an indication of his failure to appreciate the direction in which Gropius was moving the profession: toward a team-based, rationalist design that could respond to societal demands. Mies, by contrast, seemed rooted in a classical pursuit of artistic purity. It nevertheless seemed beneath Gropius's dignity, not to mention impolitic, to take any aggressive action against Johnson, a favorite of the administration and still a close friend to Alfred Barr and the Museum of Modern Art. In March of 1943 the faculty fully approved the Ash Street house as Johnson's thesis project, and after he finally passed his mechanical systems exam he was granted his architectural degree. He was, in addition, awarded the American Institute of Architecture's medal of excellence, given annually to the student whose scholarly work and character were deemed most exceptional.

The essential ideological differences between Johnson and Gropius would remain, but the two men did have a rapprochement in the coming years, initiated by Johnson. Three years after his graduation, Johnson wrote Gropius a letter of unusual grace and admiration, an apology for his behavior during his school years. "I find myself reviewing the recent history of our time and realizing more and more what an important role you played at the critical moments," he wrote. "I write these lines because my conscience bothers me at times for my 'revolutionary' attitude toward your teachings when I was at Harvard. I sometimes think that a student never appreciates a school he has attended until he is some years out. Let me repeat in what high esteem I hold you and your work."

In the spring of 1943 Johnson's living arrangements changed once more, this time in an altogether more dramatic and less lavish direction. His desire to join the war effort, frustrated so far by his unsavory history, was now answered by the broadening sweep of the draft. On March 12 he was inducted into the United States Army, a lowly private sent off to basic training at Fort Devers in Massachusetts, then on to join Company B, 3rd Battalion at Fort Belvoir in Virginia for a twelve-week training course. Nearly thirty-seven years old, he found himself one of five Johnsons in a platoon of trainee military engineers.

He was a dreadful cadet. "My age makes it hard. My lack of manual skill is still worse. My lack of previous military training makes it next to impossible," he wrote to his family. He was older than his peers but seemed less mature, more like a homesick child at sleepaway camp than a soldier facing the prospect of war. His letters home were peppered with tales of minor ailments and requests for small personal luxuries, above all "candy, Candy, CANDY!" His anxious sisters, mother, and father extended themselves for him, standing in wartime ration lines to pick up every last article he requested: fruit-flavored Lifesavers, chocolate bars, toffee, figs, apples, oranges, mineral oil (a cure for his constipation), razor blades, slippers, water-purification tablets, cash. He easily received more packages than any other draftee.

The officers were nice to him, and his fellow soldiers treated "Pops" kindly, though he had trouble finding the kind of educated company he was used to. Instead he consorted with a group he had recently disdained. "The Jews have a really wonderful philosophy worked out to take situations like this in their stride," he wrote to Alfred Barr. He had in particular taken a special attachment to one Herman Kaplan of the Bronx, "a constant example to me of how to take things."

But it was another Jewish friend who offered possible salvation. Lincoln Kirstein was a few weeks ahead of Johnson in his training but similarly a fish out of water. Upon meeting, the two reconciled, with a generous Kirstein—always a tough judge of character—now convinced of Johnson's change of heart and willing to forgive his past sins. For a while Johnson seemed to be doing better than Kirstein. By midsummer, the hard training had begun to affect Johnson positively. "I can *lift* things!" he reported proudly. "I can be *regular*." He had kicked his constipation and no longer had persistent feelings of depression or anxiety. "My interpretation is that up till now I have never had enough to do in proportion to my energy," he wrote—a curious analysis, given how often his nervous exhaustion had been triggered by the stresses of work. He spent his spare time reading: Balzac, Melville, Stendhal.

"Pops" in his tailored Army uniform in 1942.

What he would do after the training course, however, was cause for anxiety; he was useless as a combat soldier: too old, and incompetent with a rifle. But toward the end of June he saw reason for optimism; he was in line for two assignments, both of which seemed appealing. The fallback was the Army Specialized Training Program (ASTP), in which he would be trained in the interrogation of German prisoners, his language skill making him a useful candidate. The second, more appealing option was to follow Kirstein into the intelligence unit charged with safeguarding European cultural patrimony as the Allies advanced across the continent—the unit that would be celebrated as the "Monuments Men." That commission, however, would require Johnson to pass a detailed security check.

The ASTP did not look too carefully into his past, at least not at first, and so he was transferred to Camp Ritchie, sequestered on a picturesque lake in the Blue Ridge Mountains of Maryland. "The most beautiful site in America for a camp," he wrote. "Of course the army has worked hard to destroy the place." But before his training could begin, he was subjected to yet another security clearance, and his future as an intelligence officer was over before it began. It was "peculiar" that someone with "fascist tendencies" would even be considered for such work, a Department of Justice memo noted. "Naturally, the disappointment is keen," Johnson informed his mother. But that disappointment was overshadowed by a new and far more serious fear: that he would be prosecuted as an enemy of the state.

It was clear, by this time, that Lawrence Dennis was a prime target of the FBI and would be indicted for the crime of sedition. Johnson believed he might be as well.

Johnson was living with that existential crisis when he was made a barracks orderly, his duties including scrubbing floors, washing latrines, peeling potatoes, and various other KP tasks. That was unpleasant, but even worse was that he was used as a lowly assistant in the training sessions conducted for those who had been accepted into the military intelligence Battle School program. Ulrich Franzen, one of Johnson's friends from architecture school and a frequent guest at the Ash Street house, was assigned to that program. He recalled Johnson performing before a stadium of trainees, running about placing live explosives beneath demonstration bridges to be demolished. The experience, degrading and dangerous, was a humiliation. "The situation there with my old friends looking on me with suspicion was the hardest thing I have gone through in years," he wrote his mother.

A fortuitous meeting helped him keep his sanity. One afternoon after completing his duties a bedraggled Johnson, clad in fatigues, visited the camp PX for a soda, and was spotted there by a composed first lieutenant in the dress uniform of the First Cavalry Division. It was Landis Gores, his dear friend and "protégé" from Harvard, back in the United States after a year and a half overseas. Following his own training at Ritchie, Gores had been dispatched on loan to British intelligence and sent to Bletchley Park to work on the top-secret Ultra program, which cracked the ciphers of the German high command.*

As they would again after the war, Johnson and Gores found they made a useful partnership. An officer, Gores could spring Johnson from base in the evenings. Johnson, for his part, could drive Gores and his wife, Pamela, to a local restaurant (the Fox Hole being their usual haunt; he bought the steak dinners) or even to Washington for a weekend getaway, if they had leave. It was not Johnson's handsome car, a two-toned Lincoln-Zephyr, that made this offer appealing. It was the fact that Johnson had the gas to drive it: farmers were granted extra rations for running their tractors, and because the Johnsons owned a farm he never ran out.

Johnson was returned to Fort Belvoir in October of 1943, and it would remain his base until his discharge from service in December of 1944. "I seem to be back to the beginning of my army career," he noted. In fact, his past had now completely caught up with him, and he was something closer to a glorified prisoner with privileges than a genuine soldier. Many of his old fascist cronies, by this time, had been swept up by the FBI. Viola Bodenschatz and Sylvester Viereck were both convicted as enemy

---

* After the war, Gores received the Order of the British Empire for his service.

agents in 1942, and sat in American prisons. Fritz Auhagen had just managed to escape the country before he too was arrested. Finally there was Lawrence Dennis, charged with sedition and set to be the lead defendant in a group trial that would begin in April of 1944. By the narrowest margin, Johnson managed to avoid being put in the defendants' box alongside him.

The prospect that he might be, however, weighed ever more brutally on him in his months back at Fort Belvoir. Deposed for the grand jury by prosecutor O. John Rogge, he denied that he had given Dennis cash for anything but the publication of *The Coming American Fascism* and insisted that he had never taken payment from the Nazis or any of their proxies for his propagandistic efforts. (Accepting that money, or paying Dennis, would have opened him to the charge of acting as the agent of a foreign power—sedition.) "My testimony is crisp and so obviously truthful, that all are for me," he reported. Whether or not that was accurate, he had powerful friends interceding on his behalf. His father still had contacts in high places, as did Johnson himself. John Wiley, a society friend who was the American ambassador to Colombia, had already begun talk about a house, and also the possibility of an embassy building in Bogotá. His old mentor, George Howe, now the supervising architect of the Public Buildings Administration, wrote a glowing recommendation for Johnson—"His character and reputation in the community are excellent"—and arranged for a private meeting to review his case at the Washington home of Attorney General Francis Biddle, an event attended also by James Forrestal, Secretary of the Navy.

The combination of heavy-hitting support and a difficult-to-prosecute case kept Johnson out of the dock. Dennis himself would eventually walk free; after the death of the presiding judge, the case was declared a mistrial in December of 1944. That resolution came as an enormous relief for Johnson. The remainder of his service time would now be spent at Belvoir, doing mostly menial tasks (but nothing that would mean further humiliation, and with no danger of finding himself in actual combat). His only real brush with danger came from a case of appendicitis misdiagnosed by an Army doctor as the stomach flu. After surgery in a private Washington hospital and a few days of rest he was back in good health, and for the first time he began to realize just how fortunate he was to be stashed safely away in suburban Virginia, not in the line of fire or marooned at some military installation far from his idea of civilization. "On the whole I am pretty lucky," he wrote. "I might be in Europe, a prisoner, or in a fox hole; I might be stuck away in Oklahoma or Arkansas."

He spent the balance of the war shuttling between Belvoir and furloughs to Washington, resuming the playboy bachelor's life he had lived in New York years earlier, with not a little of the same debauchery. George Howe lent him the use of his apartment, as he generally returned to his own home on the weekends. Johnson had other friends in town to keep him company; the architect Eero Saarinen, working at the OSS, was someone with whom he could engage in serious discussions about his field. John Wiley held regular soirées; at one he met Vladimir Nabokov and Isaiah Berlin, the latter becoming a lifelong friend. There was also Joe Alsop, the journalist who had broken the news of his departure from the Museum of Modern Art so many years ago, now a Washington insider. With these names in his address book, Johnson made the Georgetown rounds, finding it a place so comfortable in its affluent and influential rhythms that he considered establishing himself there after the war.

Johnson thought better of it, though, because he knew, or at least believed, that if he was to launch his architectural career with the kind of prominence he desired, he would have to do it in New York. His limited duties in uniform, however unpleasant, had left him with free time to take on a series of architectural commissions. By September of 1944 he had a design for the Wiley House, and if it was a bit more conservative than he had imagined—a composition of pitched-roof pavilions—at least the client was happy. George Howe, too, expressed his approval. "It is not at all what I would do for myself, but people seem to like it," Johnson wrote. "It may even get built!" (It did not.)

Even less to Johnson's taste was the house designed for his friends Julius and Cleomie Wadsworth, whom he knew from Cambridge. Julius was a Harvard-educated foreign service officer; Cleomie, a Wellesley graduate, had met him at one of his Ash Street events. Their architectural taste, however, was traditional, if not confused. They wanted what Johnson described as a "Romanesquoid" facade, a gable roof, and a French Renaissance floor plan. "I am afraid I shall be excommunicated from the Modern brotherhood," he noted. But a job was a job—or, more accurately, something to pass the time during his waning days in fatigues. Like the Wiley House, the clients put off their plans and it went unrealized.

Johnson preferred it when he (or his father) could be his own client. It was during his days at Belvoir that he made his first stabs at a new house for himself, a two-bedroom home that several years and many iterations later would evolve into his Glass House. He didn't get very far with it, putting it aside to work instead on two projects that seemed more likely to be realized, the first a New London hospital building funded by Homer Johnson and the second a barn at Townsend Farms. The former would have been Johnson's first institutional commission. He spent considerable time formulating it, eventually arriving at a simple two-story block with rooms set off a double-loaded central corridor. It was never built, but the barn was: a small jewel of a building, a wood-framed gray rectangle with a pair of garage doors centered on the long side, and a white decorative balustrade along the roofline. If Mies had redesigned the Petit Trianon to store farm equipment, this would have been the result.

Johnson had sent plans up to New London to get the building started, and in September of 1944 he managed a furlough so he could watch as it was finished. Seeing his own work realized gave him the sense of power that had been absent in the rest of his life. "The feeling of being almost a god, for a while, a creator out of the mind is more intoxicating than wine," he wrote. "There is no feeling to equal it for an architect."

And he wanted to feel it again.

The 1949 Glass House, Johnson's New Canaan idyll. (Author's photograph)

CHAPTER 9

A New New Beginning

It is bad to insist that people be original when they can't be. Let
them copy others but refine the work and make it better.

—*Philip Johnson*

How many chances does one receive in a life, how many opportunities for self-reinvention? F. Scott Fitzgerald wrote that in America there was no room even for second acts, but by the time World War II came to a close, Philip Johnson was looking to begin his third, and that is scoring conservatively. He had been a (successful) curator and a (failed) politician, not to mention a playboy, an interior designer, a journalist, a propagandist, and a soldier. Now he would become an architect.

Lucky so often in the past, Johnson was once again fortunate in his timing. Those first postwar years were ideally suited to anyone, and an architect in particular, aiming at reinvention. The G.I.s flooding back from the fields of battle overseas were looking to the future, not a recent past that everyone was happy to escape. The same generation that Johnson had so recently condemned for its dissolute failure to live up to the needs of the nation had saved the Western world for democracy, and it would now deliver a lasting period of prosperity and optimism. A flowering American economy meant new places to live, work, and play. You could not have scripted a more propitious moment to hang out your shingle.

The question was where exactly to hang it. Johnson had enjoyed the social life of Georgetown, his prominent father looked like he might be the conduit to a steady stream of work in Ohio, and he still had the Ash Street house in Cambridge. Johnson chose none of these options. Instead it was back to New York City, to old friends who had already forgiven his sins, and to the cosmopolitan life of which he had been so deprived as a lowly private cleaning latrines and peeling potatoes in the Army.

He had his old living quarters there as well; he could move right back into Hidden House with his erstwhile roommate and sister, Theo. Her wartime marriage to Paul Blanpain, who ran a small resort hotel on the Belgian coast, had been brief, and she was now in New York, looking to revive her musical career. Soon they would be joined by another house-mate: Jon Stroup, a slim and baby-faced arts writer and editor for *Town & Country*. He was younger by a decade, pretty, and pliant; Philip had met him at a gallery opening, and in short order Stroup became his first live-in lover.

Johnson established his place of business on the nineteenth floor of an office tower on East Forty-second Street, in the shadow of the Chrysler Building. It was but a single-room sublet from the larger office of architect S. Clements Horsley, who had assisted him on the Ash Street drawings. It had a narrow terrace and enough space for a couple of desks, which was good enough for a start. Discharged from military service in December of 1944, he was up and running before the war was even over.

The source of Johnson's first commission was comforting in its familiarity: the architecture department that he had founded at the Museum of Modern Art. His relationship with the museum, and the department, had never been fully sundered, buoyed always by his friendship with Barr and his strategic generosity. In January of 1943, just months before his induction into the Army, he fulfilled his nearly decade-old promise to donate Oskar Schlemmer's *Bauhaus Stairway* to the museum. An immensely pleased Barr gave the painting, "bought from under the noses of the Nazis," pride of place in the museum's lobby. Johnson's gift also came with a Le Corbusier chair. Just a few months later, Johnson, toiling as a private at Camp Belvoir, sent five more paintings to the museum for safekeeping during the war, a trove that included his two prized Klees. All would be donated to the museum.

His rival John McAndrew was no longer there, the victim of a museum palace intrigue in which Johnson played no part. In the wake of his departure the department was being run by Elizabeth Mock, who had joined it in 1937 and was responsible for a series of popular shows on contemporary American design. (Her older sister was the affordable housing advocate Catherine Bauer, paramour of Lewis Mumford.) Johnson had been a sounding board for Mock, and his DNA was all over *Tomorrow's Small House,* an exhibition of models and plans that would answer, according to a museum press release, "the nation's need for a million-and-a-quarter new dwellings annually after the war—a challenge without precedent in American building history." Johnson himself was among the architects commissioned to contribute—a rather brazen conflict of interest that put him in the company of Hugh Stubbins (one of his Harvard classmates), Fred Keck (the Chicago architect he had finagled to design his stage for Father Coughlin), and Frank Lloyd Wright. The exhibition itself was mounted with a bit of the flair that characterized the department under Johnson, with the models mounted at eye level. "Instead of being regarded as toys, the models can be judged as actual, habitable houses," the museum touted.

The show was produced in collaboration with the *Ladies' Home Journal,* which published the entries in its July 1945 issue, the imaginary projects pitched at young suburban homemakers looking to make a new start with their husbands freshly returned from the war. Johnson's offering was an elaboration of the Ash Street House he had built for himself in Cambridge, a single-story structure with three bedrooms that looked out onto a lawn through a wall of glass. "A new high for livability through simplicity," proclaimed the *Journal's* editors. Better still, it would fulfill the modernist's dream of prefabrication, such that it could be "assembled in a single day."

The feature proved successful enough that, less than a year later, the magazine came to Johnson with a project more attuned to his interests and lifestyle: "A House for a Millionaire with No Servants." Johnson answered with a design featuring a series of rectangular pavilions (one each for sleeping, dining, living, and a garage) set asymmetrically in a U-shaped plan and linked by enclosed passages, an arrangement that formed a series of courtyards and terraces. The pavilions themselves were constructed of brick with a steel band at the roofline and floor-to-ceiling windows. The magazine rightly praised its "high degree of taste, style, and elegant simplicity," and included it in a booklet of other modern homes, including an "equal rights house"—equal, that is, between children and parents.

Johnson did not work alone on those projects. Still insecure and inexperienced, and never particularly facile as a model maker, he had hired a draftsman, Fred Bohlmeer, to help. When the magazine projects were done, so was Bohlmeer. But Johnson was immediately joined by a new figure, a junior partner who was in many ways more than his equal, his old Harvard "protégé" and occasional wartime dining mate Landis Gores. After Johnson's discharge from the military, he had contacted Gores's wife, Pamela, suggesting that upon Landis's release from the service he join Johnson's practice. Though Gores might have preferred to start his own firm, he had neither the money nor the clients. Johnson had both. And on November 21, the day before Thanksgiving, he had Gores, too.

The two spent the holiday driving through the country together with Johnson's sister Theo and Gores's wife. Their first stop was in suburban Bedford Hills, New York, to look at a site on which Johnson had been commissioned to design a weekend house on a slim budget for a young advertising executive, Richard Booth, and his wife, Olga. Completed in 1946, the single-story house was another Miesian rectangle, but with a hint of Le Corbusier. Here, walls were made of cinder block, an inexpensive alternative to the stone that Le Corbusier had used on his de Mandrot House in the south of France, which Johnson claimed as a model. The low budget forced Johnson to dispense with an office wing that would have given the house an L-shaped plan. It was, in any case, the first freestanding residential work Johnson built for someone not named Johnson, and it would be followed in the coming years by a series of progressively more sophisticated homes in a similar architectural language that rank among his greatest accomplishments.

The Booth site was only the first stop on Johnson and Gores's Thanksgiving Day excursion. They had their turkey at lunch at a diner in Mount Kisco and crossed the border into Connecticut, driving southeast to an unlikely stopping point along a broken stone wall in New Canaan. They climbed through it, then wandered down a long grassy slope to a flat meadow with large boulders fronting a precipitous drop. The view to the west stretched out over the woods. The sale of this not particularly auspicious five-acre site was already in the works. The buyer was Philip Johnson.

After months of searching the bucolic lanes of southern Connecticut for a place where he might build his own weekend retreat, Johnson had been led by a real estate agent to this woodsy site on Ponus Ridge Road. Johnson knew immediately that it was right—that once the rocks were cleared, the ground leveled, and a few trees (or more than a few trees) removed, it would suit his vision. He bought it, all five acres, without visiting another site. In the coming years he would expand it again and again, such that by 1960 its area had grown by nearly five times.

He credited the inspiration for the placement of his house on a bluff to both Mies and Frank Lloyd Wright, but he was also mining his own history, looking back to "The Queen," the whitewashed country manor his great-grandfather had built in New London, overlooking the rolling meadows of what would become Townsend Farm. It had always been his sanctuary, the place where he had found greatest peace and happiness in a life that, however luxurious and successful, had not always been peaceful and happy—even if many of the injuries were self-inflicted.

The design of the house, or houses, that would occupy that site would be years in the making, a long evolution with almost daily recalibrations. Johnson would often arrive at the office in the morning with new ideas sketched out in his head or roughly on paper, and if there was no other work, he and Gores would elaborate on them until the noon hour, when Johnson departed for a social lunch or client meeting or, most often, the Museum of Modern Art.

Though his affiliation would not become official until 1947, the prodigal son had returned to the museum in 1945, effectively resuming the position he had so cavalierly abandoned in 1934. That two-year delay was the result of his own behavior: certain members of the board were not ready to sweep his fascist activities under the museum's modern carpets. From Johnson's perspective, with his practice still in its infancy and a capable junior partner willing to carry the rather minimal load, there was little impediment to his return.

The invitation came from Barr, whose own relationship with the museum was something less than standard. Never a particularly diligent administrator, and often absent because of various health issues, Barr had run afoul of the museum's trustees, in particular Nelson Rockefeller. In 1943 he was dismissed, but Barr simply refused to leave the museum that he had essentially created, continuing to operate from a desk in the library as its de facto chief curator. He may have been a poor bureaucrat, but he was still the brains of the place—and beloved by a devoted staff. His limbo status was resolved only after the museum installed René d'Harnoncourt as its new director, in 1949. A gentle giant at six feet seven with an easy European manner (he was born an Austrian count, though he had given up the title), he understood Barr's value and allowed that he should be cosseted, not closeted.

Johnson's return to glory was celebrated the day after his Thanksgiving trip to the country at a luncheon in his honor at the Manhattan Club. Among those in attendance were George Howe, Wallace Harrison, and Edward Durell Stone, all architects with some connection to the museum. Joining them was another who had had his ups and downs with that institution, and with Johnson: Frank Lloyd Wright, all smiles in a three-piece gray suit, holding court as the others sat in rapt attention. Wright dominated the affair, but Johnson was clearly back in the mix.

Johnson had little problem steamrolling Betty Mock out of departmental control. "She was more interested—as her sister [Catherine Bauer] was—in housing and in doing good, which interested me not at all," he recalled. "She wasn't the one who would throw me out." What could she do, anyway? He had the ties to Barr and Rockefeller, and he had the money to bankroll his own position.

He had to be a bit more careful with Eliot Noyes, another Harvard-trained architect, who had come to the museum in 1940, having worked in the studio of Walter Gropius—a black mark, in Johnson's imagination. Noyes had launched the competition *Organic Design in Home Furnishings,* mounted as an exhibition in 1941, which introduced the world to the molded furniture of Charles Eames and Eero Saarinen. A designer of no small genius in his own right, Noyes had little patience for Johnson's political games and left the museum for greener pastures as the design guru of IBM. His many iconic products for that company would include the Selectric typewriter.

Johnson did inherit one territory-threatening rival. During his absent years the architecture and design department had been split in two, with command of the independent industrial-design department turned over to Edgar Kaufmann Jr. That the two had similar trajectories did nothing to endear them to each other. Like Johnson, Kaufmann was largely self-taught in the field of design; he was not even a college graduate. He also came from a family of considerable wealth: his father, a Pittsburgh department store magnate, was the client for what many considered (and still consider) the greatest of all modern houses, Frank Lloyd Wright's Fallingwater. Like Johnson, Kaufmann was gay and could be charming, though he was more often inclined to be prickly. Philosophically, their views of architecture were as opposed as their respective allegiances to Mies and to Wright, with Johnson prizing aesthetics and Kaufmann broader social concerns. Kaufmann, also, was Jewish, and unlike Johnson's other friends at the museum — Barr, Rockefeller, even Kirstein — he did not forget or forgive Johnson's decade of transgression.

His empire somewhat reduced, Johnson was nonetheless happy to be back at the museum, even with the diminished title of Consultant to the Department of Architecture. He could live with that because it did not reflect his true status as the department's effective leader. His first proposal in that capacity was timely, coming just months after the armistice in 1945: an exhibition of speculative war-memorial designs by the likes of Alexander Calder, Le Corbusier, Mies, Henry Moore, Oud, Picasso, and Wright. The idea was propagandistic, intended, he wrote Mies, to influence "the people who commission monuments toward newer ideas." The problem was a product of a Calvinist, utilitarian tradition that rejected monumental building as wasteful and purposeless. "Man needs concrete symbols of a power outside his own lonely consciousness," he wrote in an article for *ArtNews,* "What Aesthetic Price Glory?"

That was as far as the show would get. There was little institutional support from the museum, and not even Mies returned Johnson's letter on the matter. Johnson dropped the idea, and on Barr's recommendation chose a subject closer to Johnson's heart, one that would please the architect he placed above all others: a grand retrospective exhibition of Mies's own work. "We wish to make this the most important exhibition that the Department has ever held," Johnson wrote Mies in December of 1946.

That show, and the book that would accompany it, occupied much of Johnson's time over the next year, with Johnson repeatedly flying out to Chicago for consultations with the master. There were small exhibitions in the interim, including one on Frank Lloyd Wright's unbuilt house for Wall Street financier Gerald Loeb. The show featured a 12-foot-long model of the house, produced under Wright's supervision at his Taliesin West compound in Arizona, and Johnson cleverly supplemented it with a series of stereopticon viewers. A composition of interlocking spaces, with pools and terraces set on a Connecticut bluff, it shaped Johnson's thinking about his own compound barely 20 miles away. In fact Johnson almost ended up with the Loeb commission: once the financier figured out how much Wright's house would cost, he shelved it permanently and began talking to Johnson about the less expensive renovation of buildings already on the property. That job, however, never went anywhere.*

The Mies show was another matter, a monographic architectural exhibition still unsurpassed in its influence. Johnson's aspirations were grand from the start: a press release announcing its opening, almost certainly overseen by Johnson, declared, "This country may now be assisting at the birth of an architecture as expressive of the industrial age as Gothic was of its age of ecclesiasticism." Making a star of Mies, however, was no easy task. Although he remains famous for his maxims—"Less is more," "God is in the details"—he was curt with journalists. A planned *New Yorker* profile died on the vine. Mies cared principally about his work, and when it came to its presentation he was intent on taking full responsibility.

---

* Loeb ultimately hired the California architect Harwell Hamilton Harris.

Johnson with Mies at the landmark exhibition of his work in 1947. (© The Museum of Modern Art / Licensed by SCALA / Art Resource, NY)

Visitors expecting to see a standard show of small models and modestly scaled drawings and photographs were met with something that shocked: wall-size photographic blowups of Mies's projects, images so large it looked like you could walk right into them. Mies had designed it himself, the idea from the outset being that the show would be a "work of art" in its own right. The *New York Times,* in its review, called the effect "breathtaking." When original photographs were unavailable (many archives were lost during the war), the museum enlarged pictures cut from magazines—their Benday dots clearly visible, as in the paintings Johnson would later collect by Roy Lichtenstein. Such images, some as wide as 20 feet, were entirely unprecedented. "His theory was that what you don't want in a museum is a wall," said Johnson. Instead, the large pictures floated in open space, framing views around a gallery that had been taken down to its bones, with Mies's own furniture placed strategically. Mies even wanted the gallery's columns tailored to his strict vision; when Johnson promised him that once plaster was stripped away he would find them perfectly straight, only to learn that they were in fact chamfered, Mies was livid.

There was also the matter of the Barcelona chair, which the Knoll Company had agreed to manufacture in tandem with the exhibition. Johnson had original chairs from his Ash Street house pulled out of storage and sent to the company for use as models. Only Knoll had trouble producing exact replicas: the steel was thinner, and they left the buttons off the cushions. Johnson thought this was "satisfactory" but Mies assuredly did not. There would be buttons on the Barcelona chair, period.

When it finally opened, the Mies show encompassed the entire third floor of the museum, with projects ranging from his early houses right through to the new campus for the Illinois Institute of Technology, formerly the Armour Institute, where Mies had been director since 1938. Johnson's accompanying monograph existed somewhere between architectural history and hagiography, portentously tracing Mies from his birth in Aachen to his education as a stonemason at the side of his father, his apprenticeship with architect Peter Behrens, his early speculative glass towers, and his ascendance to the pinnacle of the profession. The 1929 Barcelona Pavilion, Johnson wrote, was "truly one of the few manifestations of the contemporary spirit that justifies comparison with the great architecture of the past."

Opening night came as a relief after two weeks of frantic work preparing the installation. Johnson even arranged for company for Mies: Mary Callery, a sculptor who would commence a long affair with the architect while remaining a Johnson intimate. There was another notable guest, one who refused to cede the spotlight even when he was not the subject. At the end of the evening Frank Lloyd Wright swooped in, draped in his usual cape and trailing an entourage. Mies kept to himself in a back room. If the two titans met, what they said went unrecorded.

Reviews of the show were strong. "Everything [Mies] does is soundly reasoned," wrote *Times* critic Edward Alden Jewell, who was also complimentary of Johnson's book on the architect. But the show's extraordinary impact would become apparent only over time. Not only did it reshape the way architectural exhibitions might be mounted (an example that still remains prevalent), but it firmly established Mies's presence in the United States as a builder and not just an avant-garde theoretician. His architectural language—clear, regimented, and expansive—was both suited to the corporate American moment and easily knocked off, or at least it appeared that way. Soon enough American cities would be studded with Miesian buildings, only a fraction of them actually by Mies or approaching his mastery.

Chief among those architects taking inspiration from Mies was Johnson himself—as he had been for years. Being absorbed in the architect's works during the year and a half it took to put the show and catalog together made him only more attentive to the possibilities of the Miesian idiom. It was during this period that he undertook his second residential project after the war, a weekend house on Long Island's east end for a couple referred to him by a friend of Theo's. Mr. and Mrs. Eugene Farney simply wanted a weekend house; aside from that they were hands-off clients, which allowed Johnson to proceed as he saw fit. What he gave them was drawn from Mies's unbuilt project for Stanley Resor, a vacation retreat in Jackson Hole, Wyoming defined by a broad glass window facing the Teton Range. Johnson transposed that idea to the sandy dunes of Sagaponack, with the view pointing out not on a mountain landscape but on a cedar deck overlooking the ocean. Unlike the mansions that define the region today, it was modest in scale, a small house propped up over the dunes on steel posts, or pilotis, in the style of Le Corbusier.

Above all, Johnson looked to Mies for the site he had purchased for himself in New Canaan. "The idea of a glass house comes from Mies van der Rohe," Johnson wrote in 1950. "Mies had mentioned to me as early as 1945 how easy it would be to build a house entirely of large sheets of glass." For that matter, Mies had built a version of such a house at the Berlin Building Exhibition in 1931, and that had been an inspiration for Johnson's 1943 Ash Street home. By the time Johnson began planning the exhibition of his work, Mies had a house on the boards—a weekend home for Dr. Edith Farnsworth on a wooded site overlooking the Fox River in the Chicago suburb of Plano, Illinois—that even more fully explored the potential of glass. Mies imagined a crisp, rectilinear box outlined in white-painted steel elevated just slightly above the ground. "My debt is therefore clear, in spite of obvious differences in composition and relation to the ground," wrote Johnson of his own Glass House.

The brick Guest House, the Glass House's mute twin. (Michael Moran)

In fact, Johnson spent years experimenting with different schemes for the house. Gores, who by this time had also purchased a lot for himself in New Canaan, recalled drafting some seventy-nine different versions before Johnson settled on the one he would finally build. For a time it looked like the whole exercise might remain academic. When Johnson's friend Lincoln Kirstein pushed him about the lollygagging, he replied, "Build it? I'm not that rich." Kirstein's answer: "What do you mean?"

Records suggest the number of schemes Johnson and Gores actually developed was something closer to thirty, in a process of reductive evolution. What began as a series of linked pavilions akin to his *Ladies' Home Journal* "House for a Millionaire" gradually resolved into two separate structures, one of glass, the other brick, set in contrapuntal asymmetry. Never one to privilege function over form, Johnson dispensed with the connecting pergolas between the buildings. "Anyone moving from one to another could very well go out in the rain," he told Gores. The Glass House itself took on the contours that are now familiar: a clear box with doors on center set on a shallow brick plinth, as if it were some kind of temple. What began as two brick drums, one a fireplace and the other a bathroom, he combined into a single unit. A matching brick floor was laid in a herringbone pattern, hiding a slab base installed with radiant heating. As Johnson noted, the house was firmly rooted in the ground, unlike Mies's floating design for the Farnsworth House, emphasizing both its classicism and its connection to its verdant surroundings.

The first stake was driven on the site on March 18, 1948, a Wednesday afternoon. Johnson and Gores drove out for the occasion. Though it today seems simple, or at least "simple," construction took a year. Johnson kept the interior furnishings modest, to maintain the aquariumlike openness of the space: a low wooden bar for a kitchen (he couldn't cook anything more complex than a cucumber sandwich), a shoulder-height cabinet to wall off his bed, and his Mies-designed living space. The house's jewel-like nature was accentuated by lighting designer Richard Kelly, who seductively lit the house within but also splashed light on the trees beyond, which had the dramatic effect of dissolving the walls and extending the view out into the landscape.

Kelly was brought in only after Johnson's first night at the house, on a weekend evening in November of 1948. Without the exterior lights, Johnson had found himself alone in a dark room surrounded only by his own eerie reflections in the glass walls. Frightened, he picked up the phone and dialed Gores, by then living in his own house nearby, to come over to the rescue. He didn't officially christen the place until New Year's Eve, and even then he made sure to have a companion, Mary Callery, to be there with him.

The house was an immediate sensation, one that Johnson completed before Mies could get his Farnsworth House constructed—much to Mies's irritation. On an early visit Mies could not help a snide comment, comparing the place, all lit up by Kelly's fixtures, to a "hot-dog stand." But it was more than that; he was upset by the place, upset that Johnson had appropriated his ideas, that he had either misunderstood or

The Glass House interior; inspired by Mies and furnished with his pieces. He nevertheless considered it an apostasy.

subverted them, and that he had beat him to the punch. As far as Mies was concerned, Johnson's detailing was ham-fisted, especially at the corners where the beams joined, and the idea of putting the building on the ground was antithetical to his thinking with the Farnsworth. "I just think that he felt that my bad copy of his work was extremely unpleasant," Johnson said. Mies had been scheduled to stay the night in the Brick House, but insisted instead on being driven to the Gores'. It was a bitter rebuke. It was also not particularly fair, for even if it was derived from Mies, and even if it lacked his fastidious detailing, it was something special in its own right, a statement of Johnson's own ideas about architecture, modernity, refinement, and publicity.

Johnson, anyway, could be just as cutting as Mies. In those early days a visiting neighbor informed him, "It's all very beautiful, but I couldn't live here." His reply: "I haven't asked you to, madam." Johnson loved the celebrity that came with life in a glass house, even if he was prone to throwing stones. When magazines called, he was happy to open the house up to them. André Kertész shot it for *House & Garden*. Even *Life* did a feature, "*Life* Goes to a Party." Local police had to monitor the traffic on Ponus Ridge Road, so busy did it become with onlookers. "Startled, uninvited visitors tramp about to view the results with mingled expressions of awe, wonder and indignation. They agree that nothing like it was ever seen in these parts," the *New York Times* reported. He had always been a provocateur—as a curator, in his politics, in his personal life, and now as an architect.

That taste for narcissistic controversy was evident in an illustrated essay for the *Architectural Review,* in which Johnson admitted that the design was "derivative" and outlined his various influences. Mies was the primary inspiration, but he also claimed Le Corbusier, Dutch artist Theo van Doesburg, the Athenian Acropolis, German architect Karl Friedrich Schinkel, French neoclassicist Claude-Nicolas Ledoux, and Baroque landscape generally. The placement of a circular volume in a rectangular field he credited to the Russian painter Kazimir Malevich. This came as news to Gores, who claimed responsibility for that detail but had not heard of Malevich until his appearance in the article.

Of the twenty-four inspirations listed, the most curious was the seventeenth, in which Johnson claimed that the vision of the illuminated house at night was drawn "from a burnt wooden village I saw once where nothing was left but foundations and chimneys of brick." Had he intentionally re-created the "stirring spectacle" that was the burning of Jewish shtetls he had witnessed driving through Poland with the Wehrmacht? Was that cylindrical brick chimney a sinister reference to the evils of the Holocaust? Was this a conscious (or unconscious) revelation of the anti-Semitic feelings he had expressed in the 1930s, or was it just Johnson, the insulated boy for whom violence was always a fantastic vision and never an actual threat?

It was not the only veiled reference to his past at the Glass House. Although the living-room composition was initially completed by a Miró on a vertical easel—another Miesian floating plane—it was quickly swapped out for a painting by, or at least attributed to, Nicolas Poussin.

Johnson would claim that Poussin, the most classical of Renaissance painters, was ideally suited to his modern-classic house. But the subject matter of the picture, the burial of Phocion, suggests a more personal and coyly self-aggrandizing reading: Phocion, an Athenian politician known for his righteousness, is banished and unfairly executed for his crimes against the state. For Johnson it must have seemed like a portrait of himself, the failed politician now exiled to the Connecticut hinterland.

Notably absent from Johnson's list of influences were the essential landscapes of his youth, Townsend Farms and the Buttes-Chaumont in Paris, which helped shape his vision for the property. Another snub was a bit more obvious, especially as the snubee was particularly touchy about his place in the architectural pantheon: Frank Lloyd Wright. In a telegram weighted somewhere between tongue-in-cheek chiding and outright condescension, he asked, "Philip: If you think I'm such a great architect, why doesn't your work look more like mine?" In truth Wright's project for Gerald Loeb had been an influence on Johnson, but an unstated one. When Wright finally appeared at the house, in 1956, he made a grand showing of it, arriving in his Cherokee Red Cadillac with an entourage in tow. He proceeded to tour the property, using his cane to point out those things of which he did and did not approve. In the latter category were the two papier-mâché Elie Nadelman statues that accentuated one end of the Glass House living space. These he gave a sharp rap with his cane.

Johnson put up with it, as he always had. He was happy for an intellectual sparring partner, but he also deeply admired Wright's idiosyncratic genius, even if he thought it an obsolete paradigm. In a 1949 essay, "The Frontiersman" (the title being a dig at Wright's status as a historical figure), he celebrated just what it was that made him so attached to their relationship. "Oh, it's easy to make fun of him," he wrote. "You know, he makes fun of me, and he annoys me, he annoys all of us, but he is also one of the few these days still alive that can stand up to a blank piece of paper and, in the imitation of God, can create, almost from his head alone. The rest of us have the luck of this great tradition. But he, by his own will, has none. He has formed as many architectural manners almost as he has buildings, or as the years of his life."

The essay had come following a visit to Wright's compound in the Arizona desert, Taliesin West. It was a come-to-Jesus moment—or, as Wright put it after Johnson had navigated his way through the mazelike terra-cotta complex, through its Alice-in-Wonderland gardens and tented spaces and into the dining area where the old man held court, "The Prince visits the King."

The prince, in fact, had already embarked on a mission to depose the king, or at least plunder his realm. In this instance, as in so many others, Wright had only himself to blame. At the recommendation of Henry-Russell Hitchcock, Wright had been engaged by the art collectors Burton and Emily Hall Tremaine to design a visitors' center to the mile-wide crater where a meteorite had crashed to Earth on their property in the Arizona desert, outside Flagstaff. Wright, with his winter base in Arizona, seemed a natural fit for the Tremaines, whose experimental tastes also led them to commission works from the likes of Oscar Niemeyer and Bucky Fuller. Wright, however, proposed something much grander for the site than they had in mind, which sent them to Johnson, who had also been referred to them by Hitchcock as an adviser. When Burton wrote Wright a note warning that his design was more expensive than their budget allowed, given the cost of construction, Wright replied dismissively, "your estimate of $10.00 per foot sounds like Phil Johnson who knows about as much about this kind of construction as you do." Which was to say, not a lot.

That would change. The Tremaines were not prepared to be insulted by their architect. Soon enough Johnson joined them on the Santa Fe line's *Super Chief,* riding south in style from Chicago to their Arizona ranch. From his youth he had been inspired by the grand vistas of the Western landscape, and what he found at Meteor Crater was no different. His idea, he told the Tremaines, was to amplify the inherent drama of the site: "Visitors shouldn't see the crater until they come right up to the rim," he told them. He followed that prescription and gave them something as close to Wright as he could muster within the confines of his Miesian vocabulary, using an aggregate of the desert rock preferred by Wright, with a projecting flat canopy to provide shade—another device favored by Wright and typically abjured by Johnson. Otherwise, it was Miesian: a box with large glass walls to frame the stupendous view.

That commission begat others. Burton Tremaine ran a metal and lighting firm, the Miller Company, and he commissioned Johnson to both renovate its executive offices in Meriden, Connecticut and design a line of custom fixtures. In a clever bit of self-dealing for everyone involved, Tremaine donated a set of the designs to the Museum of Modern Art. The more important commission from the Tremaines, however, was the renovation of their eighteenth-century farmhouse and barn near Long Island Sound. Here, Johnson found himself working not so much under the amiable Burton as his wife, Emily, a somewhat more forbidding character but the force behind their aesthetic ambitions. Like Johnson she had been born into middle-American wealth, and like Johnson she was known to tweak the mores of the establishment. That included the development of one of the more significant modern art collections in America. The problem was hanging it. Their old farmhouse, with its warren of small spaces, was not particularly conducive to the art of the day, in particular the abstract expressionists, whose grand ambitions were reflected in the scale of their works. Johnson's solution was to transform their barn, opening it up by installing a 35-foot, two-story glass wall on one side and plastering over the masonry walls so they might better display the collection. He also offered his design guidance on the renovation of their Park Avenue apartment, his instruction there being to remove all architectural detail and strip the place to its bones.

That commission pointed toward Johnson's new identity as a leading domestic architect for the well-heeled and forward-thinking, an arbiter of style who could translate the austerity of modernism into a language of luxury and ease appropriate for the wealthiest families in America. Of those aristocratic dynasties, the first was the Rockefellers, and their patronage—outside the Museum of Modern Art—began with a sculpture pavilion for the family estate in Pocantico Hills, New York. The job came from Blanchette Rockefeller, wife of John D. III and sister-in-law of Nelson, and she harbored a special fondness for Johnson: he was just a few years older and seemed the epitome of cosmopolitan sophistication. Johnson's glass box for sculpture, however, would never make it to Pocantico; it was too modern for her buttoned-up husband, and the family generally preferred Wallace Harrison (and his firm, Harrison & Abramovitz) for its contemporary architectural demands, as he was a member of the extended Rockefeller family by marriage.

Generally, but not always. Blanchette, with her sweet spot for Johnson, went to him for the design of a midtown guesthouse, a project that would stand among his signature works. The idea was for a meeting spot halfway between her home on Beekman Place and the Museum of Modern Art, still practically a family appendage; as the leader of the museum's Junior Council, Blanchette wanted a place beyond the institution's walls where she could host events and show off her own collection.

What Johnson gave her was an urban, and urbane, translation of his New Canaan home, a union of the Glass House and the Brick House;

Johnson's 1950 pied-à-terre for Blanchette Rockefeller, a stacking of the brick and glass houses in midtown Manhattan. (Richard Payne)

seen from the street, it appeared that he had simply stacked the former atop the latter. There was a blank brick wall with a door on center at ground level, and above it a glass pavilion with the Glass House's signature chair-height rail. It also had something in its plan of Hidden House,

Johnson's in-town digs. The project required the demolition of a brick townhouse, with a separate carriage house behind it. Johnson's design retained that arrangement: the living space in the front and the residential area in the back were separated by an open court with a reflecting pool and fountain. To get from one to the other required a trip outdoors across three travertine steps, with no canopy whatsoever. To call it impractical was an understatement—but practicality wasn't the point. "Well, Philip, we built it for art, didn't we?" Blanchette said, perhaps not entirely convinced. For Johnson she was the perfect client, largely willing to let him do as he pleased. "I don't think she knows anything about architecture, ever will, or ever did," Johnson said later.

It was Johnson's own knowledge of architecture, at least technically, that the commission put into question. Then as now, professional licensure in architecture required several years of post-graduate apprenticeship and the successful completion of a series of examinations. In his zeal to establish a practice, along with his general sense of entitlement, Johnson had not bothered with either. Gores, similarly fresh out of school, was also unlicensed. Johnson skirted the rules by having Charles Abbe, an architect who had leased him space, stamp the plans he and Gores produced. That was fine on smaller projects, but the dubious legality became a problem given the complexity of the New York building code and the notoriety of the Rockefellers, whose every move was a matter of public interest. His cover was blown in a gossip column in the *World-Telegram and Sun* revealing that one John J. O'Hare was not in fact the owner of the modern townhouse rising on Fifty-second Street, but merely a minor functionary in the Rockefeller empire, standing in as a front for his secretive employers. That was news. And word of their architect's qualifications, or lack thereof, would soon filter back to the appropriate authorities.

Johnson had by this time also begun design work for the museum itself; for the next forty years he would essentially be the house architect, a job he prized enormously and guarded jealously. His first task in this formal-informal role was the expansion of the museum itself, to the west. This new museum wing, just 25 feet wide, would take the place of a beaux arts townhouse directly abutting the museum. In the coming years, Johnson would lead a sometimes-lonely fight for the preservation of the city's historic patrimony. But now preservation was not a priority, especially with the opportunity for his first museum building in the offing. He had, in fact, agreed to do the work without fee, an act of generosity that was not without self-interest, as it placed him squarely in the good graces of the museum's leadership, in particular the notoriously penny-pinching Rockefellers.

The Grace Rainey Rogers Memorial wing of 1951: a striking Miesian contrast to the Goodwin and Stone building. (© The Museum of Modern Art / Licensed by SCALA / Art Resource, NY)

Because it is now gone, demolished in the museum's relentless westward expansion, the Grace Rainey Rogers Memorial, as the addition was called, has largely been forgotten. But it was the first glass-walled modern building to rise in New York, completed while Skidmore, Owings & Merrill's Lever House on Park Avenue—the green-glass slab considered the city's first modernist skyscraper—was still under construction. It was the Miesian design he and Barr had wanted for the museum from the outset, a seven-story grid of black steel and glass windows facing the street. Its boldness was particularly striking when viewed from Fifty-third Street, where it stood between the museum's white marble pseudo-modern original building—matching its roofline but nothing else—and an enormous French Renaissance mansion that has likewise given way to the wrecking ball in the intervening years.

Within, Johnson had his own office, an open room with cantilevered bookshelves, a sitting space defined by wire-frame lounge chairs, a glass table, and a pair of slab desks made of white plastic laminate. He also redesigned the members' lounge and dining room, in the museum's main Goodwin/Stone building, opening it up into a broad, cafeteria-style room with seating by Charles Eames.

This work coincided with Johnson's consolidation of power within the museum. In August of 1948, still acting in his capacity as a "consultant," he installed Peter Blake, a promising design critic he had met at a Mary Callery cocktail party in the Hamptons, as curator of the architecture department. Since Betty Mock's departure the architectural curator had been Mary Barnes, wife of the architect Edward Larrabee Barnes, and she was departing to build a family. Blake had zero experience as a curator, but neither had Johnson when he had started at the museum. Johnson, anyway, wanted a trustworthy protégé, not a replacement. Blake also proved a useful instrument in Johnson's political machinations within the museum, and specifically against Kaufmann, his nemesis. Johnson was not happy to have the department he had founded divided into separate fiefdoms—one architectural, the other for industrial design—and with his closeness to both Barr and Nelson Rockefeller, he was finally able to have his way. On March 1, 1949, he was formally reinstated at the museum as director of the fused Department of Architecture and Design.

While this was generally met with approval, there remained the public relations problem of Johnson's fascist history. With the Cold War intensifying, the charge of anti-American behavior was grave, and the museum — regardless of its association with the conservative Rockefeller family — was still stigmatized from its association with the Mexican muralist Diego Rivera. During the Mies exhibition, the museum had fielded complaints about the hammer and sickle that appeared on the side of the architect's 1926 memorial to German political martyrs Karl Liebknecht and Rosa Luxemburg. The presence of Johnson on the museum staff was an even more difficult matter, and his return did not pass without notice. One donor wrote in complaining of his "subversive history," suggesting also that it was not a thing of the past. "I don't want to support an institution which believes that people of Mr. Johnson's political faith should be a part of the leadership of our culture," he wrote.

The museum's response to this letter was careful — worded and reworded first by d'Harnoncourt and then Nelson Rockefeller, in whose name it would ultimately be delivered. "With equal frankness," he wrote, "I feel I can tell you that the Trustees of the Museum gave long and serious consideration to the matters you mention in your letter.... After careful deliberations and investigations the Trustees were convinced that Mr. Johnson had undergone a complete change in his view." Moreover, they felt it best not to mention the subject further, for fear that it would do no more than "open old wounds."

While Johnson, with his dubious record, was returned to the fold, Kaufmann was practically cast off the museum's org chart — and to the extent that he remained on it, he answered directly to Johnson. "All executive authority and responsibility for the Department will rest with you and with such members of your Department to whom you may delegate it," d'Harnoncourt wrote Johnson in a memo affirming the new hierarchy. Kaufmann was demoted to the position of Adviser to the Director and Research Associate. Johnson, also, would have a large salary — $9,000, more than double anyone else's in the department (even though he was essentially working half-time and claimed, throughout his career, that he never drew a paycheck from the institution).

*   *   *

The news of Kaufmann's effective demotion would have been upsetting to him if he had been aware of it, but—insult to injury—he learned of his reduced status only after returning from a European holiday, when he found Blake ensconced at the desk that had once been his. There were fireworks, and after another blowup over the summer regarding departmental territory, he offered his resignation.

That departure left Johnson in undisputed command of the merged department, which he filled with a talented young staff to whom he granted broad autonomy. Never much for bureaucracy, he was happy for the department to run itself, especially with his primary attentions directed to his own practice. Thus it was almost by default that the department became a breeding ground for future luminaries, many of them female. Among the group were Greta Daniel, a German refugee who supplanted Kaufmann as design curator; Mildred Constantine, who covered graphic arts; and Ada Louise Huxtable, a three-day-a-week research assistant who would become the first full-time architectural critic at the *New York Times,* a position that often left her reviewing Johnson's work. She had come to the museum while a graduate student at New York University's Institute of Fine Arts; once she settled in, Johnson put her in charge of the first American exhibition on Hector Guimard, architect of the Paris Métro. The office secretary was Jane Fiske, a Vassar alum, who would become founding editor of the design magazine *ID* and then an equal partner with her husband, the architect and urbanist Ben Thompson. Working together, they would design Faneuil Hall in Boston, South Street Seaport in New York, and Harborplace in Baltimore—"festival marketplaces" designed to breathe new life into languishing American cities.

Johnson's museum office was a good place to learn, not just because of the exhibition program but because it became a kind of receiving room for dignitaries of the architectural profession visiting New York. At any moment Alvar Aalto, Le Corbusier, Gropius, Mies, or Frank Lloyd Wright might pop in for an audience with Johnson (or, in their minds, to allow Johnson the pleasure of their company). For Johnson, every day was a performance. "He could be arrogant, insulting, cutting, bitchy, devastatingly nasty — and he was often all of those things. But he was never boring," wrote Blake.

The ironic result of Johnson's burgeoning career in New York was that it chased him out of the city; continuing to practice without a license left him vulnerable to civil prosecution. Charles Abbe, now successfully ensconced as a principal with Harrison & Abramovitz, declined to establish a front company under which Johnson might operate independently. For the rest of his life, Johnson would wonder just who had tipped off the state building department to his lack of credentials. Some jealous architect he had rejected or offended in his role as a curator? Someone embittered about his apostate years as a Nazi propagandist? A homophobe? He could form a line of enemies that would run from the museum to the Rockefeller's Guest House and back again. It could have been any of them.

It didn't matter, and a ready solution was at hand, one suggested by the emergence of New Canaan as a nexus of modern architectural practice. As opposed to New York with its restrictive demands, in Connecticut no license was required for the design of domestic buildings under 5,000 square feet. And so Johnson decamped to a small office on Main Street in New Canaan, a move that would prove to be both financially and intellectually profitable, and cut down on his daily commute. It also situated him among a group of forward-thinking architects who had established roots in New Canaan. That coterie included Marcel Breuer, the Bauhaus master who had been one of his few mentors at Harvard; Eliot Noyes, who had left the museum to work with IBM and build his own variegated design practice; John M. Johansen, a twinkle-eyed boy wonder who was one of Johnson's few Harvard intimates; and Gores, by now living in his own house in New Canaan and winding down his time with Johnson in advance of establishing a practice of his own.

The group, informally known as the Harvard Five, did not go unnoticed. Conservative neighbors were not pleased to see their traditional town transformed into a petri dish of modern architecture. A poem in the

New Canaan Advertiser lampooned the five "obnoxious" architects, who "Have graciously condescended to settle here and ruin the country with packing boxes / And partially opened bureau drawers set on steel posts and stanchions.../ An architectural form as gracious as Sunoco service stations." But there was positive attention, too, including a *New York Times* story by Aline Louchheim (who would marry Eero Saarinen) extolling the work of the group. And soon enough there were tours of the area's modern homes. The first, in the spring of 1949, drew over a thousand people. The showstopper, of course, was Johnson's Glass House.

But that was not the only Johnson house on the pilgrimage route; there was another one looking out over the Glass House, right across Ponus Ridge Road. The clients, Gerry and Dick Hodgson, she in advertising and he an executive with Paramount, had come somewhat indirectly, despite the proximity of the site; their family lawyer was a childhood friend of Pamela Gores. This led to something of a problem in the office, as Landis had his own aspirations for a job he had effectively

Hodgson House, built for his neighbors across Ponus Ridge Road, 1951. (Esto / Ezra Stoller)

228

delivered. Johnson, however, was paying the bills, and it was his name on the door. They resolved this dilemma by producing two schemes, one by Gores, the other by Johnson. The Hodgsons would then choose between them. The Gores design leaned toward Wright for inspiration; the Johnson, inevitably, toward Mies. They chose the latter.

It was the right decision, for Johnson gave them what remains one of his finest design achievements, a court house in gray brick of unprecedented sophistication. One wing was devoted to public space, the other to private rooms, with ceiling heights varying. A hidden martini bar was sequestered in the entry area — a feature that perhaps only Johnson, cosmopolitan that he was, might have thought to include.

Though Johnson carped that his reputation for opulence restricted his clientele as compared to the other New Canaan modernists, he was not short of commissions. Most were simple modern boxes in and around Westchester. But one was to be a bit further afield and for a pair of discerning patrons who would support his career for decades. Jean and Dominique de Menil were French expatriates who had come to the United States after the war, settling in the elite Houston enclave of River Oaks. From there Jean could run the Texas wing of Schlumberger, the family oil-services business cofounded by Dominique's father. In search of an architect, the two were referred to Johnson by their mutual friend Mary Callery. Her advice: "If you want to spend $100,000 get Mies, but if you only want to spend $75,000 get Philip Johnson." The Menils, who did not yet have unfettered access to the family fortune, chose Johnson. Callery set up a meeting between Philip and Jean over cocktails at her New York studio, a converted garage enlivened by the work of her artist friends: Picasso, Léger, and Matisse. The two men, similarly outgoing and charming when the moment demanded, were a perfect match, and shortly thereafter Johnson was flying off to Houston to meet Dominique, with his first Texas commission in hand.

Though Jean was a member of the French aristocracy — a baron — and Dominique an heiress to one of the century's great fortunes, the two were unpretentious. Jean would Americanize his name, becoming John.

A house of modest opulence for the Houston socialites John and Dominique de Menil, 1950. (Richard Payne)

Yet a place in the polite society of the Museum of Modern Art mattered to them, as did the possibility of raising the cultural bar in Houston. Johnson satisfied on both counts, a sophisticated New Yorker who could bring his cosmopolitan ways to Texas. Their devotion to the arts had been charged in the years before their emigration by the charismatic Catholic priest Marie-Alain Couturier, who would commission Matisse's murals for the Chappelle du Rosaire de Vence and Le Corbusier's landmark Church at Ronchamp.

Johnson's design was, from the exterior anyway, almost as self-effacing as the tract house in which they had been living: a light-brick single-story court house in the Miesian tradition, set back judiciously behind a curving driveway. Barely a window faced the street, and one of the few that did was an addition mandated by Dominique. Instead, light came in through a central atrium and large window walls facing the rear. Its spareness was something entirely different from the other homes of River Oaks—mansions in period flavors—that in its own way testified to the glamour of its residents. A neighbor called it "ranch-house modern," which wasn't far off.

230

The commission was not without its contentions: Dominique was not inclined to the austere interior design palette—including Barcelona chairs and other Bauhaus favorites—that encompassed Johnson's worldview. To his great displeasure, she brought in the flamboyant English couturier Charles James to pair Johnson's architecture with the kind of drawing room flavors and fabrics Johnson then considered apostasy but would eventually come to appreciate.

Whatever his disappointments, the house was at least out of sight in Houston, and it generated a series of commissions closer to home. A short ride from the Glass House in New Canaan there was a house for Dominique's sister and her husband, Sylvie and Éric Boissonnas. Completed in 1956, it was a departure from Johnson's Miesian aesthetic, a series of linked, cubic pavilions with overscaled brick piers, suggesting the influence of Louis Kahn, then teaching at Yale. He followed it with a vacation house for the couple at Cap Bénat on the French Riviera with a distinctly non-Miesian outdoor pavilion with a wavy, handkerchief roof in concrete. For the Menil family firm, Schlumberger, Johnson built a small executive office building in Ridgefield, Connecticut, a white-brick box with offices along a skylit hallway, and a library in the core adjacent to an enclosed glass court. So pristine was it that Knoll, manufacturer of modernist furnishings, used it as an exemplar of rational office design in one of its catalogs.

Johnson's domestic practice continued to thrive, serving the wealthy and well connected, mostly but not entirely within commuting or weekending distance of New York. A planned house on Long Island for Anne and Henry Ford (grandson of the auto king) turned into a glass-box addition to their saltbox home—"certainly not offensive," Ford wrote Johnson. A commission to design a house for another automaker, Walter P. Chrysler, fell through at about the same time, though Johnson had flown down to Chrysler's 250-acre Florida estate to scout the project.

These commissions and others of that period represented a progressive refinement of his Miesian architectural language. The 1951 Oneto House, on a site overlooking the Hudson River, was a simple box of similar proportion to the Glass House, but enclosed by brick for privacy. For

The priapic Leonhardt House of 1956, on Long Island's exclusive north shore. (Esto / Ezra Stoller)

The 1953 Wiley House, a box on a box. (Esto / Ezra Stoller)

Richard Davis, a Minneapolis curator and art collector, there was an elaboration of the ideas of the Hodgson House, but in red brick and with an open terrace linking the spaces of its separate pavilions. The priapic Leonhardt House, a pair of steel-and-glass pavilions set in a parallel alignment, was offset so that one of the pavilions cantilevered out over Long Island Sound.

An even more unusual project, back in New Canaan, was for the developer Robert C. Wiley. Lying atop a rectangular stone podium modeled after Le Corbusier's de Mandrot House was an enormous glass box, a double-height aquarium for living framed by massive timber beams and black steel. The built-in furnishings, immaculate in their craftsmanship, were fabricated by New London shipbuilders responsible for America's Cup yachts. "A small, contained temple in the landscape," wrote Yale architectural historian Vincent Scully, then a rising star, in an influential essay that appeared in *Art and America*. There were unbuilt experiments, too, the most dramatic being a proposal to place a series of his small court-style houses within their own glass box, as if in a rectangular snow globe. The client, William Burden, declined to build it, but he did commission Johnson for the family apartment on Park Avenue.

Johnson's success as a residential architect indicated a broader trend in the United States: the rapid expansion of suburbs in the postwar period. Johnson capitalized on this not just as an architect but as a curator. Here was an opportunity for another attention-grabbing exhibition: With the nation facing a postwar housing crisis, why not put a model home in the museum's own garden as a demonstration project? Even the frugal trustees saw the benefit of such an endeavor.

As director of the re-formed Department of Architecture and Design, Johnson could hardly tap himself as the *House in the Garden* architect. Forced to find a suitable candidate, he turned to Marcel Breuer, his former teacher at Harvard and current neighbor in New Canaan, despite the fact that their relationship was now more cordial than friendly. He referred to Breuer, who was stained by his relationship with Gropius, as a "peasant mannerist." There was also bad blood between Breuer and Mies over the assignment of patents to furniture designed at the

Bauhaus, and Johnson was prone to take Mies's side. He nevertheless chose Breuer for the job, knowing he was a trustworthy commodity whose modernist bona fides were undeniable. No doubt, the ever-competitive Johnson was also reluctant to select someone closer to his own generation for such a plum opportunity. Peter Blake, then a curator in the architecture department, speculated that the selection of Breuer, who was Jewish, was an attempt by Johnson to expiate his anti-Semitic history.

Breuer's house opened in April of 1949, after four months of construction, to great public interest. With two bedrooms, it had an unusual butterfly roof, an exterior of unpainted vertical cypress boards, flagstone floors, and nautical-style rope-and-wire railings. Breuer designed much of the furniture, both built-ins and production pieces, including a custom radio-phonograph-television unit. Also featured were designs from Charles Eames and Eero Saarinen, and paintings from the museum's collection by Hans Arp, Alexander Calder, Paul Klee, and Fernand Léger.

The curatorial intention of the project was explicit, yet another example of the museum nodding toward a social problem, the postwar housing crisis. "Recognizing as today's primary architectural problem the need for adequate housing," a press release announced, "the Museum will present this house as good and practical design in the best of materials, equipment and craftsmanship." But the idea that the House in the Garden could somehow be a solution to the housing crisis was hardly realistic. The $25,000 building budget (not including land costs) was well beyond the capacity of the typical ex-G.I., and some four times the price of the Levittown houses that were kudzuing across Long Island. The house was more of a paradigm for the junior society set — Ivy League–educated young professionals — who were the museum's bread and butter. Breuer himself described the house as a "country home for the commuter."

When the house was criticized in the press as stylistically appealing but not particularly practical, Johnson was happy to throw Breuer under his modernist bus. "We did not tell the architect what to do in building his house, any more than we would have told Picasso what colors to use had the museum commissioned him to paint a mural."

Functional or not, it was popular—more than a hundred thousand visitors paid an extra 35 cents to visit Breuer's house, prompting Johnson to revisit the program the following spring, this time with a house by Gregory Ain, a Los Angeles architect (again, not one of his East Coast peers) known for the design of modest homes for the middle class. Ain's exhibition house, with three bedrooms and sliding walls that allowed for the reconfiguration of spaces, was estimated to cost between $15,500 and $19,500, depending on the interior finishes—still considerably more than a typical builder's home but less than Breuer's first attempt. The high cost prompted even Eliot Noyes, the former museum curator, to call it an appealing but "pointless" exercise.

The next project in the museum's backyard would be undertaken by Johnson himself. In an arranged marriage that seemed destined for divorce, the museum had agreed to collaborate on a new building for the Whitney Museum that would face out toward Fifty-fourth Street but back up onto Johnson's Grace Rainey Rogers Memorial, with its eastern facade looking directly out onto the museum's garden. As part of this agreement, the two museums would share the first floor of the new build-ing. The Whitney would have its own architects for the project, but because it was on the Modern's property, Johnson was granted design authority over the building envelope. The Whitney's front, which satis-fied nobody, was a bizarre translation of the Modern's own (hated) facade into a more Miesian language. Instead of marble panels there was a brick wall with a disastrously overscaled eagle emblem and typogra-phy that, while large, was still illegible. Far more successful was the gar-den facade, composed of the same elements as the front, but with the weird appliqué removed and a clean glass-and-steel window wall at the ground level.

The principal benefit of the new building was that it helped define the space of Johnson's redesigned museum garden, which opened to the pub-lic in April of 1953. Named for the museum's queen mother, Abby Aldrich Rockefeller, this replaced the Parisian-style garden design (gravel paths, trees in a grid) of Johnson's friend-turned-nemesis, John McAn-drew. Barr had never liked that original design, which he compared to a beer garden. In January of 1949, an essay in the *Herald Tribune* noted the paucity of park space in Midtown and took the museum to task for allowing the space to wither. An international competition was recommended for a new design.

For Nelson Rockefeller, this sorry state of affairs represented an opportunity to honor his mother, who had died in 1948, with a new design. Forgoing a competition, the job was instead turned over to Johnson, who produced what remains one of his most cherished works, despite a series of alterations and the wholesale remaking of the museum around it.

The 1953 Abby Aldrich Rockefeller Sculpture Garden, an urban oasis. (© The Museum of Modern Art / Licensed by SCALA / Art Resource, NY)

Johnson's "outdoor room" was defined by a grid of slate-gray paving plates of Vermont marble, with a dining terrace at its western end. The sunken central area was divided by a pair of rectangular pools crossed by bridges, and studded with birch and cryptomeria trees. An 18-foot-high brick wall separated the garden from the street. Barr, who was intimately involved in the project, devised the sculptural program.

There were other collaborators, too, none more critical than James Fanning, a New Canaan landscape architect who worked closely with Johnson on the plantings. Johnson, however, assiduously declined to credit him in public. "People would think he designed the garden," he later admitted. Finding trees that wouldn't fail in that environment proved a challenge. Johnson also caught flak—from Aline Louchheim, in the *New York Times*—for cutting down extant trees that he considered inconvenient, a practice that would also cause problems with his Glass House neighbors. The pools leaked, a perennial problem.

If Fanning's contributions were appreciated if not credited, the same was not necessarily the case with Philip Goodwin, the museum's original architect and now a trustee. He contributed $25,000 to the commission to replace the garden that graced his most famous work. With that, he felt free to offer advice—the stone paving would make the place too hot; there was not enough room for sitting—that Johnson duly ignored, even though Goodwin used Nelson Rockefeller as his messenger.

He was wise to do so. From its first days the garden became a favorite midtown oasis, answering the call from the *Herald Tribune* that had helped to inspire it. The Rockefeller family, which shouldered $100,000 of the $164,000 budget, was especially pleased. "You have achieved something mother would have loved," Nelson wrote. "Even father, whose interest in the field of modern art has not been primary, was simply thrilled." Johnson, moreover, had given the world something unique, "the basis for a new concept in the development of a garden as a setting for sculpture" and a "focal point for the cultural life of the city."

By all rights, it was a fitting memorial to the woman who had seen potential in him when others had not, and occasionally taken a white glove to his dusty display cases.

The Seagram Building at dusk in 1958. (Esto / Ezra Stoller)

CHAPTER 10

An Apostate at Worship

I have been called Mies van der Johnson—it doesn't bother me in the slightest, and it does seem to me that if our generation is going to stand on somebody's shoulders, we had better pick the best man to start with.

—*Philip Johnson, 1958*

What did Johnson want to be when he grew up? Heading into middle age Johnson still didn't have a clear answer, or more accurately stated he had several. By the early 1950s he had set politics aside, but he was simultaneously pursuing his career as an architect and his role as director of the architecture program at the Museum of Modern Art. From that latter position he could promote his vision of architecture and the built world at a time of rapid postwar transformation. And with his practice burgeoning, he could also promote himself.

His dual roles became an issue in January of 1953, just a few months before the inauguration of the sculpture garden he had designed in honor of Abby Aldrich Rockefeller. The occasion was the opening of *Built in USA,* a postwar follow-up to the popular survey exhibition mounted during his absence in 1944. The new iteration, introduced by an enormous photomural of Frank Lloyd Wright's Johnson Wax laboratory in Racine, featured 43 buildings by 32 architects, among them two projects by Johnson: his own Glass House and the neighboring Hodgson House. Johnson attempted to insulate himself from accusations of self-dealing by offloading the vetting of projects to an advisory committee, with final judgment placed in the hands of Henry-Russell Hitchcock. Johnson likewise removed himself from the making of the catalog for the show, writing only a preface and assigning the main text to his newest deputy and protégé, Arthur Drexler, a former journalist whom he had recruited as a curator in 1951.

Despite these measures, the show was clearly a Philip Johnson production. Wallace Harrison, whose relationship to the Rockefeller family gave him influence within the museum, noted how his own projects—the Alcoa Building in Pittsburgh and the United Nations in New York—were positioned vis-à-vis Johnson's. "I notice you put your house on the good wall, and the building of mine that you showed on a back wall," he said. Wright, who had more projects in the show than anyone else and no reason to complain, was less gentle. "You can't carry water on both shoulders," he told Johnson. "You are either going to be a critic, which is fine, or you're going to be a practicing architect. But you simply can't do both." Johnson was taken aback, but he wasn't ready to abandon either pursuit.

Wright and Johnson in 1953. Wright advised that Johnson could be an architect or a curator, but not both. (Getty Research Institute, Los Angeles)

In addition to Wright, Mies, and other modern pioneers (Aalto, Breuer, Gropius, Mendelsohn, and Neutra), *Built in USA* featured the work of a younger generation of architects remaking the modern project into a distinctly American idiom, among them Gregory Ain, Pietro Belluschi, Edward Larrabee Barnes, Charles Eames, Harwell Hamilton Harris, John M. Johansen, Paul Rudolph, and Eero Saarinen. Their work, much of it residential as they began their careers, suggested a new, more open and relaxed way of living, in keeping with American values. But the show also illustrated the changing nature of an architectural profession responding to America's explosive growth in the postwar years. That dynamic required a new kind of practice to meet the large-scale demands of government, industry, and an expanding population. This way of doing business was exemplified by Skidmore, Owings & Merrill (SOM), which was born in the 1930s but had come of age during World War II as the firm responsible for the Oak Ridge, Tennessee facilities hastily assembled to accommodate the Manhattan Project. *Built in USA* featured two of SOM's new projects: an apartment complex at Oak Ridge and the forthcoming Lever House, a model of corporate capitalism on Park Avenue. Lever House was to be a green-glass slab with a single-story podium hovering over an open plaza, and that tower was to be set perpendicular to the avenue, breaking the solid phalanx of facades along Park—a bold, modernist strike. It was revolutionary when completed, but Johnson would soon be engaged in the making of a tower cater-cornered to it that would eclipse it as the ne plus ultra of corporate modernism.

The client was the Seagram Company, the liquor conglomerate founded by Samuel Bronfman, a Canadian business savant who had made a vast fortune selling black-market booze during Prohibition. In the blue-blooded world of midcentury American business, Bronfman's past and Jewish religion were considered unsavory. That his Prohibition-era dealings became the subject of Senate hearings held by Estes Kefauver in 1950 put that history in an unwanted spotlight. A new corporate headquarters on tony Park Avenue served as a response to these perceptions: a declaration of his success and arrival at the apex of American business. Put more bluntly, it was to be the world's largest washing machine, built to launder the company and family image.

Johnson was not initially involved. One of Bronfman's deputies suggested the commission go to the recently established firm of Pereira and Luckman. If anyone could build a new Lever House, it would be the firm cofounded by Charles Luckman, who had been the president of Lever during the making of its signature tower. A boy-wonder salesman who had risen to lead the company, Luckman could see the future in an architectural profession gearing up for the booming postwar economy. He quit Lever to team up with William Pereira, with whom he had studied architecture as a college undergraduate.

Luckman was a better salesman than a designer. When Bronfman included the firm's plans in a letter to his daughter, Phyllis Lambert—a recently divorced sculptor living in Paris—she responded with a missive that let him know just what she thought: "NO NO NO NO NO," it began. Following that was an eight-page, single-spaced exegesis on architectural history and civic responsibility. There was "nothing whatsoever commendable" in the proposed design, she wrote. "You must put up a building which expresses the best of the society in which you live, and at the same time your hopes for the betterment of this society." Bronfman, whose toughness was legendary, wasn't used to being lectured by anyone, let alone his twenty-six-year-old daughter, but he was impressed enough with her intelligence and her brass to invite her to return from Europe to work on the project. If he thought he could placate his daughter by letting her pick out marble patterns for the lobby, he had grossly underestimated her. "When I come to the U.S. it will be to do a job and not to sit around the St. Regis making sweet talk," she informed her mother.

It was Lambert who brought Johnson on to the project. In need of her own adviser for an architectural search, she turned to the Museum of Modern Art, the de facto headquarters of the avant-garde in the United States. Alfred Barr sent her directly to Johnson, and the two children of privilege found an immediate rapport. For Johnson her arrival represented a unique opportunity; though he may have coveted the commission, he was clearly too inexperienced to take it on. But what he was given was almost as good, and perhaps even better: the chance to act as kingmaker on a career-defining job—a skyscraper on a prime Park Avenue site for a client with enormous resources and a desire to make a statement.

In 1954 Johnson and Lambert traveled the country, visiting and interviewing architects from a list they drew up with the assistance of Eero Saarinen. He had joined the pair at Johnson's Glass House early in the process. Together they divided potential architects into three categories: those who could but shouldn't, those who couldn't but should, and those who could and should. The first group included the corporate firms that had proven capable of large-scale building projects, in particular Harrison & Abramovitz and SOM. They could but shouldn't; both were rejected as pale imitators of Mies. In the second group were Marcel Breuer, I. M. Pei, Paul Rudolph, and Minoru Yamasaki—all younger architects with the exception of Breuer, and none with experience designing office towers. They just didn't have the requisite experience. Saarinen also belonged in this category, and he had the temerity to place himself in the competition. Indeed, he thought he had it won, but his overconfidence was his undoing: Lambert found him pushy, and wanted an experienced hand.*

That left the third category, those who should and could. There were three options in this group: Frank Lloyd Wright, Le Corbusier, and Mies. But Wright wasn't actually a candidate: he had put himself forward for the job before Lambert became involved, and Seagram executives had kiboshed him, fearing he was a prima donna and would never keep within budget. The options, therefore, were Le Corbusier and Mies.

---

* Saarinen essentially built the tower he proposed for Seagram a few blocks away, the brooding headquarters for CBS known as Black Rock. Pei, Rudolph, and Yamasaki also became prolific skyscraper architects.

That was an easy decision. Le Corbusier, whatever his genius, was notoriously difficult to work with—Johnson detested him—and Lambert thought his sculptural approach lacked intellectual rigor. Mies, conversely, stood out for his refined authority. She made the decision before she even reached his Chicago office. "You know, I've made up my mind," she told Johnson after visiting with Saarinen. "I've picked Mies van der Rohe." Johnson, Mies's chief American acolyte since the 1930s, had been hoping for that all along.

Mies was acceptable to Seagram's corporate officers largely on the word of Lou Crandall, the influential president of the Fuller Construction Company, which would build the tower. He did, however, have one recommendation: Mies, aged sixty-eight and based in Chicago, should have a junior partner in New York. Grateful for Johnson's years of support and for funneling the commission to him, Mies looked past the apostasy that was the Glass House and offered Johnson the job. "Shall we make it Van der Rohe and Johnson" he asked? Their partnership became official on October 28, 1954.

The Seagram team: Johnson, Mies, and Phyllis Lambert. (© The Museum of Modern Art / Licensed by SCALA / Art Resource, NY)

The team set up in an office building on Forty-fourth Street, a short walk from both Seagram's headquarters at the time in the Chrysler Building and the new building site at 375 Park Avenue. Johnson designed the one-room office, giving it wall-to-wall carpet, which was unusual, and placing a series of cubicles along the window wall. Because the adjacent building blocked views from those windows, he put up translucent white fiberglass screens, lit from behind to give them a pleasant glow. From his Chicago office, Mies brought a model maker who was talented but often drunk, a draftsman, and, as his deputy, an affable young Texan named Gene Summers.

Johnson had his own staff, including two new hires who would be with him for decades to come. The first was Richard Foster, a friendly boulder of a man more than six feet tall, who had started with Johnson in his New Canaan office. Johnson had discovered Foster while the former was teaching a studio class at the Pratt Institute; Foster was there on the G.I. Bill, having seen combat in the Mediterranean during World War II. Sensing his talent and competence, Johnson brought him on, and for the next two decades Foster would be the firm's administrator-in-chief.

It was through Foster that Johnson found the other man who would become indispensable to him, remaining by his side for an astonishing fifty years. Like Foster, John Manley had served in the military during World War II and had later taken Johnson's studio class at Pratt. The course famously required students to design a house in three ways: in the fashion of Mies, in the fashion of Wright, and in the fashion of Le Corbusier. Manley got a D, but Foster liked him and Johnson hardly remembered him. What they both soon realized was that as a draftsman Manley was a savant; in that predigital age he could sketch out complex geometries with accuracy and speed, calculating angles in his mind where other designers might take hours slaving over numbers. Johnson described him as a "one-man office"; eventually he would take to calling him the "ice-cream man" for his ability to make any design as appealing as a sundae. But that sold him short, because Manley's contributions were so much more than superficial: as the architect Robert A. M. Stern would note, without Manley, Philip Johnson would never have become Philip Johnson.

The great miracle of the Seagram Building was that something so magnificent could rise from an environment that was so essentially dysfunctional. There were more bosses than workers, a situation exacerbated by the presence of a member of the commercial real estate consultancy that was advising Seagram on the project. In the first months, order was maintained in the office by a buxom redheaded secretary from the deepest warrens of Brooklyn, who took to patting Mies on the head like a puppy. She was replaced by an attractive brunette, who was soon in an affair with Johnson's "business adviser," Robert Wiley. He was not much of a business manager, however. Previously the client on one of Johnson's signature New Canaan homes, Wiley had gone in on a spec house with Johnson that the two hoped would develop into a business. Only one was built before Johnson discovered that Wiley was embezzling his money to the tune of nearly a quarter of a million dollars. Wiley had represented himself as a partner with the white-shoe Boston investment bank of White, Weld, but the bank had never heard of him. Upon these revelations, Johnson severed all contact. Wiley committed suicide.

The more serious problem in the office was that Mies and Johnson could not have been more temperamentally ill-suited to one another. As Manley recalled, "Mies's approach to any problem was to sit and think about it and think about it and think about it, but in the meantime it was Johnson's nature to come up with solution after solution after solution. It drove Mies crazy." Soon they weren't speaking at all. To make matters worse, Johnson didn't want to talk to Summers; he found his Texas accent irritating. The result was that two competing camps developed in the office until Foster, ostensibly the project manager, told Mies he'd walk off the job if order wasn't restored.

It was, but the issue was soon moot. In late 1955 Mies was forced back to Chicago for much the same reason Johnson had previously been relegated to New Canaan. In its infinite wisdom, the American Institute of Architects declined to approve Mies's licensing application, claiming that one of the undisputed leaders of the profession (and the director of a leading architecture school) had not received the equivalent of a New York high school education. Speculation in the office was that this was retribution from Pereira and Luckman, who were embittered at being shut out of the job. Mies was livid. He rejected out of hand the offer to take an equivalency exam; this was a man, after all, who thought enough of himself to turn down a deanship at Harvard merely because one of his rivals had been *considered* for the post.

The split allowed Johnson far more autonomy than was possible with Mies looking over his shoulder from the next cubicle, and in several critical ways the building was better for it. Already Johnson was responsible for one of the signature features of the design: the luminous ceilings, which Johnson developed in collaboration with lighting specialist Richard Kelly, who had been so instrumental in the illumination of the Glass House. Mies had planned for the lobbies to be faced in dark green verd antique marble of the type that was eventually used on the plaza ledges. Johnson thought the result would be gloomy and hard to light. With Mies absent, he switched it to bright white travertine.

That change was wisely accepted. More contentious were the plans for the plaza fronting the building. Mies, pursuing his vision of bolt-straight clarity, eschewed the traditional New York step-back skyscraper, a product of the city's zoning regulations. Instead he pushed the entire tower back from the street so it could rise directly to its full height. The plaza out front would serve a dual purpose, setting the building off as a giant *objet d'art* while acting as a grand public space.

Mies's vision of architectural nobility quickly came under assault from within. The real estate men wanted a circular driveway, and Bronfman considered erecting a pavilion on the plaza that he could rent out profitably as a bank. Keeping it clear won out, but in Mies's absence Johnson was left to manage the design. His response was an enormous, bubbling reflecting pool that would cover the entire plaza but for a small path from the avenue to the door. Manley called it the "burping fountain." When Mies saw it he replied with one word: "No." Lambert agreed, and it was reworked into two small pools.

Johnson was otherwise responsible for maintaining the integrity of Mies's design. Although it appears a model of clarity and order, the building is deceptively complex and idiosyncratic. Making a tower out of bronze was going to be expensive—nobody had done that before—and Mies's insistence on using nonstandard sizes in the design shot prices up even higher. Everything had to be custom made, and what didn't have to be was anyway. Even the typographic program was bespoke, created by the designer Elaine Lustig Cohen. When problems arose, as they inevitably did, it was left to Johnson to resolve them. "Vy don't you build it the vay I draw it?" Mies would complain in his thick accent, leaving Johnson to explain why his demand was impossible. A tour of the building reveals any number of disguised columns, beams, and braces that preserve Mies's vision of austere perfection.

The one area in which Johnson was given free rein was the design of the Four Seasons, the defining restaurant on the building's ground floor. What

The Four Seasons, the immaculate cathedral of the power lunch.
(Esto / Ezra Stoller)

would occupy that space had been a matter of some debate. An automotive showroom, a bank, and a museum were considered before the decision was made to go with an eatery. Asked for his dining preferences, Bronfman responded, "All I want is to be able to get a good piece of *flanken,* okay?"

The building would actually have two restaurants, the Four Seasons and the Brasserie, a more affordable spot where dishes were delivered on a conveyor belt. But the Four Seasons was to be the signature establishment. The cuisine, true to its name, would change in tune with nature, a commonplace idea today but unique at the time. That vision came from the impresarios Jerome Brody and Joe Baum of Restaurant Associates (RA), who had pioneered event dining with the Newarker, their restaurant at the New Jersey airport. As work began on the Seagram project, RA was preparing to open the Forum of the Twelve Caesars, an enormous themed restaurant in Rockefeller Center that might have impressed Nero for its extravagance.

The Four Seasons would be every bit its equal, but its theme would be modernity—and there would be no kitsch. At $4.5 million, it would be the most expensive restaurant the city had ever seen. The relationship between Johnson and Baum, "the Cecil B. DeMille of restaurateurs," was shaky from the outset, with Baum insisting Forum designer William Pahlmann be added to the team because Johnson lacked restaurant experience. (Pahlmann was given the Brasserie job, and otherwise consulted on the Four Seasons.) At one point Johnson walked off the job; he was convinced to return a day later.

Johnson's design divided the space into two large boxes connected by an umbilical hallway that Lambert would favor with an enormous Picasso tapestry, *The Tricorne,* purchased for fifty thousand dollars. The two spaces were then each given their own identity. To the south would be the Grill Room, the clubby bar and restaurant that would become an epicenter of American capitalism. It was here that the "power lunch" was born, the term coined in a 1979 *Esquire* piece on the restaurant's ballet of wealthy and extremely wealthy patrons. Johnson cast himself among them, taking a prime corner table (number 32) that gave him an ample view of the proceedings—and potential clients.

The northern, more refined space would be organized around a small square pool of white Carrera marble for which it would be named: the Pool Room. The idea for it belonged to Pahlmann, but the execution, with subtle lighting from below, was pure Johnson. (Accommodating the weight for the pool required additional structural theatrics.) Johnson's detailing of the rooms was impeccable, an exercise in the broad application of his exquisite taste. The Grill Room was enclosed by panels of match-cut walnut and enlivened by a freestanding bar capped by a composition of hanging steel rods by sculptor Richard Lippold. The private dining room featured a bravura ceiling of pinpoint lights — a "sparkle blanket" — conceived with Kelly and lighting manufacturer Edison Price.

Both rooms were enclosed by curtains of draped golden chain, created by the artist Marie Nichols, that waved gently in the convection currents along the windows. The effect was unanticipated, and at first Johnson feared it would be a disaster, making diners seasick. Instead it became a signature. Less successful was tableware that Johnson commissioned from his former assistant, Ada Louise Huxtable, and her designer husband, Garth. Their three-footed sugar bowls looked sharp enough to go into the Museum of Modern Art's permanent collection but proved too unstable for actual service. Their other objects were more successful, and some quite beautiful, but that was only part of Johnson's thinking; placing the Huxtables on the design team was one of his more cynical coups, figuring it guaranteed him positive coverage from Ada Louise, who was already writing for the *New York Times*. "It was done for obvious reasons. To get good notices in the *Times*," he admitted later. It did. She called the building a "sleek and shiny temple" in the paper of record. But that was inarguable.

The commissioning of Mark Rothko for a series of paintings to hang in the Pool Room proved a genuine fiasco. The idea germinated with Johnson, who admired the painter. In the spring of 1958, with the bones of the restaurant already complete, the painter joined Johnson and Lambert on the mezzanine of the Pool Room. It was agreed, shortly thereafter, that he would produce a series of paintings for the private dining room there for a fee of $35,000. In a rented loft on the Bowery, Rothko mocked up a studio with the rough dimensions of the space in the restaurant, then created three different series for the room. But he never deemed any of them appropriate and eventually backed out of the deal. Lambert figured he just wasn't comfortable having work in which he was so intellectually and emotionally invested serving as decoration in a restaurant. That was probably accurate, but in a moment of intoxicated weakness he vented to a reporter that he had accepted the job only with "strictly malicious intent" toward the restaurant's fat-cat patrons. "I hope to paint something that will ruin the appetites of every son of a bitch who eats in that room," he said. The whole sad saga would eventually become fodder for a Broadway show, *Red*. Johnson would soon have further difficulties with Rothko, but for the moment he and Lambert were stuck with blank walls.

Johnson, meanwhile, had an even more daring vision for the restaurant. In what would become the ground-floor cloakroom, he envisioned a discreet gentleman's club: a gay bar. Had it been completed, it would have been one of the more dramatic spaces in the city. Johnson imagined a room of coarse concrete walls painted a metallic gold that would be illuminated from above by dim wall-washer lights: a gloriously debauched rough room for the rough trade. This was Johnson at his most flamboyantly provocative, a winking acknowledgment of homosexuality within the newest temple of corporate America. But the idea was buried even before Lambert got wind of it, and as it turned out it was unnecessary. In the 1970s the Grill Room developed a reputation as a gay establishment, and it was enough of an open secret that the restaurant managers thought it was hurting business with the corporate types who were their bread and butter.

Johnson and the rest of the design team moved into the building well before it was completed. With construction still going on, the motley group climbed up the building, first taking an office on the third floor before moving up to the ninth and then to the thirty-seventh, which would become Johnson's permanent address. His office boasted expansive views to the east, as well as art rotated from his own collection and borrowed from the museum. The location was ideal, barely three blocks from that institution, and not much farther from the apartment house he shared with his sister. Grand Central and the train out to the Glass House were a quick jaunt down Park Avenue—and nobody walked more quickly than Johnson, who always moved at a frenetic pace.

Critics immediately understood the building as a masterwork. Not long after its opening, Susan Sontag dropped by for a television segment. The building was bronze, but her words were purple: "The Seagram building gleamed like a switchblade in the autumn sun. The elevator swished up like a gigolo's hand on a silk stocking." Lewis Mumford, the dean of American architectural criticism, was effusive in *The New Yorker,* although his praise fell principally on Mies. His review, "The Lesson of the Master," noted particularly the strength of the plaza. "It is at ground level, in the public spaces, that van der Rohe's sense of architectural order remains unqualified and supreme," he wrote. Indeed, it would become the subject of a groundbreaking study, "The Social Life of Small Urban Spaces" by William H. Whyte, which illustrated just how successful the plaza was within the city. Decades later when the building was sold, Lambert included as part of the agreement contractual language that preserved not just its architecture but the welcoming philosophy that governed it, guaranteeing that it would not become a heavily policed space reserved only for the building's occupants.

The irony was that Whyte's study was necessary only because of all the pale imitators Seagram begat. The tower-behind-a-plaza became the de facto New York model, with developers granted zoning allowances for the amenities in front of their buildings. Only most plazas lacked the generosity of the one at Seagram, resulting in broken-up streets and countless vacant and soulless spaces tearing violently at the urban fabric.

There were other issues, stemming from Seagram's astronomical price tag. "The building cost, shall we say, a little over anybody's conception of what buildings should cost," said Johnson. It was so lavish that the New York State Tax Commission took the unprecedented step of levying an additional luxury surcharge upon it, which became a point of public controversy. The editorial page of the *New York Times* weighed in, noting the perversity of penalizing architectural quality.

As an architect, Johnson grew up with Seagram. Its rise also marked a more personal rite of passage, the death of his parents. Louise Pope Johnson, who had taken immense pride in her gifted but troubled son, passed away at the age of eighty-seven in January of 1957. She had managed to survive a heart attack, but died a few days later in the hospital. Johnson was there for her, along with the rest of the family. "It could not have happened more to our liking," Homer wrote in a letter to their friends. He did not long outlive her. Louise had not been his first or even his second choice in marriage, but they had grown together over the years into a loving interdependency.

Homer, too, had come to take great pride in the son who had once been such a bitter disappointment. Unknown to Philip, for years he had stalled the Oberlin Board of Trustees in the hope that his son would achieve professional stature such that he could award him the commission for a new auditorium on the campus. His hand was forced, however, and the job went to Wallace Harrison. But Seagram showed that he had arrived. On his last trip to New York, Homer toured it with Johnson, a proud father. By that time their relationship had essentially reversed itself, with son looking after father. In Homer's final years, Philip made sure he was comfortable in his arrangements, and that he would always have the financial security that Homer had once provided to him, for his fortune had gradually been depleted—due in large part to his own generosity—over his long retirement. When he finally passed away in March of 1960, he was just three months shy of his ninety-eighth birthday. If nothing else, his son inherited his genes for longevity.

From Seagram came one of the stranger commissions of Johnson's career: The Monaco, a luxury hotel in Havana, then still under the go-go regime of Fulgencio Batista. The client, referred by executives with the Seagram subsidiary Four Roses, was fronted by a pair identifying themselves as the "Smith Brothers" from Toronto. Johnson envisioned a gridded block of hotel rooms set up on tall pilotis, with thin cables holding up Juliet balconies outside every room—a design that owed more to Le Corbusier than Mies. When the clients brought men with barely disguised holsters into the office to inspect the plans, Johnson began to have second thoughts, and these were reinforced after a trip to Havana to inspect the site. As he discovered, the "Smith Brothers" were merely fronting a syndicate of gambling operators led by the gangster Meyer Lansky. That was enough; citing scheduling problems, Johnson ducked out of the project, which was rechristened the Riviera and taken over by Miami architect Igor Polevitzky. He finished it just before Castro's revolution, after which it was transformed into workers' housing—an accident of history that made it Johnson's first and only foray into that typology.

Had he completed it on his own, The Monaco would have been by far Johnson's largest solo project to date. As it was, that honor belonged to Kneses Tifereth Israel, a temple for a small Jewish congregation in suburban Port Chester, New York, that landed in his lap as he was squiring Lambert around the country in search of an architect for Seagram. The job came to Johnson through the arts patrons Vera and Albert List, who had recommended him after he had been passed over for another Westchester synagogue commission, Temple Sholom in nearby Greenwich. Vera List, the chief conduit, had visited the Glass House and came away impressed. His unsavory history regarding Jews did not become an issue: the building committee at Kneses Tifereth knew the basic contours of his past but chose not to confront him. "How much they understood, we never discussed," he said years later.

Johnson offered to do the job at no fee, ostensibly as an act of contrition, but knowing that this would virtually guarantee him the job. He learned this lesson when he lost the Temple Sholom commission to an architect who had agreed to take it on at no cost, and he wasn't about to get burned again. "It was a lot of money," he said, "and synagogues always need money. I enjoyed that very much." Preying on the synagogue's financial situation (and taking pleasure in doing so) was a sign of his cynicism, but even that did not fully describe his opportunism. Rehabilitating his reputation was only part of the goal. With no institutional commissions on his résumé, he considered the temple a loss leader that would pad his credentials. His business adviser Robert Wiley put it to him bluntly: "What does it cost you? Thirty or forty thousand dollars? What's that to start a career? You do it and do it for nothing."

He could also recycle the ideas he had developed for the Temple Sholom proposal. The design, a rectangular white concrete box for the sanctuary with an attached elliptical entry pavilion, was essentially cribbed from the earlier project. An overblown shoebox, the sanctuary was a large, bright room with stained glass running in vertical slits down the walls, its signature element being a wavy ceiling suspended from above that appears to float through the space, like a giant ribbon pinned to the walls.

A few years later, in a catalog for an exhibition on recent synagogue design curated by a young architect named Richard Meier, Johnson explained his design strategy: "The difficulty comes from the habits of the High Holy Days when the attendance, shall we say, swells. Now the space is either great small or great large, but it can hardly act like an accordion and be great small and large. How to design a room that will be great both ways? Our solution at Port Chester was a great room, with

Johnson's atonement: Congregation Kneses Tifereth Israel, of 1956. (Esto / Ezra Stoller)

a small screen divider, because it seemed to us that most of the congregation comes on the High Holy Days and we wanted the community to enjoy the temple." The "High Holiday" problem, it should be noted, is not any different for a Jewish house of worship than it is for a Christian one, and there are certainly more creative tools at the architect's disposal to mitigate the problem: a fan layout, for instance, in which the wings can be closed off, is more amenable to shifting audience sizes. Balconies can handle overflow crowds. Johnson's suggestion that a space can either be "great small" or "great large" was essentially false, and the real problem was that Kneses Tifereth wasn't great no matter which way you sliced it. "Lou Kahn, especially, hates that ceiling," he mused, "but then I dislike some things about his work, so that's all right."

What proved most controversial, however, was the abstract sculpture set in a place of honor behind the temple's bimah. On Johnson's recommendation, the congregation had commissioned a large work of delicate and intricately laced metal from sculptor Ibram Lassaw, a Jewish artist associated with the abstract expressionist painters then reshaping the art world. Lassaw called it *Creation* and described it as a "symphony structured in space rather than sound." But to many of the temple's congregants, just a few years removed from the Holocaust, it looked a little too much like something else: the barbed-wire fencing of the concentration camp. Some wondered if it had been proposed for the space by an unrepentant Johnson. Johnson, meanwhile, had to advance Lassaw his fee for the job, as the congregation was reluctant to pay for it.

It was not Johnson's only Lassaw. Three years earlier he had purchased one for himself, then placed it on the wall above his bed in the brick guesthouse on his New Canaan estate. In 1953 he had decided to renovate that house, adapting it for his own use as a more private alternative to the Glass House that was its counterpoint. In its original configuration, the Brick House had two guest rooms separated by a small studio. Johnson combined the studio and one of the bedrooms into a large, private suite. But this was not just a case of knocking down a wall; it was a

The guest house at Johnson's Glass House compound: stern and unrevealing on the outside, a libidinous play space within.

complete interior redesign, a remaking of the bare-boned space into an extravagantly sensual pleasure den. The entire room was reframed with a pair of domical vaults sprung from delicate plaster columns that were themselves set just off the walls, which he covered with a golden Fortuny fabric. The inspiration, he claimed, was the library of John Soane, the neoclassical English architect. At the suggestion of Richard Kelly he recessed the lights behind the vaults and placed them on dimmers, unheard of in a private residence at the time. If he felt somewhat restrained about living a gay life in his glass house, here he created for himself a space that would have suited a debauched emperor.

The room was a travesty of acceptable bourgeois morality, albeit discreetly disguised. It was also an architectural apostasy. Johnson's blatantly false structure and unabashed historical references were a rebuke to the rigid purity of the Miesian modernism he had long championed, not to mention Mies himself. That Johnson could maintain these two positions simultaneously—designing with historical forms at his own home and at Kneses Tifereth while also working with Mies at Seagram—could be seen as a mark of his great intellectual dexterity or a deep character flaw, the sign of a nihilist with a detached moral compass. But this was really nothing new for him; from his youth, the congenitally insecure Johnson had been prone to biting the feeding hand and to courting controversy, for good and ill. To some critics, his placement of one of Lassaw's delicate metal traceries, *Clouds of Magellan*, above his bed was yet another, and perhaps his ultimate, transgression: an invocation of the Holocaust in the boudoir, the "scene of rituals of a very different sort," as the critic Hilton Kramer put it, rather indelicately, in 1995.

What bred such animosity was what the spaces at the Brick House and Kneses Tifereth augured for the future. Looking back, they stand as historical inflection points, two of the opening salvos in what would become the most reviled movement in architectural history—postmodernism. Conspiracy theorists who believe the development of architecture was orchestrated by Johnson and a cabal of his intimates can ascribe the origin of the movement to March 20, 1954. On that evening, a group of Johnson's peers gathered at the Glass House to discuss the direction of the field. Among them were Gordon Bunshaft, John Johansen, I. M. Pei, Paul Rudolph, Eero Saarinen, and Harry Weese. At Johnson's suggestion, Johansen brought a model of his Villa Ponte, a single-story residence roofed by three shallow vaults. That, combined with the Soane-inspired interior of Johnson's bedroom, suggested a new and more literal direction for architecture. Speaking years later at a dinner in honor of Johnson, Pei recalled the evening: "I said, 'My gosh, what's happening here?' And the two of them were trying to say, 'Well, this is the new thing. We don't like flat-roof, we want to destroy flat-roof and we put things on top of it.' And so I checked with John [Johansen], in fact, before I came here. I wanted to make sure it was correct, and he said, 'Yes, you're right. You can say that. Philip said this is the beginning of New Classicism.' I guess you know what happened after that."

At the time, however, nobody really had any idea what was coming, Johnson included.

CHAPTER 11

Crutches

I do not believe in perpetual revolution in architecture. I do not strive for originality.

—Philip Johnson, 1954

Robert Melik Finkle was a twenty-year-old student at Cooper Union in 1955 when Mildred Constantine, a family friend, ushered him into Philip Johnson's capacious office at the Museum of Modern Art. Finkle wanted to be an architect, and meeting Johnson seemed like a good idea. His protective mother hoped the visit would go better than the last time she had arranged such a meeting, when Frank Lloyd Wright was in town to open an exhibition of his work at the Guggenheim Museum. "Don't go to college," Wright told Finkle. "College merely starches you like a starched collar." This was not the kind of advice that appealed to a Jewish mother with aspirations, and she didn't feel any better about it when the exchange landed in the Talk of the Town section of *The New Yorker*.

Johnson, who had spent seven years at Harvard—and that was just his undergraduate time—was a better example, though Finkle was by then already a collegian, enrolled in New York's prestigious Cooper Union. More importantly, he was a precocious and gifted student who admired Johnson's work; indeed, he was already imitating it in his classes at Cooper. As Johnson reviewed the portfolio that had been placed on his desk, he could see Finkle's presentation drawing of the Museum of Modern Art's sculpture garden; it was, frankly, executed with more panache than anything that had come out of Johnson's own office. Next was a pool-house project, plainly inspired by Johnson's own Glass

House, that Finkle had produced for his second-year design studio. Johnson was impressed, but he didn't admit it too readily. "This is almost good," he said. How often had he heard that same critique?

Finkle's first audience at the museum was followed by a visit to the Forty-fourth Street office, where the Mies-Johnson team was at work on the Seagram Building, and shortly thereafter by a weekend trip to the Glass House. Outside the museum setting, Johnson had never adopted a protégé—he had always been too insecure in his own abilities—but in Finkle he found a plausible candidate, one in whom he could see a bit of himself. Like Johnson, Finkle was trim and handsome, with the dark hair and boyish features of a young Hollywood star. And like Johnson in his youth, there was in him a certain diffidence and vulnerability driven by confusion and guilt about his sexuality. A gay son was not an acceptable option for his traditional parents. His Romanian-born father considered homosexuality a grave illness. But Finkle was gay, even though he hadn't come to terms with the fact. Johnson knew.

Robert Melik Finkle, with whom Johnson would carry on a relationship for decades. (Robert Melik Finkle)

Crutches

His relationship with Finkle evolved rapidly from mentor-protégé to something more. On weekends Finkle visited Johnson at the Glass House, where he received an education in architecture supplemented by field trips in Johnson's gull-winged Mercedes coupe. Johnson taught Finkle to drive in that car, one of the most viscerally sexual designs ever to hit the road.

Johnson's longtime interest in automotive design had prompted a 1950 symposium on the subject, followed a year later by a landmark exhibition that presented the automobile as the ultimate designed object. That timing was deft: in the heady postwar years, the car had become America's favorite form of conveyance, one that was shaping its built landscape in ways Johnson himself would soon lament. But his exhibition touched not at all on the automobile's urban and societal implications. Instead cars were presented as objects of art—"hollow, rolling sculpture," in the memorable phrase of Arthur Drexler, who wrote the catalog for the show. It was a testament to the originality of Johnson's 1934 *Machine Art* exhibition that even now, nearly two decades later, the appearance of automobiles in a museum still seemed transgressive.

The selections, displayed on a custom-designed ramp that pushed out into the sculpture garden, illustrated Johnson's purely formal mode of thinking. There was a 1931 Mercedes SS sedan (chosen for its "heroic scale"), an MG roadster, a Bentley, a Talbot (a three-passenger French coupe), a Cisitalia (a creation of the master Italian automotive designer Pinin Farina), and three American vehicles: a Jeep, a 1937 Cord, and a 1941 Lincoln, the last two being luxury cars that Johnson himself had owned. Not one of these represented the kind of vehicle that might be appropriate for the typical American family: there was no streamlined sedan of the type an ex-G.I. might drive from his new suburban home to his office in the city; there was no family car like the one his wife might use to drop the kids at school or park in the capacious lot fronting a gleaming new supermarket.

Johnson, however, well understood the pleasures of the typical American car; he even owned one—a Buick—in which he took perverse pride. "It is a magnificent car," he told the attendees of the museum's 1950 symposium on the automobile, and then added, "I am not being funny." He had purchased it for the same reasons so many Americans were choosing their cars: because it "turned on a dime" and it could take him down the Merritt Parkway at eighty in plush comfort. He did, however, have the chrome-plated trim removed—all that needless ornamentation did not fit with his Miesian "less-is-more" aesthetic standards. Even still, he called it "the ugliest object I have ever owned." There was no hiding it, however, because the Glass House had no garage,

He was also well aware of what the automobile meant for the city, and for architecture. "The automobile is the greatest catastrophe in the history of city architecture," he wrote in a 1955 essay. "Just try to walk across the Place de la Concorde, a once beautiful area of Paris. Too dangerous; better take a taxi." Closer to home, the advent of the suburban mall was killing the small town, knocking out the places that defined it and gave it character and human scale. Architecture, too, was a victim of the car; it threw off the entire idea of procession that was at the core of Johnson's way of seeing. "You cannot get out of a car right in front of a monument of architecture," he wrote. It ruined everything.

Unexamined was his own complicity in the growth of an autocentric society. Beyond exhibiting vehicles as objects of veneration and aspiration, Johnson had from his earliest days promoted the suburban single-family home as a model for postwar American living. His own Glass House was the ne plus ultra of the typology, and that typology was dependent on the automobile. When it came to designing or exhibiting urban housing, he was disinterested.

Never immune to contradiction, Johnson fumed about the automobile's deleterious effects and then spent weekends chauffeuring his young protégé Robert Melik Finkle to the houses he had designed in and around New Canaan, to Kneses Tifereth, and to the works of his Harvard Five peers. Back in New York, they became dinner partners. Johnson, who never ate at home, preferred the Brauhaus, where he could get the German food he had enjoyed since his youth. (The Four Seasons was for business and his A-list friends.) Sometimes—too often, by Johnson's account—Finkle would end up lecturing Johnson. After one session listening to his ward ramble on, an irritated Johnson interrupted, "You know, I'm an architect too."

It was a seduction, even if Finkle didn't realize it at first. Johnson, harking back to his years as a classicist, invoked the history of the ancient Greeks, of men taking boys for lovers to educate them about sex, and he spoke of the great men of history who were also gay—Michelangelo, Wilde, Whitman, Tchaikovsky. The propaganda played on the psyche of Finkle, who was then seeing a young woman. One evening at the Glass House, he confided to Johnson that an attempt at sex with her had failed. Johnson told him this was because he was gay. "He could have said, 'That's all right, Robert—it happens.' I was in love with the girl. I told him I was in love with the girl," says Finkle. "I think he was preying on me. He saw it as an opportunity. I wish he had been more understanding, and not imposed himself on me." But he did. "I'm five-eighths in love with you," he told Finkle, his hand on his knee.

Johnson's fractional love might be explained by the fact that he was then living with somebody else. That man was John Hohnsbeen, a delicate-looking wit with a taste for finer things that he could not afford on his own. Johnson had met him in 1950, when Hohnsbeen was working in the Buchholz Gallery, which was run by Johnson's longtime friend Curt Valentin, a dealer of, among other things, Nazi-looted art. Both Hohnsbeen and Johnson were seeing other people when they met: Hohnsbeen was in the midst of an affair with the writer Christopher Isherwood; Johnson was still living with Jon Stroup at Hidden House. Both terminated their relationships—the Stroup-Johnson breakup, with Hohnsbeen in attendance, was said to be particularly ugly.

Johnson and Hohnsbeen suited each other, a pair of extroverts who enjoyed society. Johnson could bankroll Hohnsbeen's expensive predilections, which matched his own. Both were interested in modern art. (Hohnsbeen, in the future, would end up working in Venice for the collector Peggy Guggenheim.) Neither was particularly faithful. When Hohnsbeen came down with tuberculosis, requiring prolonged hospitalization, Johnson found himself free to play, which he did. It was during this period that he began his relationship with Finkle. Johnson also became infatuated with a dashing young immigrant from Yugoslavia, Peter Vranic, whose arrival spelled the end of his relationship with Hohnsbeen. (By the time it ended, they had been together for nearly a decade.)

Through it all, Finkle remained in the picture, but occluded from view. On his twenty-first birthday, Johnson gave him a gold watch. He also arranged for Finkle to study architecture at Yale, where Johnson was now a regular lecturer, using his influence with the school's dean, Carroll Vanderslice Meeks, to get Finkle admitted. Johnson paid his tuition that first year. During that time, he was still involved with Hohnsbeen. "Philip used people," said Finkle. "And if he didn't have any use for someone, he wouldn't have any loyalty."

By the mid-fifties, Yale had become one of Johnson's favorite platforms, a place where he aired his ideas in talks that were by turns impish, witty, testing, and controversial. The school's student journal, *Perspecta*, became a favorite outlet. In 1955 it published "The Seven Crutches of Modern Architecture," a lecture first delivered the previous December at Harvard's Graduate School of Design. Framed as a review of the rationalizations by which modern architects sell their souls, it read also as an indictment of conventional thinking and a statement of Johnson's own design principles, or lack thereof. As adumbrated in the text, Johnson's crutches were "history" (the beaux arts dependence on precedent), "pretty drawing" (pictures being inherently deceptive), "utility" (a shot at the functionalism of Gropius), "comfort" (in the absence of beauty), "cheapness" (self-explanatory), "serving the client" (at the expense of the architect's own prerogatives), and "structure" (allowing the ostensibly objective purity of engineering to displace the artistic practice of architecture).

The question, then, was what Johnson did believe. On that score he did not have a definitive answer. He quoted his old nemesis, Le Corbusier—"Architecture is the play of forms under the light, the play of forms correct, wise and magnificent"—an argument, in effect, for a purely formal discipline. But he did not leave things there. "I'm a traditionalist. I believe in history," he told the students. "I do not believe in perpetual revolution in architecture. I do not strive for originality." As Mies had advised him, it was "better to be good than original."

The conceit of his own lack of creativity was beginning to be just that, although the *unoriginal* tag would hang on him throughout his career, due in large part to his own efforts at self-deprecation. But there was always an air of a man who protests too much in his self-abnegation, a sense that his act was indeed an act (wink wink, nudge nudge) and that he was more inventive than he let on, or at least thought he was.

A window into Johnson's frame of mind was revealed in a 1958 study conducted by Berkeley psychology professor Donald MacKinnon. His idea was to figure out just what it is that makes individuals creative, and to do so by bringing leading architects—architecture being an inherently "creative" profession—together for a weekend of psychological testing. Johnson's initial impulse was to rebuff the invitation on the grounds that the study was ill-conceived, given that most architects were not creative at all ("Ninety-five percent of them are, of course, business men, organizers, salesman and hucksters," he wrote MacKinnon), and that in any case there was no way to truly understand something as ineffable as human invention.

Yet he couldn't resist, and neither could many of his most distinguished contemporaries, among them Ed Barnes, Pietro Belluschi, Serge Chermayeff, O'Neil Ford, Harwell Hamilton Harris, Louis Kahn, Fred Keck, John Johansen, George Nelson, Richard Neutra, Elliot Noyes, I. M. Pei, Ralph Rapson, Eero Saarinen, and Harry Weese—a veritable who's who of midcentury architecture. Over the course of three days in April, members of the group were put through their intellectual paces in a series of physical, visual, and verbal exercises designed to determine their creativity. Of the forty participating architects, it was Johnson who proved the most difficult to measure, the most combative, the most erratic, and the most intransigent. Given a checklist of adjectives to describe himself, he chose: *autocratic, bitter, boastful, bossy, complaining, cowardly, cruel, deceitful, irresponsible, intolerant, immature, moody, opportunistic, prejudiced, sarcastic,* and *unfriendly.*

According to the interviewer who performed his assessment, "he showed many classic features of the manic: self-centered, irritable, jumpy, flight of ideas, arrogant, use of humor to defend against serious consideration of anxiety-producing topics." The diagnosis squarely fit with the evaluation he had received years earlier as a Harvard student from the physician Donald J. MacPherson.

The study accurately pegged his personality, but it was also revealing about the nature of his creativity as he and his professional peers perceived it. When his fellow architects were asked to rank their colleagues according to creativity, he came in seventh out of forty. A group of architectural critics, asked to order the same group, rated Johnson even higher, in the fifth slot. Louis Kahn, who ranked second behind Eero Saarinen among both his peers and the critics, put Johnson fourth. Most telling is where Johnson placed himself: first.

Johnson's creativity was nowhere more evident than in his posturing as to both the nature of his own originality and the direction of architectural practice. "The battle of modern architecture has long been won," he wrote in the preface to the catalog for the 1952 exhibition *Built in USA*. "With the mid-century, modern architecture has come of age." But at virtually the same moment that he declared the battle for architecture won, he began refighting it from the opposite front. Modernism, which he had championed as a discrete style—"I do not believe in perpetual revolution"—would henceforth be understood as a form subject to perpetual revolution. He articulated this vision in another 1955 lecture, "Style and the International Style," this time at Barnard College. "A style is not a set of rules or shackles....a style is a climate in which to operate, a springboard to leap further into the air....it is a commonly held corpus of visual aesthetic canons, some of which can even be verbally expressed by laymen and critics."

Johnson's "climate" was variable in the extreme. In 1958 he was back lecturing at Yale, his subject being the "Retreat from the International Style." His conceit was that a generation of architects who had taken up the mantle of modernism were now pushing back against its orthodoxies. With irreverent cattiness, he poked fun at the stylistic proclivities of his peers, to the great amusement of his student audience. Gordon Bunshaft was labeled an "academic Miesian," Wallace Harrison a "structural expressionist," Louis Kahn a "neo-functionalist," Eero Saarinen a "wavy-roof boy," Paul Rudolph a "decorative structuralist," and Edward Durell Stone a "screen decorator."

He did not spare himself. Philip Johnson, according to Philip Johnson, was a "structural classicist," though he soon reclassified himself as an "eclectic functionalist." His barbs were delivered with enough self-deprecation and charm that his friends could forgive him for them. For others, his continuing status as the primary bridge to the Museum of Modern Art was too important to burn. "At this time he seems to be the most advanced candidate as the *enfant terrible* of the twentieth century," said Rudolph, one of his closest friends since their days together at Harvard. "This is not to neglect the fact that he is undoubtedly the most sensitive and intellectually creative architect we have amongst us."

A year later Johnson elaborated on his latest ideas, again at Yale, in a talk that accompanied a small solo exhibition of his work—the first of his career. "My stand today is violently anti-Miesian," he said. "I think that is the most natural thing in the world; just as I am not really very fond of my father." These consciously Oedipal words came with the paint still drying on the Seagram Building and the Four Seasons not yet open for business. "It has always seemed proper in the history of architecture for a young man to understand, even to imitate, the great genius of an older generation. Mies is such a genius. But I grow old. No respect, no respect. My direction is clear: traditionalism. This is not academic revival; there are no classic orders in my work; no Gothic finials. I try to pick up what I like throughout history. We cannot not know history." The line became one of his signature aphorisms.

The talk reflected the influence of Yale architecture historian Vincent Scully, a charismatic scholar who had become close to Johnson through Henry-Russell Hitchcock, his dissertation adviser at Yale. Hitchcock had introduced them in the late 1940s, when the Glass House was still just a concrete slab, and Scully had remained in Johnson's orbit ever since, the rare figure whose passion for and knowledge of architecture could match Johnson's own. Scully's 1954 essay, "Archetype and Order in Recent American Architecture," published in *Art in America,* was the first serious attempt to isolate the new, classically derived direction emerging in the work of second-generation modernists. It was a direction Scully himself had done much to inspire. In 1952, while he was on a Fulbright in Italy, he met Johnson and Hitchcock at Harry's Bar in Venice, the watering hole made famous by Hemingway. Scully encouraged Johnson to revisit Rome, particularly the architecture of Hadrian. As far as Scully was concerned, Johnson's Brick House bedroom—reimagined shortly after that meeting with delicately arched columns—was a direct product of that influence. Johnson never denied it, even if he credited John Soane as the primary inspiration.

Whatever its source, Johnson's so-called traditionalism was becoming increasingly evident in his independent work of the 1950s, though his efforts in this direction were not always appreciated. His proposal for a new headquarters building for the Asia Society, another Rockefeller family project, was rejected because John D. Rockefeller III (Nelson's older brother, then its chairman) found the design insufficiently modern. That proposal featured a facade of thin stone pilasters rising up six stories to a row of delicate arches at the roofline. Johnson responded with a black-glass curtain wall, but he was unhappy with the detailing of the window system, a problem resolved when Richard Foster had the bright idea to install it inside out. The steel trim was then painted white, which gave the building the pleasingly crisp appearance of a sheet of clean graph paper.

It was at this moment, in 1956, that Johnson received his first governmental commission, and from the most unlikely of sources, given his personal history: the State of Israel. He had offered up the design of Kneses Tifereth without fee as atonement for his anti-Semitic transgressions, and whether that expiation was genuine or merely opportunistic, it was accepted by Shimon Peres, then the defense minister of the Jewish state. Peres was a rising political star then, his principal achievement being the securing of military aid from France and the United States. Among his chief goals was the development of an Israeli nuclear program, and it was in that capacity that he came to Johnson, who had impressed him on a visit to the Glass House compound. Peres's aims were facilitated by the American "Atoms for Peace" program, an Eisenhower administration initiative intended to calm Cold War fears by promoting the benefits of nuclear technology to U.S. allies. For Israel, that meant a research facility along the Mediterranean coast at Rehovot, some 20 miles south of Tel Aviv. The Soreq Nuclear Research Center would be staffed by American-trained technicians who would work on an American-made "bathtub" reactor. The architect of that facility would be American as well: Philip Johnson.

What he produced was Biblical in nature, a virtual New Jerusalem for the Atomic Age. The composition was extrapolated from Egyptian and

The pharaonic Norel Soreq nuclear facility in the Israeli city of Rehovot, 1960. (Arnold Newman / Getty Images)

classical temple design. From the outside it was all but impenetrable: a rectangle composed of immense battered-concrete walls. Within was an open court, an oasis framed by an arcade of tapering, splayed columns. The centerpiece was the reactor, the holy of holies, a faceted concrete drum capped by a shallow dome that projected above the line of the exterior walls. It was both fort and temple, secret and overt—a physical manifestation of his own personality. "The Israelis are the greatest clients in the world. They have a real respect for the architect," Johnson told a reporter. "You would think that we had done a church. Maybe we have." That metaphor was picked up by all who reviewed it. "This is not a building which invites, but one which repels," noted *Architectural Forum*. "It is a temple dedicated to the new 'religion' and served by a new order of high priests."

It remains one of Johnson's most forceful designs, but even he never saw it in operation, such was the secrecy of its operations. Although it was ostensibly intended for "peaceful" scientific research only, the Israeli government used the American technical training gleaned at Rehovot in the development of atomic weapons at its Dimona nuclear research facility—which, thanks again to Peres's skillful diplomacy, was built with the assistance of France.

While Johnson was at work on the Soreq facility, he was designing a project that was a funhouse mirror to it, located not in the Middle East but in a Utopian community in the American Midwest. The client was Jane Blaffer Owen, whose oil-magnate father had founded Humble Oil (one of the parent companies of ExxonMobil). In 1941 she married Kenneth Dale Owen, a descendant of British socialist Robert Owen, the founder of New Harmony, Indiana, an experimental farming community based on his political ideals. A romantic by nature, Blaffer Owen took it upon herself to restore the ailing town identified with her new family.

As her architect she chose Johnson, whom she had come to know as the designer of the stylish modern home of the Menils. Their first meeting came when Johnson traveled to Houston to present his design for the University of St. Thomas, a local Catholic college that was building a new campus, largely paid for by the Menils. Johnson's plan for the school translated Thomas Jefferson's mall for the University of Virginia into the modernist language that Mies had developed for the Illinois Institute of Technology (IIT). Blaffer Owen was justifiably impressed — the project was generously scaled and beautifully detailed, and remains an appealing campus — but not just with the design. From their very first interaction, Blaffer Owen was besotted with him. "I immediately felt that Philip was the one with the poetry in his soul for realizing for me what was only a dream at the time," she told Texas architect Frank Welch.

"Her interest in me was physical," Johnson recalled. "And that made for a stormy relationship. She was into sex to such a degree that it inhibited one's architecture. But after a little hanky-panky, well, we got down to business." It took some time for them to agree on a plan, but when they did the concept was in its essence identical to what Johnson had

Norel Soreq's more optimistic mirror, the Roofless Cathedral in New Harmony, Indiana, 1960. (Esto / Ezra Stoller)

built in Rehovot: a rectangular compound with a shrine at the far end projecting above its enclosing walls. Where Rehovot was all about mass, the New Harmony shrine was about lightness: from afar it looked like a handkerchief draped from a brass ring. Instead of concrete, it was shingled, and suspended nearly fifty feet in the air. Beneath its oculus was a Jacques Lipchitz sculpture of the Madonna, *Our Lady Queen of Peace.*

The so-called Roofless Church was a work of extraordinary mathematical precision. In an age before computer-aided design, one of Johnson's deputies, James Padavic, was forced to spend weeks calculating the placement of each and every shingle to form the dome's curving lobes. Johnson had teased his friend Eero Saarinen, calling him a "wavy-roof boy," but here he was indebted to him, in particular to his recently completed chapel and domed auditorium at the Massachusetts Institute of Technology. In its review of the project, *Architectural Record* described it as "one of the more ironic examples of current architectural swashbuckling." Unmentioned was the far more substantial irony that

Johnson's box-of-crayons design for St. Stephen's Episcopal Church was (mercifully) unbuilt. (Getty Research Institute, Los Angeles)

Johnson had taken the design for a space dedicated to peace and good-will from one that, reading generously, promoted research based on the most dangerous scientific ideas in the history of mankind.

The Roofless Church begat a second ecclesiastical commission in New Harmony with Blaffer Owen as client. Though it was not built, Johnson's design for St. Stephen's Episcopal Church was even more "swashbuckling" than its predecessor, an agglomeration of attached concrete tubes surmounted by blunt conical spires. In model it looked unmistakably like an open box of Crayola crayons. It might have gone ahead had the Blaffer Owen–Johnson relationship not run completely aground. Johnson was up for a bit of "hanky-panky" if it meant a commission, but he was a gay man and not particularly attracted to Blaffer Owen's emotional personality, facts that apparently eluded her.

Blaffer Owen all but acknowledged this in an impassioned 1980 letter to Johnson, a winding mea culpa recalling the very beginnings of their relationship, and her decision to hire him. "When I heard you speak at St. Thomas that long ago evening in the mid-fifties, I knew you were the magician to enflesh [my] dream," she wrote. "And now, suddenly, after so many hurtings, given and received, + after the flood of tears, I am filled, to the brim, with a deep and mature love for you that asks only to be forgiven, and that you smile with joy and with pride over your church, our church.... Also know that the love which possesses me shall never harm anyone. May it bless you, always—Jane."

It was just the kind of unhinged emotion that he could not abide, an aversion grounded in his own history of suppressed feelings. And at the same time, there was another new figure in his life who was occupying an increasing place in his emotional and sexual life, even as he kept Hohnsbeen as a partner and Finkle on the side. That man was David Grainger Whitney, who would become his partner for the rest of his life, their love deep and genuine, if crossed by years of infidelity and bitterness.

Whitney fit the type that had always attracted Johnson: trim and delicately handsome, with an effete bearing and a probing intelligence he could mentor. They met in 1960 after a lecture Johnson delivered at

Brown University. Whitney, who was born in Worcester, Massachusetts, had attended the elite Lincoln Institute for high school, and was then a junior at the Rhode Island School of Design, where he was studying architecture. He was also interested in art, and in particular the emergence of a new generation of artists moving beyond abstract expressionism. He approached Johnson after the lecture to ask what had prompted him to purchase a painting that had become a touchstone of this movement, a brazen depiction of the American flag in encaustic by a young Southerner named Jasper Johns.

Johnson admired the audacity it took to ask such a question. His self-deprecating reply: he had purchased it because Alfred Barr had told him to purchase it. That was an evasion that undersold his own intelligence. The reality was more complicated. It was not Barr who had discovered Johns. In 1957 Johns had appeared in a group exhibition at the Jewish Museum, and in January of the following year he had his first solo show, at the Upper East Side gallery of Leo Castelli. Five days after its opening, Barr visited and reserved four paintings for the Museum of Modern Art. The catch was that final purchasing decisions were not up to him, but to an acquisitions committee. That group green-lighted three of Barr's selections, but the fourth was a problem. Was *Flag* intended as irony? Was it a desecration? Johnson, a member of the acquisitions committee, didn't care: like Barr, he was attracted by the painting's boldness, and he was not afraid of controversy—indeed, he enjoyed it. But the museum had been burned in the past for its associations with political artists, and with Cold War fears running hot there was concern about appearing unpatriotic. The acquisitions committee kicked the decision upstairs to the museum's board of trustees. Johnson was a member of that group as well; he had joined it that month, in recognition of his long service to the museum.

Behind closed doors, the board decided that three Johns paintings was good enough. Whether Johnson pushed in either direction is unknown. Barr, however, was not willing to let the painting go, so he and Johnson came to an understanding: Johnson would purchase it, but donate it to the museum when it became politically expedient to do so.

Johnson followed through, at least initially, purchasing *Flag* from Castelli for $1,000.* And then he decided to keep it.

Could Johnson have done more to get the museum to buy the painting for itself? It seems unlikely. But leveraging his position on the museum acquisitions committee for his own benefit became standard procedure for him, despite the dubious ethics of that behavior. He routinely purchased works rejected by the committee on which he served, the first being an oil-on-linen painting by Renato Cristiano. Next was a canvas-and-metal relief by Lee Bontecou that he liberated from Castelli for all of $600. In the years following, he acquired artworks in similar fashion by the likes of Richard Artschwager, Claes Oldenburg, and Kazuo Nakamura. Today, this kind of insider trading is strictly forbidden.

Johnson, eventually, would reveal this history to Whitney, but for the moment his evasion of why he had purchased the Johns *Flag* would stand. Their relationship accelerated rapidly, however, from that first meeting at Brown. It began with an assignation at the Glass House, which Whitney, like so many other architectural students, had asked to visit. "He was gorgeous, he was bright, he was glamorous—what's not to like?" Whitney recalled in an interview years later. "It seemed like a good idea at the time," said Johnson. They were not exclusive—Johnson was still juggling Hohnsbeen and Finkle, among others—and both would have fidelity issues in the future, but after Whitney's graduation, in 1963, they were together. Johnson arranged a job for Whitney at the Museum of Modern Art, working as an exhibition designer in the Department of Painting and Sculpture. They kept separate apartments at first, but soon Whitney moved in, and their partnership became an open secret.

Through the changes in his personal life, Johnson continued to redefine himself in opposition to Mies, his mentor, idol, and surrogate father. At the Glass House, his apostasy was implicit; the ideas were Miesian, albeit exaggerated and debased as far as Mies was concerned. Johnson's

---

* In 2014 a much later (and presumably far less valuable) Johns flag painting sold at auction for $36 million.

Munson-Williams-Proctor Arts Institute, in Utica, New York, was worse: theft compounded by heresy. The model was unmistakable: Mies's Crown Hall at IIT, a monument of glass-box modernism fronted, like a temple, by twelve travertine steps. Johnson had borrowed from Mies's IIT campus previously, for Houston's University of St. Thomas, but there the reference was reverent. At Utica, he took Mies's basic design—a rectangular box slung from oversize roof trusses—and replaced Mies's transparent facades with blank granite walls, an intentional subversion. Inside, an open central atrium, a feature that would become a Johnson calling card, was animated by a pair of formal switchback stairs, also of Miesian origin.

Munson-Williams-Proctor was the first in a series of museums Johnson designed in the late 1950s and early 1960s. Johnson was quick to recognize the cultural import of these commissions; his association with the Museum of Modern Art, and with its chief proselyte, Alfred Barr, had shown him that America was turning to a new religion that required

The Amon Carter Museum in Fort Worth, 1961, started as a memorial to its publisher namesake. (Esto / Ezra Stoller)

its own places of worship. "Today we do not build—for whatever reasons—cathedrals and temples," he wrote in 1961. "Museums, not city halls, palaces, state capitols, movie houses, opera houses, are the buildings we look to today. They play a new symbolic part in the life of our cities."

Those words, while prescient, were also self-serving, written for the dedication to his own Amon Carter Museum, in Fort Worth, yet another commission that had come to him through the Menils. That it was to be a new symbolic centerpiece for that city was the idea from the outset; the initial plan was that it be less a museum than a memorial dedicated to its recently deceased namesake, a giant of Fort Worth civic life. The memorial envisaged by Johnson answered Carter's Texas-scale mythology: a virtual pantheon on a rise looking out over the city he had controlled. Before choosing the exact location, Johnson erected a scaffold to make sure the view would be appropriately grand.

The magisterial front was defined by a loggia divided by tapering columns of limestone that shone bright white in the hot Texas sun. Johnson repeatedly traveled to the quarry in Leander, Texas to select this native alternative to Italian travertine, imprinted with the forms of prehistoric seashells. The stone was there for appearance, however, not structure: the loggia was in fact supported by steel columns over which the limestone was threaded, as in a child's stacking-ring toy.

Whereas the exterior was decidedly antimodern, the interior was unapologetically Miesian, with exquisite materials—marble, brass, glass, steel—handled with great delicacy. That modernity made it both an unlikely and revelatory setting for Carter's collection of Western art, in particular the works of Frederic Remington and Charles M. Russell, which were typically presented in Western-themed settings. In Johnson's crisp modern spaces, those works—toughened cowboys and proud Native Americans in the grand Western landscape—were granted a new authority and dignity. Johnson's influence on the museum's collection extended beyond this reframing; he sat on its board, and brought with him the Museum of Modern Art's own president, René d'Harnoncourt, who expanded the vision to embrace contemporary American work.

The Sheldon Memorial Art Gallery, 1963, distinctive for its coat-button ceiling and fabric walls. (Esto / Ezra Stoller)

The Amon Carter was followed by another museum in flyover country, the Sheldon Memorial Art Gallery (now the Sheldon Museum of Art) on the campus of the University of Nebraska, in Lincoln. Here, Johnson merged the ideas of his two previous museums into one: the blank box of Munson-William-Proctor decorated by the tapered pilasters and gently curving arches of Amon Carter. Inside was another double-height atrium space animated by a switchback staircase. The building was not without innovation, however; Johnson covered the gallery walls with a beige cotton carpet that both pleased the eye and made it easy for curators to shift works during installation. The fabric theme was carried up to the ceiling of the atrium, which Johnson defined with large indented circles with six recessed lights each. They looked unmistakably like coat buttons. This, again, was a departure from modern orthodoxy, and a challenge to conventional taste. When Arthur Drexler was asked to author an introduction to a small monograph on Johnson's work, he declined, telling Johnson, "How do you expect me to write an article about somebody that would do something like *that*?"

Johnson had a similar reaction when he saw what his clients David and Carmen Kreeger did to the home he built for them on a wooded site in Washington, D.C. It was a design of liquid spaces defined by gently vaulted roofs. Their decorator, however, thought Johnson's Barcelona chairs would make the place look like an airport waiting room, so he filled the place with period English furnishings—and not in the spare, tasteful way of Dominique de Menil and her decorator, Charles James. Carmen Kreeger wanted "coziness." The ultimate indignity was a guest room installed with wall-to-wall pink carpet and floral wallpaper that matched a pair of twin beds and a puffy lounge chair. It was enough for Johnson to claim he was renouncing residential architecture altogether.

But he didn't. Indeed, the ultimate manifestation of his style of the period was a work of residential design in the tony reaches of North Dallas, where Johnson found willing clients in Henry and Patty Beck. They

The Beck House in Dallas, 1964, a paragon of architectural opulence.
(Collection of the author)

came, like so many of Johnson's Texas clients, through the Menils, and they approached him wanting a showstopper. Henry Beck was the director of a leading construction company, and whatever he built would be an advertisement for the firm's building prowess. Underscoring that fact, Johnson was not the couple's first architect: the job had originally gone to Gardner Dailey, of San Francisco, but his design was not sufficiently dramatic. For Johnson, that was not a problem. He took Dailey's basic design, then wrapped the exterior in a two-story arcade of bright white arches. They looked like travertine but were made from concrete; Beck had them fabricated to Johnson's exacting specifications by an aerospace manufacturer. The Becks got the iconic design they wanted, but perhaps did not realize that the arcaded facade rather overtly referenced the Palazzo della Civiltà Italiana, in Rome—a monument to Mussolini's fascist experiment.

Critics were not favorably inclined to Johnson's new style, which he now referred to as "structural classicism." Reyner Banham, a frequent Johnson antagonist, called it "toe dance" or "ballet school" architecture, a cutting reference to the fey formalism of classical dance, with its pirouetting prima ballerinas. Here was its architectural equivalent: something from another time, and wrapped up in its own self-indulgent language. If modern architecture was about bold structural honesty, this aesthetic was a decorative sham. Adding insult to this injury was the fact that Johnson was placed in this school along with the likes of Edward Durell Stone and Minoru Yamasaki, architects he considered beneath his dignity.

In the future this style would have other names—"new formalism" is the current vogue designation in academic circles—though it is best understood as an incipient phase of that most reviled of movements: postmodernism. Here was the next stage in its development, building on its early manifestation in Johnson's Brick House bedroom, but now even more self-serious and unapologetic in its public performance. This was a postmodernism before the tongue-in-cheek days of the seventies, but with similar ends: a desire to move beyond modernism by taking the language of architecture—modern and historical—and warping it into something different.

That Johnson might be the patient zero of this new direction was clear to the man who would be its philosopher king, even as he grew to despise his throne. Robert Venturi first achieved national attention courtesy of Vincent Scully, who selected him for a 1961 feature on new architectural talent for *Art in America*. Notoriety followed quickly, driven by two projects in his native Philadelphia that made him a celebrity within the architectural profession: Guild House, an apartment block for seniors, and a house built for his own mother. Both toyed with the language of architecture, making ironic references to both classical and modern orthodoxies. Among the most controversial provocations: placing a giant television antenna atop the facade of Guild House, as if it were a sculpture—a wry commentary on the state of American domestic life.

Johnson was naturally inclined to anyone willing to offend the gods of architecture, and Venturi was especially appealing as his path out of modernism seemed a good deal more inventive and sly than Johnson's own pretentiously grave direction. They were introduced by Scully, who brought Venturi with his partner Denise Scott Brown and their toddler son to visit Johnson for the afternoon at the Glass House. It was the beginning of a long and sometimes frustrating friendship, with the host at his charming best. "He was perfectly generous and kind," Scott Brown recalled. "He said it's all very good for children around here, and of course there was a precipice thirty feet away. But it was a very kindly situation." So kind, in fact, that he would pass along to them Peter and Sandy Brant, a young couple who had come to him for a house, a commission he didn't want for himself. "He didn't think they were going to be some of the great art collectors in the country, and pretty soon too, and he soon regretted it," said Scott Brown. "It was a typical kind of project he liked to give to a young architect, because it would not compete with him." Venturi and Scott Brown ended up building three houses for the Brants.

Propelling Venturi to the forefront of the profession was not just his work but his writing, specifically the self-styled "gentle manifesto" he had begun during his time as a fellow of the American Academy in Rome in 1954. *Complexity and Contradiction in Architecture* was finally published in 1966 by the Museum of Modern Art as the "first in a series of occasional papers," with an introduction by Scully, whose wife, Marian, was its editor. Johnson supported it financially. The insularity of this project was reinforced in its first pages, where Johnson's work was used to establish Venturi's central thesis. His famous "less is a bore" twist on Mies's "less is more" maxim was actually directed at Johnson's Wiley House, in New Canaan, with its glass-box living room perched over a stone base. Venturi's argument was that this division was so simplistic that the house was uninteresting. But Johnson was hero as well as goat: the Wiley House was contrasted with the Glass House—which, according to Venturi, appeared to be straightforward but was actually highly complex, given all the different functions forced into its apparently simple volume.

Johnson, then, had given postmodernism its start, and sponsored its bible. As for its chief lesson, that had always been with him: never be boring.

CHAPTER 12

Cocktails on the Terrace

We are all the product of our age and not without this gnawing
sense of guilt. I hope you are not bothered with it.

—*Philip Johnson*

W e're having a fire today, sir. Please call back tomorrow."

Whether a receptionist actually delivered those words or the story is apocryphal, the Museum of Modern Art's cocoon of privileged safety was ruptured on August 8, 1958. The museum, in a perpetual state of expansion from its very inception, was then in the midst of a mechanical renovation that included the installation of a new air-conditioning system. A construction worker's cigarette butt ignited a small pile of trash that in turn set fire to open cans of paint. A cloud of black smoke soon billowed through the museum. The Fire Department arrived quickly, smashing through windows as patrons and staffers rushed out, some carrying priceless works to safety. Among the rescued paintings was Georges Seurat's *A Sunday on La Grande Jatte,* some seven feet long and five hundred pounds in its frame. It was on loan from the Art Institute of Chicago, that museum's signature work. Losing it would have been a catastrophe—and might have severely compromised the museum's ability to borrow art.

Johnson was in his office in the Seagram Building when he received word of the fire. He left at once, running the three blocks west to find Fifty-third Street jammed with thirty-five emergency service vehicles that had responded to the three-alarm call. By that time a woman had already been retrieved from his own fifth-floor office at the museum; terrified, she had found her way there through the smoke, broken the window, and thrown her shoes and purse out to capture the attention of the firemen below, who raced up to the rescue. Rubin Geller, an electrician working on the renovation, was not so lucky. In the thick black smoke he could not find a way out. According to an investigative report by the National Fire Protection Association, he had left claw marks in the walls in his desperate and futile efforts to free himself. More than thirty firefighters were treated for injuries, most resulting from smoke inhalation. Miraculously, no other staffers or patrons were injured.

That could not be said about the collection. Nine works were destroyed beyond repair, including two prized canvases by Monet. Scores required conservation to remove the residue of black smoke. The works Johnson had given survived without permanent injury, but the event sent him into a deep funk. When a secretary expressed her relief that there wasn't more human cost, Johnson replied, "I don't care about the people. It's the art that I'm worried about."

As it turned out, the disaster inured to his benefit. By the time the museum reopened, in early October, it was clear that a major new expansion was required in response to the growing popularity of its programs and its holdings. At the time of the fire, the museum had space to exhibit less than 15 percent of its permanent collection. In this sense, the timing of the fire was fortuitous, for it roughly aligned with the museum's upcoming thirtieth anniversary, in November of 1959. That marked the perfect occasion to launch a $25 million capital campaign—an astronomical figure at the time, the largest ever undertaken by an American museum—and to unveil the model for the expansion that this money would support. Who better to produce this new design than Philip Johnson, the celebrated house architect, who had been with the museum since its earliest days and now sat on its board of trustees?

The proposal Johnson answered with was, in a word, disappointing, especially insofar as Frank Lloyd Wright, whom Johnson considered a superannuated figure, was upending the very idea of what a museum building could be with the Guggenheim, just a short trip up Fifth Avenue. The principal feature of Johnson's proposal for MoMA was an eight-story building that would face Fifty-fourth Street and serve as the new primary entry to and gallery space for the museum, completely reversing its polarity. Were it completed, the original building by Philip Goodwin and Edward Durell Stone that Johnson had considered a personal and architectural affront would have been relegated to back-of-house status, with its entry lobby reconfigured for special exhibitions.

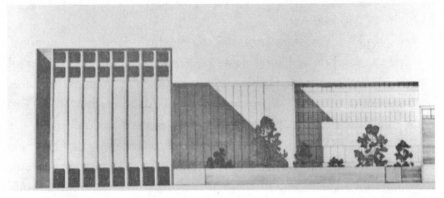

Johnson's plan for the expansion of the Museum of Modern Art on its thirtieth anniversary. Eerily similar to Ed Stone's gallery for Huntington Hartford. (Collection of the author)

This act of architectural retribution might have passed muster if Johnson's own design wasn't so banal. Johnson's new wing was a massive, windowless block skinned in white travertine, with pilasters running up the sides, an extrusion to eight stories of his Sheldon Memorial Art Gallery. The concept seemed like the product of satire: the Museum of Modern Art, the quintessential New York institution, modeled on a building in, of all places, *Nebraska*. Functionally it was a nonstarter. There was nothing to advertise the new entry, merely an open arcade at the base. At the very top were two rows of square windows in rounded frames, bringing natural light only to floors reserved for offices and facilities for the trustees.

The irony of ironies was that this design bore a striking resemblance to the museum that Edward Durell Stone was designing concurrently for a site on Columbus Circle, which was itself intended as a rejoinder to the Museum of Modern Art. The so-called Gallery of Modern Art was the progeny of Huntington Hartford, heir to the A&P supermarket fortune, a collector of nineteenth- and twentieth-century art, but not of the abstract variety favored by the likes of Alfred Barr and Philip Johnson. To build the museum that would house his collection, Hartford commissioned Stone on the grounds that he was both a practitioner of the "ballet school" form of modern classicism reviled by the doctrinaire modernists he detested, and because hiring him was a thumb in the eye to the Museum of Modern Art.

Yet Stone's design for Huntington—which would be famously derided by Ada Louise Huxtable as a "die-cut Venetian palazzo on lollypops"—appeared remarkably similar to Johnson's rebuke to Stone's original building for MoMA: both were blank travertine boxes with open arcades at the base, punctured by rows of windows only at the top. Stone's was more kitschy, but the principal difference was that the trustees of the Museum of Modern Art were not so foolish as to build Johnson's fantasy. Indeed, one of their prime objections was that it would have cast Johnson's own sculpture garden in permanent shadow. Johnson had to be saved from himself.

Johnson was sent back to the drawing board, but in the meantime the design brief changed. In 1960 E. Parmelee Prentice, the daughter of John D. Rockefeller (Abby Aldrich Rockefeller's aunt), agreed to will two beaux arts townhouses directly east of the museum to the institution upon her death, which came less than two years later. Johnson's professed dedication to the principles of historic preservation did not preclude him from demolishing those nineteenth-century buildings, which he replaced with his own new East Wing. With it, the original Goodwin and Stone museum now had Johnson-designed bookends: the 1951 Grace Rainey Rogers Wing to the west, and this new wing to the east, which mirrored that previous addition of blackened steel-and-glass, but this time with gently rounded windows Johnson compared to televisions. Behind it, the eight-story travertine block Johnson had originally proposed was reduced to a two-story structure, the Garden Wing, fronted by broad steps that extended the sculpture garden up to a rooftop terrace.

The 1964 East Wing expansion of the Museum of Modern Art, with television-shaped windows. (© The Museum of Modern Art / Licensed by SCALA / Art Resource, NY)

Ada Louise Huxtable—hardly the most objective source, given her history with both the museum and Johnson—extolled the design's virtues in the *Times*. "If steel can be said to be subtle and sensuous, it is here," she wrote. "The all-glass and metal facade has not been handled in such handsome fashion since the vogue for cast-iron fronts in the late nineteenth century." Her praise extended beyond the facade to every aspect of the building, from its negotiation of programmatic elements — in particular, the expanded lobby — to its relationship to the street. "The word for all this is professional, in its highest and most knowledgeable sense; the ultimate compliment in a field rife with uneasy dilettantism." For Johnson, that was the ultimate compliment, for it cut against his deepest insecurity: his sense of inferiority, that he was just a fake, a follower, a man without originality. In years to come, however, she would use just that word, dilettante, against him.

Johnson had other figures from his past that he could count on, not least being the newly minted governor of New York, Nelson Rockefeller. He remained the final authority at MoMA, even after his 1959 election. It was through him that Johnson was able to secure the job of remaking the museum, despite talk of insider dealing. There was also Lincoln Kirstein, who Johnson now considered his closest friend. Kirstein had fully forgiven him for his fascist *rumspringa,* and his respect for Johnson's intellect and talent had grown to the point that he considered him America's preeminent architect. Their aesthetic proclivities were neatly aligned. When Kirstein founded New York City Ballet as a vessel for Russian-born choreographer George Balanchine, it was to serve as an outlet for his vision in which the modern and the classical were conjoined. This duality was plainly evident in two of the choreographer's most celebrated recent works: *Allegro Brillante,* a sixteen-minute distillation of classical ballet with a score by Tchaikovsky, and *Agon,* an exercise in high modernism with black-and-white costumes and a score by Stravinsky.

Given their friendship and shared sensibility, it was natural that Kirstein chose Johnson to design a theater for his ballet company. Johnson already had some experience in this direction; in 1946 he renovated the public spaces for the associated School of American Ballet, a small, pro bono job.

The discussions between Johnson and Kirstein about what a theater for dance might look like had begun back then, but with little agreement. Kirstein, the company director, cared little for public space; his concerns were for back-of-house functions such as rehearsal space, dressing rooms, and offices. Johnson cared not a whit for these things; he was not a dancer and had little taste for the medium. The performance he cared about was that of the audience. He made this clear to Kirstein in a letter of 1949. "In regard to the attitude toward designing theaters, you say that I design too much for the 'house' and not enough for the action behind the proscenium. I see what you mean of course, but....I think it enhances the emotional pleasure of the parting of the curtains to be sitting in an emotionally arousing space....I would almost say that you

The Promenade of the State Theater, one of New York's great rooms. (Esto / Ezra Stoller)

The New York State Theater at Lincoln Center, 1964. Authoritarian pomp with a side of cosmopolitan glamour. (Esto / Ezra Stoller)

cannot enjoy a spectacle if there is nothing but the focus of the performance. You must have ambiance."

More than a decade later, when Johnson built that theater for Kirstein, the design emphasis unquestionably tilted toward "ambiance." Although the two had imagined it on its own in the city—Kirstein wanted it plopped into Central Park—it was now to be a part of Lincoln Center, the performing arts complex to be built on a vast urban renewal site cleared by Robert Moses on New York's Upper West Side. What had begun as a plan to find a new home for the Metropolitan Opera had expanded to include a theater for the New York Philharmonic, a repertory theater, a home for the Juilliard School, and a permanent home for Kirstein's City Ballet. The man conscripted into the job of making this massive complex a reality was John D. Rockefeller III, an unlikely choice in that his only significant achievement in philanthropy had come in leading the Asia Society through the making of its Johnson-designed headquarters. Given the larger portfolio, he proved an able director and fundraiser, though for the ballet theater he had the assistance of his younger brother, the state's governor.

Nelson Rockefeller had been close to Kirstein and Johnson for three decades, originally drawn together during MoMA's founding days, three family scions on the make. The three had even started a business together, Art International, to sell souvenir tchotchkes of Rockefeller Center while it was still rising out of the ground. This endeavor was quashed by the Rockefeller family before it became a reality—this was a bit too lowbrow for the family name, and Nelson was not then in a position to argue. At Lincoln Center, the three could collaborate on a real building, not one that would fit in a snow globe. To help pay for it, Rockefeller siphoned funds dedicated to the 1964 World's Fair, with the understanding that the theater would be used as a performance venue during that event. It would be named the New York State Theater, in honor of the people whose taxes paid for it.

Johnson's ambitions extended beyond the design of his own theater to the entire Lincoln Center complex. In that he was not alone. The designers of the different facilities constituted a list of architectural eminences jockeying for turf. Wallace Harrison, a member of the extended Rockefeller family, had been given the prime Met commission, and his partner, Max Abramovitz, the Philharmonic. Eero Saarinen got the repertory theater; Gordon Bunshaft, the presiding force at Skidmore, Owings & Merrill, the performing arts library; and Pietro Belluschi, the dean at MIT, the building for Juilliard. Johnson called them a bunch of "pushers-arounders."

Meetings of this group were held at the rarefied private clubhouse of the Century Association, an Italianate palazzo designed by McKim, Mead & White. The environment was gentlemanly but the behavior wasn't. Everyone wanted to be in charge, except for Harrison. He had been through the wringer as leader of the United Nations design team and was reluctant to place himself in the same unhappy position on the other side of town. Acrimony centered on the disposition of buildings on the site and the design guidelines to which the entire group would conform. That he was the least experienced member did not preclude Johnson from trying to impose his own ideas. "Being young and much too brash—I mean, I blush now thinking of the meetings we went to—I just assumed I might as well take over everyone's job," he recalled.

Among Johnson's rejected proposals was one that would have placed his theater on the site given over to Juilliard. The idea was to achieve added prominence for his theater by setting it apart. Given that extra breathing room, Johnson proposed a semicircular glass facade fronted by delicate concrete columns. The idea was shot down by the other architects, who were irritated at his hubris. Meanwhile, discussions about the overall site plan were complicated by Robert Moses's insistence that space be set aside for a park. This precluded the most obvious solution, which would have been to push all the venues to the perimeter of the superblock.

In a sly bit of strategic thinking, Johnson showed up at the meeting scheduled to break this impasse with a new master plan already drawn out, a move that infuriated his colleagues. "When I walked in with *that,* all the architects said, 'Well, Philip is trying to kill us all,' which of course

The embattled builders of Lincoln Center in 1959: (left to right) Edward Matthews, Johnson, Jo Mielziner, John D. Rockefeller III, Wallace Harrison, Eero Saarinen, Gordon Bunshaft, Max Abramovitz, and Pietro Belluschi. (Arnold Newman / Getty Images)

I was." That plan, with the three principal theaters clustered around an open plaza, became the point of departure for future discussions; it was largely adopted, along with Johnson's proposed design guidelines. These included the use of white travertine, matching scale for all theaters, and columns separated by twenty-foot bays for the theaters fronting the plaza. They all agreed, but nobody was particularly happy. That frustration was visible in a photo taken on November 28, 1959, with the prime movers arrayed around a model of the complex. By that time the architects were no longer on speaking terms. "Everybody pretty well hated everybody," Johnson remembered. "We just sat there glaring at the camera."

In addition to the site plan and guidelines, Johnson managed to secure the design of the central plaza. This was achieved through attrition—a slow wearing down of the others until they were willing to wash their hands of it. There was also a bit of horse-trading; Saarinen agreed to back Johnson in exchange for Johnson's giving Saarinen the freedom to design the space in front of his own building. It was an ugly process, but it turned out for the best. Johnson delivered what was then and remains one of the most pleasing public spaces in the city, with spokes and concentric circles of travertine emanating from a dancing central fountain. With its broad granite ledge at perfect sitting height, it became a favored meeting point for generations of visitors to the center, until it was needlessly replaced during renovations to the complex in 2010.

When it came time to design the New York State Theater, Johnson was given free rein. Balanchine's sole requests were a large proscenium and a large stage; other than that, he and the company staff had little meaningful contact with Johnson and his design team. This was fine by Johnson, who considered Balanchine an idiot savant concerned only with dance. That condescension extended to the ballet company—a collection of "blithering idiots," according to their architect. The lack of communication resulted in a series of design miscues—the wrong kind of stage floor, a too-small orchestra pit, offices and classrooms without natural light—only some of which could be corrected. Urbanistically the building was a disappointment, leaving a long blank wall facing Amsterdam Avenue.

But in other, more important ways, the theater proved a success. Although it appears to be a simple box, it is in fact quite complex; a structural tour de force, with hidden steel trusses spanning its width to support a giant cantilevered upper gallery of five hundred seats. That structure was disguised—a Miesian no-no—behind the theater's gilded ceiling, itself marked by a massive globe of circular lights. To stand beneath it was to be enclosed within an enormous jewel box. The "continental" orchestra seating, with no central aisles and extra legroom between rows, was also highly unusual for an American theater. The arrangement meant the most valuable real estate in the theater could be given over to seating, not circulation. While some patrons complained they had to climb over one another to get to their seats, the design fostered a sense of community within that audience, and indeed developed a reputation for initiating long-term friendships among ballet subscribers.

That sense of community was masterfully achieved in the theater's second-floor promenade, one of New York's great public rooms. Ascending to it from below was, like one of Balanchine's ballets, an exercise in movement and drama. Patrons entering the building in the compressed space of the lobby were swept up a pair of grand staircases at either end of the room. These deposited them in the multistory space of the promenade, watched over by Elie Nadelman's woozy oversize sculptures and surrounded by balconies fronted by brass filigree. Johnson was unabashed in the inspiration: the Paris Opera of Charles Garnier, the sine qua non of beaux arts magnificence. He had won his debate with Kirstein, and the theater would be defined, both for good and for ill, by the decision to privilege the spectacle of theater over back-of-house functionality.

Critical reception was mixed, though the voices that mattered most were effusive. Henry-Russell Hitchcock celebrated it as the heir to Grand Central Terminal. Ada Louise Huxtable, who generally held Lincoln Center in disdain as a reactionary "artistic failure," could not help admiring Johnson's building, in particular its grand public room. "Like the rest of the theater, the promenade is sumptuous, elegant, sophisticated and seriously beautiful," she wrote. The only real sour note came from Virgil Thomson, who compared the promenade to a prison courtyard.

The impeccable Dumbarton Oaks, 1963, gallery in Washington, DC.
(Esto / Ezra Stoller)

During the prolonged design and construction of Lincoln Center, Johnson undertook and completed another job that came to him through the auspices of Kirstein: a new wing for Harvard University's Dumbarton Oaks Research Library and Collection in Washington, D.C. Kirstein had been an important figure in the Harvard arts community since his undergraduate days as founder of the journal *Hound & Horn* and the Harvard Society of Contemporary Art. When the school turned to him to build a new home for the pre-Columbian art collection of Robert Woods Bliss and Mildred Barnes Bliss—whom he knew socially—he again looked to Johnson.

The gallery for Dumbarton Oaks remains one of Johnson's most satisfying and beloved designs. The space was divided like a tic-tac-toe board into nine squares, but with rounded corners. Each square was capped by a shallow dome and supported by thick columns trimmed in dark wood. The central square was left as an open atrium, and the exterior walls' floor-to-ceiling glass looked out onto dense woods. It was, in truth, not the easiest place to mount work, but as architectural space it conveyed a sense of sybaritic leisure that verged on the illicit—a conflation of a sultan's playroom with an art gallery. "A small, sophisticated jewel of a modern building," wrote Huxtable, "it gives pleasure in every sense; visually, tactically, spatially and as a setting for a collection of exceptional artifacts."

The unstated subtext of much of the commentary on this building, and on the flamboyant State Theater decorative program, was that these spaces reflected Johnson's homosexuality. Whether that was meant approvingly or not was a matter of differing perspectives, both architectural and cultural. That Johnson was gay was at this point an open secret, but only now was his sexuality beginning to show publicly in his architecture. The Brick House boudoir, with its walls of golden fabric and lights on dimmers, was an unabashedly erotic space, but it was private. The hidden gentleman's club tucked into the Four Seasons was never more than a fantasy. But the baubles of the State Theater and the seductively curvaceous forms of Dumbarton Oaks were right out in the open, and those paying close attention noticed.

Reviews, both positive and negative, inevitably addressed this

The false-scale pavilion on the pond at Johnson's New Canaan estate, 1962. (Esto / Farrell Grehan)

character with coded language that hinted at homosexuality without stating it. *Time,* for instance, described Johnson's lighting fixtures at the State Theater as "Cyclopean rhinestones." For Johnson, breaking out of modernism was not just an aesthetic choice or a means of rattling the status quo; it was a declaration of his own self through design. He paid a price for doing so. It was no accident that, unlike so many of his peers and despite his high professional standing, he had virtually no corporate clients. His fascist history didn't help, a sensitive topic for corporations, especially those—Ford and IBM, for instance—that had their own uncomfortable wartime histories of complicity with Nazi Germany.

Because Johnson was Johnson, he couldn't help reinforcing the perception that he was a provocative threat to norms—the very opposite of the stable, heterosexual company man sought after by corporate America. The toy pavilion he built for himself on his New Canaan estate in 1962 was an embodiment of this attitude in arched, precast concrete. It was, ostensibly, a means of testing the arcaded forms he planned to employ at Lincoln Center. Set by the pond in the valley beneath the Glass House, it had a pinwheel plan, with four arcaded arms extending out over the water. But the trick of it was that it was made to false scale, with six-foot ceilings; viewed from the grassy terrace of the Glass House, it looked far bigger than it was in actuality. The visual joke became a physical one when visitors stepped into the compressed space under its gold-painted ceiling.

His inspiration, he claimed, was the chambers for the court dwarfs at the Ducal Palace of Mantua. "The aim is to make giants of the visitors," he said. "The design is aimed at the amusement we all feel of the miniature and the complicated; the pleasure of hiding among a forest of columns." There was also a broader purpose: "I wanted deliberately to fly in the face of the 'modern' tradition of functionalist architecture by tying on to an older, nobler tradition of garden architecture," he claimed. *Dwarf's chambers? Nobler?* This was something, coming from Johnson, the erstwhile champion of Mies van der Rohe's austere minimalism.

Not everyone saw the humor. According to one critic, the pavilion was "one step further along the road to complete architectural decadence." The author was just getting rolling. "It is indeed hard to believe that this is the same man who once designed and built the thirteeen-year-old famous glass house, in which he still lives, or that a former admirer and collaborator of Mies can, in a few years, come to conceive such feeble forms as these." Johnson responded, tongue in cheek, that he was flattered by the attention, with its "overtones of Puritan disapproval," and begged for more: "We need more of this pointed, beautifully written criticism in this country!"

Johnson continued the expansion of his New Canaan grounds with an art gallery to maintain his rapidly growing collection, in particular the Pop works that spoke directly to him. "It is the most important art movement in the world today," he told *Time* in 1963. "It is a very sharp reaction against abstract expressionism, and as such, it is a great relief to see, because we recognize the pretty girls and the pop bottles." Inasmuch, it was an analogue to his own work, which was moving beyond the doctrinaire abstraction of modernism to a new place of representation and provocation. From 1960 to 1965, when the gallery opened, he embarked on an epic buying spree, acquiring scores of works, among them pieces by Lee Bontecou, John Chamberlain, Jim Dine, Mark di Suvero, Dan Flavin, Lucio Fontana, Robert Indiana, Jasper Johns, Donald Judd, Roy Lichtenstein, Robert Morris, Claes Oldenburg, Larry Poons, Bridget Riley, James Rosenquist, Lucas Samaras, Frank Stella, Paul Thek, Wayne Thiebaud, and Andy Warhol.

Some of these works—Warhol's portrait of Marilyn Monroe on a field of gold, Lichtenstein's girl with a beach ball—would be donated to the Museum of Modern Art and become defining mainstays of the collection. He purchased these works on his own, because they spoke to him, and not because he was told to by Alfred Barr—a common misperception—or by his young partner David Whitney, who began working at the Castelli gallery after a failed attempt striking out as a dealer on his own. "Philip made his own judgment every time," said Ivan Karp, who was then associate director at Castelli and sold Johnson many of the works he purchased there. "He was a singular presence in the gallery, because he looked at things with such intensity and passion and perception."

Johnson's underground art gallery, 1965, with entry modeled on the Treasury of Atreus. (Esto / Ezra Stoller)

To display and safeguard his treasures, Johnson built what was effectively a large vault into a berm on his estate. The entry to this gallery, between sloping walls of red stone, was modeled on the approach to the Treasury of Atreus in Mycenae. Through its front door was a compressed corridor that led into the gallery proper, which was defined by four intersecting circular spaces, each a different diameter, so that in plan it had the appearance of a distorted cloverleaf. To compensate for the relatively small space, Johnson mounted the paintings on floor-to-ceiling, carpet-covered panels that could be rotated like the poster displays of a museum gift shop. It was a neat effect, but there was something inherently disturbing about this bunkerlike space; for those who knew about his Nazi period it was hard, very hard, not to think there was, at least subconsciously, some reference to the dreaded architecture of Hitler. This perception was only reinforced with the appearance of Frank Stella's *Brzozdowce I*, from a series inspired by Polish villages destroyed by the Nazis. That took some kind of perverse hubris; Johnson had claimed the Nazi annihilation of Jewish shtetls as inspiration for the design of the Glass House. Now, in his own art bunker adjacent to it, he could look upon another aesthetic response to those atrocities, albeit by a Jewish artist.

The art gallery was one of a several subterranean projects Johnson built at the time, of vastly differing scales and for purposes that bore no relation to one another. In central Arkansas there was a library for Hendrix College, a small liberal arts school, and in the Cincinnati suburbs a private home, the Geier Residence, for a wealthy contractor. The projects were so dispersed that his peers and the critical world barely noticed, but within the Johnson office there was concern: what exactly was Johnson doing burying his work underground? The truth, he admitted privately, was that the three projects reflected a crisis of confidence. He was perceptive enough to see that, in the wake of Lincoln Center, his brand of "ballet school" modern classicism was an architectural dead-end. A second-rater like Edward Durell Stone might continue with it, but for Johnson that in itself was proof that it was the wrong track. But what would come next? He admired Venturi, but he simply did not have the design acuity for the kind of "complexity and contradiction" that

The futuristic New York State Pavilion for the 1964 World's Fair, like nothing else in Johnson's career. (Esto / Ezra Stoller)

characterized the work he was doing with Denise Scott Brown. Without any clear direction, he pulled an earth blanket over his head, hoping nobody would notice while he figured out a path to the future.

The search for a new and more robust architectural expression was first evidenced in the New York State Pavilion for the 1964 World's Fair, another commission that came to Johnson through Nelson Rockefeller. There was no precedent for this unique, and uniquely weird, structure in his catalog, and there would be nothing like it after. The "Tent of Tomorrow" was envisioned as something approaching a fair within the fair, a colossal oval pavilion that could host all manner of events and activities: music, dancing, theater, receptions, displays, vendors for food and drink. Inside it was a whirl of color, the floor a map of New York State sponsored by Texaco. Structurally the pavilion was a daring showpiece defined by sixteen immense concrete piers, each 100 feet tall. Multicolored plastic panels, suspended from a system of steel cables, formed a glowing canopy

302

over the 50,000-square-foot space below. This "velarium," according to its own hype, was the largest "rigid suspension roof" in the world.

Standing next to this spectacular structure were three stalklike towers—60, 150, and 226 feet tall, respectively—with glass-enclosed elevators running up their sides. A trip up deposited visitors on broad, disc-shaped platforms with restaurants and observation decks. The whole thing looked like an assembly from outer space, a docking station for flying saucers. (Indeed, Barry Sonnenfeld used it for exactly that purpose in his 1997 film, *Men in Black*.)

A third element to the pavilion complex was a drum-shaped "Cyclorama" theater for the projection of films in 360 degrees. Though far less interesting architecturally than its neighbors, it was this structure that created controversy—though the problem wasn't the design itself but what Johnson tacked onto it.

Robert Moses, the power-broking fair commissioner, had shown so little concern for the visual arts that the day after Christmas in 1961—three years before the fair opening—the editorial board of *Art in America* dispatched a letter to him, complaining that this absence constituted an unacceptable failure of purpose. Among its signatories were numerous individuals with connections to MoMA, among them Ada Louise Huxtable, James Thrall Soby, Beaumont Newhall, Dorothy Miller, and John McAndrew. Moses caved, and Johnson was given rein to commission a series of large-scale works for the Cyclorama's exterior.

He was, contemporaneously, responsible for the art program at the State Theater. Each case was an obligation that gave him pause. "Commissioning decorative works of art for monumental buildings is dangerous in any age," he wrote. Artists did not like to be subordinate to architects, and architects did not like to be subordinate to artists. The works he selected for the State Theater, for the most part, successfully balanced this dynamic. Among the highlights was a Lee Bontecou assemblage that, in his words, fit "as well as a baroque statue in the niche of a baroque hall." His one regret concerned the piece that was and remains the great masterpiece of that collection, a vertical Jasper Johns numbers composition in metallic silver that he placed uncomfortably in a space better suited to a horizontal work. "We will fix it—some day," he wrote. Alas, it remains in the same awkward position, and now behind protective glass to boot.

For the exterior of the Cyclorama, Johnson looked to the younger generation of artists who were coming to dominate his personal collection. There was one of Roy Lichtenstein's inflated cartoon women, a study in geometry and color by Ellsworth Kelly, a bent metal "cartouche" by John Chamberlain, and a sign that read EAT from Robert Indiana, along with works by Robert Rauschenberg, James Rosenquist, and—temporarily—Andy Warhol. "I frankly love my choices," Johnson wrote in *Art in America*. But the affection was not universal. It was Warhol's submission—a grid of screened mug shots of New York's most wanted criminals—that was at issue. The state's lawyers were concerned that the work could somehow provoke legal action. Warhol's proposed response was to replace the mug shots of criminals with mug shot–style portraits of Robert Moses. That, obviously, was a nonstarter. The ultimate decision was to whitewash the work with silver paint, with Warhol publicly claiming that he had voluntarily withdrawn it—a half-truth at best.

The controversy blew over quickly, and it left little mark on the reception of the pavilion. Huxtable, as was becoming routine, extolled the virtues of a Johnson project in the *Times*. A "sophisticated folly," she called it. "This is 'carnival' with class." Perhaps that was pushing it, but it was popular and remains a kind of derelict monument even today. Johnson, for his part, was exceedingly grateful to Rockefeller for his patronage, both for the pavilion and the State Theater. "I have always wished I could express to you in some way what you personally have meant to my career, but surely the crowning experience is this spring with not only these two buildings, but our beloved museum as well," he wrote. "Please be assured of my continuing gratitude for your faith in me. How well I remember the beginning of Art Incorporated, back when we were both too young to know what we were doing. It has been a wonderful life ever since."

That sentiment was appealing, and while it was accurate insofar as the generally charmed nature of Johnson's existence, it did not fully reflect the reality of his present. In his practice he was still searching for direction, shoving buildings underground as he tried to reinvent himself.

(Ironically, *Esquire* named him one of America's "decisive dozen" in July of 1960, along with television executive Robert Sarnoff, baseball commissioner Ford Frick, publisher Alfred A. Knopf, and New York machine politico Carmine DeSapio, among others.) That aesthetic struggle was accompanied by a broader sense of despair about the direction of America in the postwar years. For some time Johnson had been warning about the destructive nature of the automobile, "the greatest catastrophe in the entire history of city architecture." He now saw that danger compounded by urban-renewal programs that decimated the urban fabric, and by a decline in the quality of building.

Johnson responded with an activism, in public and within professional circles, that was reminiscent of his political conversion in the 1930s. In his lectures he criticized America's business-oriented culture and the so-called military-industrial complex. In particular he railed against real-estate speculation, which he blamed for city-destroying, low-quality architecture that could be quickly flipped for profit. "Is it right to buy land as cheaply as possible and to build a building on it and, in six months, to move out and to make 200% to 300% profit, if you can?" he asked, in 1965. "That is not considered stealing. It is not considered bootlegging or whore-mongering. They're always considered worse. I can hardly understand that; I didn't know whoremongers made that much money."

Was it any wonder his small firm was struggling to attract large clients and skimming along on the margins of solvency? Abstract attacks on speculation might have been excusable, but Johnson excoriated America's leading corporations by name. General Motors, General Electric, and Pan Am all came under fire for putting up buildings he considered cut-rate. There was a veiled anti-Semitic subtext to his argument, "speculation" being coded as a putatively Jewish endeavor. There was irony, too, for it was bootlegging that had made possible the building he considered the prime counterexample to this trend and an exemplar of civic virtue. That was the Seagram Building, commissioned by the Jewish Bronfman family, whose fortunes blossomed with illicit trade during Prohibition.

Johnson's statist, Keynesian economic prescriptions also harked back to his wayward years of the 1930s, though they were now stripped of the more unsettling eugenic, political, and militaristic ideas of that time. "We can never go bankrupt hiring our own people to work," he said. He called for a massive public works program to be funded by a new $1,000 tax on automobiles, a halving of the federal budget for road building—"spend it on places for roads to go to"—and a 10 percent "tax on war," by which he meant the military budget. The Johnson who had once thrilled to the spectacle of the Wehrmacht's blitzkrieg into Poland had matured and was now opposed to war on principle. With this infusion of capital into the public coffers, Johnson would bring beauty back to the American landscape— urban, suburban, rural—and free it from the dual curses of finance capitalism and the automobile. He could build twenty Lincoln Centers a year, monuments that would be remembered for generations, like the pyramids. "What dream cities we could build," he wrote. "What a heaven on earth."

Johnson's own hypocrisy undercut his criticism of American business culture. He freely admitted his own culpability in the system he decried. "I realize I am as great a sinner as the rest of them," he wrote. He had engaged in speculation himself, using the proceeds to build his art collection. His own Glass House, in suburban Connecticut, would not have been possible without the automobile. In 1966, when Buick wanted to advertise the new Electra 225 on the Glass House lawn, with newlyweds pictured in the background and two boys using his Jacques Lipchitz sculpture as an obstacle in a game of tag, he was more than happy to cash the check. Admitting his own guilt had always been Johnson's strategy for neutralizing those who called him out for his cynicism. When a Yale student, at an event hosted by Vincent Scully, stood up and accused him of being "nothing but a cocktails-on-the-terrace architect," Johnson replied—after a suitable pause for effect: "That is the nicest compliment I have ever received."

It was one thing to disarm a college student. But as the 1960s progressed, Johnson had increasing difficulty ducking accountability for his cynicism, even among his own acolytes. At a 1961 panel sponsored by the Graham Foundation, Peter Blake, one of his protégés, excoriated him for celebrating the "creative, delicious chaos" of cities from the safe distance of his New Canaan estate. The friendly-fire attack posited that not only had he retreated in person, but intellectually; that a sense of nihilism had prompted him to wash his hands of architecture's societal obligations so he could devote himself entirely to the art of building. "I like to build for myself now," he told Yale students in 1965. "I should not be so old that I have to retire from the battle, but that is the way you get, if you let these facts of American life get you down."

In February of that year CBS aired "This Is Philip Johnson" in prime time, the first in a series of what it called "action biographies" of cultural figures. Johnson was shown at work and at play at the Glass House, and if there were any allusions that he might be a man of the people, his performance dispelled them. Philip Johnson, according to Philip Johnson, didn't believe in mistakes—an assertion that came as news to anyone who knew him. As for architectural advice, he allowed that every American should own a gazebo. The *Herald Tribune* pilloried him as "a glib torrent of witticisms and clichés."

Like so much with Johnson, the talk of retirement and the superficial chatter was an act disguising his insecurity. He had, in fact, not retired. The very idea was antithetical to his personality. And in a genuinely uncynical manner, he had mounted an active defense of America's architectural heritage, put under siege in the name of progress and profit. He put his time, his money, and his reputation into the endeavor, and before it was fashionable to do so. In New York the situation was especially dire, with destruction ranging from people's palaces like Ebbets Field and the Polo Grounds to the Fifth Avenue "Gold Coast" mansions of Gilded Age society. Johnson could be a culprit, as he was in the expansion of the Museum of Modern Art, but he was also a compelling advocate, an elegant spokesman who could straddle both the modernist and the traditionalist factions. Among the leading defenders of the city's beaux arts history was his old friend from Harvard, John Barrington Bayley. Ivan Karp, the art dealer who sold him Pop paintings for Leo Castelli, formed the Anonymous Arts Recovery Society, dedicated to salvaging architectural details from the city's condemned buildings.

Johnson's advocacy extended beyond New York. He made headlines in Omaha, Nebraska, for his plea to save that city's 1892 post office, a magnificent pile in the style of H. H. Richardson, which was threatened with replacement by a generic modern box. "If Omaha allows that fine old building to go, you people will be kicking yourselves around the block for years," he told the *Evening World Herald*. In Chicago, he put his own money behind an effort to save an actual Richardson landmark, his 1886 Glessner House, a masterwork of Gilded Age opulence. "All Americans should help to save Chicago's architectural landmarks in the same manner that all of France would help save Notre Dame if it were doomed for destruction," he told the *Chicago Tribune*. To that end he offered to pay fifty percent of the purchase price, up to thirty-five thousand dollars, if a local nonprofit would match it. That proposal fell through, but when a preservation group arranged to buy it at a lower price, he chipped in ten thousand dollars to make it happen.

At home in New York, the preservation movement galvanized around the fight to save Pennsylvania Station, the monumental beaux arts train depot that architects McKim, Mead & White modeled on the Roman Baths of Caracalla. By the early sixties the building had been under siege for some time, a victim of ill-conceived renovations and general neglect. Writing in *The New Yorker*, Lewis Mumford lamented that "no one now entering Pennsylvania Station for the first time could, without clairvoyance,

The Action Group for Better Architecture in New York (AGBANY) rally to save Penn Station, with Jane Jacobs, Aline Louchheim Saarinen, and Johnson on the barricades. (Walter Daran / Hulton Archive / Getty Images)

know how good it used to be in comparison to the almost indescribable blotch that has been made of it." After years of speculation about its future, in 1961 plans were announced to demolish the old station, still owned by the Pennsylvania Railroad, and replace it with a complex of retail, office space, and an arena, the relocated Madison Square Garden.

Backlash from the architectural community was immediate. A group of young architects, led by Norval White and Elliot Wilensky, formed the Action Group for Better Architecture in New York, or AGBANY, as a protest organization. They recruited Johnson to lead an advisory committee of heavy hitters that would include the architects John Johansen and Paul Rudolph, along with cultural figures such as Mumford, Eleanor Roosevelt, Alfred A. Knopf, and Fannie Hurst. Johnson's prominence and savvy with the press prompted the group to make him, along with Aline Louchheim Saarinen, one of its two official spokespersons. His first opportunity in that capacity was August 2, 1962, the blazingly hot afternoon on which AGBANY held its first protest, with several hundred marchers parading before the station's enormous Tuscan columns. Johnson was there, front and center in a dapper gray suit, photographed alongside Saarinen and Jane Jacobs. He had not come alone, either. With him was his friend Eliza Bliss Parkinson from the Museum of Modern Art board, a genuine member of New York society manning the barricades.

The press was receptive if somewhat condescending, the protesters treated like well-meaning aliens despite the presence among them of representatives from the city's blue-blooded aristocracy. "One of the city's strangest and most heartening picket lines," the *Times* called it. Of all the coverage, it was only the article in *Time* that AGBANY's leaders found wanting. The quote from developer Irving Felt was particularly galling: "Fifty years from now, when it's time for our Center to be torn down, there will be a new group of architects who will protest."

AGBANY's best efforts were not enough to stop the destruction of Penn Station. Demolition alone took years, beginning in the fall of 1963 and ending only in the summer of 1966. Its replacement is universally loathed, an architectural pox that would engender little outcry if it were to be erased from the urban fabric, Felt's admonition notwithstanding. Vincent Scully, better than anyone, summed up the pathetic trajectory that began with the annihilation of the old pile: "Through it one entered the city like a god. Perhaps it was really too much. One scuttles in now like a rat."

The repercussions extended far beyond the loss of the station. The fight effectively launched the preservation movement in America, galvanizing a public appalled by the wanton destruction of local and national history. Johnson, instrumental in the fight, would continue to be an active participant. It should be no surprise that he found himself on both sides of the battle.

Johnson inspecting the wreckage of the plane that crashed with him on it in 1966. (Getty Research Institute, Los Angeles)

CHAPTER 13

Third City

Architecture in the twentieth century can only mean city building.
—Philip Johnson

On the evening of Friday, August 19, 1966, Philip Johnson was in a rush, as usual. He was stuck in Washington, D.C. with Richard Foster, his chief deputy, trying to get a flight back to New York after a client meeting. All the commercial airlines were booked or delayed. Impatient and looking for alternatives, he was tipped off to a charter flying into Danbury, Connecticut. It seemed like a perfect solution: Danbury was a short ride to the Glass House in New Canaan, and also convenient for Foster, who lived in nearby Wilton.

Five businessmen and a pilot were on board the Piper Cherokee when it took off at five thirty. Two hours later, with the plane cruising over Connecticut, its single engine gave out and the craft veered sharply down. "There was no fear, no panic," Johnson told the *Stamford Advocate* the next morning. "We tightened our seatbelts and started gliding because we had no motor." The pilot, moonlighting from his regular duties flying for United Airlines, diverted to nearby Westchester Airport. Johnson was glib in recounting the experience. "The pilot said, 'Gentlemen, we're going to make it.' Then a little later he said, 'Gentlemen, we're not going to make it.'" The plane clipped a pear tree on approach, and came down hard just short of the runway. The pilot survived uninjured, but Foster and one other passenger were hospitalized. For the next year, Foster had trouble moving. Johnson walked away unscathed.

The episode encapsulated Johnson's life in the tumultuous sixties: as the world around him seemed to come apart, he carried on, inconvenienced and unsettled but essentially unharmed. In his own work he was still unmoored, searching for a new style or idiom to adopt as his own. The "ballet school" modern classicism that he had taken up was no longer fashionable, and increasingly discredited as fascistic, a particularly damaging association given his personal history. But as he found himself out of step with the times, Johnson faced more than just an aesthetic crossroads. He was now questioning the entire modernist project. His criticism dovetailed with that made by journalist-turned-advocate Jane Jacobs in her 1961 book and cri de coeur, *The Death and Life of Great American Cities*. Though its reformist goals were benign, the modern movement had to answer for disastrous towers-in-the-park housing projects and decimated downtowns that privileged cars over people.

"Our Ugly Cities" was a lecture Johnson delivered repeatedly in the mid-1960s. The title said it all: the city had been grievously harmed by highways and the demolition of historic architecture, by cheap building and crass advertising. "Ugliness, ugliness, ugliness." Beyond speeches, he took on a greater role as a public advocate. He had been nominated to President Kennedy's Commission on Fine Arts in 1963, a nomination that was stalled for an investigation into his behavior during the 1930s. "He has repented, I am told, and is over-compensating for his earlier point of view," wrote Dan H. Fenn in a memorandum to Kennedy. Arthur Schlesinger also spoke on his behalf. But Johnson, perhaps fearing rejection, recused himself from the appointment before a decision could be made in his favor.

Just a few years later, when President Lyndon Johnson chose more than 100 panelists for a conference on "natural beauty," Johnson was left off. Worse still, no architect was invited to speak, an insult that left Johnson "humiliated for the profession." It was a diminishment he ascribed to architecture's failure to address the changing nature and scale of the issues facing the discipline. "The new problems of today are those of urban design," he told an audience of professionals at the Architectural League of New York. "It is *the* problem of our time." In a new climate of intensive speculative and public development fixated on costs, architects, once visionary, were now dismissed as effete stylists, incidental members in the cast of building professionals. Johnson was complicit in this transformation. It was he, after all, who had defined the architect as a stylist in his work as a museum curator, and his fame as a designer himself rested largely on his own house, an unrivaled exercise in suburban aesthetics. Now he wanted more: to be a city builder, to design streets and parks and housing developments, and to do so freed of the imperative of finance capitalism.

The president passed over Johnson, but the New York governor, Johnson's old friend and patron Nelson Rockefeller, did not. When he launched his own conference on natural beauty, in 1966, he made Johnson a leading figure, the chairman of a committee on urban planning. Among the far-reaching prescriptions it advocated: a tree bank, tax incentives for good landscaping, the shielding of gas stations on highways, urban traffic calming, landscape preservation, mixed-use building, use of water both for transportation and as an amenity, a ban on the sale of public land to private investors, special commissions for Times Square and Harlem, education for planning boards, and the teaching of urban design and aesthetics in high school. "We believe," Johnson wrote, "that our towns should be designed for the humans who live in them, that we must keep the communities from falling prey to highways and other bulldozers, on the one hand, and to bad architecture and faceless acres of buildings perpetrated even without architects, on the other. We recommend immediate action." Today, more than fifty years later, those proposals are either accepted wisdom or still pipe dreams among progressive advocates.

This was an intellectual about-face—and an entirely new direction for Johnson. His only practical experience in urban planning up to that point had been a 1955 design for a small uranium-mining town carved into the Canadian wilderness. The client was industrialist Joseph Hirshhorn, who would later endow an eponymous museum for modern art on The Mall in Washington, D.C. Johnson's plan was never realized, but a decade later he had a grander opportunity at city planning, and in the very neighborhood that was already the battleground over the future of the city: Greenwich Village. Jane Jacobs and other neighborhood advocates had recently won a major victory when they put a halt to Robert Moses's plans to expand vehicular traffic through Washington Square Park. The zone of contention now shifted to the south, in a protest against the proposed Lower Manhattan Expressway, an elevated highway that would run straight through the heart of SoHo.

Johnson opposed that project, but he wasn't quite so sensitive when it came to his own work in the area. Once again, his entrée was through an institutional client, New York University, which brought him in to take its motley collection of buildings around Washington Square Park and somehow create a unified campus. Johnson's solution to this challenge was a three-block-long, glassed-in pedestrian arcade that would stretch all the way from the park to Broadway. Flanking the arcade would be a series of what Johnson described as "fairly anonymous" academic buildings in red limestone, the centerpiece being a new library. The projected cost was $100 million.

Neighbors saw the proposed scheme for what it was: an attempt by the school to appropriate the park—and the entire Village—for itself. The flashpoint became the design of the library, a dreary red box inflated to ten stories. "All the glamour of Philip Johnson won't save that corner of the park from gloom," wrote Jacobs, an ally in the fight to save Penn Station but a fierce opponent here. By the time the library design was approved, in August of 1966, nearly thirty advocacy groups had joined forces against it. A lawsuit, with Jacobs and future mayor Ed Koch as sponsors, was tossed out of court. Delayed by controversy, the library didn't open until 1973.

When it did, it was bereft even of Johnson's putative "glamour." Dull on the exterior, the library was even more depressing within, where it was defined by an enormous full-height atrium, from which students could look up to see open floors guarded by carceral aluminum railings. The marble atrium floor, laid in a Escher-like pattern so that it appeared three-dimensional—an effect borrowed from the Renaissance—exacerbated the destabilizing nature of the space. When Virgil Thomson had accused the promenade at the State Theater of feeling like a prison courtyard, the attack seemed unfair, but here the analogy was unmistakable. In the early

Bobst Library, a book prison for New York University, 1973. (Esto / Ezra Stoller)

2000s the atrium became a disturbingly frequent place for student sui-cides. There was something about the space—oppressive and lonely—that contributed to a feeling of hopelessness. The run of deaths forced school administrators to glass in the building's open balconies. Even John-son knew it was a failure. "The big room started out all right. But some-how the marble floors and the stone walls don't go together," he would admit in the 1980s. "I mean it is very boring, indeed, just to pile up a lot of balconies. I didn't think it would be. The proportions are off. It's too tall for its width and the materials are funny. I don't know what else is wrong, probably a lot of things."

Washington Square managed to survive Johnson's architecture and remain a vibrant place. The dream of a pedestrian arcade—the most appealing part of his plan, though its mall style seemed out of spirit with the city—was never realized. The only building of serious merit to emerge from Johnson's work for NYU was the Hagop Kevorkian Center for Near Eastern Studies, a spare, five-story block with a taut asymmetric geometry that gave it a monumental presence despite its rather small size. Similar in form and affect, but somewhat larger in scale, was the Kunsthalle Biele-feld, his first institutional work on foreign soil. The museum, completed in 1966, was a red sandstone block with a cantilevered superstructure.

Taken together, these two buildings represented a new direction in Johnson's architecture, and not just in the attempt to work at an urban scale. The restrained transparency of Mies and the decorative classi-cism of his "ballet school" work was replaced by a tougher and more forceful blocky aesthetic defined by hard surfaces and simple geometries. The origin of this new aesthetic was unmistakable: Louis Kahn, the Philadelphia-based modernist who developed a cultlike following among architects for his gnomic aphorisms and the almost mystical power of his work. Kahn and Johnson were never close, but they came to know each other while teaching at Yale. Johnson never much bought into Kahn's guru act—and he did think it an act—but like just about everyone else he was enamored of the boldness of Kahn's vision.

Kahn's Richards Medical Research Laboratories at the University of Pennsylvania and his Salk Institute in La Jolla, California suggested a potent way forward for modernism that did not rely on the crutch of his-tory. His forms were simple, almost archaic, and his material palette raw. From brick or concrete he could conjure spaces of physical and emo-tional power, an ability that appealed directly to Johnson and that he wished to appropriate for himself. But he also freely promoted Kahn. In one of the more unlikely episodes of Johnson's career, he managed to secure a commission for Kahn as designer for a Holocaust memorial to be built in New York's Battery Park. Johnson, of all people, had been among three members of a jury assembled by the Committee to Com-memorate the Six Million Jewish Martyrs to select an architect for this project, which was never realized.

At the time, Johnson was engaged in a memorial project of his own, to commemorate the recently assassinated American president, John F. Kennedy. The commission came to him through Stanley Marcus, the luxury retailer who transformed his family business, Neiman-Marcus, into a global arbiter of fashion and cosmopolitan glamour. Marcus was more than a retail genius. He was among a group of civic leaders who were the public conscience of Dallas, and this put him in a minority who felt compelled to memorialize the murdered president. The majority simply wanted the ugly event to vanish from history, along with the "City of Hate" stigma it left behind. The memorial, it was argued, belonged in Washington, D.C. The location that Johnson was eventually given reflected this ambivalence; Dealey Plaza, site of the assassination, was left untouched as a working road. Instead, the memorial became an excuse for the clearance of a nearby block in the name of urban renewal. When it was finally dedicated, the county judge leading the proceedings didn't even mention Kennedy's name.

The memorial itself was disappointing. Johnson's brief was to keep things simple and dignified. What he delivered, in his own less-than-inspiring words, was something "devoid of expression or moralizing"

Johnson's memorial for John F. Kennedy in Dallas: an empty vessel, 1970. (Esto / Ezra Stoller)

and "monumental in its empty presence." In practice, this meant a box of white concrete pillars that floated above ground on steel feet. Within, there was a marble slab inscribed to the dead president. It was supposed to look austere and dramatic but instead just looked forlorn, like a plinth missing its statue. The whole project had a dreary rather than melancholy air. It was also unoriginal; the entire scheme—a room with a square memorial tablet—was taken straight from an unbuilt Mies project. Jacqueline Kennedy, whom Johnson counted as a friend, could not bear the idea of visiting, though it was not his design that kept her away. A return to Dallas was something she just could not countenance.

The Kline Biology Tower at Yale, 1965, a sculptural interpretation of the Seagram Building. (Richard Payne)

Johnson's move to a more robust architecture of tough materials and stark geometries could be seen in a series of science buildings for Yale, most prominently the Kline Biology Tower, which he set before a broad plaza enclosed by a pergola. It looked as if he had taken the red brick exterior of Kahn's library at Phillips Exeter Academy and crossed it with the Seagram Building. Mies's external I-beams, which "expressed" the steel-frame structure of Seagram, were here replaced with hollow brick columns that carried the mechanical systems required by the scientific program. Champions, including Vincent Scully, congratulated him for its sensitive positioning and generous public spaces. Henry-Russell Hitchcock, being overly optimistic, said it would prove "the most aesthetically durable" of the recent signature buildings commissioned by Yale President A. Whitney Griswold, among them Kahn's Yale Art Gallery, Eero Saarinen's David S. Ingalls Rink, Paul Rudolph's Art and Architecture Building, and Gordon Bunshaft's Beinecke Library—all of which, unlike Kline, remain touchstones. Critics, meanwhile, called it over-sized, fascistic, and heavy-handed, and derided his plaza as decorative rather than pleasant. Another project for Yale, an Epidemiology Laboratory, was even more butch, a nearly windowless limestone box with all the character of a detention facility—which is basically what it was: the building's top six stories were designed for the breeding and accommodation of thousands of mice, monkeys, geese, and other animals to be used in medical testing.

The completion of the Yale projects coincided with a significant professional milestone, the first serious monograph on Johnson's work, with an introduction by Hitchcock. The only part of the book Johnson authored himself was the acknowledgments, in which he managed to misspell the name of his old friend and associate Landis ("Landes") Gores, thanked unconvincingly for his "loyal collaboration during the difficult early years." Although Johnson didn't write the book, he did review it, at once demonstrating his great wit and equally great capacity for self-dealing. The editors at *Architectural Forum* thought he might prove an entertaining critic, and Johnson did not disappoint. "It is always good in our decadent world to see a well-designed, sumptuous book come onto the market," he wrote. "This is one." Elaine Lustig Cohen's book design? "Cocktail tables look handsome with it." Hitchcock's text? "Faultless." As for the work itself, he pleaded the Fifth, but noted it would be "a plus for the historian" to have a record of it. He closed by chiding himself for shifting styles, and for failing to practice the various philosophies that he preached.

It was a nifty bit of intellectual jujitsu, an attempt to defang criticism by acknowledging it without addressing it substantively. Cynical, nihilistic, patronizing, frustrating, irreverent—Philip Johnson was happily stepping into the role of "Philip Johnson," a public persona that he cultivated and refined, now augmented by the owlish glasses that he had begun to wear, another borrowed statement, this time from Le Corbusier, an architect and polemicist who, for all his flaws, could never be accused of being apologetic.

A major new commission confirmed the rise in Johnson's professional fortunes: an addition to the Boston Public Library, a beaux arts masterpiece on Copley Place designed by Charles McKim of McKim, Mead & White. For many, Johnson among them, it represented the high point of nineteenth-century American classicism. "My task is to honor that

Boston Public Library addition, an overbearing mausoleum behind Charles McKim's beaux arts masterpiece. (Esto / Ezra Stoller)

beautiful building, to pay obeisance, so to speak," Johnson told the *Boston Globe,* promising, of his design, "its keynote will be modesty."

This was a poorly kept promise. The Johnson addition, stuck behind the McKim original, had the distinct flavor of a bunker. In a vain attempt at Kahn's monumentality, Johnson proposed an imposing granite box that matched the historic building in scale and material but possessed none of its refinement. McKim's original had the distinguished elegance of a gentleman at the opera; Johnson's contribution was more a lunk from the docks. From the street it appeared looming, an effect magnified by massive granite screens that blocked visibility into the building from the exterior. Within, it was more interesting: enormous roof trusses—the work of structural engineer William LeMessurier—allowed for a towering atrium in the center of the space, which had a simple, tic-tac-toe plan.

There was, deservedly, considerable negative response. "Before it's too late, can nothing be done to change the hideous exterior of the Boston Public Library addition?" wrote one concerned citizen to the *Boston Herald* in 1967. But the steps taken made the situation worse: due to budgeting issues, a bronze-and-granite building became an aluminum-and-granite building. Various issues with cost and design pushed the project back for years. Although Johnson was awarded the commission in October of 1963, the library addition did not open to the public until December of 1972.

When it did, Johnson could still count on his old protégé, Ada Louise Huxtable, for a full-throated, well-argued defense. "The library is outstanding," she told readers of the *Times* in one of the more gushing reviews of her career. "It poses, and solves, a number of functional, structural, environmental and esthetic problems with mastery, and represents the kind of unity of program and solution that is what the best architecture has always been about." Johnson was less sanguine about the project. He knew it was dull—"it doesn't have any emphasis," he admitted—and that its clunky monumentality was neither effective nor suited to his own nature. Aesthetically, he remained unmoored. "You never know what period you're in or why you're doing things," he said of that time in his career. "I was very tired."

*   *   *

The library addition was at least deferential to the landmark beaux arts building by McKim, which was left unscathed, at least in its principal facades and spaces. Despite Johnson's public advocacy of preservation, elsewhere he could be considerably less sensitive. There was no better example of this than his plan for the redevelopment of Ellis Island, a commission that came to him through the offices of Stewart Udall, the Secretary of the Interior. The island had ceased functioning as an immigrant gateway in 1954, and there had since been a series of unfulfilled plans to transform it into a park, the most dramatic coming from Frank Lloyd Wright, who imagined a bizarre playground of towers and domed theaters floating on a grassy plane suspended from tensioned cables.

Johnson's scheme was somewhat more rational, but that was hardly an advertisement. His plan was the exact opposite of landmark preservation: rather than restoring the historic Main Building, a fine beaux arts structure that was the symbolic heart of the island and a place of memory for millions of American immigrants, Johnson proposed that it should be partially dismantled and then left as a romantic ruin. On the opposite side of the island, he would build a new monument, "The Wall of the Sixteen Million." This was not actually a wall, or at least not in the conventional sense. Instead, it was to be an enormous white cone-shaped drum, more than ten stories high, with ramped walkways spiraling around its exterior. Etched into the wall would be the names of the immigrants who had passed through the island. The center of the drum would be, in what was becoming a Johnson habit, a void space, with a reflecting pool at ground level.

The plan was both obscene and preposterous, but Johnson could again count on Huxtable's support. In words that seem to have been suggested by him, she compared his proposal to make an artificial ruin of the Main Building to the restoration of European churches ravaged during World War II. "The romantic ruin can evoke a more immediate and emotional sense of the past than the most accurate reconstruction." Huxtable wrote those words in the *Times,* but she did not speak for the paper. An editorial noted that a wall was a distinctly inappropriate metaphor for a monument celebrating immigration, especially at a time when the Berlin Wall was doing just the opposite. Neither was the editorial board impressed with Johnson's circular structure, which it dismissed as a "rheostat cast in concrete." The plan was eventually scrapped for lack of enthusiasm and funding, and the island lay essentially dormant until 1990, when the fully restored Main Building was opened as a museum to universal acclaim.

The failure to get the Ellis Island project off the ground was indicative of a broader difficulty for Johnson. Although he was among the most visible figures in the profession, with an impressive list of clients, there was precious little actual work to keep his office in operation. Part of the problem was that it appeared as if he was busy when he wasn't: the Boston library and NYU projects spent years in limbo, stalled as advocates and budget cutters took their shots. The office, at one point, was down to Johnson, Foster, Manley, an office manager, and a couple of draftsmen just out of architecture school.

And then, to make matters worse, he was abandoned by Foster, who had grown tired of living in Johnson's shadow. He wanted to establish his own practice, and he had become exasperated by Johnson's blasé sense of professionalism, in particular his penchant for wandering into the drafting room—Foster's territory—and meddling with settled designs, often undoing finished work and throwing projects off schedule. The last straw came at a presentation of the NYU library at which Johnson neglected to mention his name.

With no other trustworthy deputy, Johnson elevated Manley into Foster's position as second-in-command and chief of daily operations, a position to which Manley was ill-suited; he accepted it without enthusiasm. Manley liked his job as chief draftsman, a position from which he could magically transform Johnson's sometimes poorly conceived ideas into plausible reality. In that role he was exalted both by Johnson and by the rest of the office. Personnel management was a lot less interesting to him, and he did not aspire to see his name above the door. Worse still, Manley's shyness made him uncomfortable dealing with clients at a time when Johnson needed someone who could schmooze the corporate suits who had always shied away from him. But there was nobody else, so Manley it was. Johnson delivered the news over lunch, and not even at the Four Seasons, promising that he would, in the future, stay out of the drafting room. "You won't mind if I don't believe you," said Manley, and they laughed together at the uncomfortable reality. Their relationship was professional only. "I respected him and he respected me, but I couldn't say we were friends," said Manley. "I wasn't to the manor born, for one thing. He asked me once what my father did, and dropped the subject entirely when I said he was a railroad engineer."

Johnson with John Manley, his trusted "ice-cream man" of fifty years. (Collection of the author)

The lack of work was less an economic problem for Johnson, still insulated by his personal wealth, than a psychological one. For a time he considered shuttering the office altogether so he could found an organization that would do architectural and urban advocacy. He never went through with it, however. The museum was still there for him, and the idea of giving up as an architect was more appealing in theory than in reality. His ambition remained. In a story for *Life,* he told the journalist and political historian Theodore H. White of his dream to become the nation's urban-building commissar.

The interview came in the context of the 1965 mayoral campaign of John Lindsay, a Kennedyesque progressive running as both a Republican and a liberal. The race pitted him against Democrat Abe Beame, a charisma-free accountant, and right-wing pedant William F. Buckley, who ran as a conservative. The magnetic Lindsay promised a revolution in governance—an end to the Tammany Hall political machine that had long ruled the city—and to bring an optimistic, can-do spirit to an office associated with corruption, incompetence, and stagnation. His campaign was animated by a series of reformist task forces and committees that would infuse his administration with new ideas and energy. Architecture and urban design were central to this agenda, and he tapped Johnson to chair his committee on municipal architecture.

It was in this capacity that Johnson was interviewed by White, who was impressed by the scale of the atchitect's vision. "When he speaks, he makes one behold the city as it might be," White told readers of *Life*. "Can the soot-grimed, green-rotted waterfront be restored to beauty? Can the waters be used to bind rather than divide the city? Can the barricades of automobile junking yards, the rusty derelict coaling stations, the decaying pier sheds be torn down to reveal the beauty of the islands again? Sketching future vistas, Johnson makes one see how an *architecte du roi* could create of New York's natural beauty something more splendid even than Paris."

Once elected, Lindsay sought to put these visionary ideas into operation, establishing a Task Force on Urban Design to be led by William Paley, the president of CBS. The committee was stacked with heavy hitters from the business and philanthropic world, along with four architects: Johnson, I. M. Pei, and two ambitious recent graduates of Yale, Robert A. M. Stern and Jaquelin T. Robertson, who would play significant roles in Johnson's professional life ever after. Robertson was the more worldly of the two; he could (and did) take credit for the very existence of an urban-design task force. A son of the Virginia aristocracy, with the Southern airs to match, he was headed for a life in politics but, while on a Rhodes Scholarship, decided he preferred architecture. By sheer coincidence he had run into Lindsay in the Bahamas not long before Lindsay declared his candidacy for mayor, and on a fishing trip convinced him that urban planning should be a significant part of his campaign strategy.

Stern would play a larger role in Johnson's life; indeed, he was already being seen as a protégé, though he would never work for him. Johnson first met him at Yale, where Stern was a standout student and the editor of *Perspecta,* the school's influential journal, which Johnson supported financially and as a contributor. According to Vincent Scully, who introduced them, it was a relationship Stern pursued. "He made himself indispensable to Johnson," he recalled. "By being always around. Respecting Johnson. Admiring him. Learning from him. Not a lot of people would admit to doing that. Johnson was not quite respectable." Like Johnson, Stern would fashion a career as both a provocateur and a builder, with critics ambivalent about his work in both of those endeavors.

It was clear, conversely, what Johnson saw in Stern: himself. Trim and short, with an appealingly nasal voice and unbridled energy, Stern was a smaller, Semitic version of Johnson: an intellectual omnivore with a steel-trap memory, endless ambition, and an unquenchable taste for gossip. Theirs was a relationship of outsiders—Johnson a gay Clevelander, Stern a Jewish Brooklynite—desperate to prove their station in the social and corporate worlds of Manhattan.

Johnson was a useful mentor. When Phyllis Lambert, who after building the Seagram Building decided to become an architect herself, transferred from Yale to the Illinois Institute of Technology to study with Mies, Johnson arranged for Stern to rent her New Haven townhouse. (A promising but impoverished art student, Richard Serra, lived rent-free as the house cleaner and handyman.) Upon Stern's graduation, Johnson arranged for him to receive the Architectural League's J. Clawson Mills Scholarship, which would allow him to develop a course of independent study under Johnson's supervision.

In the interim, Stern had become a regular presence at Johnson's side, a frequent guest at Johnson's Glass House salons, which were becoming a thing of legend in art and architectural circles. In a notable photograph, taken in 1965, Stern sits on a Barcelona chair, intently leaning forward as Johnson chats with Andy Warhol while David Whitney gazes at the ceiling, either bored or irritated by the proceedings. By then Stern had cracked his way into Johnson's circle, marrying into the Gimbel family of department store wealth. This put Johnson and Stern together both in society and in geography: Stern's new in-laws had an estate in nearby Greenwich from which he was often eager to escape.

The Lindsay campaign's urban-design task force met weekly in Paley's boardroom at CBS. Paley ran the show, demanding that its report be concise and contain objectives that could be easily understood by the general public. The group answered with *The Threatened City,* a 62-page analysis of the urban condition, with prescriptions for its improvement. Design journalist Walter McQuade ghosted the document, but Johnson's fingerprints—and aphorisms—were all over it. "Style is visual wit," it proclaimed, a locution that sounds distinctly Johnsonian. Its primary assertion also carried Johnson's argument for an expansion of the role of architecture and design within the political sphere. "Design is not a small enterprise in New York City today, nor should it be considered narrowly as merely a matter of aesthetics, a frail word. In our increasingly crowded man-shaped urban world, aesthetics must now include not only the marble statue in the garden but the house, the street, the neighborhood, and the city as a cumulative expression of its residents."

The study's concrete proposals included the rehabilitation and development of the city's waterfront (a Johnson preoccupation); improvement of the subway system (described as "the most squalid public environment of the United States"); the development of a new business district centered on 125th Street in Harlem; preservation of historic neighborhoods; and above all expanding the personnel, budgets, and authority of city-planning agencies.

These ideas seem visionary today. Johnson's dream of New York as a waterfront city was not implemented until the Bloomberg years—when park building could be yoked to massive increases in real estate value—but at the time the plan was controversial, taking hits for being unrealistic in its ambitions and dangerously misguided in its solutions. Most stinging was a rebuke from the editorial page of the *Times,* which claimed the report's "conventional brand of nineteenth-century esthetics has limited value for the dynamic disorders of the twentieth-century city." That prompted a terse letter in response from Johnson, who wrote: "If by 'nineteenth-century esthetics' you mean access to the waters' edge for all, imaginative design for our major avenues, an over-all plan for plazas and parks, then we are for it." Like the paper's editors, he wrote, the group believed in "design as a tool for the city's future."

Johnson was willing to engage those ideas as an architect, at least on a theoretical level. While he was arguing for architects to expand their role as city planners, and specifically for the reanimation of Harlem as a business center, his office took up that crusade in the guise of a project that was the most brazenly far-fetched and ill-conceived of his career. This was Third City, an urban-renewal scheme that would have razed an entire square mile of Harlem, where poor living conditions and a lack of political power had provoked destructive rioting. Johnson proposed wiping the unraveling center of African-American life clean—an

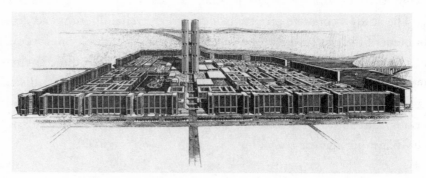

Third City, Johnson's 1967 urban renewal scheme to raze and rebuild a square mile of central Harlem. (Getty Research Institute, Los Angeles)

erasure that also included a bit of his controversial past. Replacing it would be an entirely new community centered at 125th Street, where a pair of 150-story towers would rise to the heavens. The perimeter of this city-within-the-city would have been lined with a phalanx of twenty-story apartment towers, making it appear as a walled-off, fortified zone. Within would be low-scale housing, amenities, and offices. Accentuating its separation from the city around it, all through traffic would have been routed onto an underground grid of streets and avenues.

The name, Third City, suggested a modernist's view of progress: the first "city" was the farming community of Colonial-era upper Manhattan; the second was the existing Harlem; the third was this new vision built from a blank slate. Johnson had come to propose it as a supplementary project to be included in an exhibition on urban renewal at the Museum of Modern Art. That show, *The New City,* was brought to curator Arthur Drexler via a group of young architects and academics who had formed an organization, the Conference of Architects for the Study of the Environment, or CASE, by which they might address the urban condition. The ringleader was Peter Eisenman, a theoretically minded architect then teaching at Princeton, and he was joined by his peers Michael Graves, John Hejduk, Richard Meier, and the ubiquitous Robertson, along with critics Kenneth Frampton and Colin Rowe.

There was no way for Johnson the preservationist to justify the demolition of an entire neighborhood, much of it occupied by historic architecture, for his own new city built from scratch. He didn't even try. After elbowing his way into the show, he decided that he didn't, in fact, want to be too much a part of it. When a dissatisfied Drexler asked him to elaborate his design, he flatly refused. "I'm not the kind of designer to work on Utopian ideas," Johnson told him.

The truth was that his participation was conceived as a make-work endeavor for the office at a time when there were few active commissions to keep it occupied. Sensing the possible political fallout of the show, Johnson told Drexler it was best that the museum "under-emphasize" his work lest it be accused of "nepotism." The model the office had spent months building was dismantled and put away. More critically, the entire nature of the project was whitewashed, removing the potentially incendiary implication that the city's black population be placed in a walled-in ghetto. Displayed at the museum, there was no indication that the project was intended for Harlem. Instead, it was simply billed as a placeless "project for a community of 150,000."

There was good reason for this shift. As Johnson was at work on his project for a fantasy Harlem, he was commissioned to work on a major new project in the real one. The job, as so many before it, came from Nelson Rockefeller, and it was for a new state-office complex to be located almost exactly where Johnson had envisioned his 150-story towers. The idea was to spark development in Harlem, where private investment was lacking, with a major public initiative. Johnson responded with a plan for a series of buildings including an office tower and a cultural center. But what might have seemed like an altruistic plan was immediately attacked by community groups, with cause, as a paternalistic intrusion over which they had little control. Johnson gave up his work on the project, turning over the design of the tower to a minority-owned firm that ran into troubles of its own. "I was convinced it wasn't very good politics for a white man to do a building [in Harlem]," he admitted in a 1973 interview. "The blacks won't even let a black architect do a building up there." That was the year the State Office Building finally opened; by then it was known, with all the affection its acronym suggests, as the SOB. By then, too, Johnson had long since washed his hands of it. "I don't care who builds a monument for blacks," he said. "Who cares?"

The SOB was among a series of significant civic commissions of the period that seemed promising but went nowhere. Downtown Junction, an urban-renewal scheme for Bedford-Stuyvesant that tied a large mall to a transit hub, died of its own overly grand ambitions. More interesting, and closer to realization, was Chelsea Walk, an enormous middle-income housing complex to be built on a platform above the railroad tracks leading into Penn Station. Johnson's plan called for four concrete towers set in parallel rows, like soldiers at roll call, with the rear rank (at thirty-eight stories) peering over the front (at twenty-five) out toward the Hudson. Balconies animated the facades in irregular patterns, such that the whole promised a dynamic interplay of vertical and horizontal lines, as if a painting by Mondrian had been translated into reinforced concrete. It was to be a community in itself, the buildings separated by a park set over a parking deck, with retail frontages at street level. Johnson even included a nursery school for resident children. This was subsidized housing, with controlled rents arranged under the aegis of the New York Redevelopment Companies Housing Program. The financing, however, never materialized, and the site remained unimproved until the 2010s, when it was built out — on a vastly larger scale, and for profit rather than as affordable housing — as the Hudson Yards development.

Johnson couldn't get his own buildings built, but he did manage to put a halt on one designed by his former teacher, Marcel Breuer. The project was for a tower to be built over Grand Central Terminal, arguably New York's greatest work of architecture, even more beloved than the sadly demolished Penn Station. The idea of either razing or building over Grand Central had been in the air since the 1950s for essentially the same reasons: a desire to cash in on valuable real estate conjoined to a misbegotten notion that the station was obsolete. Johnson was appalled by the idea, and had rejected an overture to see if he might be interested in the commission. "I didn't want to be responsible for ruining a landmark I had worked so hard to defend," he told Ada Louise Huxtable. As far as Johnson was concerned, the Pan Am (now Met Life) Building was already a titanic disaster for the terminal, a looming gray eyesore that was the progeny of his longtime nemesis Walter Gropius. Johnson thought the city should have bought its site for a park.

What Breuer proposed for Grand Central was even worse: a monumental concrete slab of a tower that would have sat right on top of the terminal. It was so immense that it would have dwarfed even neighboring Pan Am by some 150 feet. In response, Johnson teamed with

Jacqueline Onassis to form the Committee to Save Grand Central Station, their combined forces giving them immense cultural and political clout. They were memorably photographed in front of the station in the winter of 1975, along with future mayor Ed Koch and the political operative (and former Miss America) Bess Myerson. Their efforts, unlike those in defense of Penn Station, were successful, although resolution came only after legal proceedings that went all the way to the United States Supreme Court.

Johnson, meanwhile, continued with his own major urban projects. In upstate New York he built a vast convention hall just blocks from Niagara Falls. Featuring a series of office buildings around a pedestrian mall leading to the riverfront, it was intended to jump-start the moribund local economy. Johnson's contribution was an immense arched hangar, a 100,000-square-foot exhibition space with concrete buttresses holding up a steel space-frame engineered by Lev Zetlin. Little of the other promised development materialized, and today the large open space has been converted into the floor of a casino.

Johnson's most significant and most successful attempt at city building came with the reimagining of Welfare (previously Blackwell's, now Roosevelt) Island, the two-mile landing strip in New York's East River that for generations had been a depository for the city's contagious, deranged, and unwanted. Through the early 1960s, the city batted around ideas for what to do with it, ranging from a towers-in-the-park housing scheme to a public park. Con Ed hoped to use the southern end for a nuclear power plant. Johnson rejected all of these ideas. "The isolated block in the park—fuck that," he told one interviewer. "I am interested in the quality of life of the people in our century with no money."

He presented his alternative vision in a master plan accompanied by an exhibition, *The Island Nobody Knows*, that opened on October 9, 1969 at the Metropolitan Museum of Art. It called for a car-free, pedestrian-scale, family-friendly community for twenty thousand low- and middle-income people. Though they had battled over his work for

NYU, Johnson freely admitted the proposal was influenced by the ideas of Jane Jacobs, particularly in its focus on providing day care, schools, play spaces, and shopping. "I put the school right in the center of the town," he said, "I want so much to get the life of the babies, crying babies, right up into the offices." To offset the linearity of the island, Johnson produced a series of spaces that cut horizontally, opening up view corridors to the Manhattan skyline while providing access to the water, which was fronted by a promenade. The centerpiece was a large, glassed-in mall in the style of the shopping arcades of Italy and France, and what he had proposed for NYU. But overall the concept was intentionally modest, built at a town scale and with inexpensive materials—concrete and brick. "There's no place for monumentality," he said. "I'm not interested in the architecture."

The Johnson master plan was received with general praise. Huxtable called it a "showpiece" and her erstwhile mentor a "late-blooming urbanist of notable sensibilities." His vision was never quite realized, or not fully. Bureaucratic infighting, finances, politics, and myriad other factors chipped away at the plan's integrity. Implementation was left to the direction of Ed Logue, director of the New York State Urban Development Corporation, who doled out design work to a series of architectural firms; Johnson was given the town square, but the proposed shopping arcade was budgeted out. The technical job of overseeing the project fell from the office of the architect to a large engineering firm that, Johnson complained, "had a vice president for everything."

Today, the relative success of Roosevelt Island (it was renamed in 1971) is a matter of debate. That it never fully lived up to Johnson's dream of a vibrant town is undeniable. Yet it did realize much of his vision of a pedestrian-oriented community for mixed-income families, and that is a considerable accomplishment.

Just as Johnson was bringing the small town to the big city, he was bringing the big city to the small town. On July 1, 1967, he opened the Glass House for a benefit in support of the Merce Cunningham dance company, with entertainment by Andy Warhol's in-house—or rather, in-Factory—band, the Velvet Underground. Attendees at what *Vogue* described as a "lark on a summer evening" included John de Menil (a cosponsor of the proceedings), Alfred Barr, Claes Oldenburg, and Jasper Johns, along with New York Senator Jacob Javits and some four hundred members of New York society—each of whom had paid $75 for the privilege of attendance. Here was the ultimate downtown-meets-uptown scene; so far uptown, in fact, that it was in the most WASPy of Connecticut suburbs. Cunningham called it a "Country Happening."

The main event was a performance by Cunningham's troupe, on a shallow stage set up on the lawn adjacent to the house. Cunningham, in a seaman's striped jersey and white leggings, led dancers in a series of pieces of antic choreography. The costumes were by Robert Rauschenberg; the score, commissioned from and played live by John Cage, included viola, gong, radio, and noises from three automobiles. Upon the conclusion of the performance, the dancers took a collective bow, descended from the stage, and packed into a waiting station wagon, which summarily drove them off the grounds.

The guests gave them a standing ovation, then picked up wicker baskets filled with pâté, prosciutto, cheeses, bread, chocolate mousse, and bottles of Beaujolais for a picnic dinner on the grounds. (The provisions came courtesy of the Brasserie.) Then it was up to the Velvets to entertain, playing songs off their recently released first album, with its now-famous Warhol-banana cover, while the assembled poured onto the stage for dancing of the more casual variety.

High and low, serious and playful, patron and artist; the event was nothing if not a demonstration of Johnson's ability to marry opposites in a way that seemed almost natural, and redounded to his own benefit. At the age of sixty-one, Johnson was still a formidable cultural arbiter. Yet he was also removed from that culture, safely apart from it in the rarefied environment he had created for himself. He had the Velvet Underground, but that most avant-garde and angsty of bands was deracinated, tamed into providing dance music for an upper-crust lawn party. There was no burning of draft cards, and the riots of the inner city were out of sight and out of mind.

The local police did bust up the party—politely, to be sure—upon noise complaints from some of the neighbors. The guests left for their suburban homes, the Velvets returned by limo downtown, and Philip Johnson went to sleep in the Glass House, his world intact.

Company men: Philip Johnson and John Burgee. (Esto / Roberto Schezen)

CHAPTER 14

Towers and Power

*What I look for now is, I regret to say, something we used to call
expressiveness, before it became a dirty word.*

—*Philip Johnson*

If Philip Johnson was going to be the kind of architect Philip Johnson
wanted to be, he wasn't going to be able to do it by himself. The office
could float on, but Johnson didn't have the business acumen to make it
blossom into something more, and neither did John Manley. But in 1967
Johnson found a man who could change things. His name was John Burgee, and he was tall and masculine and self-assured, with a no-nonsense,
take-charge attitude, the kind of man a captain of industry could trust
implicitly.

It was Burgee who would help Johnson reinvent himself as a master
builder of skyscrapers and the unrivaled celebrity face of the architectural profession. Their partnership would reach extraordinary heights—
literally, figuratively, financially—before a bitter professional divorce
some twenty years in the future would sunder their relationship. What
ruined them for each other was what they shared: unquenchable ambition paired with an inherent inability to share a spotlight that would
grow increasingly hot as their success mushroomed.

Burgee was born into a family of architects. His father had been a
partner at Holabird & Root, one of the Chicago firms that had invented
the American skyscraper in the late-nineteenth century. His brother was
an architect at that firm, which is where he, too, had started his career,
after graduating from Notre Dame. He left it to join the corporate practice of C. F. Murphy, which had been awarded the commission to build

337

O'Hare Airport and seemed like a place where he could make his mark. It was a good professional decision, and also fortuitous; Johnson was known to drop in on the firm's Chicago offices to visit his friend and former Harvard classmate, Carter Manny, the partner in charge of the O'Hare project.

Johnson barely noticed Burgee on their first meeting in the early 1960s; he was never particularly interested in the lives of junior staff. That changed when Johnson decided to enter the competition to remake the Philadelphia airport in 1965. Until that point, his only experience in airport design had been unproductive. In 1959 he had been one of five architects selected to enter proposals for a terminal for National Airlines at Idlewild (now JFK) Airport. This opportunity would have placed him in the same field as SOM (designing the International Arrivals Building) and Eero Saarinen (whose TWA Terminal would become a jet-age icon). In his own effort at boldness, Johnson chose not to segregate arrivals and departures, instead dumping everyone into a "Great Room" inspired by Grand Central Terminal. The result would have been utter chaos, and he was passed over for I. M. Pei.

Johnson had gone to see Manny in an effort to avoid repeating this experience in Philadelphia, proposing that C. F. Murphy collaborate with him in the competition, coupling his prestige with Murphy's airport bona fides. Manny agreed and put Burgee in charge of the project for the company. Johnson liked him immediately—and tried to poach him while their proposal was still in bureaucratic limbo. Burgee declined, thinking he was on track to take over Murphy one day. A year later that was appearing a less likely prospect, especially after the Philadelphia job didn't come through. So when Johnson again approached him to take over the number-two role that Manley had unhappily inherited from Foster, he accepted. But Burgee was not content simply to join the firm as second-in-command. In what should have been a red flag for Johnson, the thirty-three-year-old wanted to be made a partner, with a share of the profits.

Johnson made him wait for that title, and at first Burgee's share in the firm's profits was nominal—2 percent—but Johnson was frankly happy to turn over the office to him. Burgee was the new kind of architect that the corporate, postwar era demanded; not the bow-tied dandy who would design your dream house, but a company man in a sharp blue suit who knew how to squeeze every ounce of profit from a project while making clients feel like they were in reliable hands. "The businessmen always feel much relieved when he appears on the scene," said Johnson. Gerald Hines, the Houston developer who would become Johnson's greatest patron, put it bluntly: "Without John Burgee he would not have gotten commissions. Johnson could not have gotten the work by himself. There wasn't the confidence level. He didn't have a reputation for building commercial buildings. . . . He was an aesthete." Burgee made men like Hines comfortable. That is just what Johnson needed, and when he found it he acquired it. Johnson had dreamed of being the *architecte du roi,* and Burgee was the man who could put him before America's corporate kings.

The only problem was there wasn't any work, or hardly any that paid, when Burgee arrived at the Seagram Building in 1967. A new headquarters project for Mercedes-Benz that Johnson had promised was but a phantom, never to happen. Burgee was shocked, and upset that he had been sold a bill of goods. Making the best of it, Johnson assigned him the languishing Boston Public Library job, which had grown to be so over-budget that all work had come to a halt. Burgee pushed it back into action, cutting costs and cajoling the Boston bureaucracy with his persistence and executive skill. In the meantime, he cleaned house in the Johnson office, installing a team, many imported from Chicago, that would answer to him while removing those of longer tenure who might not be loyal. Only a handful remained, most prominently Manley, the only one who could effectively translate into buildable reality the ideas Johnson scribbled onto yellow tracing paper over weekends at the Glass House. He was indispensable to Johnson, and would forever remain with him.

Without much other work, the subject of Johnson's latest drawings was another structure for his New Canaan estate, a sculpture gallery that would serve as a showplace for his growing collection of three-dimensional work, and as a pendant to his cryptlike painting gallery. The need for the space reflected his changing interest in artistic media—"Sculpture interests me much more than painting," he told *Art in America* in 1966—and his allegiance in particular shifted from Pop to the group of minimalist artists emerging in New York. David Whitney was his conduit to many of these artists, among them Richard Artschwager, John Chamberlain, Mark di Suvero, Dan Flavin, Donald Judd, Robert Morris, and above all Frank Stella. From Judd he commissioned a site-specific work for the Glass House compound, a concrete ring completed in 1971 that looked more like an accidental work of infrastructure. (It makes a rather forlorn welcome to the dynamic composition between the Glass and Brick houses.)

Johnson's relationship with these artists was not always easy—despite his wealth and reputation as a patron, he had a history of miserly behavior with artists that dated back to his earliest purchases of Mondrian and Schlemmer. When he was rather obscenely late to pay for a conceptual piece by Morris, the artist responded by sending him a "statement of aesthetic withdrawal." Johnson doubled down, paying his debt (all of $300) and then having Morris mount the letter and turn it into another "work"—which he also purchased.

Johnson suffered over the design of the gallery for months; his early schemes included a series of linked pavilions that stepped down the sloping ground of his property. Eventually he collapsed those pavilions in on themselves, landing on a design that zigzagged into the ground around a squared-off staircase. From the outside it had the unremarkable appearance of a maintenance shed, a whitewashed brick structure with an asymmetrically slanted roof. To walk inside it was a dramatic revelation. On a sunlit day, the beams of what turned out to be a greenhouse roof cast zebra-stripe shadows across the red brick floors and white walls. Sculptures were mounted along the stairwell, which had a deviously low ledge, adding an additional sense of drama to the proceedings. Johnson claimed the whole thing was inspired by the ragged geometry of one of Stella's polygonal abstractions.* Writing in *Time,* critic Robert Hughes

---

* In 1990 Johnson acquired Stella's massive assemblage work *Raft of Medusa, Part I,* which has since held pride of place in the gallery.

called it "a brilliant attack on the problem of how to avoid a long, boring, enfiladed room."

The dramatic whiteness of the sculpture gallery was replicated in a landscape that could not have been more different: the shoreline of Corpus Christi, a sleepy industrial city on the Texas Gulf Coast known not for its cultural advantages but for its vast petrochemical works. That this might change, at least somewhat, was the idea of Patsy Singer, a member of the local gentry and friend of the Menils. Envisioning a museum for Corpus, Singer thought the charismatic Johnson, with his blue-chip museum pedigree and Texas building record, was the man for the job. At first he didn't much agree. She arrived at his Seagram Building office with the offer of a commission but not much of an idea of what should go in it—and no money to pay for it either. Johnson told her to come back when she was bankrolled, thinking that was the end of it. But to underestimate the powers of a Texas socialite was a grave error.

Bold forms at the Museum of South Texas, in Corpus Christi, 1972. (Esto / Ezra Stoller)

Singer did return, and Johnson responded to her brief with a work of architectural sculpture, a building of bold geometries in hot white concrete that shimmered against the rich blues of the sea and sky. Inside it was bright and open, with a concrete floor. The appearance of solidity was telling: the walls were fourteen inches thick, to protect against the frequent hurricanes that tore along the coast. One hit during the early stages of construction, wiping away a work building and site model built by Johnson's Texas associates, Howard Barnstone and Eugene Aubry. Johnson had known Barnstone and his partner Aubry for decades; Barnstone was the "house architect" of the Menils in Houston and an unabashed Johnson champion. But it was Aubry who took over the Menil-sponsored Rothko Chapel project, a job Johnson had renounced in 1967 after drafting its basic design. (Rothko accepted Johnson's octagonal brick structure but didn't like the chimney-like skylight above it; Johnson, having been burned by the painter at the Four Seasons, turned the whole thing over to Barnstone and Aubry, who were more pliable.)

When plans for the inaugural show at the museum in Corpus fell through, Johnson stepped into the breach, deputizing David Whitney to mount an exhibition celebrating three artists who also happened to be among Johnson and Whitney's friends: Jasper Johns, Frank Stella, and Andy Warhol. To celebrate the occasion, Warhol produced a large portrait of Johnson, actually a grid of nine screened prints of Johnson looking deeply serious in a buttoned-up work shirt with the woods of his New Canaan estate in the background.

Excitement was largely confined to Corpus; the Art Museum of South Texas might have been better known and more widely celebrated if not for a bit of unfortunate timing that had seemed propitious at the moment. Its opening, in 1972, coincided with the debut of another Texas museum, Louis Kahn's Kimbell Art Museum in Fort Worth, which was immediately hailed as one of the great masterpieces of modern architecture, a work of nearly mystical monumentality and spatial drama. This was an impossible act to follow, especially for a building in an even more provincial corner of the state. Johnson's museum inevitably fell into the Kimbell's shadow, a situation exacerbated by the fact that the two institutions collaborated on a publicity campaign in a joint effort to bring journalists to Texas.

The geometric reductiveness and brazen whiteness of Johnson's museum projects reflected the influence of a circle of young architects, all based in New York, who had emerged out of the CASE group that had originated the *New City* exhibition. Their names were Peter Eisenman, John Hejduk, Michael Graves, Charles Gwathmey, and Richard Meier. In an effort to keep in touch with the coming generation, Drexler had invited this group to use the Museum of Modern Art as a venue to present their work to one another (and to a few scholars) in closed-door meetings. Although they were beginning to branch out in ways that were individually distinctive, at the time their work could still be seen as of a piece: a next-wave modernism inspired by Le Corbusier. The mood was quite different from the CASE sessions, which were driven by the reformist impulse to address the problems of the city. Here, at the height of the war in Vietnam and the struggle for civil rights, the group of five had turned inward, producing an architecture of unrelieved formalism that acknowledged nothing but its own Euclidean language. That work was published in a monograph, *Five Architects,* that branded them as stars on the rise, an architectural Brat Pack — the New York Five.

Johnson was a part of none of this, at least not at first. A great deal of misinformation surrounds the group, beginning with the fact that it was initially six architects, not five. William Ellis, who met the group while on a fellowship at Cornell, participated in the show-and-tell discussion but was deemed beneath the level of the group by the remaining five. They left him out of the book, and he was subsequently erased from the group's history. Another incorrect assumption is that the museum held an exhibition of the group's work. It did not, nor did it publish the book, though Drexler wrote the foreword. Johnson did not enter the picture until *Five Architects* had become a phenomenon, and at that point he understood it was time to put his imprimatur on it. And so for its second edition, Johnson pitched in with a "postscript" that allowed him to assert his authority over the group by offering his endorsement, along with a tongue-in-cheek *précis* on each of the five subjects. Eisenman, the ringleader, was "weighted down by erudition" and prone to incomprehensible theorizing; Graves was a "painter-architect"; Gwathmey a builder in the Miesian sense; Hejduk a "theoretician's designer"; and Meier the most commercial. His descriptions proved to be entirely accurate.

The rise of the New York Five engendered a response, and it came from another set of Johnson acolytes. In May of 1975 *Architectural Forum* published "Five on Five," in which the anointed group came under the assault of five architects whose proclivities leaned more heavily in the postmodern direction, chief among them Robert A. M. Stern, a Johnson protégé now building his own reputation. Stern excoriated the five for work that was "puritanical" and "hermetic." He compared their formalist vision unfavorably to that of the husband-and-wife team of Robert Venturi and Denise Scott Brown, whose book *Learning from Las Vegas* suggested architecture's path forward was not to look inward, but outward at the vernacular forms of the American landscape. The New York Five became "The Whites" and their postmodern antagonists "The Grays," and their ensuing intellectual battle inured entirely to Johnson's benefit. He had no need to take sides, for he was on all sides at once—the generous paterfamilias supporting all of his unruly children. His association with them kept him engaged and affirmed his position above all.

Conversely, the kids eagerly latched onto his bespoke coattails, Stern and Eisenman in particular. The two looked past their ideological differences and together spearheaded the 1979 publication of a book of Johnson's writings, a handsome white volume with a vellum jacket designed by Massimo Vignelli, who had become something close to Johnson's house designer on important projects. The more theory-minded Eisenman provided the introduction to the book, and Stern, with his encyclopedic knowledge of history, wrote brief commentaries on each of the pieces they compiled. These included Johnson's 1933 essay "Architecture in the Third Reich" but none of the more incendiary pieces of his fascist years, in particular his anti-Semitic, eugenic arguments in *Social Justice* and *Today's Challenge*.

Johnson's patronage extended to Eisenman's most significant project, the Institute for Architecture and Urban Studies, or IAUS, which Johnson backed financially. Having been denied tenure at Princeton, Eisenman chose to open his own institution in midtown New York, a combination think tank and teaching program for avant-garde architecture. The clubhouse—and it was as much a club as anything—was on the penthouse floors of 8 West 40th Street, looking out over the unregenerate Bryant Park and the New York Public Library. With the CASE group at its core, it became the center of New York architectural intellectualism, with a cast of luminaries (Rem Koolhaas, Rafael Moneo, Bernard Tschumi) and a host of talented young professionals and academics who saw the institution as the base of a burgeoning avant-garde. The IAUS produced *Skyline,* a tabloid-style newsletter with reviews, gossip, and other features (Johnson paid the salary of its editor), and *Oppositions,* a heavy-duty journal of theory in which the institute's distinguished fellows and other leading thinkers might explore their ideas. (The joke, of course, was that no opposition viewpoints were allowed in *Oppositions.*) Its ninth issue was devoted to Johnson, a Festschrift for the man who had helped bankroll the entire operation.

When he was a younger man, or even a few years earlier when pickings at the office were slim, Johnson might have thrown himself into the goings-on at the institute. But instead he could act as its sugar daddy and gray eminence, because Burgee had remade his practice into a profitable, going concern, and soon enough there was so much work they were expanding.

The shift began with the largest commission of Johnson's career, his first true skyscraper, and it was Burgee who made it happen. The job came through one of Johnson's own contacts, Kenneth N. Dayton, the design-minded chief executive of Minneapolis-based retail giant Dayton-Hudson (now Target). Impressed with Johnson's elegant house in the lakeside Minneapolis suburb of Wayzata for curator Richard Davis, Dayton had attempted to commission a residence of his own from Johnson. In his efforts to move beyond his reputation as a society architect, Johnson had declined. Dayton returned in 1967, however, this time with a bigger prize. He had persuaded the banking giant Investors Diversified

Services (IDS) to go in as the lead partner with Dayton-Hudson on a combined new headquarters tower in downtown Minneapolis.

On the morning Dayton and the IDS executives arrived at Johnson's Seagram Building office, they were not looking for an architect for their projected fifty-story tower—they already had one, Ed Baker, a Minnesotan with a long history with Dayton-Hudson—but merely a prestigious name who could slap a decent-looking facade over it, giving it an aesthetic boost and promoting their status as patrons. Johnson had no great qualms about such an arrangement. A fifty-story tower was already several orders of magnitude larger than anything he had ever designed, and he was perfectly happy to concentrate on aesthetics while Baker worried about interior space planning and where to put the mechanical systems. But before he had a chance to comment, Burgee stepped in abruptly with a statement that shocked everyone in the room, Johnson included: "Gentlemen, I'm sorry, we're not building decorators, thank you very much. If you'd like us to be your architects we'd be pleased to do it."

Johnson was stunned but didn't say anything. At lunch at the Four Seasons, Burgee apologized for overstepping his bounds. "I'll do whatever you want to do," he told Johnson. In the meantime, Dayton and the executives from IDS spent the day shopping their project to other blue-chip architects, including I. M. Pei and Skidmore, Owings & Merrill. But Burgee's confidence and Johnson's reputation brought them back for another meeting later in the afternoon. "You can have the whole building," they said. Baker would act as their local subordinate. That meant an enormous bump in fee (and work), but more critically it redefined the entire practice. Henceforth they would be genuine skyscraper architects.

Burgee was not finished expanding the firm's role in the job, and indeed the job itself. At the time, IDS had acquired a prime half-block site adjacent to the Nicollet Mall, recently transformed into a pedestrian-only public space by landscape architect Lawrence Halprin. Burgee realized this site was simply not large enough to accommodate Johnson's ambition to build something more than just a tower, but a true civic space in the heart of downtown. To accomplish this, they needed the

IDS Tower in Minneapolis, 1973. The Miesian skyscraper revised. (Richard Payne)

entire block. A few weeks into the project, Burgee made that pitch to the executives at IDS, playing on their desire to create a dramatic signature for Minneapolis (and on that city's Midwestern rivalry with his own hometown). "That's how we do it in Chicago," he told them. "We don't have a bunch of other stuff in front of your building."

It was precisely the kind of bold, business-oriented move that Johnson was too timid to contemplate on his own, and it was precisely why he valued Burgee. IDS accepted the advice and paid dearly for the rest of the block, held up by owners who had all the leverage in the negotiations. Johnson also paid a steep price: flying back from Minneapolis after this coup, Burgee again raised his demand for partnership and a fifty percent stake in the firm. "You got it," Johnson replied. It would be years before he realized just how steep a cost that was.

The expanded site allowed Johnson to build not just an office tower but a composition of four buildings—the fifty-one-story tower, a nineteen-story hotel, an eight-story office annex, and a two-story retail building—clustered around a grand public atrium, the "Crystal Court." The model for this pentagonal space was the Piazza San Marco in Venice, arguably the world's grandest public space, though here it would be indoors, as a protection against Minnesota's brutal winter cold and intolerable summer heat. It was Manley, however, who came up with the atrium's signature design: a roof of cascading plastic panels that, seen from below, had the appealing look of a jumble of ice cubes. Although it became one of the hallmarks of the project, it was incorporated against Johnson's wishes: IDS executives saw a preliminary model in the office and were thrilled. The problem was that Johnson was out of town and had not seen it himself. When he returned, he was livid, and tried to replace it with his own design, which didn't work.

Upon its 1972 opening, IDS became one of the city's defining structures, and the Crystal Court a beloved public space. On the ground the complex was connected to Halprin's pedestrian mall, and on its upper levels skybridges linked it into the city's extant above-ground pedestrian

The Crystal Court of the IDS Center, a civic crossroads and urban oasis. (Richard Payne)

system. The hotel brought visitors—each room had a Warhol print—and the retail spaces attracted shoppers. When they arrived, the pentagonal plan made for a pleasing diversity of paths, a genuine urban scene. It was Johnson's finest public space since the opening of the sculpture garden at the Museum of Modern Art, and his most successful realization of the planning principles he had been promoting for the last decade. "There is more of a there, there now," Johnson averred. Its status as a civic icon was affirmed when it was added to the opening credits of that quintessential touchstone of we're-gonna-make-it-after-all urban progressivism: *The Mary Tyler Moore Show*. Before tossing her beret, Moore could be seen gazing down from a balcony table on the court's seventh story.

The focal point of the IDS composition, and its raison d'être, remained the tower—still the tallest building in Minneapolis, and at some 2.3 million square feet nearly triple the area of the Seagram Building. As with the Crystal Court, much of the actual design came from Manley. Burgee acted as a kind of editor, managing the job and piping up when necessary on matters of finance, internal organization, and logistics. To the extent his recommendations related to design, Burgee was essentially ignored; Johnson would thank him and move on as he saw fit. When he was not within earshot, the design staff could be dismissive of his role. Manley considered himself responsible for sixty percent of the design, Johnson for fifty percent, and Burgee "minus ten percent."

Johnson had originally wanted the building to spiral up in a series of steps; he had attempted a similar plan for a project that had recently fallen through, Logan's Circle, a large commercial development project for Philadelphia. This turned out to be a logistical nightmare, so Manley suggested that instead of stepping up as it rose, they could translate those steps into the floor plan. Johnson agreed, the result being a rectangular blue-glass prism with a zigzag in each corner. (Johnson called them "zogs.") From the outside this gave the building a crisp and distinctive shape, accentuated by reflective windows set in a dense grid—a Miesian tower, but of a friendly rather than forbidding sort. Within, the saw-toothed design meant each floor could have thirty-two corner offices, answering a perennial need in a management culture. (That element alone was widely imitated.) The top floor was opened as an observation deck and the floor just below for a restaurant, so the public was welcomed not just in the pleasant environment of the Crystal Court but at the highest levels, where they could enjoy views across and beyond the city.

The success of IDS begat Johnson's next skyscraper commission, which inaugurated a relationship that would benefit him for decades and reshape skylines across America. It came from Gerald Hines, an Indiana native with a mechanical engineering degree (from Purdue) and an adopted drawl (from Texas) who had cut his teeth developing anonymous commercial buildings but moved on to larger things. The first was Houston's immense Galleria mall, followed by One Shell Plaza — a fifty-story, tapering shaft wrapped in white travertine that projected a lavish glare in the hot Texas sun. The design was by Bruce Graham, a principal in the Chicago office of SOM, and it suggested to Hines that there was immense profit to be made if blue-chip architecture could be coupled to rigorous budgetary forecasting and cost controls. That philosophy appealed directly to Hugh Liedtke, the chief executive of Pennzoil, who approached Hines to build a "distinctive" tower for his company in Houston.

Hines's first impulse was to return to Graham, who responded with a structure similar in character, though only half as tall, as his Sears (now Willis) Tower in Chicago. "It was a building that was very austere," Hines said. "I was not convinced." Neither was Liedtke. He didn't want another upright glass "cigar box," and he wasn't interested in building the tallest tower in town, because it would inevitably be eclipsed. "Distinctive" was the operative goal. And Hines was already at work with another architect who could provide that elusive quality: Philip Johnson.

Their connection came through a most unlikely source, Ike Brochstein, a Jewish immigrant from Palestine who had begun his career as a teenage cabinetmaker and built a millwork firm revered in Texas and beyond. Brochstein had supplied the teak paneling for Johnson's Amon

Carter Museum in Fort Worth, and the two men, equally persnickety about craftsmanship, impressed each other. It happened that Brochstein had acquired a large parcel of land in close proximity to Hines's Galleria mall, and when he wished to develop it, he sought out Hines to go in on the project. Hines, concerned that Brochstein might build a competing retail center, advocated an office park. He made a short list of potential architects, among them Graham, Pei, and Kevin Roche (successor to the deceased Eero Saarinen). But Brochstein remembered his work with Johnson in Fort Worth and asked that he be added to the list. When the other candidates either dropped out or were crossed off, Johnson was the last man standing.

Johnson's first proposal for the project was a translation of the Chelsea Walk project: concrete towers set on top of a deck with parking and retail. Hines didn't like it, not least because he'd have to build the whole thing all at once, not one building at a time—a financing issue. Johnson came back with something more acceptable: three stepped glass towers with horizontal window bands and rounded corners that could be built in phases. For their inspiration he had reached back to New York's 1931 Starrett-Lehigh Building, a masterpiece of industrial architecture that he and Hitchcock had included in their landmark Modern Architecture show of 1932.

The so-called Post Oak project was still in its infancy when Hines turned to Johnson for the Pennzoil job, which now had an added complexity: a second major tenant. The Pennzoil business had actually grown out of another company, Zapata Oil, which Liedtke had founded with his younger brother and George H. W. Bush, the future president. Together Liedtke and Bush represented a new era in Texas oil; the older, wildcatting generation that lived large and lost big was being supplanted by a Brooks Brothers breed that kept their eyes on spreadsheets and their loafer-clad feet off oil derricks. Liedtke and Bush eventually split their business in two, with Liedtke re-forming under the Pennzoil banner and Bush keeping the Zapata name. It was Zapata that was to be the second tenant in Liedtke's proposed tower.

How to put two signature tenants in a single building? Johnson's first

Pennzoil Place in Houston, 1976, Johnson's impeccable twin tower scheme. (Hines Interests Limited Partnership)

attempt, a cool Miesian tower modeled on the Seagram, was rejected—too boring. The solution, prompted by Manley, was deceptively logical: build not one but two towers, and connect them at the base. Sitting with Hines in his Seagram office, Johnson sketched out a diagram that looked like NBC's pre-peacock logo, a pair of kissing trapezoids. That was how the buildings would look from above, except they would not actually kiss—there would be a slim gap between them, with a soaring glass-house atrium bringing them together at street level. Hines approved, but when a model was shown to Liedtke he was still dissatisfied. The buildings had flat roofs—boring. A quick-thinking Johnson plucked one of the wedge-shaped atrium blocks from the model and stuck it atop one of the towers. "Yeah, *that's* it," said Liedtke.

Hines was also happy. Although it seemed to defy conventional wisdom, Johnson's paired thirty-seven-story towers cost 20 percent less than the fifty-five-floor building Graham had proposed: the shorter buildings required fewer steel columns and allowed for more parking. Using an architectural version of the "trust but verify" system, Hines had all the drawings prepared in the Johnson office completely redone in Houston, auditing them for cost efficiency. (Johnson clients who neglected to follow similar procedures tended to deeply regret it.) Fears that the top floors, with their angled walls and diminishing floor spaces, would be hard to rent proved to be exactly wrong. Hines could actually charge a premium for those unique "prestige" spaces. Liedtke himself occupied the top floor of the Pennzoil building.

The sharp Miesian appeal of Pennzoil was not entirely the product of Johnson, or even Johnson and Manley, but a new figure who had emerged in the office. Like Burgee, Eli Attia had come from the Chicago offices of C. F. Murphy, recommended by Johnson's old classmate Carter Manny. A native Israeli trained at the prestigious Technion in Haifa, he had all the stereotypical characteristics of the Sabra: he was brash, aggressive, tough, and deeply intelligent. Those traits had put a brake on his upward mobility at Murphy, and they were plain on the day in 1970 that he interviewed with Johnson. Mies may have been a great designer, Attia told Johnson, but his buildings were boring shoeboxes. Attia claimed he knew how to break that mold, which was exactly what Johnson wanted to do himself. Attia began working on Pennzoil and was soon leading its design development.

Burgee, Manley, Attia: Johnson didn't care where the ideas were coming from or who did the work. He was the one with the final decision and he was the one who would get the lion's share of the credit, the one who would be hailed as a genius. And there was no shortage of encomiums. Pennzoil Place was received with nearly universal praise in the press, depicted as a marriage of high design and good business, a generous addition to Houston's downtown, and a sculpturally daring twist on a Miesian aesthetic perceived as frigid and inhumane—a friendly new kind of modernism for America's corporate aristocracy. Huxtable proclaimed it a "towering achievement" and a "synthesis of structure and style." She was not the only *Times* writer to cover it glowingly.

Johnson had his eye on a new journalistic protégé, a bright Yale graduate from Nutley, New Jersey, who had recently taken a junior position at the *New York Times Magazine*. Johnson was introduced to Paul Goldberger by Vincent Scully, who was then acting as an informal adviser to a student publication of which Goldberger was an editor. Scully had suggested Johnson might be a willing financial backer, so Goldberger visited him at his Seagram Building office and Johnson was impressed enough to send him along with a check for $500. A visit to the Glass House followed, with Goldberger and three friends receiving a short course on architecture from Johnson over a bottle of scotch.

Johnson kept an eye on Goldberger in the interim—Goldberger had written a few articles on architecture for the magazine, though he was then a generalist—and when he learned that *Architectural Forum* was planning to dedicate a special issue to his work, he recommended Goldberger to the editors as its principal author. The issue was published in January of 1973, its cover not the usual building but the lionizing Warhol multiple portrait made for the opening of the Corpus Christi museum. Goldberger's feature, "Form and Procession," ran across seventeen pages, analyzing and celebrating Johnson's recent work, in particular IDS and Pennzoil.

That the entire issue was dedicated to Johnson signalled his changing place in the profession. It was a shift marked as well by the Museum of Modern Art: he had shown his work at the museum on occasion, most recently in the *New City* show, but in October of 1970 Drexler featured the man who was very much his superior in a three-person exhibition, *Work in Progress: Philip Johnson, Kevin Roche, Paul Rudolph*. The three, according to Drexler, were "making major contributions to the American scene." Of Johnson in particular he wrote, "his insistence on fine craftsmanship and materials has helped to associate him with the design of elegant single buildings isolated from their surroundings, yet most of his recent work has sought to provide public spaces that would relate buildings to each other and to the street."

With those words, Drexler may have had in mind a project that was not shown in the exhibition, but on which Johnson had been at work for several years, namely another major expansion of the museum itself. Johnson's previous expansion of the institution, which opened with the World's Fair in 1964, had been something of a half-measure, and within only a few years the museum had grown out of it. Drexler himself had drawn up his own designs for a grand new museum addition, a terraced concrete megastructure that would have replaced Johnson's sculpture garden. That went nowhere, but in the meantime the museum's trustees had landed on another plan. Although it was considered the child of the Rockefeller family, and thus not just financially secure but rich, the museum in fact operated at an ever-growing deficit that outpaced even the growth of its popularity. The solution to this problem was to go into the real estate business, to take the property directly west of the museum and build a speculative office tower, of which the museum would occupy the bottom floors, leaving those above to be leased for profit.

Johnson worked through a series of feasibility studies for an expansion. In 1969 a planning report, authored by Drexler, was submitted to the trustees outlining Johnson's vision. Its centerpiece was not a new tower but the sculpture garden, now enclosed under a six-story glass atrium, an analogue to the Crystal Court at IDS or the proposed arcade for NYU. This would become the new entry to the museum, a quasi-public space that would be, according to Drexler's report, "the most spectacular public room in the world." For Bill Paley, the board chairman, it was a bit *too* spectacular. A following proposal for raising the sculpture garden a level and ramming several gallery levels beneath it was set aside as both too expensive and too challenging technically. In 1976, after years of equivocation, the trustees decided to move ahead on a plan for a speculative tower. And they decided that Philip Johnson, for the first time since his return from fascist banishment, would not be the museum's architect.

The decision came from the very heights of a stratified board: there was a lower tier on which Johnson sat, and then a more elevated level of Rockefellers and Paleys that held ultimate power. The justifications for passing over Johnson were several: there were three other distinguished architects on the museum board—Ed Barnes, Gordon Bunshaft, and Wallace Harrison—and it would be unfair to choose among them. Of course, this hadn't stopped the museum from doing so before, or from having Johnson spend years working on feasibility studies for the project. Technically Johnson, as a member of the board, was excluded from participating in the project on the grounds that it would appear as insider-dealing. There was irony here, too: the very mechanism that allowed the museum to use its air rights to build a tower was the product of thinking that could be traced back directly to the Task Force on Urban Design, on which Johnson was an influential figure.

Johnson did not for a moment believe that the reason he was passed over was due to some potential legalistic indelicacy, and his decades of work for the museum—never mind his generous gifts of both cash and art—plainly argued against the idea that he could not be granted the commission because there were other architects on the board. For weeks he held out hope that his allies could sway the decision back in his favor. His key protectors in the museum administration, however, were gone; Barr had finally retired in 1967 and René d'Harnoncourt died a year later. A fellow trustee who reached out to Paley on Johnson's behalf was treated to one of his infamous screaming tirades.

Whether it was a perception that he could not keep to a budget, a distaste for his design, or some other offense—and he certainly committed more than his share—the decision was the decision, and the museum's architect would not be Philip Johnson. He was instead allowed to serve on the selection panel for the architect who would get the job. The choice came down to three: I. M. Pei, Mitchell Giurgola, and César Pelli. With Johnson's blessing and active support, the committee chose Pelli, an architect of political dexterity whom the trustees could trust to carry out their vision without headache. He came out of the office of Victor Gruen, America's preeminent mall architect, and that is essentially what he made of the museum: a shopping center for art, with a high-end condo tower stuck in the middle. In going ahead with that project, the trustees altered the very nature of their institution while hamstringing their ability to remake it in the future.

For Johnson, it was a devastating blow—the worst of his career, a betrayal from which he would never fully recover. He remained on the museum's board; he retained his position as chair of the architecture department; he would even purchase a pied-à-terre for Whitney and himself in Pelli's tower, which he thought well constructed. But the rejection changed his relationship with the museum, an estrangement that would last for years and permanently alter the way he disposed of his estate, and in particular his coveted art collection. His donations to the museum, up to that time, accounted for well over two thousand works, including many of the institution's signature pieces: Dix's *Dr. Mayer-Hermann*, Schlemmer's *Bauhaus Stairway*, Johns's *Flag*, Rauschenberg's *First Landing Jump*, Warhol's *Gold Marilyn Monroe*. It is hard to fathom the Museum of Modern Art without these works; they define it. Johnson, thereafter, turned off the spigot—with a few significant exceptions, namely Lichtenstein's *Girl with Ball* in 1981 and, a decade later, Warhol's *Orange Car Crash Fourteen Times*. But those were exceptions that almost cruelly kept the museum hoping for more.

Johnson never forgave the museum its trespass, though it had forgiven his. "I gave them a whole collection," he said. "What did they expect? That I would like just being thrown out like that?" He tethered the bulk of his collection to the Glass House, which he donated to the National Trust for Historic Places; the gift was valued at $2 million, and he supplemented it with an endowment of $1 million, which he later doubled.* There were other beneficiaries, as well. In 1982 he donated the archives of his drawings to Columbia University, and he would eventually gift his papers to the Getty Research Institute in Los Angeles—institutions to which he had never had any connection. If MoMA wouldn't let him build its museum, he would have one of his own, and disperse his records so no single institution could claim him.

At least he had other work. Among the projects in which the office was engaged in the early 1970s was an urban landscape project that had come to him through Ruth Carter Stevenson, the daughter of Amon Carter and patron of the museum Johnson designed in his honor. This was to be another gesture of civic patronage, the renewal of four and a half blocks between Fort Worth's convention center and its railroad station into a grand urban amenity and linchpin for a revitalized downtown. The inspiration was the work of San Francisco–based landscape

---

* Today, with the rise of the art market, its value is higher by many orders of magnitude.

architect Lawrence Halprin, who had remade Nicollet Mall adjacent to Johnson's IDS Tower. Halprin's terraced concrete forms and water features on the streets of Portland, Oregon were the prime model for Johnson in Fort Worth. Johnson unashamedly borrowed Halprin's palette, creating a concrete topography that traded on the tropes of the Western landscape, with mesas and ravines and narrow canyons that opened into surprising views. At its core was a vast, unprotected concrete square intended for public events but in practice so hot in the Texas sun as to be uninhabitable for much of the year.

The Active Pool at the 1974 Fort Worth Water Gardens, where "safe danger" could become just plain danger. (Author's photograph)

The chief attraction of the Fort Worth Water Gardens, as its name implied, was water, which Johnson presented in a variety of states. There was a placid "Quiet Pool," set in a sheltered area surrounded by towering cypress trees, and an "Aerating Pool," from which forty dancing jets sprayed a cooling mist into the air. But the true centerpiece was the "Active Pool," a stepped, pentagonal well in which roaring whitewater crashed down nearly four stories before gurgling under a small platform.

Daring visitors could visit this platform, and effectively stand in the midst of the waterfall, but to do so one had to traverse a path of table-shaped steps with no rails, and these were often slick from the spray of the falling water. Those who made that journey were in for a thrilling sensory experience, a combination of physical, aural, and visual pleasure. Johnson called this effect "safe danger," the idea being that it provided an adrenal rush with no genuine risk. Which was true until it wasn't. The inevitable came on June 16, 2004, when three children and an adult who tried to rescue them were sucked underwater and drowned by the pool's recirculation pumps. A memorial plaque now pays tribute to their loss, and to prevent further deaths the pool's depth has been reduced to a level that is no longer lethal.

The projects of the early 1970s changed the way Johnson was seen by his fellow professionals and brought his name to the executive offices of corporate America. The firm's next job made him a genuine American celebrity, the controversial face of postmodernism, with his picture on the cover of *Time* magazine. The story of how it came into the office is one of legend verging on the apocryphal, though facts support its essential contours. It is a story that begins with the arrival in the mail of a questionnaire for prospective architects. This was summarily dumped in the trash by either Johnson or Burgee — both laid claim to the deed — on the principle that replying to over-the-transom inquiries was beneath the firm's dignity. Of the twenty-five firms receiving the survey, however, they alone did not reply, and this piqued the interest of the executives who had sent it. They were from AT&T, then the largest corporation in the world, and they were not used to having their missives go unanswered. They called for an explanation and were routed to Johnson, who responded with characteristic condescension. "We threw it away," he said. "We don't like questionnaires." Unbeknownst to him, they were planning a new headquarters in midtown Manhattan and looking for an architect to build it.

The unintentional hard-to-get act was successful enough that

Johnson and Burgee made it down to the final cut, pitting them against two others, the corporate behemoth HOK and Roche Dinkeloo, the successor firm of Eero Saarinen. The three made their presentations on the same day, Johnson and Burgee going last. The first two entered the company's boardroom loaded down with models and plans and photographs demonstrating what they might do. Johnson and Burgee had taken another tack. Doubling down on their air of cool superiority, they brought only three images: the Seagram Building, IDS, and Pennzoil. If AT&T was looking for something equally distinctive, they would be happy to oblige.

They bought it, mostly. In response to a question about how AT&T's corporate culture might be translated into the design of an office building, Burgee promised that the architects would meet personally with all of the company's top executives. The concession may have won them the job, but it irritated Johnson no end, as it meant several weeks of glad-handing a parade of mid- and upper-level managers in whom he had exactly zero interest. There was, in any event, only one individual who really mattered: John DeButts, the hard-charging chairman of the company. He wanted "the world's greatest skyscraper for the world's greatest corporation," and he wanted Johnson, whom he considered an outright genius, to build it. When Johnson got the call that the firm had won the job, he jumped up and down with giddy excitement. He had landed the project that would allow him to redefine himself yet again.

Even a putative genius was going to be hard-pressed to satisfy the conflicting demands of AT&T. DeButts wanted a distinctive tower, but he didn't want a glass box. And though he wanted an architectural statement, there was a sense that it couldn't be too much of a statement. The institutional culture of Ma Bell was one of plainspoken apple-pie practicality, and there was an abiding concern that a flashy Manhattan office would turn off the company's mom-and-pop clients and shareholders. For that reason, the company had gone to immense pains to secretly cobble together a site for the building on Madison Avenue—then still off the beaten track for a corporate tower—rather than ritzy Park Avenue, where it would sit alongside prestige buildings such as the Seagram.

Johnson's solution was to look back to history, to the stone-clad towers of an earlier era. This was, of course, an about-face from the firm's recent steel-and-glass designs, which had been interpreted as a development of the language of Mies. What Johnson here proposed was nothing short of apostasy, and the greatest provocation was its Chippendale-style pediment, which gave it the patently ludicrous profile of an overgrown eighteenth-century highboy. No building had made so distinctive a mark on the New York skyline since the early 1930s, when the Empire State and Chrysler buildings had fought for aerial supremacy. This was going

The AT&T Tower, 1994.
A postmodern rebus.
(Richard Payne)

to be, according to an effusive Goldberger writing in the *Times,* the "first major monument of post-modernism."

Just how Johnson had arrived at that design became a matter of contention that was almost as famous as the design itself. According to Manley, it came from a grandfather clock Johnson spied while sitting through a meeting in Washington, D.C. Denise Scott Brown was sure it was a reference to the broken pediment at the house her husband and partner, Robert Venturi, built for his mother in the Philadelphia suburbs. Others thought it looked like the cradle of an antique telephone headset. Everyone had an opinion, most of them unflattering. Johnson himself was coy — "I'm not sure, but it did not come from a Chippendale clock," he wrote in a *Times* op-ed defending the design. That in itself was a sign of its controversial status: an architect defending his work on the opinion pages of the paper of record was not an everyday occurrence. It was, in part, necessary because the project was so long on the drawing boards. Johnson and Burgee junked AT&T's questionnaire in 1975. The company didn't move in until 1984, giving both critics and public nearly a decade to air their opinions on the controversial design.

Whatever its intellectual origins, Johnson suffered over the particulars, sketching out a variety of options before landing on the familiar version that would solve the dual purpose of putting his own signature on the New York skyline while engendering no end of controversy — a win-win scenario. The tower's backward-looking vision was conceived as an homage to the grandeur of New York's prewar masonry skyscrapers, and Johnson likewise enrobed his tower in stone. To be precise, he chose pink Stony Creek granite, cut from the same quarry used for the construction of Grand Central Terminal. He even sent one of his trusted deputies, Judith Grinberg, to measure the stones at the terminal so he might copy their proportions. When complete, the building was cloaked in 160,000 cubic feet of granite, a weight so immense that the tower's renowned structural engineer, Les Robertson, was forced to design a special mounting system to support it.

The cost was enormous, estimated at $200 million, making it arguably the most expensive skyscraper in the world, at least per square foot, an extravagance that was antithetical to the company's corporate culture. The immense cost came not just because Johnson had dressed the building in expensive stone — which, in theory at least, would lead to energy savings — but because it was a thirty-six-story building in sixty-story clothing. Johnson convinced his client that the building should have ten-foot ceilings (eight was standard in an office building) to account for the company's technical needs and because he wanted the extra height for aesthetic purposes. The executive suites, on the top three floors, were even taller and more luxurious: twelve-foot ceilings with teak paneling, bespoke furnishings, and an open central stairwell connecting the levels—a corporate mansion in the clouds. One ascended to those heights from a white-marble "sky lobby" elevated six stories above ground level, a trick that allowed Johnson to create a monumental public arcade at street level. From there one entered the main-floor lobby, a tomblike gallery with a soaring vaulted ceiling covered in gold leaf. At its center was sculptor Evelyn Beatrice Longman's *Genius of Electricity,* a twenty-two-foot-tall winged male nude draped in cabling and with a fistful of lightning bolts held heroically above his head. *Golden Boy,* as it was known, had been taken from its privileged spot atop the company's erstwhile headquarters on Broadway.

Johnson's idea, as at both IDS and Pennzoil—and before them the Seagram Building—was to create not just an office building but an urban amenity, a public space where the office worker might walk and shop, have lunch or coffee (or perhaps even a cigarette), people-watch, or otherwise while away an afternoon. AT&T's narrow lot made a front plaza out of the question, so Johnson effectively propped the building on stilts, opening the space beneath and connecting it to a covered atrium that ran along its rear side.

What exactly did it all add up to? Was the Chippendale cap Johnson being playful—a wink-wink, nudge-nudge exaggeration of historical precedent? What about the base? The rather dark and monumental arcade beneath the building wasn't very funny at all—nor did it prove to be much of an amenity, except for the homeless. The top said "joke" and the bottom said "serious" and Johnson—who liked to have things all ways at once—said whatever seemed to be the right thing at the moment. "Philip Johnson has always talked a good building, and AT&T is no exception," quipped one critic. Goldberger, who could hardly be described as a Johnson antagonist, warned during construction that "a joke is being played with scale that may not be so funny when the building, all 660 feet of it, is complete."

That physical incongruity belied an intellectual absurdity: that Johnson had reached back into history to design a work of architecture for a corporation driven by modern technology. This was especially galling, as there was another skyscraper going up half a world away that was also breaking cost records, and it was everything AT&T seemed to reject. That building was Norman Foster's HSBC Tower in Hong Kong, an aggressively technical structure with an exposed skeleton supporting prefabricated steel modules and fantastical hanging gardens. Johnson knew it well; he had been one of Foster's early champions, dating back to the 1960s, when Foster and his friend and future partner Richard Rogers were students together at Yale. In an incident that became lore at the school, Paul Rudolph, who was then the dean, criticized a project on which the two English students had collaborated. Johnson agreed, and proceeded to rip out the offending portion of their model and toss it summarily on the floor. "There, now it's great," he told the stunned students.

Johnson was harsh, but he also gave Rogers the break that launched his career—and changed the face of Paris. In 1971 Rogers and Italian architect Renzo Piano went in together on a submission for what was the most important design competition of the period, for a new modern museum on the Plateau Beaubourg in Paris. Their proposal, one of nearly 700, was for an antic building that wore its colorful innards on its outside. Johnson, who was on the jury, joined French architect Jean Prouvé in fiercely advocating for their submission. This was more than a bit ironic, because Rogers and Piano almost didn't enter the competition as they feared Johnson's presence indicated it would go to a more experienced architect with a more conventional design. But they decided to submit anyway, and that was a smart choice. Notwithstanding his own work, Johnson was fairly ecumenical in supporting the new and the innovative, and all the more if it allowed him to generate controversy, excitement, and attention. That he could do this in staid France was a bonus, for he reserved a Germanophile's special disdain for that nation. "Sex, food, and art are the only important things," he said. "The French know about food."

*   *   *

Johnson could dish it out, but he was easily injured when forced to take his medicine. It stung the most when it came from Huxtable, his erstwhile protégé. Of all the critiques of AT&T, hers was the most damning because she was the one he most respected. "It is impossible to write about this building with mixed feelings," she wrote in April of 1978. Though she described her mentor as a grand intellect, she lambasted AT&T as a "monumental demonstration of quixotic aesthetic intelligence rather than of art." It was "pastiche" and Johnson was now a "dilettante." It was a critique that zeroed in on his deepest insecurity—his suspicion that he had no real gift as a designer. It effectively ended their relationship, despite decades of mutual support and admiration. For Johnson, she had crossed a line that could not be uncrossed.

Her criticism was shared by much of the professional establishment, and especially those in its more progressive quarters, who viewed Johnson's willingness to turn away from Mies not only with aesthetic distaste, but as emblematic of a moral deficiency and essentially nihilistic worldview. Chief among his antagonists was Michael Sorkin, a young New York architect who served double duty as the brash architecture critic of *The Village Voice*. Sorkin had little taste for the more egregious pretensions of the avant-garde set Johnson supported at the IAUS, and in the acerbic-wit department he could return—or just plain open—fire with all of Johnson's nerve, and then some. When it came to AT&T, he was downright ruthless: "The so-called 'post-modern' styling in which AT&T has been tarted up is simply a graceless attempt to disguise what is really the same old building by cloaking it in this week's drag, and by trying to hide behind the reputations of the blameless dead."

As revealing as who didn't like it was who did. In the making of his documentary series "The Shock of the New," critic Robert Hughes had visited Albert Speer, Hitler's chief architect and logistician, in Heidelberg, where he had returned after serving the sentence for crimes against humanity imposed on him at the Nuremberg trials. "Speer talks of you with great respect," Hughes wrote to Johnson on Speer's personal stationery. "I am

365

directed, so to speak, to send compliments from the Masterbuilder to the Formgiver." The two had never met, but Speer was particularly impressed with AT&T, which he considered "more in the spirit of his own work than anything he had seen by an American architect since 1945." Given Johnson's history, this was particularly unsettling, and Hughes happily needled Johnson with it. "I will *try* not to put this story in circulation," he wrote, "or would you prefer a straight cash arrangement?"

The ultimate and entirely unintended irony of the AT&T Building was that the corporation for which it was named effectively ceased to exist while the building itself was still in development, making it obsolete before the first slab of Stony Creek granite had been hoisted into place. DeButts had been in and out of the very first presentation Johnson and Burgee had made to AT&T's executives, called away to deal with the lawsuit that would eventually lead to the divestiture of the company, in January of 1982. By then DeButts was gone, replaced by Charles "Charlie" Brown, a second-generation AT&T manager who exemplified the company's aw-shucks, small-town ethos. Brown tried to kill the project, and when he couldn't, he did what he could to nickel-and-dime it into submission. The reduced company did eventually move in, but by 1984 it was an entirely different business, with a management structure half as large as when the building was commissioned. In 1992 AT&T sold the tower to Sony, which enclosed the lower-level arcade. Its peculiarities have always made it a difficult fit for business; Sony dumped it in 2013 to a developer with plans to transform it into luxury condominiums and a boutique hotel. That plan never materialized, and the "world's greatest skyscraper for the world's greatest corporation" is now that most rare of rarities: a vacant orphan in the heart of midtown Manhattan. A plan to reanimate it by ripping off the facade at its lower levels was met in 2017 with blowback by preservationists, who rightly understood the building as a landmark of postmodern architecture and essential to the character of New York.

Whatever its status now, AT&T propelled Johnson to a new level of stardom and made him, after decades as a glorified backbencher, the face of the architectural profession. In 1978 he was awarded the Gold Medal of the American Institute of Architects, the professional organization's highest accolade. The year following he was the recipient of the inaugural Pritzker Prize, established as an architectural equivalent to the Nobel. Its citation hailed him for his "consistent and significant contributions to humanity and the environment," which was perhaps a stretch. Savvy observers noted that it might not have been the most objective of juries, given that it included Arthur Drexler, his direct subordinate at the Museum of Modern Art; César Pelli, to whom he had just awarded a career-defining commission; and Carleton Smith, his freshman roommate at Harvard.

But nothing quite testified to Johnson's new position quite so much as his appearance on the cover of *Time* magazine, always a sign of supreme cultural relevance. He stood glowering with a gray overcoat draped over a banker's suit, holding the slab-like model of AT&T as if it were a tablet delivered from the heights of Mount Sinai. In a way, he did bear a new covenant. As Hughes wrote in the accompanying story, "Johnson did not create the way of thinking that his building reflects, but he helped bring it about, and now he has given it a degree of public validity that cannot help affecting other corporate clients."

This was undeniably true, but he did more than give this new way of thinking "public validity." Indeed, he was responsible for another iconic postmodern tower that was perhaps even more reviled than AT&T. The architect was Michael Graves, whom Johnson had come to know as a member of the New York Five. Graves had always been an outlier among that group; where the others stuck mostly to white-box modernism, he had moved away. His drawings, in colorful pastel tones, incorporated classical elements and were at once cartoonish and timeless. Johnson, who had no artistic ability, admired him immensely. When Johnson was offered the design of a Madison Avenue gallery, a job too small for consideration, he turned it over to Graves.

But that was just the beginning of his patronage. When the city of Portland, Oregon held a competition for a new municipal building, Johnson was asked to serve on the jury. He had been recommended for that post by Graves, and he returned the favor by promoting him for the job. The pivotal moment came at Johnson's Seagram Building office (the committee met there because Johnson could not be bothered to travel to Portland), with other jury members concerned that Graves was too inexperienced for the project. Johnson pointed out that Graves had gone into partnership with the corporate architects Emery Roth & Sons for the job. To emphasize the significance of this point, he pulled the committee up to his office window. "See that building there? See that building there? See that building there? Those are all Emery Roth."

Graves ended up with the job, and delivered a fifteen-story polychrome cube with punch-cut square windows. The whole thing had a two-dimensional effect, like one of Graves's drawings, but blown up to titanic scale. If its aesthetics were a matter of taste, its functionality, or lack thereof, wasn't: the project never had a significant enough budget for its scale. It did, however, open before Johnson's own AT&T building. Johnson didn't mind—he had all the notoriety he could handle—and when insurance company Humana came to him looking for an architect to design its new headquarters in Louisville, he once again recommended Graves.

Johnson couldn't take it on because the firm was just too busy. The boom times of the Reagan era had arrived, and city skylines across the country were being reshaped by towers with tacked-on columns and pediments and any number of historical references. For that Johnson was responsible, and nobody took greater advantage.

CHAPTER 15

The Head of the Circle

I do not believe in principles, in case you haven't noticed.
—Philip Johnson, 1982

Philip Johnson began his design career as a society architect in the late 1940s, transformed himself into a man of institutions and government in the late 1950s, and finally remade himself as the corporate architect par excellence in the 1970s. It had not happened quickly, and it had not even begun until he was in middle age, after he had already succeeded in one career (curation) and failed in another (politics). The final transition had been the most difficult if the most rewarding, placing organizational demands on him he had never faced before while also elevating him to a level of genuine celebrity. As the 1970s began and Johnson entered his mid-sixties, the tensions implicit in this new role conspired with his martinis-and-foie-gras lifestyle to take a toll on his health, fragile since his sheltered youth.

His friends noticed, as did his colleagues. Johnson, who had always seemed to be rushing, could no longer maintain his usual pace. When he darted about the office or across the city's streets, he found himself short of breath. He speculated that it was emphysema. Burgee and Manley had to make house calls to review projects, visiting him at the Rockefeller Guest House, his Manhattan pied-à-terre from 1972 until he and Whitney took an apartment in another one of his projects. He had designed the luxurious if spartan townhouse on East Fifty-second Street for Blanchette Rockefeller, but ownership had since passed through the museum, which had received it as a gift, and on to the wife of his former client, Robert Leonhardt. It made for a stellar landing pad, a place to entertain parties both grand and intimate. But by the fall of 1974 he was so exhausted that he checked himself into St. Luke's Hospital for examination. According to his physician, Myron Wright, he was often fatigued, and felt a "sense of pressure with hurrying or with emotional stress or strain." Tests there proved inconclusive, but Mary Lasker, a philanthropist he had come to know through her support for urban beautification projects but who was better known as a patron of medical research, suggested he consult pioneering heart surgeon Michael DeBakey at the Baylor College of Medicine in Houston.

Johnson had a speech to give in Houston, so the timing worked out; he arranged an appointment with DeBakey, who determined that he needed a bypass—and thought it dangerous enough that he should operate the following morning. He admitted Johnson to Baylor and arranged for a private room, from which Johnson phoned Burgee at home to notify him of the situation. Burgee considered the decision rash and jumped on a plane to Texas, where he convinced a fearful Johnson that he should hold off on the advice of the father of modern vascular surgery and return to New York, where he could take his time and solicit other opinions. "Let's not get rushed into this," he told Johnson, who hadn't even conferred with Myron Wright. Burgee's framing of the decision as something that affected both of them indicated the conflation of his genuine concern for Johnson's health with his own existential crisis: without Johnson, there would be no Johnson/Burgee.

Afraid and congenitally indecisive, Johnson deferred to Burgee. Back in New York he saw a series of specialists who were divided on surgery, until Johnson finally decided to go ahead. Once again he admitted himself to St. Luke's, this time for double-bypass surgery, which was successful. He recovered quickly and was back to his frenetic self in a matter of weeks. But the office he returned to was changing. The small atelier he had opened in the wake of World War II—just he and Landis Gores in a shared space—had grown into a corporate office occupying two floors of the Seagram Building. The extra bodies were necessary to do the large projects the firm had taken on, but with them came not just bureaucracy and management responsibilities but internal dynamics that Johnson considered both inconvenient and beneath him. The same Philip Johnson who had once fashioned himself as an American political leader was reluctant to engage in the politics of his own architectural practice. This was a large part of why he had partnered with Burgee, but Burgee's ambitions were such that he above all needed to be managed with care.

Johnson's distaste for the mechanics of office culture was compounded by his desire for the practice to be seen purely as the product of his personal aesthetic vision and leadership, even as it became larger and responsibility was dispersed. This reluctance to share credit was a product of his native insecurity and desire for attention. It also made him indispensable: if the office was synonymous with Philip Johnson, Genius, then it could not survive without Philip Johnson.

This was troubling to Burgee, some thirty years his junior, who imagined himself an equal partner in a going and growing concern that would presumably survive Johnson's retirement or death. Burgee's concerns on this front led to a change in the firm's name as he tried tied to assert his own role in the partnership. Back in 1968 the firm had been renamed Philip Johnson & John Burgee Architects. But now, in the summer of 1979, it was rechristened as Johnson/Burgee Architects. Part of the problem had been the sheer length of the name, which led people to drop the second half for linguistic convenience, thereby eliminating Burgee. The removal of first names also conveyed a move to a more corporate footing and away from a cult of personality.

Still, Johnson's inability to share the spotlight made it difficult for the firm to retain talent. "Philip, while he liked people to take his instructions, he didn't like too much contribution," said Burgee. "It was always a toe dance to keep good people in the office." For every John Manley, who was content to remain in the shadows, there was a Richard Foster, irked by a lack of recognition and upward mobility. Eli Attia, the Israeli-born architect who had joined the firm during the design of the Post Oak towers, was among that latter group. His relationship with Johnson was variable: Johnson repeatedly asked Burgee to fire him, which Burgee was reluctant to do. Conversely, Johnson generously countered job offers when he sought to leave, allowed him paid time off for research, and

even invited him to stay at the Glass House compound with his family —
virtually unheard of for an employee.

As Attia would have it, he and not Johnson — and certainly not
Burgee — had been responsible for the firm's aesthetic vision during his
ten years at the firm. More than a decade after his departure, this became
a matter of contention when Attia claimed credit for a series of the firm's
designs, among them Pennzoil Place. Johnson responded with an open
letter claiming that while Attia was an "important member" of the
design team, his claim of credit was, "to put it mildly, a gross exaggeration." Attia complained and Johnson recanted, writing a second letter,
composed in consultation with Attia, stating that "the buildings he lists
in his brochure are his main achievements" and that his decade-long tenure was "wonderful."

Among the jobs for which Attia took credit was the Crystal Cathedral, the Orange County church built for televangelist Robert Schuller.
A charismatic visionary attuned to the possibilities inherent in postwar
modernity, Schuller began preaching in 1955 from the roof of a snack bar
at a drive-in movie theater, with his wife playing an organ pulled by the
family station wagon. He understood California's automotive culture,
and he was quick to embrace television as a means to reach an ever-wider
flock attracted to his sunny, optimistic message. Schuller's popularity,
and his taste for architecture, was such that in 1959 he commissioned the
modernist Richard Neutra to design a church where congregants could
listen to his sermons from the parking lot without leaving their cars. He
called it "a twenty-two-acre shopping center for Christ."

By the late 1970s Schuller needed to upgrade from shopping center to
full-scale mall, a space that could accommodate his prodigious congregation and make a fitting impression on the small screen as the setting
for his "Hour of Power" broadcast, which drew three million viewers on
Sunday mornings. These aspirations led him to Johnson, whom he had
seen in a *Vogue* magazine spread about the opening of the Fort Worth
Water Gardens. When he found himself in New York, he called the office
to "talk about a job" only to find Johnson out of town. Burgee, figuring

he was an architect looking for work, tried to dodge him. But Schuller showed up at the office anyway, and after a conversation worthy of a British comedy of manners, Burgee grasped what Schuller had come to offer. "I have only one question," Schuller asked. "Do you think I will have a spiritual experience with Johnson?"

Johnson, spiritual? It was a ridiculous notion, but Johnson did his best to feign piety in Schuller's presence, even allowing him to conduct prayers with the design staff when he visited the office. That was enough for Schuller to declare that he and Johnson were on a "harmonious wave-length." It didn't really matter, anyway, for the two were kindred spirits, a pair of natural salesmen with a shared ambition to build on a grand scale and achieve inspiration through architecture.

The firm's first attempt to attain that result failed spectacularly, how-ever, leaving Schuller uncharacteristically speechless over lunch at John-son's corner table at the Four Seasons. A Spanish Mission–style church, clad in stucco with a red-tile roof, was definitely not what Schuller had in mind. It should have the spirit of California, he told Johnson, recalling his start at a local drive-in. Why not embrace that experience, and bring the outside in?

The design that followed satisfied all of Schuller's aspirations, and then some: Johnson's response, filtered through Attia, was an enormous box of reflective glass panels — 10,900 of them — in the shape of a flat-tened diamond, pinched in at the sides. As with Neutra's previous facil-ity, the building could be opened up with a 90-foot-tall door, inspired by NASA's hangar at Cape Canaveral, to allow Schuller's sermons to reach an overflow crowd in the parking lot. Inside the space was bright, cheer-ful, and orderly, with the altar facing the short axis, so the congregation (and the television audience) would feel close to the pastor. For Johnson, the Gothic cathedral was the ultimate form of architecture, and here he had achieved something on a scale of those structures of yore, a genuine Chartres of televangelism.

Its opening was a ceremonial event par excellence, with the Goodyear blimp overhead and a personal message from Ronald Reagan. As Paul

The Crystal Cathedral, 1980. The Chartres of televangelism.
(Richard Payne)

Goldberger noted in the *Times,* it was the most significant debut in Orange County since the opening of Disney World. Those two places had much in common: both offered a temporary escape from reality within a sunny constructed environment. Whether this was praiseworthy was a matter of opinion. As Italian critic Manfredo Tafuri noted derisively in the journal *Domus,* Johnson "has decided to live in an imaginary museum where all tragedy has been banned. The noise of the world does not penetrate his Crystal Cathedral." Others complained that its mirrored-glass facades were more appropriate to a nondescript corporate office than a religious facility. That cavil was a misreading of the intentions of both the architect and Schuller, who wanted nothing so much as to introduce the sacred into the everyday. As Goldberger wrote in the *Times,* "If this is not the deepest or the most profound religious building of our time, it is at least among the most entertaining."

Above all, it was the quintessential Johnson project, in that it could be read in any number of entirely contradictory ways; it was unabashedly

Johnson's faux-Mansard facelift of 1001 Fifth Avenue. A joke without humor, 1979. (Richard Payne)

modern yet decidedly kitschy; it was fascistic in its relentless celebration of order but bathed in the sybaritic optimism of Southern California. Empty it was cold; filled with Schuller's congregants it came alive. And then there was the question of its authorship. Attia would claim it, and the structure was inarguably composed of the gridded glass that he favored. But Johnson was never averse to taking the design of another and making it his own. And here the decisive and perverse presence was his and his alone.

Attia was not long for the office; he was a modernist to his core, with little tolerance for Johnson's postmodernism. He found opportunity in the client of one of the firm's more egregiously shallow projects, a facelift for 1001 Fifth Avenue, a residential tower that butted up against 998 Fifth, perhaps the single most revered apartment house in the city. That McKim, Mead & White masterpiece was built by the grandfather of Jackie Onassis and had been home, over the years, to a succession of Astors, Rockefellers, and Vanderbilts. On its opposite side, it was sandwiched in by a handsome beaux arts mansion. Philip Birnbaum, 1001's principal architect, chose not to compete with these landmarks on their own terms, and proposed a generic modern design. This was rejected as beneath the dignity of the block by the powerful neighbors, who convinced the developer, Peter Kalikow, to bring in Johnson, a figure who could presumably bestow on Birnbaum's frame a more tasteful exterior treatment and lobby. Following these instructions, Johnson dressed the building in limestone and copied the stringcourse lines of its more distinguished neighbors, but this was putting lipstick on an inglorious pig. Worst of all was the faux mansard roof—a false front supported by struts—that Johnson placed at the top of the building, a postmodern joke that wasn't funny. The firm's own monograph described it as a "last-ditch effort at sensitivity" before concluding that it was "reasonably neighborly" but "not innocent." Critics were far less generous.

Among the ramifications of that job was to connect Attia, who worked on it, with Kalikow. The two got along well enough that the developer had him begin work on a speculative office tower that would rise on Park Avenue, just south of Grand Central Terminal. In a meeting with Burgee, Attia proposed that he would bring it in to the firm if he was made a partner, something the principals previously had resisted. Burgee was furious and refused outright. Attia left, taking both the Park Avenue project and Kalikow with him—a bitter pill for the firm.

Johnson had no illusions about 1001 Fifth, but he moved into the building nonetheless, taking a one-bedroom apartment with David Whitney. It was a decided step down from the Rockefeller Guest House, but as the 1970s turned into the 1980s and Johnson moved into his seventies, a more domesticated life with Whitney seemed to be in order. Their respective infidelities had taken a toll over the years. Johnson's occasional assignations with Robert Melik Finkle had ceased only in the mid-1970s, and then it was more because the idealistic Finkle was appalled by Johnson's turn to postmodernism. Whitney, for his part, had a reputation for belligerence and drink, often together. The apartment they shared at 1001 Fifth was kept fastidiously, with Jasper Johns prints on the walls and Andy Warhol's cow-print wallpaper in the bathroom. The refrigerator was eternally empty, because they never cooked. When

Warhol, on a visit, noticed a pair of underwear out on a bedroom chair, he considered it such a rare breach of decorum that he noted it in his diary: "It was the first time I've ever seen a piece of clutter in their apartment."

Warhol was a regular fixture with the couple, because Johnson collected his work and Whitney curated it. Whitney's interest extended beyond art, or even friendship. His infatuation became a matter of public record with the publication of Warhol's diaries, a tabloid sensation in 1989. Johnson and Whitney appeared throughout the occasionally titillating but generally tedious compendium of the artist's daily maneuvers. Those who turned to the date of December 4, 1983 found the three protagonists at a Four Seasons event celebrating Johnson. Whitney, after one too many martinis, informed Warhol of his plan to take up with him after Johnson's (presumably not-too-distant) death. "As soon as Philip popped off he and I could get together," Warhol recounted. "I laughed it off, but later he said I had to kiss him on the lips. I really didn't know he actually felt this way about me!" This became a routine: whenever Whitney was around Warhol in a social situation, he'd get drunk and declare his intentions. "It's scary," wrote Warhol the following August. A few months later Whitney again told Warhol of his plan for when "Pops pops off." Warhol wasn't interested, and suggested that, given his penchant for drink and high living, Whitney would "probably pop off before Pops."

Johnson's lack of faith in Whitney, and perhaps his concern over his drinking, was plainly evident in his decision to trust the dependable Burgee with instructions on what to do in the event of his death. "I wish you to be in complete charge of the obsequies, your responsibilities ending with the final disposition of the remains," he wrote in a 1985 memo.

That was mordant thinking at a time when business was very, very good. Thanks to Burgee's business acumen, by the early 1980s the headcount at the firm had grown tenfold. It was an unusually happy place to work, and especially appreciated by women with young families, as Johnson insisted employees keep strict banker's hours. He didn't like to pay overtime, and he still clung to a gentleman's idea of the profession, and with it the notion that one should have time for a personal life. Other corporate firms, by contrast, had—and still have—a tendency to expect junior architects to work the same hours as their contemporaries in law and business, but at far lower compensation.

Much of that new work came from a single source, the Houston developer Gerald Hines, who had found such success with the Pennzoil towers. With the economic crisis of the 1970s past, he embarked on a spate of building across the country, much of it designed by Johnson/Burgee. The first in this series was San Francisco's 101 California Street Building, a granite-and-glass megastructure with a stepped circular plan— imagine the IDS Center forced through a tube —and exposed concrete columns at the base. The building was largely forgettable until it achieved an unwanted notoriety in 1993, when a deranged gunman, Gian Luigi Ferri, took an elevator to the 34th floor, donned protective headgear, and embarked on a killing spree that was then unprecedented.

It was the last Johnson tower that could be classified as "modern," and not coincidentally the last on which Attia played a significant design role. Henceforth Johnson's skyscrapers would lean in to history with progressively more zeal, beginning with the Transco (now Williams) Tower, another production for Hines, this time on a site in Houston near the Galleria mall and the Post Oak development. As with Post Oak, Johnson looked back to New York's prewar history for inspiration, to the Beekman Tower, an Art Deco jewel he could view from the window behind his desk in the Seagram Building. The Beekman was built of warm beige brick with vertical channels and stepped setbacks at its crown; Johnson's interpretation more than doubled it in size, from twenty-eight to sixty-five stories, and sheathed it in reflective glass, though not entirely: in a bid for additional grandeur, Johnson tacked on a monumental granite entry gate at the base that was dramatically at odds with the rest of the building. Urbanistically it couldn't have been further from the Beekman, which was set within New York's dense street grid. With an open site in Houston, Johnson fronted his building with a linear park bordered by oaks, a composition that culminated at a large hemispherical fountain set behind Palladian arches. In case anyone

PPG Place in Pittsburgh, 1984, a black glass fantasia inspired by the British Houses of Parliament. (Richard Payne)

failed to notice this new addition to the scene—and with its priapic vertical form it was intentionally hard to miss—Johnson installed a rotating searchlight at its top, marking its place in the sprawling Houston landscape.

Johnson took a similar aesthetic approach for PPG Place, a development spread across more than five acres of prime downtown space packaged by the Pittsburgh Redevelopment Authority. The anchor of the complex was a forty-story headquarters building for the Pittsburgh Plate Glass Company, which determined the principal material used throughout: black mirrored glass—more than a million square feet of it—set off in grids of aluminum, and all done up in a pointed neo-Gothic style based on the Houses of Parliament in London. There were six buildings in all, arranged around a central plaza marked by a Napoleonic obelisk of Johnson's own design. The idea was to create something like a medieval village within the city, with the office tower in place of the cathedral—that alone being a rueful

The Republic Bank Tower in Houston, 1984, with a stepped-back Dutch Gothic cap, to preserve the views from neighboring Pennzoil Place. (Hines Interests Limited Partnership)

commentary on American values—and the surrounding buildings in support. It has been a relative success in that capacity, a happy and largely occupied hub of activity in the city core, and one with a strong visual identity, although distinctly apart from and unrelated to its neighbors.

Transco and PPG took the forms of history and dressed them in modern materials; Johnson's massive Republic Bank Center looked back to history—specifically, to the Dutch Gothic of the seventeenth century—but without the modern drapery. The composition, developed by Hines, sat on a full city block directly across the street from Pennzoil Place, and initially Johnson thought to match it with a complementary design. Hines rejected that proposal in the interest of contrast. There were other demands, among them that it be built around a switching station, and that it not block Pennzoil chairman Hugh Liedtke's skyline view. At 780 feet it towered over its neighbor, but Johnson solved the view-corridor problem by giving the building three pointed gables that stepped back as it rose, so that by the top it was far reduced in bulk. Instead of glass, its facades were of red Swedish granite, giving it the impression of an immense, scale-less mass at ground level. Marked on the skyline by its stepped roof, at the street it was defined by an enormous banking hall—actually a separate but attached building. This was an essay in architectural decadence, an immense box with 167-foot-high ceilings, as well as arches, columns, and arcades in marble and ebony. Overscale antique-style street lamps and clocks were set about to give the place some semblance of urbanity. But this was a far cry from IDS, with its Crystal Court, or even AT&T: here the public space only masqueraded as such, a pantomime of a civic gesture.

It looked rich, however, and that was the look of the moment in the burgeoning Reagan era. It was morning in America, and Johnson's solid buildings, with their familiar architectural elements—columns, pediments, vaults, gables, and so many other details jettisoned as extraneous by modernists—spoke to a conservative clientele open to a corporate language that corresponded to the white-picket-fence suburbs to which they returned after work. Soon Johnson/Burgee had towers going up across the United States at a rate that was astonishing for what was still, in essence, a boutique partnership. Atlanta, Boston, Chicago, Dallas, Denver, Detroit, Louisville, New York, San Francisco. There were towers everywhere, a string of similarly forgettable buildings, unless one happened to live or work in one of those cities, in which case their pharaonic scale and retrograde presence made them unavoidable touchstones, generally unforgiving to the pedestrian. Each one had some distinguishing characteristic: Atlanta had pergolas. Dallas got barrel vaults. Denver got Palladian windows that looked like wallpaper. Louisville's was capped by a hemispherical dome. Chicago and Detroit got gables at the skyline, San Francisco a mansard roof with kitschy sculptures.

They had one thing in common: they were all profitable. The little firm that once struggled to land residential work in the Connecticut hinterland was now pulling in nearly $20 million annually in billings, with seven-figure salaries for the partners. For the first time, Johnson could claim to be rich of his own accord. What happened to the Philip Johnson who pilloried development driven by speculation and the corporate degradation of the city? The Philip Johnson who considered ditching his practice to go into nonprofit urban advocacy? That figure was now but a distant memory.

No project better illustrated the ultimate cynicism of this output than One International Place, a complex of three stone-clad towers (of forty-six, twenty-seven, and nineteen stories) on the low-rise fringes of Boston's financial district. The buildings were patently overscale for the site, the grid of Palladian windows on the smallest towers an absurd affectation. "The project is ridiculous," declared the *Boston Globe*, "a jumble of unrelated buildings standing in isolation."

The harshest criticism came not from the press but from Johnson's peers, at a private conference whose proceedings became public (by design). The setting was the most grand in American architecture: under the dome of Thomas Jefferson's Rotunda at the University of Virginia, in Charlottesville. The venue was furnished by Jaquelin Robertson, lately installed as dean of the university's architecture school, but it was really a substitute for the Institute for Architecture and Urban Studies, which the event was supposed to celebrate on its tenth anniversary. Political turmoil within the IAUS, however, precluded it from acting as host. The institute's board, in an effort to establish financial and curricular discipline, effectively destroyed the freewheeling openness that had made it so attractive to thinkers of an avant-garde bent. Johnson was a party to this in all ways—he was its most devoted benefactor, and a mentor to Peter Eisenman, its deposed founder—though he tried to keep a safe distance by installing Burgee as his surrogate on the board.

Robertson acted as host, but the prime mover behind the Charlottesville event was Eisenman. (Robertson and Eisenman, close friends but divergent philosophically, had a short-lived architectural practice together.) Invitations to the secret proceedings went out with the not-so-cryptic signature *P3*, the *3* being a flopped *E*. It did not take an Einstein to figure out the source. The guest list was intentionally exclusionary, the idea being that this would add to the event's (and the participants') cachet while fueling interest in the mysterious goings-on. To ensure that it would be recorded for posterity, the editor of the publisher Rizzoli was on hand to see it into book form.

Beyond narrow self-promotion, the stated, if dubious, agenda was to reclaim control of the direction of the profession for architects themselves, steering it away from what Eisenman called the "hegemony of the writer." The cast was drawn from the CASE and IAUS groups, with some older hands thrown in (Kevin Roche, Paul Rudolph) and figures from abroad, most of whom had some association with the institute (Toyo Ito, Arata Isozaki, Rem Koolhaas, Rafael Moneo). In all there were twenty-five architects, embracing architecture's full ideological spectrum, from the most postmodern (Graves) to the relentlessly modern (Meier).

As intriguing as who was there was who was not. The most conspicuous absence, given his role as theoretical godfather, was Robert Venturi, who had a distaste for such pugilistic gatherings. Absent also was his partner Denise Scott Brown, who rather enjoyed them. She was not invited, because no women (or minorities) were to be invited to this stag party. "It was all very male, a special one of those 'boys club' events," wrote Robertson in his introduction to the book that documented the proceedings. Over two days the group sat around a long conference table, with each architect being allowed a ten-minute presentation of a single unbuilt project, followed by twenty minutes of discussion. According to Robertson, "it was a time of both high-minded objective criticism and the settling of a number of old and new scores."

First up were Johnson and Burgee, and the project they presented to this contentious audience was One International Place. The inquisition that followed began gently with a diplomatic question from Bob Stern but devolved rapidly. Roche wanted to know how the buildings responded to their context, and Johnson freely admitted that they didn't, that their scale was grossly inappropriate—"two million square feet that should not be in this part of Boston." Eisenman called it a "pastiche." Koolhaas eviscerated him for the design's pretension. "What baffles me is the contradiction between your casualness and the extreme uptightness, the awkward elements," he said. When he followed up with a question about the thinking by which Johnson chose his forms, the reply was irritatingly flippant, "Oh, there isn't any." César Pelli, also pursuing this line of

One International Place in Boston, the project that begat Johnson's "I'm a whore" proclamation. (Richard Payne)

inquiry, got a more telling response: "I do not believe in principles, in case you haven't noticed."

That was a cop-out that revealed his insecurity: if he wasn't trying to be good, if he admitted to his cynicism, then the criticism couldn't reach him. But the response that inevitably caught the public's attention, and would follow him for the rest of his career, came in reply to Rob Krier, an architect and polemicist who advocated a return to classical design principles, and whose recent book, *Urban Space,* argued that tall buildings were inherently destructive to a city. With this assumption in mind, Krier wanted to know how Johnson could justify the building of skyscrapers. The nihilism of Johnson's response was brazen in its nakedness. "I am a whore and I am paid very well for building high-rise buildings."

This was the architectural equivalent of the "I was only following orders" defense—poor optics for Johnson, with his inglorious past—though even worse, as it implied a willingness to please, just so long as the check was large enough, and damn the consequences. As Robertson demurred in the introduction to the publication of the proceedings, this was "not an encouraging strategy for those interested in building more appropriate, practical, elegant, and just cities." Michael Sorkin, who was becoming Johnson's principal nemesis in print, skewered him (and the entire conference) mercilessly in Shakespearean verse:

Philip: Here's a building that should make a buck.
The Others: It's ugly as sin.
Philip: I don't give a fuck.

Johnson, of course, knew he was courting controversy; he did so intentionally. The question was why, and the plausible explanations were contradictory. Robertson suggested it was a facetious ruse, speculating that Johnson's real intent was to illustrate the profession's lamentable powerlessness in the context of American corporate culture. The problem was that once Johnson's "facetious" ploy was rendered into two million square feet of actual building, it was no longer droll. Any real explanation would have to account for the fact that Johnson's buildings were not just jokes but actual places in the city. More plausible was the idea that Johnson had always operated under the assumption that, as P. T. Barnum was said to have said, there is no such thing as bad publicity. More acutely, the philosophy allowed Johnson to satisfy several conflicting imperatives: his paradoxical desire to be both an *enfant terrible* within the profession and a source of establishment conformity to his clients, and also his atavistic need to be the center of attention.

Johnson liked to be at the head of the table, and indeed that is where he was seated at the gatherings that had precipitated the Charlottesville conference and continued on a regular basis in the years following. These took place on Monday evenings at the Century Association. The club was exclusive—no women were admitted until 1989—its roster made up of the city's cultural glitterati since its founding in 1829. Johnson himself had almost been rejected: Max Abramovitz attempted to blackball him. (Whether his objection was Johnson's fascist history, his behavior during the planning of Lincoln Center, or simple distaste is unrecorded.) The idea for a small colloquy of architects over dinner had actually come from Richard Meier, who broached the subject with Johnson over a lunch at the Four Seasons. Johnson approved, and together they made a list of invitees, defining the "in crowd" then and there. The stalwarts were, in addition to Meier and Johnson, Eisenman, Graves, Gwathmey, Robertson, and Stern, and they were typically joined by other architects and critics of acceptable pedigree. Among the very few women invited were Denise Scott Brown, Zaha Hadid, and Phyllis Lambert, but it was almost always an all-male event.

As Meier, Johnson, and several other initiates were members of the club — "Centurions" — it was deemed an appropriate place for the private gathering, and even better still to hold it in the library of the architect Charles Adams Platt, which had been donated to the club in 1942. Its 450 volumes — documenting, primarily, the history of European architecture — made for an especially apt backdrop for discussions frequently veering into the application of that material in contemporary practice. The dinners were black tie and began at 6:30 because Johnson, already in his seventies when they began, liked to be home and in bed early. The format called for each dinner to have a principal subject for discussion, often determined by a guest of honor. After a brief presentation, there would be open discussion. Seating was assigned, usually by Meier, who diagrammed who would be next to whom. In all of Meier's drawings Philip Johnson was at the top, in the place of honor — "the head of the circle," in the words of Michael Graves.

The content of these dinners was of significantly less import than the simple fact of their existence. "It was always less interesting than everyone who didn't get invited thought it would be," recalled Stern. But that was the point and the essential theme: exclusion. From the very inception of the idea it was about the establishment of a favored circle, a power play. Those within its borders were the chosen few — the ones who would be asked to lunch at the Four Seasons, the ones who would have their work displayed at the Museum of Modern Art, the ones who would benefit from Johnson's direct and indirect patronage. Nobody stood to benefit more than Johnson, the gatekeeper-in-chief, for the proceedings both magnified and advertised his status as the profession's ultimate kingmaker and elder statesman.

The notoriety only helped business, never mind the stinging rebukes from his peers and the press. The brazenness of his own cynicism became ever more shameless, his projects achieving what appeared to be an ever-increasing level of nihilism, a rejection of all the ideals that had defined both his more recent writing on urbanism and his earlier built work. The sharp modernism of his Miesian period had given way to a coy postmodernism and finally to something altogether worse and without intellectual pretension or rigor, an architecture of staggeringly indelicate historic detailing slapped onto leaden structures that made negative contributions to civic space. With IDS, Johnson had tied corporate modernism to a sense of progressive urbanism. Now he had unapologetically retreated

The Crescent in Dallas, from modern to kitsch, 1985. (Richard Payne)

from that goal, instead offering up his name and his reputation to any client willing to foot a large enough bill.

This reached its egregious apogee in Dallas with the Crescent, a luxury mixed-use development dressed up like a steroidal Parisian *hôtel particulier,* with rusticated stone walls and mansard roofs. In an attempt to claim a regional identity for the project, patterns for iron filigree railings and finials were borrowed from the landmark Victorian buildings of Galveston, which recently had been celebrated by noted architectural photographer Ezra Stoller. The eighteenth-century terrace architecture of Bath, England was also cited as an inspiration. In the *Times,* Goldberger called it a "marvelous confection," but as architecture it was

The 1985 School of Architecture at the University of Houston. An imitation where originality was called for. (Author's photograph)

bloated and absurd, an unfortunate confirmation and reification of the stereotype of Dallas as a city of outsize arriviste pretensions.

Aside from bad taste, the Crescent's crime was urbanistic. Here was an opportunity to make a genuine civic space at a crossroads of the expanding city, but instead Johnson created what was in essence a self-enclosed superblock: more than a million square feet of space spread over ten acres. Within was a five-star hotel, three class-A office buildings, a luxury mall, and more than four thousand parking spaces. As *Dallas Morning News* architecture critic David Dillon wrote, "the Crescent fails in its attempt to reconcile the competing claims of city and suburb." It was a generous assessment.

The Crescent's institutional equivalent in cynicism could also be found in Texas. In 1983 Johnson and Burgee received the commission for a new architecture school building at the University of Houston. Like the Crescent it was of inflated French origin, though here the ideas were drawn from the imagination of neoclassical visionary Claude-Nicolas Ledoux; the building was an unashamed reproduction of his House of Education, a speculative project for an ideal city drawn in the 1770s. The faculty was opposed to it from the outset. That an institution promoting creativity should not create something original seemed, at its very essence, anathema. "Why does an architecture building have to be a COPY???" asked one campus poster. Judged on its own terms it was a failure, a postmodern pastiche. Venturi had called for an architecture of complexity and contradiction; Johnson responded with the unambiguous and uninteresting, four cookie-cutter stories of open space lighted by windows designed for their outward symmetry rather than the needs of architecture students. At the center was his signature: a giant skylit atrium bereft of energy and signifying nothing.

Burgee had not even wanted to take on the project, fearing it would be a black hole of time and energy at a moment when resources were better spent on more profitable work, and not a prestige undertaking that would enhance Johnson's reputation. That was indicative of a growing problem. Success exacerbated the firm's internal dysfunction. From Burgee's perspective it was caught in a slow-moving existential crisis; as Johnson aged, Burgee became more concerned about its future and his ability to keep it a viable concern when Johnson finally walked (or was carried) away. This was a moment he had been anticipating since 1967, when he partnered with Johnson and became his heir apparent. Johnson was sixty then, Burgee nearly three decades his junior. But the passing of the torch never happened, and as time wore on, Johnson's flame burned only brighter. This was Burgee's worst fear: that the firm would be so closely identified with Johnson that it would be unsalvageable when he finally withdrew. And by the late 1970s it had begun to dawn on Burgee that succession was never going to happen, despite Johnson's promises over the years. "He never really meant it. But I bought into it. Several times," he said, later. The very idea of torch-passing was antithetical to Johnson's understanding of architecture as an art practiced by singular form-givers; if this was the case, once the form-giver was gone, there was no practice left worth retaining. It was the architectural version of *"L'état c'est moi."*

Johnson was nevertheless forced to balance his intellectual prerogatives with the pragmatic concerns and needs of Burgee. The 1979 decision to collapse the firm's name to Johnson/Burgee was Johnson's attempt to solve this problem typographically, as if bringing their names into closer physical proximity might bridge the yawning gap in their stature. Four years later, with Johnson pushing eighty, he made another concession to Burgee's desperation, agreeing to rename the firm yet again, this time to John Burgee Architects with Philip Johnson. On the surface it was a solution ideal for all parties. Burgee wanted his name at the top of the corporate masthead, and Johnson—tired of traveling and glad-handing clients—was happy to focus his energies on design. He knew that what came out of the Johnson office would be identified with Philip Johnson, no matter whose name appeared first on the stationery.

As this slow-motion drama unfolded, another obstacle blocked Burgee's path to sole possession of the practice. That obstacle was Raj Ahuja, who had joined the firm in the early 1970s as a draftsman. In 1984 he became a partner, despite the fact that neither Johnson nor Burgee wanted him on the company masthead.

Born in Lahore in 1941, Ahuja emigrated to India after partition in 1947. He studied architecture there and then made his way to New York, where a friend landed him an interview with Johnson. It turned into a job, and in 1973 he returned to India with Johnson, who had been commissioned to design a theater, the National Center for the Performing Arts, in Bombay. The job had come through Zubin Mehta, conductor of the New York Philharmonic, who was born in Bombay and had worked with Johnson on the renovation of Avery Fisher Hall at Lincoln Center. That theater, designed by Johnson's rival Max Abramovitz, had been an acoustic disaster since its unveiling, a problem Johnson's alterations did not solve.

In Bombay, Johnson and Ahuja toured the city's colonial British architecture, which would serve as inspiration for the complex, then met with Indian industrialist J. R. D. Tata, the chief benefactor of the project, who had his own design thoughts. During their meeting Tata presumed to draw out some of his ideas; he was a man used to dictating orders. Johnson, however, was not used to taking them. In a break of decorum that was almost unthinkable, he grabbed Tata's pencil, broke it in two, and tossed it down. "I'm the architect. You talk and I draw. You don't draw for me." Tata, chastened, agreed. The product was a taut, boxy exterior in Johnson's Kahnian concrete idiom. It was not especially dynamic, but the theaters inside were of the dramatic jewel-box variety Johnson had mastered for the State Theater at Lincoln Center.

In August of 1975 Ahuja was dispatched from New York to Tehran to open a satellite office for the firm. There was opportunity aplenty in prerevolutionary Iran; the Arab oil embargo had spiked profits, and architects were flooding the country to cash in. The Shah's wife, Farah Pahlavi, had studied architecture at the École Spéciale d'Architecture in Paris, and her presence made for a climate encouraging to the international design set. At the center of that rush was Johnson's good friend

Jaquelin Robertson, who was the chief designer for a massive new redevelopment project for central Tehran, Shahestan Pahlavi. (It was never
built, due to the fall of its namesake.) Robertson, with his genteel Southern charm, could make anything sound enticing, and soon enough Johnson had likewise caught what Robertson called "the Iran disease." When
Johnson visited Tehran, Robertson made sure he was feted by the city's
elite. Johnson, erstwhile champion of the American *volk,* was happy to
work in the shah's notoriously repressive regime.

Two significant projects emerged from that time, both in the city of
Isfahan, the once-magnificent Persian capital some three hundred miles
south of Tehran. One of them, a luxury apartment building overlooking

The picture that defines the partnership: Raj Ahuja, separated from
Burgee and Johnson, in a 1987 press photograph. (New York Times)

the seventeenth-century Khaju Bridge, was built. The other, a large commercial development off the Chahar Bagh, the city's grand boulevard, was not. With revolution in the air, Ahuja returned to the New York office, but he was a man out of place, having become accustomed to the perks of life overseas: a free apartment, an expensed Mercedes. Back home he was like anyone else at the firm, except for the fact that his colleagues did not trust him, seeing him as an ambitious interloper. Johnson and Burgee didn't quite know what to do with him. For long stretches, it seemed that he just sat at his desk, idle.

Eventually he was moved to the fifty-story Peachtree Tower project in Atlanta, one of the firm's works for Hines. He was an excellent manager, and particularly adept at keeping costs in line, which made him the rarest of birds at the firm and endeared him to its clients. Indeed, he went out of his way to ingratiate himself with those clients, in particular at the Park Tower Group, the development company of George Klein. "That was the problem with Raj," said Burgee. "He thought he was playing at a level higher than he was." Still, he was undeniably efficient. He managed the building of 33 Maiden Lane, a twenty-seven-story tower in New York's financial district. Built for Klein's Park Tower Group, it was grim and gray, with a monumental arcade at the base and limestone facades marked by projecting cylindrical turrets—a nod to the castle-like Federal Reserve Building next door.

Ahuja's impressive organizational ability left him with a trump card when Johnson and Burgee finally needed someone who could complete the firm's signature AT&T commission, which had dragged on endlessly, always with some new hiccup precluding completion. Sensing he had the upper hand, Ahuja demanded a piece of the partnership. Johnson, never really concerned about the slipping of budgets or the whims of clients, strongly advised against it. But Burgee, worried about business, relented and Ahuja got his minor partnership, though not his name on the masthead. It was a decision Burgee would soon deeply regret. The two principals' discomfort with it was plainly evident in a promotional photograph taken shortly thereafter. The three partners posed behind a table with large models of the firm's many projects, with a smiling

Burgee in the center and an avuncular Johnson over his shoulder. Ahuja stood by himself to the side with his arms folded, separated from the others by one of their recent towers. It seemed as if he was his in his own unrelated photo.

Ahuja's elevation was followed by another alteration of the firm's identity: a change of address. Johnson had moved into the Seagram Building while it was still a construction site, and though he had shifted floors, it had never stopped being home. It was ideal, of course: the Four Seasons, his personal cafeteria, was downstairs; it was convenient to the museum and to Grand Central's service to New Canaan; clients were impressed by the austere monument, a reminder to them and (perhaps more importantly) to him of his association with Mies. But in February of 1986 the office picked up and moved two blocks east to the firm's latest contribution to the city skyline, 885 Third Avenue, better known as the Lipstick Building.

The Deco-style "Lipstick Building," an icon for New York's prestige-deprived Third Avenue, 1985. (Hines Interests Limited Partnership)

The name came naturally to it; it resembled an enormous tube of lip-stick, its telescoping cylindrical shaft accented by horizontal bands of red granite and shiny stainless steel. Chanel was not the intended reference. For Johnson, it was yet another nod to the city's deco tradition, though it seemed out of place on down-market Third Avenue. For the developer, Gerry Hines, it was absolutely essential because Third Avenue was the "boondocks" (Johnson's word) as a location for class-A office space. A signature design was therefore necessary to attract tenants east from tonier addresses along the likes of Park Avenue. Johnson was thus the perfect target, and Hines lured him over with a deal for the second floor, never the most popular lease. It was a match made in heaven.*

The Lipstick Building helped transform Third Avenue, but as that project was under way the firm became involved in a work of New York urban reinvention on a far grander scale: the redevelopment of Times Square. Entrée into this urban-design soap opera came through Klein and his Park Tower organization. The glamorous "Crossroads of the World" had been in fitful decline since World War II, its historic theaters buffeted by the emergence of movies and television and the flight from the city to the suburbs. The louche titillation of Ziegfeld's dancing girls gave way to the tawdry peep show, introduced in 1967. By the 1970s Times Square was a wreck: dilapidated and infested by drugs, prostitution, and street crime. Even as New York rebounded from the economic ravages of the 1970s, it remained a national symbol of urban dysfunction, the sordid heart of the American city.

Times Square had always had a tawdry underbelly, and nobody knew that history better than Philip Johnson, whose life had been nearly upended by an assignation gone bad with an underage rent boy at the Times Square Hotel back in the 1930s. This made him an unlikely, or at least ironic, vessel for the area's cleansing, but contradiction, as he so frequently demonstrated, was not something that troubled him. In part because of his prominence, and in part because the mechanics of the

---

* It would later achieve considerable publicity from another newsmaking tenant: Bernie Madoff.

development were so complex, Johnson became the public face of the renewal plan, which situated four massive new office towers—fifty-six, forty-nine, thirty-seven, and twenty-nine stories, respectively—around a barren wedge-shaped plaza then occupied by the historic Times Tower. Upon the announcement of the plan, in December of 1983, Johnson and Burgee appeared before the press, beaming but dwarfed behind scale models of their proposed buildings.

Only they were smiling. Beyond the bitter pill that Johnson, the noted preservationist, was advocating the demolition of the Times Tower, one of the city's defining buildings, there was the fact that the proposed towers could not have been less compelling as architecture or more inappropriate for the site. But for their heights, they were virtually identical, with monumental granite bases and giant glass mansard roofs topped by spiky pinnacles—references, in theory, to the long-departed Astor and Knickerbocker hotels. The facades were essentially glass, but with limestone overlays that looked like children's drawings of skyscrapers.

The intention was to create something cartoonish for a cartoonish place. But even crediting that ambition, the result was disappointing: a cartoon without humor or wit, and at immense scale. Apart from being dull, the buildings exhibited a blatant disregard for the established design guidelines they were supposed to meet, which included the retention of the Times Tower, setbacks to minimize bulk, and the application of signs and reflective materials to maintain the character of the "Great White Way." As New York magazine's Carter Wiseman wrote in a cover story critical of the design and planning process, "the idea is not merely to rebuild its physical fabric but also to redefine its social identity, by making a massive transfer of 'upscale' uses into thirteen battered acres where many New Yorkers now fear to tread."

The design proposal was both lazy as architecture and a grave intellectual miscalculation. New Yorkers wanted Times Square tamed, but they did not want it neutered and replaced by dull monuments to corporatism. Times Square was supposed to be an escape from that realm of conformity, a place with the frisson of danger. The plans were thus received with broad public and critical derision. Huxtable, who had warned of "the perils of commercial blandness" in Times Square back in the late 1960s, saw in the Johnson-Burgee plan a confirmation of all her worst fears. "Oversized commercial packages wrapped in a bit of quasi-historical trim," she wrote. More damning was Brendan Gill, of the typically staid *New Yorker*. To him the project was "a heinous misadventure," the buildings "exceptionally repellent."

The only mitigating voice came from a diplomatic Goldberger, who worried about the scale and repetitive nature of the projects but suggested they were "likely to be the most striking additions to a skyline that has had its share of striking things." That equivocation prompted its own Sorkin column in the *Voice,* "Why Paul Goldberger Is So Bad," in which he pilloried Goldberger as a Johnson toady and the "embodiment of the aesthetics of Yuppification."*

It was a demonstration of just how powerful a hold Johnson had on the media that the *Times*'s architecture critic was loath to cross him, and that Johnson was the point of controversy in a battle of architectural criticism. That uproar would make an impact, but it was slow in coming. Even as other critics and the public rejected it, the plan retained support in the back rooms where decisions were made. From the outset, it was a baby of the pro-development mayor, Ed Koch, who felt little need to defend it. "I, for one, have never felt it necessary to explain why we improve something," said Koch, who was not typically at a loss for words. The *Times* brass were also for it, cheered by the prospect of improving their neighborhood and dramatically increasing the value of their own property. (The paper was then based not in the Times Tower, which it left in 1913, but in a large building on West Forty-third.) Nevertheless, public blowback was strong enough to sideline the project, and in the ensuing years, as the architects worked to refine their scheme, the Johnson-Burgee partnership would fundamentally change.

---

* Goldberger fired right back, claiming Sorkin's writing "is to thoughtful criticism what the Ayatollah Khomeini is to religious tolerance."

Johnson and David Whitney, together at the Glass House. (Getty Research Institute, Los Angeles)

CHAPTER 16

Things Fall Apart

*If you'd indulged every one of your whims that you had when you
were a kid, you wouldn't be here with a job either.*
                                        —*Philip Johnson, 1993*

Though he couldn't pinpoint when the problem started, Philip Johnson
was not well, and hadn't been for months, if not longer. He was routinely
fatigued and out of breath, frequently napping in the office; the same
symptoms that had dogged him ten years earlier had resurfaced again.
On June 7, 1986, he was admitted to New York Hospital for his second
heart surgery. It was doubly depressing because the procedure took place
a day before a scheduled Glass House blowout to celebrate his upcoming
eightieth birthday. That party went on without him: two hundred of his
friends wandering his New Canaan estate in the summer rain, doing
their best to make light of the guest of honor's absence. Whitney acted as
host along with Johnson's sister Theo, who had found a new husband,
an amiable New York dentist named Scott Severns. The two had married in 1960 and lived in a luxurious Central Park West apartment in the
Dakota—a wedding gift from her beloved older brother.

This time Johnson was slow to recover from the angioplasty, and
when he returned to the office he was lethargic and lacking in enthusiasm. The practice, once a boutique atelier, was now a factory churning
out boring corporate towers. For a man with flagging energies in his
eightieth year, it seemed to have grown too large, to be moving too
quickly. Management and organization had never been his strengths—
that was why he had needed Burgee, and before him Foster, and before
him Gores—but for the first time he felt divorced from the work that

bore his name. He and Burgee had for several years been in conversation about Johnson's reducing his role in the firm, about finding a way to pass the torch. On this front Johnson had always been equivocal. But now his mind was changing. "I'm tired. I don't want to do this rat race anymore," he had told Burgee, even before the surgery. "Can't we slow the practice down?" For Burgee that was a nonstarter; he was in his prime running a gangbusters office, what he had always wanted. Johnson understood Burgee's predicament, and in his reduced state was powerless to force his hand, so he agreed to the unthinkable: to fully take his name off his own firm, while retaining his share of the partnership.

That arrangement lasted all of two months. It was not in Johnson's DNA to walk away, to cede control, to voluntarily step out of the spotlight. His friends had been calling in to the office, and when the receptionist answered, "John Burgee Architects," they presumed he was dead. That wouldn't do. In search of a better solution, Burgee turned to public relations king Howard J. Rubenstein, a specialist in high-stakes damage control. Johnson resisted his interference from the outset; when it came to publicity, he didn't need much assistance. Rubenstein agreed with that assessment, but he did help the two men sketch the contours of how their

Johnson's study/library, set in the Glass House meadow, 1980. (Collection of the author)

future relationship might operate, and he led them to a settlement on what it should be called: John Burgee Architects, Philip Johnson Consultant. It was a wordy, awkward half-measure, but it suggested the independence Burgee demanded and it meant Johnson could assume the more avuncular, design-oriented role he wanted. Johnson would be paid a retainer for his services on the order of $200,000 a year. It effectively ended their partnership.

Among the benefits of the new arrangement was that Johnson could spend more time at the Glass House with Whitney. He had always been most at peace on his New Canaan estate, and he had continued to build on it, erecting a series of new buildings and follies that augmented his carefully manicured landscape. The largest new addition was a combination study and library set a short walk across the grounds from the Glass House. The path to it was unmarked and unpaved, so that he had

The Ghost Pavilion at the Glass House Compound, inspired by Frank Gehry and Robert Venturi and Denise Scott Brown, 1985. (Michael Moran)

to walk through a meadow to reach it—a throwback to his youthful days on the rolling hills of Townsend Farms. The building itself was a charming little cartoon inspired by Italian postmodernist Aldo Rossi, whose abstract historical forms toyed with the architectural imagination. Johnson's homage was a small box surmounted by a cone and a squared-off chimney. At the apex of the cone was a skylight, and under it was Johnson's desk. His books lined the walls, arranged neatly by subject. There was no phone, no bathroom, no kitchen; it was purely a place for work and reflection. "Everything about this little building helps me concentrate," he told a reporter after he finished it. "The light is glareless, the colors are gentle, I'm surrounded by books, and I can't be distracted by anything going on outside."

A large picture window looked out toward another new addition to the estate, the so-called Ghost Pavilion, which Johnson erected in 1984 on an abandoned stone foundation found at the woods' edge. The pavilion, a gabled structure divided into two and made of chain-link fencing, answered Johnson's question, "What would a child's idea of a house look like if it was split down the middle?" The idea for it had several sources: Venturi and Scott Brown had built similar "ghost" structures in Philadelphia, and the split-gable top referenced the landmark house Venturi built for his mother in suburban Chestnut Hill. (As far as Scott Brown was concerned, Johnson had also stolen that split-gable motif for Pennzoil Place and the Chippendale cap of the AT&T Tower.) The chain link came from a different source, however, a young Los Angeles architect whom Johnson had taken under his wing: Frank Gehry.

They were an unlikely pair, to say the least. Johnson was a man of champagne and Dover sole. Gehry looked like a guy who made donuts and liked to sample his product. Canadian and Jewish (his given name was Frank Goldberg), he cut a disheveled figure, with an untrimmed brush mustache, oversize eyeglasses, and oxford shirts rolled to the elbows. Their first meeting was memorable chiefly for Gehry's inability to remember it: on a visit to Los Angeles in the early 1970s, Johnson had arranged to visit Gehry's recently completed home and studio for painter

Ron Davis. Both Gehry and Davis considered the arrival of so distinguished a patron a coup, and this made them nervous, and—this being the 1970s—they decided to calm their anxieties with a little weed. Which became a lot of weed. Johnson came, and then he left, and in the aftermath neither Gehry nor Davis had any recollection of what he had said about the building or the paintings within it.

From that inauspicious beginning, their relationship would grow to be one of great personal devotion. At its core was Johnson's conviction that Gehry was an immense talent. The Ghost Pavilion was a testament to that growing friendship; Gehry had famously used chain-link fencing on the jumble of a house he had made for his young family in Santa Monica, an old bungalow wrapped in unlikely materials. Johnson's version lacked Gehry's messy vitality, but the fencing had other benefits, and one in particular that pleased him: it kept the local deer off the flower beds he planted within the pavilion's walls.

A year later, in 1985, another monument to friendship rose on Johnson's New Canaan estate, this one less transparent in form and less opaque in meaning. The honoree was Lincoln Kirstein, his on-again, off-again friend for half a century. Long stretches would pass when they would not even speak to one another. At other times the relationship between the two high-strung men could be difficult. In September of 1982, after one such episode, it was Kirstein who wrote seeking absolution. "I don't know why you should forgive my churlish behavior, but I suppose you will, and for that I am very grateful," he wrote. "I don't know why I behave to old friends the way I do, but it is a curse which burdens my later days, and there seems to be no cure for it." However bad his behavior, Kirstein had certainly forgiven Johnson for worse.

Part building and part sculpture, Johnson's monument to Kirstein was composed of small concrete cubes that climbed in an irregular jigsaw pattern—imagine a three-dimensional Tetris game—to a height of thirty-five feet. Johnson gave it a place of honor, on a hill behind the toy pavilion, so that it could be seen marking the landscape from the Glass House. But it was best experienced up close; Johnson arranged the blocks so you could corkscrew your way to the top, albeit carefully, as there were no railings. This was, like the Fort Worth Water Gardens, an exercise in the principle he called "safe danger," in which the experience of architecture was amplified by the sense—though not the serious reality—of physical risk. It was a perfect metaphor for his relationship with Kirstein, which so often had seemed like it would end in disaster but somehow survived.

His partnership with Burgee was proving to be less sustainable. The Rubenstein-engineered détente remained a gentleman's agreement until the morning of April 15, 1988. With Johnson's blessing, Burgee had formulated a three-page memorandum in which he set forth terms and conditions that they had spoken of only informally. What Johnson received was altogether more severe than what he had expected. In Burgee's precise and orderly prose, the terms they had casually discussed appeared not gentlemanly at all, but by turns condescending, draconian,

The monument to Lincoln Kirstein and the toy pavilion: a pair of follies. (Michael Moran)

The Tetris-like monument to Lincoln Kirstein, 1985, illustrating Johnson's idea of "safe danger." (Michael Moran)

unrealistic, and self-defeating. It was not so much a memorandum as an ultimatum, and for Johnson it read like a professional death sentence:

> First it has become clear in a variety of ways that the perception of the firm is such that it would or could not continue without your total and central involvement. This obviously is not acceptable to me as I must prepare for the time when this is not possible. It is also apparent that we may have already waited too long to project the shift. Any longer would only worsen my problem of continuity. The most drastic action which I feel I must take if nothing else will work is to become totally independent now with your immediate retirement and take my chances now instead of later which in my judgment would not be possible or certainly much more difficult. I would rather have a chance now that [sic] face it in emergency conditions in 2-5-10? years.

This would be difficult for both of us however, and I would really like to make the transition as pleasant and easy as possible. I really can't imagine you in retirement but I also am not sure if you can work in a more subdued, restrained way. Personalities are what they are and habits are not easily changed and our method of working must change if we are to go on. While I'm sure it will be awkward and difficult as we attempt to work it out I'm willing to try, for a limited time, if you are.

What I propose is that you really become a "design consultant": consulting with the firm on design issues just as other consultants consult on lighting design, landscaping, graphics, etc. It is a different role than you have had in the past and will require modification of working process.

If that had been all it might have been acceptable, but Burgee continued, adumbrating how Johnson would be allowed to operate in public, with clients, and in the office. According to the terms set forth, Johnson would be barred from: public appearances and interviews, including exhibition openings; any unsupervised contact with clients; and any contact with employees of the firm without Burgee, Ahuja, or another senior staffer present. Moreover, any interaction with staff or clients would have to be preapproved by Burgee, who concluded: "This is meant to be a very perceptible change in the firm and will require a change in habits if it is to work. As your role is reduced you may find you don't need to be in the office as much and can spend more time in the country or at other activities. We will schedule design reviews as conveniently as possible. I know it won't be easy and I'm not sure it's possible, but I truly want it to work and hope you do too."

The idea that Johnson would or could entirely retreat from public view was absurd. It ran counter to his persona, and it was an effective impossibility. Even if Johnson accepted Burgee's conditions with respect to the firm — which he had already proved congenitally incapable of doing — he remained a trustee of the Museum of Modern Art, and since 1981 he had been chairman of the Trustees' Committee on the

Department of Architecture and Design. In 1984 the museum dedicated its architecture gallery in his name. "His contribution to the life of this institution, as to the life of architecture, is incomparable," Arthur Drexler proclaimed on that occasion.

Johnson, to state the obvious, could hardly be expected to absent himself from exhibition openings held by his own department in the gallery that bore his name—especially if he himself was the curator. That fact pointed to the essential disingenuousness of Burgee's demand, because he was fully aware, when he issued his memorandum, that Johnson was putting together an exhibition that would open at the beginning of the summer. And this was not a usual happening. Although Johnson had been a constant presence at the museum over the years, it was to be the first show he had personally curated since 1954, when he had turned over the reins of the department to Drexler.

Johnson's return to the museum in that capacity was prompted by his sense of displacement and lack of interest in his own firm. But more critically and not unrelatedly, it was spurred by his desire to reimpose himself on the profession in his eighty-second year, and to reinvigorate the museum department he had founded half a century earlier. In the years since Drexler had taken over, Johnson had assumed an increasingly hands-off role in its programming, both because Drexler was a shrewd political tactician within the museum and because Johnson was focused on his architectural practice. When cancer forced Drexler to step down in 1985, Johnson initiated a search with Richard Oldenburg, the museum director, but defaulted to the man Drexler picked as his successor, Stuart Wrede, a scholarly, Yale-trained architect. In truth Johnson had long been unhappy with the direction under Drexler, feeling it was insufficiently provocative and generally boring—cardinal sins. Wrede, in his estimation, proved to be more of the same, but worse. "The Museum is the most powerful institution in the world in architecture, and he's not breaking new ground, or there's no excitement generated," Johnson complained in an oral history of the museum.

That changed emphatically on June 23, 1988, with the opening of *Deconstructivist Architecture.* Johnson's return was not physically large, really just one claustrophobic room with ten projects by seven architects, but what it lacked in scale it more than made up for in notoriety. To the public, the works on display looked nothing like architecture as they knew it. Instead there were practically indecipherable models and drawings for structures, most of them unbuilt and unbuildable, that had been sliced and diced and folded and punctured. Even before it opened it was the talk of the town; the *Times* had run a series of articles on this radical new architecture known as "deconstructivism"—a portmanteau of deconstruction (the literary theory) and constructivism (the Russian art movement)—and the architectural profession had speculated for months about what the show would offer, and who would be included.

The exhibition followed the core curatorial principle Johnson had proposed before the museum even opened: that "every show should have a point." But aside from commandeering attention for himself and generating controversy within the world of architecture, Johnson was coy about exactly what that point was in this case. He was quick to deflect comparisons to the *Modern Architecture* show of 1932, which had established the International Style as the defining aesthetic of its era. "However delicious it would be to declare again a new style, that is not the case today," he wrote in the preface to the show's catalog. "Deconstructivist architecture is not a new style." What exactly was it, then? To those who parsed Johnson's wordy explanation—"It is a confluence of a few important architects' work of the years since 1980 that shows a similar approach with very similar forms as an outcome"—it sounded a lot like a new style. Exactly like one.

In truth, the show had not even been Johnson's idea. The initial impulse had come from a pair of Chicago-based architects, Paul Florian and Stephen Wierzbowski, who had unsuccessfully sought funding for an exhibition, *Violated Perfection,* of recent architecture defined by fragmented geometries. Their idea was appropriated by an ambitious young architect-writer, Aaron Betsky, who broached the subject of an exhibition with Johnson over lunch at the Four Seasons. (He had also pitched a book on the subject to the publisher Rizzoli.) At the same time, another architect-writer, Joseph Giovannini, was working on a book on the same direction in architecture, and he too had broached it with Johnson. The term "deconstructivism" was Giovannini's formulation.

That the theme was in the air was undeniable. "There was nothing to invent," Johnson claimed in retrospect. "It was common property." He knew Betsky and Giovannini were not likely to complain about his appropriation, given their own ambitions; Wrede's status as the department's director was still very much provisional when discussion of the exhibition began. (He was elevated from "acting" director only in March of 1988.) For Johnson, a man who lived by the Miesian credo that it's "better to be good than original," where an idea came from was a lot less interesting than how it was applied.

In that he had help, principally from Mark Wigley, an architectural theorist from Princeton who came to him through Eisenman. Those three, with input from Betsky and Giovannini, performed the vital function of selecting, or perhaps anointing, the chosen few architects who would be included. Wigley was assigned the catalog essay, something to give intellectual cover to the endeavor, and also left to do much of the groundwork, for which he was credited as the exhibition's "organizer" because Johnson was not prepared to share his curatorial title.

What visitors found when they arrived at the exhibition was an anteroom installed with works by the Russian Constructivists—Kazimir Malevich, Lyubov Popova, Alexander Rodchenko—from whom the work on display was ostensibly derived. Hanging over the entry, like architectural mistletoe, was a construction by Vladimir Tatlin. Within were projects by Eisenman, Coop Himmelb(l)au (the partnership of Wolf Prix and Helmut Swiczinsky), Frank Gehry, Zaha Hadid, Rem Koolhaas, Daniel Libeskind, and Bernard Tschumi. Of this group, only Hadid could lay any serious claim to an association with the actual constructivists. Her fantastical drawings, with their dramatically plunging planes, drew self-conscious inspiration from the Russian artists of the early twentieth century, albeit without the political implications that animated their work. The Peak, the project she exhibited, was for a private club in the hills of Hong Kong, hardly a redoubt of prole-tarianism.

What drew these architects together, aside from superficial similarity, wasn't clear. Rem Koolhaas's hypermodern complex of tilted towers in Rotterdam had no relationship to the charming jumble of a house Gehry had cobbled together for himself out of chain-link fencing and corrugated metal in Santa Monica. Wigley's turgid catalog essay didn't help. Deconstructivist architecture, he wrote, "puts the pure forms of the architectural tradition on the couch and identifies the symptoms of a repressed impurity." Stripped of its jargon, it was an argument for subversion, but so broadly defined as to be meaningless: "It is the ability to disturb our thinking about form that makes these projects deconstructive."

Among the most perceptive, and most critical, reviews of the exhibition came from a critic of growing prominence writing for *The New Republic*. Herbert Muschamp would become one of Johnson's staunchest guardians, but his first significant column on his work was not generous. While acknowledging the radical nature of the architects included in the show, he pilloried Johnson and Wigley for their shallow reading of what made their work subversive, for stripping them of their ideas and presenting them merely as paradigms of a new aesthetic. "What is truly challenging about this work has been neutralized by as conservative a brand of architectural thinking as you are likely to find outside Colonial Williamsburg," Muschamp wrote. This, of course, was the exact same critique made against Johnson fifty years earlier, when he and Hitchcock had drained the radical context from the work of the early modernists in the interest of promoting the movement they dubbed the International Style.

A more fruitful direction might have included an examination of the work presented in the context of the exhibition's alternate namesake, the literary "deconstruction" promulgated by the theorists Jacques Derrida and Paul de Man, among others. A loss of subjectivity within capitalist culture would have been a pertinent framework to look at the projects presented (and might have suggested other work to exhibit). But

Johnson and Wigley went out of their way to avoid such a discussion, instead choosing merely to cash in on a superficial association with a fashionable mode of academic inquiry. The works in question were "not an application of deconstructive theory," Wigley wrote. "Rather they emerge from within the architectural tradition and happen to exhibit some deconstructivist qualities." If anything, the exhibition seemed almost a repudiation of the French school of thinking. What Roland Barthes described as the "death of the author" was here reversed into a celebration of the architect—an auteurist theory of design dedicated not to the many ways a building might be perceived but to a valorization of the singular genius who created it. If the exhibition could be said to have launched a movement, it was not one based on aesthetics, but celebrity: it was the show that gave the world starchitecture. For the next two decades, the profession would be defined by a chosen few jet-setting international figures building ever grander and more expensive monuments designed to capture public attention. That had always been Johnson's goal.

To look at the work of John Burgee Architect, Philip Johnson Consultant, it was easy to see why Johnson felt the need to get back into the curatorial game. The bloated postmodern towers that littered American cities could be criticized with a variety of labels—corporatist, reactionary, clunky, and anti-urban, to name just a few—but above all they were boring architecture, and for Johnson this was always the worst crime. And there was an example right around the block from MoMA, so visitors to the *Deconstructivist* show could see just how pale was his own work in comparison. The building in question was the Museum of Television and Radio, a fussy white limestone tower that had the look of an inflated neoclassical bank. It "couldn't be more bland," wrote *Times* critic Paul Goldberger when it opened. Johnson countered that it was contextual, that there was "no place" for a modern building on West Fifty-second Street, a ridiculous assertion given his own history of modern building for MoMA in exactly the same context on Fifty-third. Indeed, it was his building that was truly inappropriate. As with the design for AT&T, Johnson paid no heed to the very inspiration for the building—television and radio—and

411

instead looked back to a time before those technologies existed. As architecture, it was pure anachronism.

When Johnson, as Burgee's so-called consultant, tried to tack from postmodernism to something congruent with the formal language of his anointed favorites, the results were dispiriting. Nowhere was the nihilism of this turn more apparent than in the return to the design of Times Square, a project that had lingered for years in political, economic, and bureaucratic stalemate. In 1989 the project was once again resurrected: developer George Klein sent Johnson and Burgee back to their drawing board, with instructions to remake their rejected scheme in a way that more deftly responded to prescribed guidelines and answered their critics. But after Burgee's 1988 memorandum, the two were uncomfortable bedfellows, and hardly speaking. Indeed, Burgee wanted to freeze Johnson out of the Times Square work entirely, but Klein wouldn't have it. He wanted Johnson on the project for the weight carried by his name and because he respected him as a design authority.

What the two drummed up, however, was hardly commensurate with the idea of a redesign. The "new" scheme was essentially the old scheme, with the postmodern trimmings stripped away and replaced with pasted-on elements that Burgee, now acting as front man, described as "New Modern." Instead of four overscale towers with limestone facades, the New Modern design had four overscale towers with mostly glass facades set off here and there by random protrusions and bedecked at their lower levels with high-wattage electronic signage. It was, once again, savaged in the press. Goldberger, the most lenient in his estimation of the new design, nevertheless called them "token changes."

The most perceptive review once again came from Herbert Muschamp, in a column written shortly after he joined the *Times* as an architecture critic in 1992. Muschamp derided the original postmodern Johnson/Burgee Times Square scheme as "abysmal" but was no greater a fan of their second attempt. "The new design of Mr. Burgee and Mr. Johnson simply applied a new veneer to the same set of jumbo panels. Here was evidence, if more was needed, that for all its appeals to history and tradition, postmodernism was often no more than modern formal-ism in period dress." That was by then accepted wisdom; what Mus-champ contributed was an acknowledgment that architecture was more and more a product of celebrity. The Times Square redevelopment plan was "the apotheosis of architecture as entertainment for the star struck." It was Johnson who minted the star architect, and none more so than himself.

The Times Square plan collapsed of its own dead weight, but the con-fused entity that was John Burgee Architect, Philip Johnson Consultant produced several additional designs in the "New Modern" vein before it completely came apart. In Toronto there was a headquarters for the Canadian Broadcasting Corporation, a large box defined by slightly tilted walls, grids of windows, and a glazed wall that cut at a slight angle through the composition. This was Deconstructivism lite, its pantomime of radical design, as at Times Square, being almost entirely superficial. In Madrid the attempt was more forceful but equally egregious: a pair of stumpy, twenty-story gridded towers that leaned in toward each other over a barren plaza. Not only did critics hate the scale-less "Puerta de Europa," but the failure of the project's Kuwaiti developers threw all of Spain into economic turmoil.

The failings of those projects reflected not just flawed architectural thinking but the fracture within the firm. While Johnson had initially complied with the portions of Burgee's memorandum that applied to his role in the company, it was not long before he was up to his old tricks. A particular frustration, for Burgee, remained Johnson's penchant for vis-iting the drafting floor and making changes to settled designs. In response, Burgee instructed Ahuja to command the drafting teams to disregard Johnson's orders. This put the junior staff in an untenable position—many of them were loyal to Johnson, for whom they had deep respect—and especially infuriated Ahuja, who thought Burgee's treat-ment of Johnson was potentially catastrophic (and didn't care to be dic-tated to himself, given his 25 percent stake in the firm). "We should have let him gracefully get older and share design work with other people in the firm, and capitalize on his name," Ahuja told the *Wall Street Journal,* after the firm finally broke up.

While that outcome was clearly on the horizon, the two principals were loath to accept it. Once again Johnson and Burgee arranged for a détente—or, more accurately, a separation without a formal divorce. In exchange for his noninterference, Johnson would be allowed to operate as his own independent entity, with a separate office on the ninth floor of the Lipstick Building and a skeleton staff, his overhead covered by the firm. It was an arrangement bound to fail, and it did when Johnson and Burgee started hunting for the same jobs. The first conflict came over a proposed addition to the public library in Cleveland, Johnson's home town. Sensitive to this fact, Burgee asked Johnson to go in on the project with him, despite their agreement to act separately. Johnson demurred, telling Burgee he wasn't interested and he could have the job to himself. After Burgee had submitted, however, Johnson informed him that he had changed his mind, and—worse—that he was submitting in partnership with a local Cleveland firm. "This was a real double cross, he really was screwing me," Burgee said. Sabotage was the only explanation.

Johnson didn't win that job, but he did successfully submarine another Burgee commission—and walk away with the prize for himself. The site was one that carried significant historical meaning in recently reunified Berlin: Checkpoint Charlie, the famed gateway between East and West. The commission was for an office building to promote American business interests, and it was backed by a consortium that included cosmetics magnate Leonard Lauder. Burgee was tapped for the project and traveled repeatedly to Berlin to move it forward. But on a scheduled review of his models for the building, Lauder summarily replaced him with Johnson. The two, Johnson and Lauder, had become friends through the Museum of Modern Art board. Over lunch at the Four Seasons, Johnson had pitched himself for the job, and Lauder had accepted.

The episode marked the formal end of the Johnson and Burgee partnership. The firm, without its founder, didn't last much longer. Forcing out Johnson had cost Burgee much of the company's business. His attempt to push out Ahuja was catastrophic. Burgee, in this effort, had offered to buy out Ahuja's partnership for $1.8 million, or one year's share in the company profit. But Ahuja quite understandably saw no reason to walk away with a single year's check—he had a quarter share of the company, after all. He took Burgee to arbitration, and in April of 1992 he was awarded $13.7 million. The judgment forced Burgee into bankruptcy. Johnson walked away free and clear.

Within the profession, the presumption was that Burgee was responsible for his own downfall, it being a product of his own hubris. Though there was truth to that reading, Johnson did nothing to discourage it; he made no effort to protect the man who had transformed his limping practice into a powerhouse. Without Johnson, the profession's in crowd had no reason to stand by Burgee: he was not a designer's designer but a businessman architect, a manager of projects that, thanks to Johnson's postmodernist predilections, had become widely disdained. Now Burgee, like postmodernism, was another thing Johnson could abandon.

He dumped Burgee but kept the Berlin job. The site was memorable, but the building Johnson designed for it was an uncomfortable attempt to have his postmodernism and his deconstructivism at once. The exterior was nondescript: a clunky seven stories of black mirrored glass overlaid with gray Brazilian granite. The glass panels intermittently sliced out to create canopies (deconstructivism!), while the granite formed an abstracted peristyle (postmodernism!). Within there was a grand triple-height lobby drawn from the work of Heinrich Tessenow, the German architect of the Weimar era. That was the spoken precedent; unmentioned was the fact that the square-coffered ceiling had another, more sinister reference in the work of Tessenow's infamous protégé, Albert Speer, who had also borrowed Tessenow's design for his Reich Chancellery of 1939. Hitler's architect had registered his approval of Johnson through the intermediary of Robert Hughes in 1979; a decade later, Johnson returned the favor.

Johnson's coy attitude to his past was evident in a lecture on the reconstruction of Berlin that he delivered in the reunified city in June of 1993. "As a foreigner, I have had three separate and distinct experiences here: first, at the end of the Weimar days, when I spent the better part of three

The exterior of the American Business Center in Berlin, in Johnson's "deconstructivist" style, 1992. (Richard Payne)

The interior hearkens back to Heinrich Tessenow, and his student, Albert Speer. (Richard Payne)

years here. The second was in the fifties, when Berlin was unbearably sad. The third is this year, as I take a small part in the rebirth of Berlin," he told his audience. This, of course, was omitting a certain other time of "distinct experiences" in the city, namely the period of National Socialism. That conveniently ignored, he instead focused on his Weimar days, a period of self-discovery when he drank in the city in all its cosmopolitan dimensions. "In my intoxication with Berlin's modern life, I completely missed the underlying political difficulties that were developing. I knew no outspoken communists or outspoken Nazis, though maybe they just did not tell me, I floated on the wonders of the new culture and most of all the new architecture." This was, as best, disingenuous.

The basic contours of Johnson's fascist foray had long been public knowledge — especially after the publication of William Shirer's *Berlin Diary* — but that memory had receded. Out of politesse and Johnson's own efforts to bury the past, his activities were generally forgotten. The threat of their resurfacing in ugly fashion emerged in the early 1980s, and from a source within Johnson's own orbit. Arguably, he was himself the culprit. Beginning in 1982 he sat for a series of recorded interviews with Peter Eisenman, interviews he understood to be the basis for an as-told-to biography. The two discussed Johnson's fascist years at length, including the pathetic tale of his encounter with Czech modernist Otto Eisler, who had been tortured by the Gestapo. Unbeknownst to Johnson, Eisenman began marketing the book to publishers, and when word got back to a concerned Burgee, he confronted Eisenman at a cocktail party. According to Burgee, a tipsy Eisenman told him that he was "going to get" Johnson, and that he had photographs of Johnson riding in a German officer's car and wearing a Nazi uniform. Eisenman categorically denied that he had ever made such a threat and disputed the existence of such an incriminating photograph. That last claim, at least, had the ring of truth, however titillating the idea. Whatever his sympathies, if Johnson had been caught impersonating a German officer he would have been subject to summary execution, and that kind of courage was not in his makeup.

Photo or not, Burgee was deeply concerned. Eisenman was a wild card. Burgee himself had been a victim of Eisenman's notorious cruel streak: on first meeting Burgee's wife, Eisenman had suggested that Burgee was a closet homosexual. He also told Johnson that Burgee's ambitions were driven by a cocaine habit—an accusation Burgee vehemently denied. Johnson juggled their personal enmity because each gave him something that he valued: Eisenman was his gatekeeper to the New York avant-garde; Burgee ran his business. The taped interviews threatened that balance. Burgee had always known about Johnson's past, but having it paraded in the press would be deeply upsetting to a partner he cared for (however troubled their relationship), not to mention bad for business. Burgee insisted Johnson put an end to the project and get the tapes back.

As it turned out, Johnson had not agreed to have Eisenman's oral-history project go public. "As you know, when we first began our conversations, it was never my intention that at one time they would be transcribed and edited in a biography which you would then seek to have published," Johnson wrote Eisenman in February of 1983. The letter was written with his attorney, Arthur H. Christy, who was not to be trifled with: as a federal prosecutor, he had put away Vito Genovese and Frank Costello. In three pages, it stipulated the conditions by which Eisenman would be allowed to continue with the project, among them that Johnson retain sole right to edit the work as he saw fit; that Johnson would retain right of final review; that the completed manuscript and all tapes would be delivered to Christy, who would hold them until the time of Johnson's death; and that Eisenman would be prohibited from submitting any portion of the work for any purpose until Johnson's death. In exchange for surrendering the material as directed, Eisenman would be paid $10,000.

That agreement shut down Eisenman, who never retook the project. But there was another writer anxious to reveal Johnson's history, and it was someone whom Johnson could not control. In October of 1988 Michael Sorkin, his greatest antagonist, returned Johnson's unsavory activities during the 1930s to public attention in the pages of *Spy*, the satirical journal of New York culture and politics. "Where Was Philip?," the piece asked in its title. If Sorkin had recounted only Johnson's departure from the museum to join up with Huey Long—or even resurrected Shirer's accusation that Johnson was a Nazi mole—the piece would have been damaging enough. But Sorkin also reprinted ugly snippets from Johnson's writings in *Today's Challenge* and *Social Justice*. Old stories and accusations could be parried. But his own anti-Semitic, eugenicist words, in black and white for all to see, were indefensible.

The BBC picked up on the Johnson-as-fascist-mafioso theme in a 1993 documentary, *Philip Johnson: Godfather of American Architecture*. In response to so many attacks, Johnson adopted a contrite air, at once accepting responsibility for his past but also evading it by blaming it on his youth (although his fascist period extended well into his thirties) and even his wealth. "If you'd indulged every one of your whims that you had when you were a kid, you wouldn't be here with a job either," he told television host Charlie Rose. "It was the stupidest thing I ever did, and I never forgive myself and I never can atone for it. There's nothing I can do."

As evidence of his repentance and his lack of bigotry he could point to his close friendships with the Jews (Lincoln Kirstein, Eddie Warburg); his mentoring of Jewish architects (Eisenman, Gehry, Meier, Stern); his design of Kneses Tifereth Israel; and his design of the Soreq Nuclear Research Center in Israel. He advocated for Lou Kahn, promoting his design for a Holocaust memorial in lower Manhattan. He was an active benefactor of the Israel Emergency Fund of the United Jewish Appeal. In the early 1970s, he befriended Jerusalem mayor Teddy Kollek and lobbied in the *New York Times* for progressive design in that city. "Jerusalem awaits its twentieth century, its Israeli shape," he wrote in an editorial. He considered Shimon Peres a close personal friend. "I've always been a violent philo-Semite," he said, an awkward locution frequently repeated.

And yet, throughout his life, Hitler remained a philosophical touchstone. "Personally I think the Nazis were better than Roosevelt, but I haven't had time to dig up the truth," he wrote to a Columbia professor in 1964. He often quoted the Führer—especially in private—and while he publicly rejected Hitler's anti-Semitism and general barbarism, he waxed in admiration of his ability to build at great scale.

In the realm of legacy management, Johnson could be his own worst enemy. Such was the case with his falling out with two of his closest advocates over the publication of a book of interviews. The author was Rosamond Bernier, a raconteur of great panache who charmed audiences with firsthand tales of life in Paris with the likes of Picasso and Matisse in the years after World War II. Johnson was one of her many prominent friends in the arts; the two had been so close that in 1975 Johnson hosted her wedding, to *New York Times* chief art critic John Russell, at the Glass House. Aaron Copland gave her away, and Pierre Matisse (the painter's youngest child) was best man. Leonard Bernstein and Virgil Thomson came out for the event, and poet Stephen Spender flew in from London. Over the years Johnson and Bernier appeared frequently together on stage, a "brother-sister act" in which they bantered about art, architecture, and the grand lives they had led. Eventually they took their conversations to television in a series of interviews broadcast on CBS. These talks were to make up the bulk of a book, *Listening to Philip Johnson,* that Bernier sold, with Johnson's consent, to a Doubleday editor who happened to be a close friend to them both: Jacqueline Onassis.

Then Johnson pulled the plug. He had, it seemed, contracted with another writer for a virtually identical book, *Philip Johnson: An Architect in His Own Words,* to be published by Rizzoli. Bernier was incensed—not just because he had killed the book, but because of the brazen arrogance with which he had done it. "With no word of warning or explanation, Philip summarily refused to allow Doubleday to publish my book," she wrote to David Whitney. "Nor did he have the decency to inform me himself. I learned of it weeks later, at third hand, since it had never occurred to Jacqueline Onassis, the book's editor, that Philip would be too craven to tell me himself.... Mrs. Onassis is as mortified as

I am by his conduct and disregard for even the most elementary of courtesies." Bernier continued on to accuse him of other episodes of "false friendship" that she had forgiven in the past. But she wouldn't this time, and neither would Jackie O. Henceforth, he was dead to them both. "On your word of honor you will never speak to Philip Johnson again," Onassis instructed Bernier, who agreed. "She never spoke to him after that," recalled Bernier. "Nor did I. I lived up to my word. It was outrageous."

It was another of Johnson's many contradictions: though he was obsessive about his image, he had achieved a status whereby he felt uninhibited in expressing his condescension even for friends. His conjoined flippancy and desire for attention led to any number of self-inflicted wounds. In a 1993 profile for *Vanity Fair*, Kurt Andersen found him denigrating a series of his powerful friends, including Gerald Hines, his greatest patron. He was, according to Johnson, "the world's dullest man." Hines didn't care. "I let it slide off my back," he said. "He was always looking to jar people and shock them. That was part of his personality." But not everyone was so gracious.

Johnson also miscalculated, at least in his own mind, on his selection of an authorized biographer. His choice was Franz Schulze, a fastidious German-born architectural historian who had published a well-received biography of Johnson's architectural lodestar, Mies van der Rohe. Schulze had not shied from Mies's own opportunistic behavior during the early years of the Third Reich, but his treatment was fair-minded and scholarly and above all deeply respectful of Mies's immense achievement. Johnson, wrongly, considered it "hagiography," but for his purposes that was an advantage in a biographer. Given that background, he allowed Schulze complete independence to write a "warts and all" treatment of his history—though as a protection, publication would have to await Johnson's death. Schulze accepted that condition: after all, Johnson was then well into his eighties, with a long history of heart trouble.

The problem was that Johnson refused to die. Schulze was forced to sit on the manuscript, until finally Johnson—at the age of 88, and still going strong—allowed him to publish it. He had not read it, however, and when he finally did it was an unpleasant shock, and not because Schulze had exposed Johnson's fascist period yet again, with more depth. It was the rest of *Philip Johnson: Life and Work* that upset him. He thought Schulze had grown to dislike him and that a sense of condescending antipathy had permeated the book; that he had gotten his facts wrong; that he had focused excessively on his sex life; and that Schulze had not sufficiently addressed his architecture, the book being too much "life" and not enough "work." Most critically, he did not see himself in the book. The scholarly Schulze, he felt, had failed to capture his playful and witty nature. "I'm not in there. My personality just doesn't show, good or bad," he complained in a Museum of Modern Art oral history.

To a considerable extent those cavils were unfair, a combination of Johnson being unhappily confronted with ugly truths about his life conjoined with a misunderstanding of the essential project of biography. Reviews of the book were mixed, but there was a consensus on one point. Schulze had difficulty capturing Johnson's antic presence, a fact that was reinforced by the nearly simultaneous publication of *Philip Johnson: An Architect in His Own Words*. As Goldberger wrote in a review of the two books in the *New York Times Book Review,* "in the biography Mr. Schulze sets out, conscientiously, on a task that resembles capturing a butterfly; in the other book we just watch the butterfly soar."

That flight, however, was nearing its conclusion.

Johnson gets the full Trump experience in Atlantic City in 1992.
(Harry Benson)

CHAPTER 17

The Irresistible Allure of the Fantastic

Johnson's faults have always been at least as stimulating as his virtues.

—*Herbert Muschamp, 1993*

The sordid tale of the dissolution of Philip Johnson's partnership with John Burgee and Raj Ahuja landed on the front page of the *Wall Street Journal* on September 2, 1992. It was a painful day for Johnson, but one person saw opportunity in his humiliation. "From your standpoint, I loved the article," wrote Donald J. Trump, an expert in falls from professional grace, in a letter. Just a few years earlier Trump had been some $900 million underwater, but he had managed to pull himself out, at least mostly. In Johnson he saw another fallen idol, and he wanted to help in the only way he knew how—by helping himself. "Now that you are 'free.' I have a very exciting project for you in Atlantic City," he wrote. "I will be redoing the front boardwalk façade and the main porte cochere entrance to the Taj Mahal Hotel and Casino." He was looking for "a feeling of opulence," and he knew exactly who could provide it. "It has always been one of my great ambitions to work with Philip Johnson, the legend."

His admiration for Johnson could be read in his signature property, Trump Tower, a glitzified imitation of Johnson's IDS Tower in Minneapolis, right down to its zigzag corner and retail atrium. Trump had in fact engaged Johnson's services earlier, in the mid-1980s, for the design of a sixty-story condo tower on Madison Avenue to be known as Trump Castle. Johnson, in his postmodern phase, had embraced the theme, imagining a Disney-style jumble of cylindrical towers with crenellated battlements and pointy roofs covered in gold leaf. "Very Trumpish," Johnson told the *Times*. The most theatrical gesture came at ground level: to enter the building, visitors would have to cross a drawbridge over a moat patrolled by live alligators. It is hard to imagine that passing muster with city regulators, let alone Trump's budget minders, but it didn't matter—the project died before it could come to that.

Atlantic City was another chance for the two icons to collaborate, but with an even better storyline: Trump as savior, a white knight in a black helicopter, ready to make Johnson great again. The press would eat it up, and they were invited along when he whisked Johnson off to Atlantic City by chopper for a whirlwind tour of his properties. On the short hop from New York they talked across each other, Trump on golf, Johnson on architecture. In the limo to the Taj, Trump offered his philosophy of women:

Trump: You have to treat 'em like shit.
Johnson: You'd make a good mafioso.
Trump: One of the greatest.

Johnson, dressed in a gray Armani suit, had an expression that rated somewhere between mortified and revolted as Trump ushered him through his plastic-and-mirror palace. "As you probably have heard, the Taj has become the most successful hotel and casino anywhere in the world," Trump had bragged to Johnson. The latter almost certainly had not heard, but now that he was a captive audience, Trump could soliloquize on the fabulousness of the Taj, which he deemed superior to its namesake in India. Johnson, in turn, proposed a "Crystal Palace" on a pier over the ocean—anything to get away from Trump's gaudy monstrosity. The day ended with an impromptu press conference on the boardwalk at which Trump introduced his architect: "Does everyone know Philip Johnson? A total legend. And ladies, he's available."

Johnson never built that porte cochere for the Taj, but the connection led to more significant work, beginning with a series of towers for Trump Place, an insta-neighborhood to be constructed overlooking the Hudson

River on the Upper West Side. Trump had been devising schemes for the vast site since the 1970s, and in 1985 he floated plans for Television City, a mega-development anchored by a 150-story tower. The proposal met with near-universal disdain among critics (Sorkin: "boneheaded") and even less enthusiasm from its would-be neighbors, who organized against it with a vengeance. By the early 1990s, however, Trump had negotiated the development down and won approval for a series of residential towers; four of them were turned over to Johnson, who was partnered with Costas Kondylis, a Trump favorite experienced in residential design. Johnson would do the exteriors, and Kondylis the apartment layouts for the project, now known as Riverside South. What they came up with was the product of a morass of codes, regulations, and design mandates that largely precluded what creativity they might have brought to the endeavor. By law, the towers were to be set back and in the moderne style that defined the beloved apartment houses of Central Park West. But these seemed like cut-rate, overscale versions, a phalanx of boring, cookie-cutter apartments thrown up in a lifeless enclave divorced from the rest of the city.

While they were under construction, Trump engaged Johnson on a more prominent project, the remaking of the Gulf + Western Building on Columbus Circle. Trump had acquired the forty-four-story tower with the aim of transforming it into a combination apartment house and hotel, and this meant a virtual reconstruction, as the building was visually unappealing and notorious for swaying in the wind. Johnson found a solution to these problems on the way back to his office after a site visit with John Manley. On that trip the two had walked past the accordion-fold facade of the Hilton on Sixth Avenue. Triangular projections, inspired by the hotel, would both stiffen the tower and add visual definition to new facades of gold-tinted glass, chosen to achieve the requisite Trumpian gaudiness. Herbert Muschamp, in the *Times*, derisively compared the remade tower to both an upright gold ingot and a slot machine. "Refinement was never this building's point anyway," he wrote.

The collaboration between architect and developer was difficult almost from the outset, though you wouldn't have known it for their public behavior. Trump sponsored the luncheon when Johnson was given the New York Landmarks Preservation medal of honor in 1994. Following Richard Serra on the toast list, he saluted Johnson in classic Trump fashion: "Ladies and gentlemen, oh Philip, what an honor, what a great gentleman, what a great man and your best work is yet to come, 'cause of a lot of it's going to be mine." Johnson was effusive in return. "I never worked with anyone as bright and as quick and as decisive as Donald Trump," he told Charlie Rose. But behind closed doors he fumed at Trump's *arriviste* taste and lack of professional deference. At one early meeting, after Johnson had made an impassioned plea for one of his decisions, Trump called in his secretary for a second opinion. Johnson was flabbergasted but said nothing.

Much of the acrimony between the two revolved around the building's public spaces. Johnson was vexed that Trump limited the lobby height to twelve feet while insisting on grand crystal chandeliers that Johnson considered inappropriate generally, and all the more so given the low ceilings. He was even more irritated when Trump plopped an imitation Unisphere in front of the building, then demanded that Johnson replace his rather restrained stainless steel marquee with something more garish. Johnson caved, but not without issuing a backhanded compliment. "After thinking for some time, it seems to me you should have your bronze entrance," he wrote. "It is sort of a signature of your work everywhere and this is a good place to demonstrate it." Trump gladly accepted. "Thank you," he replied. "You are truly a great person to work with — despite your genius!"

The dustups eventually led Trump to dismiss Johnson from the Riverside South development, but by then they had gotten what they wanted out of each other. For Trump, the son of an outer-borough developer of low-income housing projects, it was Johnson's imprimatur as the sine qua non of blue-chip, blue-blood taste. Who better to add credibility to his palaces for the newly landed, and with a name that would draw the paparazzi and allow him to upcharge units? Johnson wanted the work, craved the attention Trump was so expert at delivering, and was glad to perpetuate his image as an architectural *enfant terrible* by association with New York's most craven developer.

Johnson and Trump got together one final time, gathering at the Museum of Modern Art at Muschamp's invitation. The critic, in an effort to make amends with two men he admired as embodiments of New York celebrity, had called for a trilateral meeting with the developer and the architect. His idea was to convene in front of Andy Warhol's *Gold Marilyn Monroe,* the iconic painting Johnson had donated to the museum and that Muschamp had likened to Trump himself. "Glitz packaged as class holds strong appeal for those who appreciated the idea of putting a soup can in a museum," he wrote. Trump, like Warhol's *Marilyn,* was campy, a "caricature of a tycoon." The problem was that Trump, cartoonish as he may have been, also happened to be an actual person, and one not particularly invested in Muschamp's contrived summit, except insofar as it served as a promotional opportunity. When he arrived, he tossed his coat on a Donald Judd sculpture as if it were a coffee table and spent much of the group's time extolling the myriad virtues of his properties—in particular his recently acquired Florida estate, Mar-a-Lago. Johnson didn't say much at all.

Despite the harsh review of the Trump International (né the Gulf + Western), Johnson had in Muschamp another ally leading the architecture coverage at the *New York Times.** Despite the gulf in their ages, the two had a good deal in common: both were precocious gay men who had come from working-class northern cities (Muschamp was from Philadelphia) to New York, drawn by the promise of glamour and cosmopolitan dynamism. Upon arrival, Muschamp had fallen into Andy Warhol's circle of acolytes, and that relationship put him in the orbit of Johnson and Whitney. Even before the contretemps with Trump, Muschamp had authored a sympathetic and perceptive profile of Johnson (then eighty-seven years old) for the *Times.* "Johnson long ago perfected the art of self-deprecation as a shield against attacks by others," he wrote. That

---

* Muschamp became chief critic when Goldberger left for *The New Yorker* in 1997.

was not a particularly original observation, but his exculpatory defense of Johnson's architectural enterprise was both canny and vexing at once. It had "the irresistible allure of the fantastic, an apparition, a dream," he wrote. "Even if Johnson were to blow away tomorrow, the issues raised by his work would remain to haunt us. Slight though much

Da Monsta, Johnson's derivative folly, was lauded by Herbert Muschamp but never worked for its intended purpose. (Michael Moran)

of his work may be, it nonetheless challenges us to rethink the prospects for architecture as a social art." For Muschamp, who believed that "conflict is the most important cultural product a city puts out," this was highest praise.

Muschamp's irrational exuberance for Johnson was best evidenced by his fawning review of Da Monsta, the visitors' pavilion Johnson erected in 1995 at the Glass House, envisioned for a time when the estate would be turned over to the National Trust as a museum. More folly than serious building, it consisted of two separate galleries, one vertical and one horizontal, pushed together, with not a right angle in sight. The lower volume was painted jet-black, the taller one deep cherry red, and the interiors bright white. Johnson credited the artist Frank Stella as an inspiration, but the more obvious debt was to Frank Gehry. (Johnson thought it looked like a monster, but called it "Da Monsta" because it sounded more urban, or at least au courant—it debuted just after the off-Broadway smash, *Bring in 'da Noise, Bring in 'da Funk*.) On a practical level it was a disaster: acoustics inside were so bad that it was impossible to have any kind of programming in the space, and the plan to use it as a welcome center had to be scrapped. Muschamp, nevertheless, extolled it in the *Times* as a "masterpiece" and "radically novel," which was ludicrous; architects had been making spray-formed non-Euclidean buildings for decades. Only Johnson could earn that kind of encomium for a rich man's derivative folly that was an abject failure on functional terms.

The intellectual glue that most tightly bound the architect and the critic was an absolute belief in architecture as an art. As Muschamp memorably put it, Johnson "will take architecture in any form so long as it's only form." He picked on Johnson for his blind spots when it came to the social and political dimensions of architecture, but the truth was that he was not particularly interested in those themes either. Nor were either of the two especially attuned to issues of environmental responsibility, resilience, sustainability, urban context, or regional identity. This made it easy (and not inaccurate) to lump them together as partisans of a jet-setting cabal of international stars, the architects Johnson considered his "kids."

On July 8, 1996, that celebrity set converged at the Museum of Modern Art to celebrate Johnson's ninetieth birthday. The list of attendees included more than two hundred figures from the worlds of art, architecture, industry, media, and society—all dressed to the nines. They mingled at a reception in the museum's atrium, then gathered for a dinner in the members' dining room, decked out for the evening with a sea of votive candles and centerpiece models of Johnson's greatest works rendered in steel. There was, of course, a ceremonial cake topped with a frosted Glass House and a pair of his signature owl-frame glasses. Writer

Christopher Mason sang an ode to Johnson composed to a medley of Beatles hits:

> Bold International Style he directed it.
> He fostered it and practiced and protected it.
> Then caused a mighty stir and rejected it.
> ...
> He's an energetic and enthusiastic pup
> A wondrous boy who never grew up.

The evening's singular moment, however, came when a tipsy David Whitney managed to scandalize the man who lived for scandal. Speaking of his partner of more than thirty years, he announced, "There is something I want to say about Philip's and my relationship. Even though he is ninety years old, is deaf and has false teeth, he is still great in the sack!" The room exploded in laughter. The comment was the talk of the architecture world for weeks, not that his homosexuality was any longer a secret; just two months earlier he had appeared on the cover of *Out* magazine. Johnson's own remarks at the dinner were not particularly memorable, though he did make the assembled an offer: "When I'm 106 I'll retire and let you all come see me." For one night at least, it seemed plausible.

The museum's "gift" to Johnson was an exhibition of *his* gifts to the museum, *From Bauhaus to Pop: Masterworks Given by Philip Johnson.* The show included some eighty of his most important donations, including Dix's *Dr. Mayer-Hermann,* Schlemmer's *Bauhaus Staircase,* Rothko's *Number 10,* Johns's *Flag,* and Warhol's *Gold Marilyn Monroe.* A separate installation of his contributions to the architecture and design department was placed on view, and Johnson himself selected 21 works for display in the sculpture garden, including a Jacques Lipchitz "portrait" of Gertrude Stein, which he and Whitney posed with for a celebratory article in the *Times.*

The evening following the museum's party, Johnson and his "kids"

Johnson's "kids" celebrating his ninetieth birthday at the Four Seasons in 1996. Back row: Charles Gwathmey, Terry Riley, David Childs, Frank Gehry, Rem Koolhaas. Middle row: Zaha Hadid, Bob Stern, Hans Hollein, Stanley Tigerman, Henry Cobb, Kevin Roche. Front row: Michael Graves, Arata Isozaki, Johnson, Phyllis Lambert, Richard Meier. On the ground: Peter Eisenman, Jaquelin Robertson. (Timothy Greenfield-Sanders)

gathered in black tie for a more subdued celebration in the private dining room of the Four Seasons, an event commemorated by photographer Timothy Greenfield-Sanders, who assembled the initiates for a group portrait. Johnson sat in the center beside Phyllis Lambert, who had made the Seagram Building and the Four Seasons possible. Circled around them were fifteen of architecure's most luminous luminaries. Most had already contributed appreciations of the architect to a special Festschrift edition of *Any* magazine, the journal of architectural avant-gardism that was the baby of Eisenman and his wife, Cynthia Davidson.

There was but one unfamiliar figure in the Greenfield-Sanders photograph. Standing in the back row was Terence Riley, whom Johnson had plucked from obscurity and installed as the new director of the museum's Department of Architecture. Johnson had never been a fan of Wrede, and his departure "to pursue personal interests" allowed Johnson to choose his own man. His short list consisted primarily of young theoreticians, among them Michael Hays, Jeffrey Kipnis, and Mark Wigley, the presumed frontrunner given his work on the *Deconstructivist Architecture* show. Johnson had even interviewed Michael Sorkin for the job, minding the adage that one should keep one's enemies close. But he chose none of these figures, landing instead on Riley, who had captured his attention and his admiration with a show he had organized as director of exhibitions at Columbia University's school of architecture. It was no wonder Johnson admired it, because it was a reconstruction of his own landmark, *Modern Architecture: International Exhibition,* the same one Johnson had curated with Henry-Russell Hitchcock back in 1932. What better compliment could there be?

In Riley, Johnson had found the perfect deputy, an inexperienced acolyte who shared his worldview and would remain safely in his pocket. Members of the department thought Riley deferential to Johnson in ways that neither Drexler nor Wrede had been. They spoke almost daily on the phone—an intrusion neither of his predecessors would brook but which Riley actively sought. Under his aegis, the department produced retrospectives of Johnson favorites including Rem Koolhaas and Bernard Tschumi, a show on trendy private residences, and the Berlin work of Mies. All bore Johnson's fingerprints. When Johnson was no longer around as adviser and protector, the *Times* turned on Riley, assailing his "lack of leadership" and bemoaning a "sense of inertia" in the department.

Johnson had a harder time finding a replacement for John Burgee. He had never been able to run a firm by himself, and the idea that he would be able to do so at such an advanced age was a nonstarter. Once again he tried to promote Manley, but he was neither interested in nor capable of assuming that responsibility, given that he was now pushing seventy and managing his own fragile health. Instead Manley was given leadership of the drafting room, while Donald Porter, an effective manager, was elevated to associate and left to run the business. But Porter was more interested in design than in dealing with clients, and with large projects still in the office—in particular the towers for Trump—Johnson felt he needed more experience. As he was casting about, one of the firm's consulting engineers recommended David Fiore and Alan Ritchie, architects who had worked for the Johnson-Burgee firm but had left to start their own practice. A lunch at the Four Seasons convinced him that they were the answer to his problem, and so Johnson Fiore and Ritchie was born. But it didn't last long. Barely two years in, Fiore quit architecture altogether. He had been the managerial partner of the duo, and the one Johnson had been chiefly interested in when he joined forces with them. Ritchie was more of a design architect, though not a particularly inventive one, and Johnson already had Manley in that capacity. But now he was left with him.

Among the projects undertaken by the remade firm was a town hall for Celebration, Florida, the white-picket-fence town manufactured out of whole cloth by the Disney Corporation as a bedroom community for its Orlando theme park. The very idea of a "town hall," with its suggestion of democratic freedom, was something of a misnomer, as the place was largely ruled by its corporate parent and the stringent codes it set down for life in its "ideal" town. The concept was a product of the New Urbanist movement, which inveighed against the planning sins of modernism (all those towers-in-the-park) and argued for pedestrian-friendly towns that harked back to an imagined better America. The problem was that this better America was in many ways a fantasy, one without diversity (Celebration was notorious for its lack thereof) and only nominally invested in walkability, because it was still a suburban model that required cars. Johnson, who had spent so much of the 1960s as an urban reformist, avoided wading too heavily into this debate; he was happy to have the commission, and to be contributing to a project along with the likes of Michael Graves, and Robert Venturi and Denise Scott Brown. His building was about as modern as one could get within Disney's constraints: a simple box set within a forest of squared pillars holding up a pitched metal roof—a tropical temple for the modern age.

Texas, where Johnson had always found a willing public, continued to be a place from which he could count on patronage. There was a major expansion of his Amon Carter Museum in Fort Worth, and in Dallas a

The Chapel of St. Basil, a return to the University of St. Thomas, in Houston, 1995. (Author's photograph)

fine-tuning of Thanks-Giving Square, a small urban park with a corkscrewing cylindrical chapel modeled on the ninth-century Mosque of Samarra in Iraq. That was an unlikely inspiration, but it was a weird project generally. From its debut in the 1970s it had never quite been a success, though it was unclear whether the problem was Johnson's design (an oasis walled off from the city) or Dallas itself, which had a tendency to treat pedestrians as if they were a civic nuisance.

Johnson also returned to the University of St. Thomas in Houston, the campus he had designed in the Miesian idiom in the 1950s. His new

Chapel of St. Basil was given pride of place at the head of the main quadrangle. The design aped the language of deconstructivism; it was a white cube capped by a golden dome, with a black wall that appeared to guillotine through the whole composition at an angle. The entry was a slice in the cube that looked like a tent flap. Compared with the rest of the stolid Miesian campus, it lacked gravitas—an attempt at provocation that was too clever by half. There was nothing heartfelt about it, a fact made plain by the defining feature of the interior: a tilted, backlit crucifix that was actually a cut in the wall. Johnson had appropriated Christianity's most sacred symbol and subordinated it to the interest of formalist gamesmanship.

He redeemed himself for this apostasy in a no-man's-land of car dealerships, auto-repair shops, and strip-mall flotsam and jetsam on the road to Love Field in Dallas. This airport-access route was an unlikely place to find god, but it happened to be home to one of the fastest-growing religious institutions in the country, the Universal Fellowship of Metropolitan Community Churches, a Protestant denomination that catered to the LGBT community. As the center of gay culture in the southwest, Dallas had the largest congregation in the church, with a membership of over 1,500. To accommodate this population, minister Michael Piazza turned to Johnson, having been attracted by the Crystal Cathedral in California. The setting was similar and the cathedral's brightness appealed to Piazza, but there was something more. The church had been ravaged by the AIDS epidemic; more than a thousand of its congregants died in the plague years of the 1980s. Piazza felt there was something in Robert Schuller's optimistic message that could help heal his community. For Schuller, Johnson designed a Crystal Cathedral. Piazza wanted a Cathedral of Hope.

That was, from Johnson's perspective, reason to decline the job. Although there were elements in his architecture that could be read as provocatively "gay"—the almost palpably libidinous bedroom of his own Brick House, for instance—in the postwar years he had assiduously avoided making public reference to his homosexuality. He could justify this behavior as a protection against further embarrassing the museum, which had forgiven him for so much in the past, and he could also tell himself that it was necessary if he was to remain a plausible architect for conservative corporate America. For a time those may even have been legitimate concerns, but the culture, by the late 1990s, had caught up to and passed him. That fact had been brought home to him

The cloudlike Chapel of Hope, a sweet cartoon among Dallas auto dealers, 1995. (Author's photograph)

years earlier at a dinner thrown by society stalwart Kitty Carlisle Hart. At Johnson's table were Jackie Onassis and Barbara Walters, the latter of whom confronted him about his behavior. Why, television's most famous interviewer wanted to know, was he always escorting female beards to such events instead of Whitney, whom everyone knew was his partner? From then on, that changed. Still, he was reluctant to engage with gay organizations, even in the depths of the AIDS crisis.

The prospect of designing a cathedral, however, was too good to pass up, and Johnson was charmed by Piazza, who introduced him to the congregation along with Whitney, his "spouse." "It seems only fitting that the largest gay and lesbian church in the world should inhabit a building designed by the greatest living architect, who also happens to be a gay man," Piazza announced. With that, the congregation erupted in cheers. How could Johnson refuse? What he created for them was a faceted white block, a great iceberg floating through a sea of urban detritus. It was a grand vision, but it never happened; the congregation could not fund it.

It did, however, manage to realize two parts of Johnson's composition: a bell tower and a separate chapel, also a free-form building in white. In contrast to the hard lines of the unbuilt cathedral, the chapel was soft as a cloud, a bright little cartoon of a building that evoked the joy and optimism that defined the church.

The design was yet another indication of the degree to which Johnson had been influenced by the work of Frank Gehry. For that metter, Johnson was now peppering the landscape with Gehry-style objects. There was a torqued clock tower sponsored by a watch company in front of Lincoln Center, and a cluster of sculptural shapes at Case Western Reserve University in Cleveland. His relationship with Gehry had blossomed since that first meeting back in the early 1970s, when Gehry and painter Ron Davis had gotten themselves stoned to the point of unconsciousness to alleviate their anxiety over his imminent arrival. That Johnson and Gehry met in the company of an artist was fitting. For Gehry, it was a mutual interest in contemporary art that allowed them to bond. "I was attracted to him originally because he was the only architect I knew or heard about who was interested in contemporary art, that was having anything to do with living artists who were pushing their work forward into the unknown," he said. "He was both a supporter and a collector of those works."

Over the ensuing years, the two developed a rapport that was unlike anything Johnson had with any of the other "kids." Johnson admired Eisenman for his theoretical bravado and Stern for his encyclopedic knowledge, but Gehry he considered a truly great architect. More important, they took pleasure in each other's company. And just as Johnson had promoted Gehry early in his career, once Gehry achieved his own stature he returned the favor, acting as a protector for the elderly Johnson. "I enjoyed him. He got on with my family. We just had fun together talking about architecture," said Gehry. "I liked him in my life and I went overboard to include him in stuff."

It was a reversal of polarity, with one of the "kids" feeding him work instead of the other way around. This included a joint commission for insurance magnate Peter Lewis, who had hired Gehry to design a residence in suburban Cleveland. As this was Johnson's hometown and Lewis admired him, Gehry had little problem persuading Lewis to bring Johnson aboard. "He won't admit it, but the back and forth between us, the one-upmanship, the preemption of moves, the studied juxtapositions, the continuously upping the ante, was one of the most joyous architectural experiences of my life," Gehry would recall. The problem was that the employees of their respective firms were a lot less enthusiastic about the collaboration. "They resented the fact that we were even involved, and didn't hesitate to show it," said Manley. A bigger problem was the constantly changing nature of the Lewis design, which comprised a collection of related buildings. Every time Johnson's office thought they had something done, Gehry's office made a change that required a reconsideration. Johnson's most notable contribution was for an octopus-shaped "ghost" building that was derived from the work of Bauhaus expressionist Hermann Finsterlin.

In the end, none of it was built — it was all too fanciful, too excessive, too complex, and above all too expensive. By the time Lewis put the kibosh on it, the estimated price tag had risen to $82 million, which would have made it far and away the most expensive private residence ever built at the time. For Gehry, it had become less a possibility to build than an experimental opportunity run amok. In *A Constructive Madness,* a documentary on the project, narrator Jeremy Irons portentously (and pretentiously) called it "a primeval incubator of architectural vision."

The vision that it realized, or helped to realize, was the Guggenheim

Bilbao, Gehry's magisterial essay in liquid titanium and soaring space in the Basque capital. "The word is out that miracles still occur, and that a major one has happened here," Muschamp wrote in the *Times*. The Guggenheim Bilbao was the ultimate realization of Johnson's vision of architecture: an unabashed work of personal genius that celebrated the architect's power as a place-maker and shaper of experience. It was immediately hailed as the building of the century, and its impact reshaped the culture industry and cities around the world. In an effort to capture some of the same economic and promotional glory, institutions and municipalities everywhere looked to build their own architectural showstoppers. The so-called Bilbao Effect was a boon to the class of architects Johnson had promoted, who were ready to cash in on this newfound desire for their work. Of course, there could be only one Bilbao, which meant any number of cities and institutions overextended themselves in efforts to attract a world that became increasingly jaded and finally decided the whole endeavor was intellectually and economically bankrupt.

But Johnson did not waver in his enthusiasm. When he first visited Bilbao, it was with Gehry and casino impresario Steve Wynn, who flew them and Charlie Rose across the Atlantic on his private jet. (Wynn had hoped to engage the two on a hotel in Atlantic City, a project that fell through.) Rose's cameras caught Johnson as he entered the soaring entry gallery of the museum. He began to cry. "Architecture is not about words. It's about tears," he said. The building was like nothing he'd ever seen, but it was everything he imagined architecture could be. "There's nothing that Frank Lloyd Wright ever did that had that emotive power," he said. "Gehry is so far the greatest architect that you almost can't talk about the rest." Later, speaking about the experience on Rose's program, he elaborated on what he thought made the building so extraordinary. "It's so full of contradictions and fun and games and excitements that there's never a dull moment." He might as well have been describing himself.

It was, overall, a happy time in his life. He had work at the office that kept him interested, control over his department at the museum, and a comfortable domestic routine with Whitney. He seemed invincible, but of course that was not true. Shortly after Johnson's ninetieth birthday gala, in July of 1996, he was back in the hospital for heart surgery, this procedure requiring the replacement of an aortic valve and the insertion of a pacemaker. The event left him in a "semicoma" with a breathing tube. There were repeated bouts of pneumonia, and serious questions as to whether he would survive. Eventually he began to recover, and with the help of a physical therapist who would remain with him for years he made it out of his wheelchair and began to walk around his estate. He rarely saw anyone, including his friends, during what he described as his "vacation." Whitney was especially protective of him. He didn't return to the office until the following March—an absence of eight months.

There was a brief revival. The press still courted him. His return to work generated a Talk of the Town item in *The New Yorker*. He appeared on the cover of *Metropolis* magazine for an interview that focused on the influence he had once exerted—and arguably still did—over the profession. The headline was classic Johnson: "What, Me? Power?"

There was work, too. Among the jobs in the office was a complex commissioned by Ronald Lauder that would be sited in the Israeli desert. Like the Lewis project, it was to be a series of free-form residential pavilions, but here arranged around a palm-ringed reflecting pool. Off to the side was a synagogue, which had the look of a rounded-off stone standing on end. Known as the Oasis, it was to be something like an Israeli version of Camp David, a safe and luxurious retreat for the country's leadership. It was never built. Other projects ranged from the zany (a Gehry-style children's museum in Guadalajara) to the banal (the conversion of an office park in White Plains, a bank in Boca Raton). An addition to the rear of the Chrysler Building—three glassed-in pyramids dubbed "The Trylons"—didn't work particularly well, but were inconsequential enough not to do serious damage to their estimable neighbor.

The best of these late works was designed for himself and Whitney, and looked back to his postmodern days. For their West Coast retreat at Big Sur, he designed a house that looked like something out of *The*

Flintstones, with a tower shaped like a wobbly rook and wildly organic furniture by Swiss designer Mattia Bonetti.

The last, great high point came closer to home, in Long Island City. To launch its collaboration with the art space PS1, in 1999 the Museum of Modern Art inaugurated an annual architectural competition for young architects, who would be given free rein to design an outdoor party space in the institution's courtyard. But in that first year the commission went to an architect who was only notionally "young"—the ninety-three-year-old Philip Johnson. Fifty years earlier he had designed the museum's beloved outdoor party space, the Abby Aldrich Rockefeller Sculpture Garden, and now that the museum was branching out, the idea was that he could once again bring it a sense of style and star power. The rough-edged design was a debauched nightclub version of an Italian hill town, with towers made of scaffolding and metal screening. Johnson deputized the society-party impresario Robert Isabell as the "coordinator" of the production, and their combined efforts made it the hottest ticket in town, a velvet-rope club for the art-and-architecture set. And of course, on opening night, Johnson was there to take it all in from the DJ booth as the in crowd danced the night away in New York's post-industrial hinterland.

It was a glorious night, but the reality was that the end was near. Early in 2000 Johnson called Ritchie and Manley into his office to say he thought he should resign. They persuaded him not to, but the truth was that he didn't have much left to offer. He came in only once or twice a week, always accompanied by his physical therapist, and spent most of his time in his office doing nothing of import or sleeping on a lounge bed. When he did interact with clients, there always had to be somebody with him. His last major project, completed posthumously, was the Urban Glass House, a downtown condominium tower that capitalized on the recent zeal for high-end fishbowl residences of glass and steel. The trend had begun just a few years earlier and a few blocks away, with a development by one of Johnson's protégés, Richard Meier. In a final irony Johnson was once again a follower, but this time to a movement he himself had launched more than half a century earlier when he built his own Glass House.

Mostly Johnson spent time in New Canaan with Whitney, a pair of charming older gentlemen who cared deeply for one another. In lieu of cell phones, they dotted the estate with Post-it notes scribbled with endearments — "XOXO" — and other personal messages. Johnson designed a small doghouse for the fluffy Keeshonds, Alice and James, who followed the two around the grounds. Whitney gardened and collected art and ceramics, in particular the work of George Ohr, the "mad potter of Biloxi." They mostly kept to themselves, out of the spotlight, seeing only their closest friends.

When the end finally came, in the winter of 2005, Johnson had ordered there be no great obsequies, no grand memorial service. The man who courted attention and publicity his entire life wanted none that he could not experience himself. His end was a private affair. "Death is nothing, you see — it just happens and that's the end," he said. He had designed simple classical headstones on the New Canaan estate for himself and for Whitney, but he was not buried there. Instead his ashes were quietly spread in the garden Whitney kept behind Calluna Farms, an eighteenth-century farmhouse on the estate that he used as his own residence while Johnson was in his Glass House.

The closest thing to a eulogy had come from Gehry, and Johnson was there when it was read at his ninety-fifth birthday:

During his recent hospitalization, I was forced to deal with the possibility of his not being here, and I started thinking about what Philip means to me and what he means to architecture. He has a very public persona, he has aired all his dirty and clean laundry for all to see. He is and has been out there. He has received every possible criticism and accolade that could befall a human being in a lifetime. What does he do? What does he mean to us, his work, his life, his contribution? He is notorious for trying everything, for trying every movement, style, language, architecture, trying it on for size, regurgitating and spitting it out, studying it, understanding it, making it his own, making it his way.... No one else of his stature in architecture spends so much time nursing, cajoling, involving themselves in an effort to inspire younger people, to help younger people, to help colleagues, to worry about colleagues, to spend time with other architects, to promote other architects. It's a very compelling history that points to only one thing, this incredible love for the profession of architecture by this one man and his willingness to give of himself, and his time and his effort. This is beyond what one could label as self-serving. This is a whole life of support and interest and love of architecture and the people that make it. It's way, way beyond, and there's nobody alive today in architecture that does that.

Absolutely no one.

Johnson at the Glass House, 1998. (Michael Moran)

Epilogue

In the winter of 2017 news of a developer's proposed alteration to Manhattan's 550 Madison Avenue circulated through the architectural press. In chirpy, promotional language a press release described changes that would include stripping the lower portion of the building's granite facade and demolishing its opulent, marble-floored lobby. Outrage rapidly mounted among architects and preservationists, and a campaign to halt those alterations and grant the building landmark status gained momentum. It was already too late for the interior. Before those efforts could wind their way through the city bureaucracy, the lobby was gutted—a bitter blow against one of the city's most significant, if notorious, buildings. Although its address, 550 Madison Avenue, might not be familiar, its granite profile and skyline-marking Chippendale cap surely are. Most people know it by its original name: the AT&T Tower.

There was a time not that long ago when no one would have complained. For much of its life, and even when it was still on a drafting board, the AT&T Tower was the most reviled work of architecture in America, the poster child of postmodernism, that most gleefully despised of architectural movements. The building was vilified, the movement was vilified, and so was its architect: Philip Cortelyou Johnson.

But time has a way of shifting perspectives, and in the intervening years the AT&T Building has become a genuine icon. Not necessarily beloved, but appreciated as historically significant and worthy of preservation. In the 1960s and 1970s, Johnson rallied in the streets to save Penn Station and Grand Central Terminal; now, more than a decade after his death, crowds gathered on Madison Avenue with signs reading SAVE AT&T and HANDS OFF MY JOHNSON.

This unlikely turn of events, the shift from one pole to its opposite without any explicit rejection of that previous position, suited Johnson's nature and career. He was a man of contradictions, and that included his advocacy of preservation, which came to a halt when his own interests were involved. If expanding the Museum of Modern Art meant knocking down two beaux arts townhouses, fine. His vision for Ellis Island would have turned its iconic main building into a ruin. And then there was Third City, his plan to raze a square mile of historic Harlem and replace it with a walled city of his own design.

Johnson's contradictory nature was more than intellectual gamesmanship. Duality was his essential makeup, the product of the psychological condition—a form of bipolar disorder—that had afflicted him since he was young. For much of his life there were two Philip Johnsons, one manic and animated by possibility, the other profoundly damaged, lost, diffident and insecure. Being gay in a time when homosexuality was unacceptable, and certainly unacceptable to his father, only exacerbated the problem. There had to be multiple Johnsons, one intimate and disguised, the other a public performance.

Johnson was magnanimous—with his art, with his money, with his time—but also casually cruel and deceitful. He held grudges, sometimes for no reason other than pettiness, jealousy, or ambition. That he was a serial hit-and-run driver in his youth reveals an essential cowardice and an appalling lack of interest in the welfare of others. Of all his repellent traits, the most damning was his willingness to use people and then dispose of them when they were no longer of consequence to him. He did so throughout his life, in both his personal and professional worlds. Jan Ruhtenberg, Jimmie Daniels, Landis Gores, Jon Stroup, Robert Melik Finkle, Rosamond Bernier, John Burgee—those names are only a few on a long, dark list.

Well into middle age, he was a virulent anti-Semite and racist advocate of eugenics. For decades he sought to bury his sordid fascist behavior during the thirties and forties. He was never publicly confronted with the full evidence of his complicity—that he was more than a Nazi sympathizer, but an unpaid agent of the Nazi state. In his defense he could boast of his deep and lasting Jewish friendships, Lincoln Kirstein and Eddie Warburg chief among them; his advocacy for any number of

Jewish architects, from Louis Kahn to Frank Gehry; his synagogue building; his support for Israel. Shimon Peres, the Nobel Peace Prize winner who negotiated Israel's relationship with postwar Germany, considered Johnson a close friend.

His actions and relationships were tainted by his cynicism and by his opportunism, but they were also in many ways genuine—another Johnson paradox. Is it possible to forgive him? Perhaps it is more useful to ask what prompted him to such drastic and misguided ideas and behavior. He inherited the prejudices of his father, and of middle-American white privilege, but he pushed those beliefs to obscene extremes. That was surely part of his goal, an Oedipal rejection of his father, an immature desire for attention and power masking his own insecurities. He acted as if the rules that applied to others did not apply to him, that he was above the common man even as he made populism his cause.

As an architect, a theorist, and a critic, he was notoriously unfaithful. Because he was restless and his mind was nimble, he could not resist the narcotic draw of the new, and the opportunities for self-aggrandizement the new presented. And so he dispensed with one idol for another, one way of thinking for another, tacking with the zeal of an America's Cup champion. In the world of architecture, a profession of idealists and romantics who would impose their visions on the world, his inconstancy was perceived as a grave moral flaw.

The story of Johnson's power and influence began at the Museum of Modern Art with the landmark *Modern Architecture: International Exhibition* of 1932. That show nearly didn't happen; that it did was a testament to the enlightened patronage of Abby Aldrich Rockefeller and Alfred Barr, and to Johnson's own energy and intelligence. It introduced European modernism to the American public, presenting work by Le Corbusier, Walter Gropius, Mies van der Rohe, and others who had developed a new architecture that responded to the materials, technologies, and conditions of contemporary life. But Johnson's vision of this new architecture was deracinated. He presented modernism as a style, a new aesthetic, rather than a progressive way of thinking about the built environment. At the height of the Depression, Johnson only reluctantly addressed architecture's obligations to relieve a mass housing crisis and to build a more equitable society. There was nobody more critical of Johnson's worldview than Frank Lloyd Wright, who castigated Johnson for his "propagandistic" formal agenda even as he benefited from it. Johnson loved that controversy. He was not afraid of intellectual pugilism; it showed him that he was on the right path.

From the success of that show, the museum's department of architecture was born. Johnson immediately expanded its purview with another exhibition of lasting influence. After proving that architecture was a museum-worthy subject, he did the same for design. The *Machine Art* show of 1934 was groundbreaking in suggesting that there was artistry in everyday objects, from a ball bearing to a microscope, and in how those objects were displayed—on pedestals, as if they were religious relics to be venerated. He pioneered a vision of design as a consumable product, a marketable quality to be exploited in a commercial age.

As important as what he favored was what he did not: architecture for families, architecture and the environment, regional and vernacular architecture, mass housing. Social responsibility was boring, and for Philip Johnson to be boring was an unforgivable crime.

Johnson's identity was inextricably entwined with the museum. Although he did not design its main building—that happened during his prodigal fascist years—he became the house architect in the 1940s and remained so until the museum rejected him in the 1970s, the biggest blow of his career. But in that long period he contributed two handsome modern wings (one remains) and what is indisputably the museum's architectural masterpiece, the Abby Aldrich Rockefeller Sculpture Garden. The collection within the museum's walls is also unthinkable without Johnson's contributions. What would the place be without Lichtenstein's dotted girl with a beach ball, or Warhol's shimmering gold reproduction of Marilyn Monroe, or the encaustic flag of Jasper Johns? These works define the museum.

He shaped that collection just as he shaped the world of architecture. He began as a "propagandist" for modernism, and his campaign was a success. The Miesian glass box became the de facto paradigm for the skyscraper, a model that was easily and inexpensively reproduced by an America increasingly dominated by corporations. With Mies, Johnson designed the ne plus ultra of these towers, the Seagram Building, and he followed it with several others—IDS, Pennzoil Place—of great delicacy and urbanity. His domestic work of the 1940s and 1950s, when he was building refined homes for the wealthy—not least himself—may be his most consistent period of excellence. If these works were not entirely original, they were gracious, attuned to their moment and to the mores of his clients, and impeccably made.

When Johnson tired of modernism, when he felt he needed to forge a new identity in opposition, he experimented with historical elements and precedents. There was something unsettling in his Ballet School formalism, for it not only rejected what he had so recently promoted but was unmistakably fascistic in its insistence on classical order and authority. With his history, that connotation was especially disturbing. When Robert Venturi pushed that direction in ways even he had not imagined, and then provided a theoretical foundation for it, Johnson was supportive, though it didn't stop him from experimenting with other idioms— notably Louis Kahn's monumentality—as he sought an architectural language for himself. But it was postmodernism that proved the best vehicle for shaking up the profession, and for making himself into a genuine American celebrity.

Postmodernism was a lot like Johnson himself: controversial, deplored as amoral, and ubiquitous. In the late 1970s and 1980s postmodern towers sprouted in cities across the country, many of them designed by Johnson, who had established the paradigm with the AT&T Tower in New York. If that was Exhibit A of corporate postmodernism, Exhibit B was Michael Graves's Portland Building, and Johnson had made that possible, too. But pomo's lifespan was blessedly short, and when it was no longer the outrageous new kid on the block, Johnson pivoted again. Deconstructivism would be the new architectural style of the day, and if it lacked intellectual coherence as a movement it didn't matter. What did matter to Johnson was staying relevant and retaining his position as a tastemaker and a kingmaker.

His career mirrored American life of the postwar years, marked by increasing corporatization and the concentration of power and wealth among a privileged few. By the time of his death, celebrity had become the chief form of public currency. It was no accident that Donald Trump was the most prominent patron of his later years. Both craved attention, and they knew that their collaboration would generate it in boldface type.

Johnson himself became something of a human Rorschach test; the animus directed at him could reveal as much about those critics as it did about him. By birth he had been granted every conceivable privilege. When he squandered his advantages, he was given chance after chance to redeem himself, and despite his missteps he accrued more power and more privilege. For those who had not been so entitled—which is to say, just about everyone else—the idea that such profligacy could be rewarded was hard to swallow. This was compounded by the feeling that he had wasted his gifts and failed to achieve what he could and should have. This made him an especially ripe target, a figure onto whom all flaws and inadequacies might be projected.

The legacy he did leave extends beyond his architecture into art, design, and urban affairs, but his buildings remain his most visibly enduring markers. These works are so disparate in style and quality that it can be hard to believe they were generated under the direction of the same individual. The architect of aesthetically modest modern residences of the mid-century became the designer of aesthetically bombastic postmodern towers as that same century came to a close. In between there were moments of enduring civility and dignity offset by works that were overblown, nihilistic, and crass.

Yet there is a through line that holds all of this work together, a theme that recurs continually in Johnson's vast oeuvre. When he spoke on the nature of architecture, he returned again and again to the theme of procession, to the idea that architecture should be experienced through the unfolding of movement and time, a lesson he ascribed to his first visit to the Acropolis in Athens.

But Philip Johnson's work was rarely defined by procession. If there was any single hallmark to his designs, any defining characteristic, it was the void. His buildings resolve themselves in grand empty spaces, in open rooms, courts, and atriums. These are spaces one comprehends not through time and movement, but by standing still and gazing out, by stasis. The Glass House, the building that was his most intimate and personal architectural statement, is in essence an empty container, a simple open room.

Johnson imagined these voids as spaces of social interaction, and at their best they could achieve great energy and civility. Between the sculpture garden at the Museum of Modern Art and the promenade at the State Theater, he was responsible for two of New York's greatest rooms. Even the Glass House was a salon of intellectual and physical exchange.

But when emptied of human presence, stripped down to its bones, Johnson's architecture feels barren and inert and lonely, despite its refinement and extravagance.

That was Johnson in architecture and in life: an exquisite, fragile, and empty vessel, always in search of a charge.

Acknowledgments

All works of architecture are collaborative endeavors, and the same is true for books. In the many years it has taken me to complete this project, I have benefited from the generosity of a great number of individuals and institutions, and they all have my gratitude.

It is dedicated to John Manley and Robert Melik Finkle, who knew Johnson intimately and spent many, many hours with me sharing their insights and memories. I regret that John was not able to see it completed, but hope it honors his memory, and all the many other men and women who supported Johnson in his professional and personal life.

This project began in a conversation with my agent, Sarah Burnes, whose integrity and intelligence are inspiring, and with the sharp-thinking, optimistic Chris Parris-Lamb. It began life at Little, Brown under Michael Sand, and blossomed under the exceptional editorial guidance of Michael Szczerban, who shaped it into its final form. A reunion with Katharine Myers, a colleague from my own days in publishing, was a special joy. Thanks also to Nicky Guerreiro, Allison Warner, Michael Noon, and Ashley Marudas.

This book would not have been possible without a grant from the Graham Foundation for Advanced Studies in the Fine Arts. My early research was assisted by Julia Cooke, a Columbia University Hertog Fellow. My thanks to her and to Chris Beam for welcoming me into that program.

I completed the manuscript for this book while on Loeb Fellowship at the Harvard Graduate School of Design. I think John Petersen, Sally Young, and my fellow fellows for their support and ideas.

For their instrumental early support and insights, I am indebted to

Barry Bergdoll and Robert A. M. Stern. Irene Shum helped me discover Johnson's Glass House and other New Canaan work. The staff of the Glass House has been gracious in providing me access and information on Johnson's home and life. Philip Dempsey, Johnson's nephew, was an invaluable source of family material and knowledge.

Many of the photographs appear here courtesy of two friends and mentors, Erica Stoller and Michael Moran. I am indebted to both.

To the many archivists and librarians who have assisted me, my gratitude is unmatched. My special thanks go to Michelle Elligott, Michelle Harvey, Paul Galloway, and Jennifer Tobias at the Museum of Modern Art. At the Getty Research Institute, I was grateful for the work of Lois White and Peter Bjorn Kerber. Russell Flinchum guided me to Johnson's files at the Century Association. I am otherwise thankful to archivists at Columbia, Harvard, Oberlin, the University of Pennsylvania, The Rockefeller Foundation, Tufts, Wellesley, and the Western Reserve Historical Society.

In the course of research, I benefited from interviews and discussions with countless friends, associates, scholars, and clients of Johnson. I am saddened that many are no longer alive to see it finished. The list of those I was privileged to speak with includes: Raj Ahuja, Donald Albrecht, Eli Attia, John Belle, Rosamond Bernier, Denise Scott Brown, John Burgee, David Childs, Elaine Lustig Cohen, Corky Cunningham, Raymond Dowd, Martin Eidelberg, Peter Eisenman, Norman Foster, Ulrich Franzen, Belmont Freeman, Alexander Garvin, Frank Gehry, Rosalie Genevro, Paul Goldberger, Alex Gorlin, Pamela Gores, Joe Giovannini, Michael Graves, Judith Grinberg, David Hanks, Gary Hildebrand, Gerald Hines, Gerald Horne, Scott Hughes, Ada Louise Huxtable, K. Michael Hayes, Barbara Jakobson, Stover Jenkins, John Johansen, Ivan Karp, Henry Krotzer, Phyllis Lambert, Neil Levine, Carter Manny, Richard Meier, Christopher Mount, Si Newhouse, Victoria Newhouse, Joan Ockman, I. M. Pei, Jonathan Petropoulos, Vidya Preya, Terry Riley, Alan Ritchie, Jaquelin Robertson, Les Robertson, Richard Rogers, Vessel Ruhtenberg, Vincent Scully, Douglass Shand-Tucci, Martin Skrelanus, Suzanne Stephens, Barbara Stokes, Jane Thompson, Brendan

Tobin, Kazys Varnelis, Robert Venturi, Nicholas Fox Weber, Frank Welch, and Robert Wojtowicz.

Many of the ideas developed here were first tested in publications including *Architect, Architectural Record, Architectural Review, Design Observer, Landscape Architecture,* and *Metropolis.* I am grateful to my editors for their generosity and wise counsel.

I thank my colleagues at the University of Texas at Arlington, in particular Brad Bell, Don Gatzke, Kathryn Holliday, and Adrian Parr for their support and ideas.

At the *Dallas Morning News,* my critical home, I thank Mike Wilson, Tom Huang, Christopher Wynn, and Mike Merschel for their patience and encouragement. Rick Brettell shared his memories of Johnson with me, and was a generous sounding board and friend.

For their many indulgences, I am grateful to Kurt Andersen, Christopher Bonanos, Ruth Franklin, Chris Hawthorne, Sarah Herda, Karrie Jacobs, Mark Lee, Kevin Lippert, Michael Morse, Emmanuel Pratt, David Ulin, and Tom Vanderbilt.

I am fortunate that three of the brightest critical minds in architecture also happen to be three of my dearest friends. For their years of support and collaboration, I thank Andrew Bernheimer, Alexandra Lange, and Philip Nobel.

Above all, I thank my family: my parents-in-law Mark and Valeria Kuchment; my parents Hal and Jane Lamster; and my wife Anna Kuchment and daughter Eliza Lamster.

Notes

Prologue

xiv "If I had all the money": Johnson to Louise Pope Johnson, 20 June 1930. Philip Johnson Papers, Western Reserve Historical Society (WHRS), Cleveland.

xvii He could let go: Martin Skrelunas, telephone interview with the author, 7 June 2011.

Chapter 1: The Master's Joy

4 Metropolis on the rise: On Cleveland Heights, see Marian J. Morton, *The Overlook of Cleveland and Cleveland Heights* (Charleston: Arcadia, 2010).

4 "The smoke of prosperity": William Ganson Rose, quoted in *Cleveland: A Concise History 1796-1996* (Bloomington: Indiana University Press, 1997), 77.

5 "Pretty chutzpahish": Johnson, taped interview with Peter Eisenman, 19 October 1982. Glass House Archive (GHA).

6 "The sweetest old girl": Homer Johnson to Nettie Whitcomb, 6 November 1886. Oberlin Archives, Homer H. Johnson files, series I.

8 "Very intimate friends": Louise Pope to Cousin Sally, 27 September 1901. Oberlin Archives, HHJ files, series VIII, box 5.

8 J. Milton Dyer: On Dyer, see Franz Schulze, *Philip Johnson: Life and Work* (New York: Knopf, 1994), 15–16.

8 Louis Rorimer: On Rorimer's design, see Leslie A. Piña, *Louis Rorimer: A Man of Style* (Kent, Ohio: Kent State University Press, 1990), 101.

9 Records suggest: According to his birth certificate, Louise Pope had given birth to one child "born alive and now dead" at the time of Johnson's birth, in addition to his two living siblings. This would also account for the gap of three years between the births of Alfred and Philip, whereas the interval between the other three births was only a single year. GHA, Johnson Papers.

12 Down-home, American charm: On the history of the house, see Andrew S. Dempsey, "A Greek Revival House in Ohio: 1840," unpublished paper, 18 January 1955. Collection of Philip Dempsey. Andrew Dempsey was the son of Johnson's sister Jeannette. The paper was produced for an art history class at Yale.

13 Homer's attempted remedy: Johnson's early schooling, stuttering, and Homer's response are recounted in Schulze, *Johnson,* 22–23. See also GHA, Johnson-Eisenman tapes.

15 "Mule dealer": Homer Johnson, quoted in "Oberlin's Damon-Pythias," Cleveland *Plain Dealer,* 26 March 1960. See also Edwin B. Parker, *Final Report of the United States Liquidation Commission* (Washington: Government Printing Office, 1920).

16 Just "sightseeing": GHA, Johnson-Eisenman tapes, 19 October 1982.

17 "Widespread anti-Semitic prejudice": Report of Henry Morgenthau, Sr., Mission of the United States to Poland, American Commission to Negotiate Peace, Paris, 3 October 1919.

17 This did not suit Johnson: Morgenthau's report did not satisfy his fellow commissioners, nor did it satisfy many in the Jewish community, who felt it too soft on Polish political leadership.

18 "None of these excesses": Report of Brig. Gen. Edgar Jadwin and Homer H. Johnson, Mission of the United States to Poland, American Commission to Negotiate Peace, Paris, 31 October 1919.

18 Themselves to blame: Homer's sympathy with the postwar Polish government contrasts with his lasting distaste for the American South in the wake of the Civil War. Noting the continued discrimination against blacks, he advocated against any aid to the Southern states during Reconstruction. See Johnson college paper on Reconstruction, 3 February 1879. Oberlin College Archive, HHJ Papers, series IX.

18 "Able and conscientious manner": Robert Lansing to Homer Johnson, 19 December 1919. Getty Research Institute (GRI), Los Angeles, Philip Johnson Papers, family scrapbook 7.

18 "Corruption of sources": Homer Johnson's remarks as reproduced in the *Pinehurst Outlook,* 17 March 1920.

19 "The intellectual type": Hackley *Annual,* 1922. GRI, Johnson Papers, box 28.

19 "The master's joy": Hackley *Annual,* 1923. GRI, Johnson Papers, box 28.

19 "Interest in current problems": Hackley *Annual,* 1923. GRI, Johnson Papers, box 28.

20 A male role model: Johnson to Louise Pope Johnson, 14 February 1926. GRI, Johnson Papers, box 25.

20 Automatically accepted: Harvard maintained a similar arrangement with many of the top preparatory schools.

20 "A boy of sound character": Walter Gage, Personal Record and Certificate of Honorable Dismissal for Philip Johnson, 30 June 1923. Harvard University Archives (HUA), Philip C. Johnson Student File.

20 "Has very high ideals": Hackley *Annual,* 1923. GRI, Johnson Papers, box 28.

Chapter 2: From Saul to Paul

21 "The only thing I lack": Johnson to Homer Johnson, nd (1927). WRHS, Johnson papers.

22 "Hopeless amount of things": Johnson to Louise Pope Johnson, 19 February 26. GRI, box 25.

22   "I think he will learn": Homer Johnson to Prof. C. N. Greenough, 10 September 1923. HUA, Philip Johnson Student File.

23   The Battle Creek System: J. H. Kellogg, *The Battle Creek Sanitarium System: History, Organization, Methods* (Battle Creek, Mich.: J. H. Kellogg, 1908).

23   "I was an outsider": GHA, Johnson-Eisenman tapes, 19 October 1982.

23   "As he would his parents": Johnson, letter to the editor, *Harvard Crimson,* 5 April 1924.

24   Not a congenial place: On the purge and its effect on gay life at Harvard, see William Wright, *Harvard's Secret Court: The Savage 1920 Purge of Campus Homosexuals* (New York: St. Martin's Press, 2005). On Lowell and his Harvard career, see Andrew Schlesinger, *Veritas: Harvard College and the American Experience* (Chicago: Ivan R. Dee, 2005), 152–176. On gay life at Harvard generally, see Douglass Shand-Tucci, *The Crimson Letter: Harvard, Homosexuality, and the Shaping of American Culture* (New York: St. Martin's Griffin, 2003).

25   "Very narrow and behind the times": Johnson to Louise Pope Johnson, 14 February 1926. GRI, box 25.

25   "Son, this is all": GHA, Johnson-Eisenman tapes, 19 October 1982.

27   "Think of greater things": Johnson to Louise Pope Johnson, 14 August 1925. GRI, box 25.

27   Not the tourist destination: In 1920, Yellowstone received fewer than 80,000 visitors. Today the annual number is around three million.

28   "The ideal of a National Park": Johnson to Louise Pope Johnson, 21 August 1925. GRI, box 25.

29   "I'd rather be a coward": Johnson to Louise Pope Johnson, 14 August 1925. GRI, box 25.

29   "The guide is a Jew": Johnson to Louise Pope Johnson, 14 August 1925. GRI, box 25.

29   "By moonlight": Johnson to Louise Pope Johnson, 30 August 1925. GRI, box 25.

30   "Out of words": Johnson to Jeannette Johnson, 13 October 1925. GRI, box 25.

30   "It is the purest mess": Johnson to Jeannette Johnson, 13 October 1925. GRI, box 25.

31   "It was a gory thing": Johnson to Louise Pope Johnson, 14 February 1926. GRI, box 25.

31   "Their mentality is so inferior": Johnson to Louise Pope Johnson, November 1925. GRI, box 25.

31   "An innocuous person": Johnson to Johnson family, March 1926. GRI, box 25.

32   "Convenient nervous breakdown": Johnson to Theo Johnson, 19 February 26. GRI, box 25.

32   "Fairy godmother": Johnson to Louise Pope Johnson, 19 January 1926. GRI, box 25.

32   "Think how much we judge": Johnson to Louise Pope Johnson, nd. GRI, box 25.

33   His wife, Rosalind: Sarton dedicated a poem to Greene, "For Rosalind," in her 1971 collection, *A Grain of Mustard Seed.*

34 "They look so much better": Johnson to Louise Pope Johnson, July 1926. GRI, box 25.

34 "Little Saffron": The name was a reference to the Essex town of Saffron Walden, which he had visited, not to the color of the car.

35 "I have no convictions": Johnson to Louise Pope Johnson, 31 January 1926. GRI, box 25.

37 "Surpass, ye higher men": Friedrich Nietzsche, *Thus Spake Zarathustra: A Book for All and None* (New York: Macmillan, 1896), 420.

37 "I never could understand it": GHA, Johnson-Eisenman tapes, 19 October 1982.

37 "I get mixeder up": Johnson to Louise Pope Johnson, nd (1927). WRHS, Johnson Papers.

37 "Acute stage of cyclothemic reaction": Dr. Donald J. MacPherson to Dean Robert M. Bacon, 2 December 1927. HUA, Philip Johnson Student File.

37 "I have had a slight nervous breakdown": Philip Johnson, petition to the Harvard College Administrative Board for leave of absence, 12 December 1927. HUA, Philip Johnson Student File.

38 "Why don't you buck up?": GHA, Johnson-Eisenman tapes, 19 October 1982.

39 "Doubtful ethics": Johnson's history of these events was related to Oberlin President Donald M. Love at a private meeting at the Johnson house in Cleveland on 25 October 1936. Love recorded them under the headline "The Inside Story" in a memo he marked as "confidential." "Conversation with H. H. Johnson," Oberlin College Archive, Donald M. Love Papers, series IV, subseries 1, box 5.

39 Gross breach of trust: On the Aluminum Company restructuring, see George David Smith, *From Monopoly to Competition: The Transformations of Alcoa, 1888–1986* (New York: Cambridge University Press, 2003), 143–59, 494–97.

40 That resolution: Smith, *From Monopoly to Competition,* 143–59, 494–97.

40 Everything he had ever built: Exactly how large was Philip Johnson's fortune? In 1940, after the Depression had sapped its value, the FBI still estimated it at roughly half a million dollars. His secretary told the FBI his private income was roughly $5,000 a month.

42 "Neurasthenia": Kellogg, *Battle Creek Sanitarium System,* 170–71.

43 "Enjoy the tropical scene": Kellogg, *Battle Creek Sanitarium System,* 27.

43 A handsome actor: Johnson described his second visit to Battle Creek and subsequent affair and trip to the Finger Lakes to Franz Schulze. See Schulze, *Johnson,* 41–3.

43 He changed his concentration: Technically, the classics concentration was "Philosophy-Classics."

43 "Without a return": Donald J. MacPherson to Johnson, 19 April 1929. HUA, Philip Johnson Student File.

44 "Architecture should be devoid": Henry-Russell Hitchcock, "The Architectural Work of J. J. P. Oud," *The Arts* 13 (February 1928), 97–103.

45 "Whatever situation": Lincoln Kirstein, quoted in Martin Duberman, *The Worlds of Lincoln Kirstein* (New York: Knopf, 2007), 36.

46　Proselytizer for the new: See Alfred H. Barr, "Boston Is Modern Art Pauper," *Harvard Crimson,* 30 October 1926.

47　Something altogether new: The inspiration may well have been the 1927 "Abstract Cabinet" designed by El Lissitzky and curator Alexander Dorner for Germany's State Museum in Hanover. Barr saw it, and so did Johnson—both considering it critical. See Joan Ockman, "The Road Not Taken: Alexander Dorner's Way Beyond Art" in Robert E. Somol, *Autonomy and Ideology: Positioning an Avant-Garde in America* (New York: The Monacelli Press, 1997), 80–121.

47　*coup de théâtre*: On the exhibition, see Nicholas Fox Weber, *Patron Saints: Five Rebels Who Opened America to a New Art* (New York: Knopf, 1992), 61–67.

47　"I disliked it very much": Johnson, quoted in Fox Weber, *Patron Saints,* 67.

48　Submit to a quiz: The test is reprinted in Steven Watson, *Prepare for Saints: Gertrude Stein, Virgil Thomson, and the Mainstreaming of American Modernism* (New York: Random House, 1998), 94.

48　No other class like it: On Barr's class, see Sybil Gordon Kantor, *Alfred H. Barr, Jr. and the Intellectual Origins of the Museum of Modern Art* (Cambridge: MIT Press, 2002), 101–103.

48　The trip was a revelation: On Barr's trip to Europe, see Alice Goldfarb Marquis, *Alfred H. Barr Jr.: Missionary for the Modern* (Chicago: Contemporary Books, 1989).

49　"Why not include architecture?": Marquis, *Alfred H. Barr Jr.,* 88.

49　A small design exhibition: On the exhibition, see "Exhibitions: 1929 [May 2-23] Modern European Posters and Commercial Typography." 10S Museum, Exhibitions File, Wellesley College Archives.

Chapter 3: A Man of Style

51　"I certainly have swallowed": Johnson to Louise Pope Johnson, 18 August 1929. GRI, box 25.

51　"What I like about the Black Forest": Johnson to Louise Pope Johnson, 13 August 1929. GRI, box 25.

51　"I shall never conceal myself again": Johnson to Johnson family, 29 August 1929. GRI, box 25.

52　"My final judgment": Johnson to Johnson family, 28 July 1929. GRI, box 25. To be precise, Johnson's original wording read, "There are two many unfunctional decorations and too little use of solid colr, + too much convention in chairs."

52　He "hates the people I hate": Johnson to Louise Pope Johnson, 18 August 1929. GRI, box 25.

52　"The French are awful": Johnson to Johnson family, 13 August 1929. GRI, box 25.

52　He preferred Germans: There were various other excursions, often with Alfred Kreusel, a German friend with little interest in architecture, and members of the Schutz family, with whom he lodged.

53　"If I could build a house": Johnson to Louise Pope Johnson, 18 August 1929. GRI, box 25.

54 "The Parthenon of modern Europe": Johnson to Alfred H. Barr, 16 October 1929. Archives of American Art (AAA), New York, Barr Papers.

55 "Sacrifice the best buildings": Johnson to Louise Pope Johnson, 22 September 1929. GRI, box 25.

55 "Properly thrilled": Johnson to Louise Pope Johnson, 3 October 1929. GRI, box 25.

55 "Only a very young": Christopher Isherwood, *Berlin Stories* (1945; reprint: New York: New Directions, 2008), xviii.

56 "The only thing": Johnson to Louise Pope Johnson, 24 November 1929. GRI, box 25.

57 Photographer Helmar Lerski: On Lerski, see Lynne Warren, ed., *Encyclopedia of 20th Century Photography*, vol. I (New York: Routledge, 2006), 925–927. Lerski tried to make it in the United States as an actor and free-love advocate before taking up photography and returning to Europe. His images were popular with the fashion press, though he typically chose unfashionable subjects, transforming working-class Berliners into figures of great sculptural power.

58 "Bohunks, I calls em": Johnson to Louise Pope Johnson, 26 October 1929. GRI, box 25.

58 "All things in this world": Hannes Meyer, "My Expulsion from the Bauhaus: An Open Letter to Lord Mayor Hesse of Dessau," in *The Bauhaus: Weimar, Dessau, Berlin, Chicago* (Cambridge: MIT Press, 1969), 164. Also "Building," p. 153.

61 "Kandinsky is a little fool": Johnson to Alfred H. Barr (November 1929). AAA, Barr Papers.

61 "The simplicity of a great man": Johnson to Alfred H. Barr (November 1929). AAA, Barr Papers.

61 Several works by Ruhtenberg's wife: There is no record of the fate of Johnson's works by von Helmsing, who was killed in Allied bombing during the war.

62 "It sounds rather ugly": Johnson to Louise Pope Johnson, 3 October 1929. GRI, box 25.

62 "Hardly disentangle": Johnson to Louise Pope Johnson, 8 November 1929. GRI, box 25.

62 "Get lots of new ideas": Johnson to Louise Pope Johnson, 8 November 1929. GRI, box 25.

62 "What I want to experiment": Johnson to Louise Pope Johnson, 24 November 1929. GRI, box 25.

63 "I heard something disquieting": Johnson to Johnson family, 18 November 1929. GRI, box 25.

63 The renovation of her living room: On the Johnson living room at Pinehurst, see Piña, *Rorimer,* 110–11.

63 "I will have to hump myself": Johnson to Louise Pope Johnson, 8 November 1929. GRI, box 25.

64 It was astonishing: On the "Three Ladies" and the founding of the Museum of Modern Art, see Russell Lynes, *Good Old Modern: An Intimate Portrait of the Museum of Modern Art* (New York: Atheneum, 1973).

64 Their first order of business: On A. Conger Goodyear, see Lynes, *Good Old Modern,* 8–9.

65 Another fixture was Margaret Fitzmaurice-Scolari: They were introduced by Sachs protégé Agnes Mongan, whom Barr knew from Harvard. AAA, "Oral history interview with Marga Barr concerning Alfred H. Barr," 22 February–13 May 1974.

65 "It was a fantastic atmosphere": AAA, Marga Barr oral history.

66 Junior Advisory Committee: The name of this committee was initially the "Advisory Committee" and its members "Junior Trustees." It had become known as the Junior Advisory Committee by 1934.

66 The first chairman: There are conflicting reports as to whether Howe was the chair of the committee or merely a leading member of it.

67 "New York appeals": "The Bachelors of New York," *New York Times,* 9 September 1928. The single-female population was roughly 700,000. See George Chauncey, *Gay New York: Gender, Urban Culture, and the Making of the Gay Male World, 1890–1940* (New York: Basic Books, 1994).

67 Cory Ross was the product: Martin Eidelberg, "Living International Style," unpublished ms., 2012.

68 Ross was not interested: The episode is drawn from notes made by Barr in 1977 and recounted in Schulze, *Johnson,* 59.

68 "You are the only one": Marga Barr, quoted in Schulze, *Johnson,* 59.

69 Film producer George Kates: Kates would later suggest the inclusion of film set designs in the *Modern Architecture: International Exhibition* show, an idea rejected by Johnson.

69 "An Austrian Jew": Johnson to Louise Pope Johnson, 7 July 1930. WHRS.

70 They would collaborate on a book: Exactly when the two began working first on the book and then on the exhibition is a matter for conjecture. There are even differing accounts of when and where Johnson and Hitchcock first met (either in New York in the spring of 1930 or Paris in the summer). The preponderance of evidence suggests they met in Paris. It is difficult to believe that at that time, in their conversations with Barr, they did not at least broach the subject of an exhibition, though other histories have suggested they arrived at the decision to collaborate later on their trip.

70 "I find that if I contradict": Johnson to Louise Pope Johnson, 7 July 1930. WRHS.

71 Published in German: The provisional German title was *Also doch ein baustil.*

71 "The most charming man": Johnson to Louise Pope Johnson, 20 June 1930. WRHS.

72 "I think you can leave it": J. J. P. Oud to Johnson, 22 July 1930. Curatorial Exhibition Files, Exh. #15. Museum of Modern Art Archives, NY.

72 Come in and restore it: The restoration led to some confusion. Mondrian, in his repainting, incorrectly dated it "P. M. 25." That date stood from then until the 1980s, when curators determined it was in fact painted in 1929.

73 "It was not the least my fault": Johnson to Louise Pope Johnson, 4 July 1930. WRHS.

73 "Dried wine and cockroaches": Kirstein quoted in Duberman, *Kirstein,* 28.

74 "The things he liked": Johnson to Louise Pope Johnson, 6 August 1930. WRHS.

75 "All I saw was the girl flying": Johnson to Louise Pope Johnson, 22 August 1930. WRHS.

75 To the city of Brno: Johnson described it as "a fantastic city of squalor and modernism."

75 The two met Otto Eisler: On Eisler, see *Otto Eisler: 1893–1968* (Brno: Obecni dum, 1998), 23.

76 Sutton Place: The neighborhood transformation was brought to screen in William Wyler's 1937 hit *Dead End*. The film stars a young architect, played by Joel McCrea, who must navigate these two worlds.

77 "He keeps his distance": Johnson to Louise Pope Johnson, 1 September 1930. WRHS.

Chapter 4: Show Time

79 "After all what I want most": Johnson to Alfred H. Barr (summer 1931). CUR, Exh. #15. MoMA Archives, NY.

80 "Now, ladies and gentlemen": This, at least, is how Johnson remembered this meeting. If his memory was not always perfect (or honest), in this case it has the sense of truth and is bolstered by the weight of evidence. MoMA Archives, Philip Johnson Oral History (1990–91), 25, 42.

80 "American megalomania": Johnson, "The Skyscraper School of Modern Architecture," *Arts* (May 1931), 569–75; reprinted in Philip Johnson, *Writings* (New York: Oxford University Press, 1979), 39–42. Johnson first mentions his intended battle against the skyscraper in a letter to his mother from Berlin on 21 July 1930.

81 Also named to this committee: Also proposed for the committee was Swiss art collector G. F. Reber, who was sympathetic to the exhibition plan.

83 "While the architect accepts the machine age": Note that Johnson, Hitchcock, and Barr were subtly reformulating the three principles of the International Style such that a "functional plan" was now being replaced by an emphasis on volume — that is, another aesthetic position.

84 The Bowmans were chosen: See "All Metal Apartment," *New York Times*, 6 July 1930.

84 A necessary evil: In a letter dated 24 February 1931, Goodyear suggested that Rockefeller Center be presented in model form, ostensibly as a demonstration of the timeliness of the show. CUR, Exh. #15. MoMA Archives, NY.

84 "Wright was a great pioneer": Johnson to Lewis Mumford, 3 January 1931. University of Pennsylvania Rare Book & Manuscript Library, Lewis Mumford Papers.

86 While the writing of the book: Their presumption was still that it would be first published in German.

86 "Shopworn": Johnson, "Modernism in Architecture," *The New Republic,* 18 March 1931, 134.

87 "Urban's admiration": Johnson, "The Architecture of the New School," reprinted in Johnson, *Writings,* 33–36.

87 The show's Gold Medal: Technically, the Gold Medal was awarded to the firm of Shreve, Lamb, Harmon, but it was for the Empire State Building.

87 It was catnip to the press: "Young Architects Stage Rival Show," *New York Times,* 21 April 1931.

88 That one had been designed: The Lindbergh House appeared in the Harvard Society's Bauhaus show in December 1930, presumably in the form of drawings and/or plans loaned by Barr, who had somehow acquired them from the architects.

88 A breeding ground for young moderns: In the year following, after Howe & Lescaze's submissions to the show were rejected, the architects publicly resigned from the league, which denied it was retribution in a story that ran on the front page of the *Times.* Meanwhile, the Philadelphia Savings Fund Society tower was prominently featured in Johnson's show at the museum, which ran concurrently. "Architects' Show Bars Two Moderns," *New York Times,* 28 February 1932.

89 "Exhibitions should have a definite purpose": Johnson to Mrs. Cornelius J. Sullivan, 27 March 1931. CUR, Exh. #15. MoMA Archives, NY.

89 "His inferiority": Lincoln Kirstein, unpublished diaries, 1930–31, 119. New York Public Library for the Performing Arts, Lincoln Kirstein Papers. Johnson would in fact become the head of the Bauhaus's American "circle of friends" during the coming summer.

90 "I am not a stylist": R. M. Schindler to Johnson, telegram, 9 March 1932. CUR, Exh. #15. MoMA Archives, NY.

90 A techno-charlatan: Technically, he was right. Fuller was not yet an architect, though he would grow tired enough of hearing this cavil that he would go and get his degree. Of course, Johnson wasn't an architect at the time, either.

90 "The motif at the top": Johnson to Raymond M. Hood, 27 May 1931. CUR, Exh. #15. MoMA Archives, NY.

91 "Probably not meet": Johnson to Frank Lloyd Wright, 22 May 1931. CUR, Exh. #15. MoMA Archives, NY.

92 "The grotesque decadence": Julien Levy, *Memoir of an Art Gallery* (New York: Putnam, 1977), 67.

92 *The International Style*: It was published in the United States, by Norton.

92 "I shall only send it": Oud to Johnson, 14 August 1931. CUR, Exh. #15. MoMA Archives, NY.

94 Jewish architect: Mendelsohn had traveled through the United States in the twenties and published a book of his impressions, *Amerika* (1928). On the Nazis, Berlin, and Mendelsohn, see especially Thomas Friedrich, *Hitler's Berlin: Abused City* (New Haven: Yale University Press, 2012), 229–236.

94 "Doesn't know the first thing": Johnson to Hitchcock, quoted in Schulze, *Johnson,* 73. In fact, Johnson was critical of the two Mendelsohn projects illustrated in *The International Style,* unfavorably remarking on the New York–style setbacks of his Schocken Building and an "unsatisfactory" stair tower in his German Metal Workers Building.

94 "You don't seem to mind Jews": Johnson to Alfred H. Barr, summer 1931. CUR, Exh. #15. MoMA Archives, NY.

95 "The Utopian race": Helen Appleton Read, "A New Architecture," *Vogue* (October 1931), 98.

96   "This type of display": On Reich as exhibition designer, see Matilda McQuaid, "Lilly Reich and the Art of Exhibition Design" in McQuaid, *Lilly Reich: Designer and Architect* (New York: MoMA, 1996), 9–46.

96   "You know very well": Johnson to Hitchcock, quoted in Schulze, *Johnson*, 80.

96   The housing section: It is not coincidental that patrons to the housing section of the exhibition included the Jews Alexander Bing, A. E. Kazan, Herbert Lehman, Henry Moskowitz, Joseph Proskauer, Aaron Rabinowitz, and Albert Stern, along with the Catholic former New York governor and Democratic presidential candidate Al Smith.

96   "I rather doubt the value": Johnson to Bowman Brothers, 1 December 1931. CUR, Exh. #15. MoMA Archives, NY.

97   As was par with Wright: In his essay on Wright in their exhibition catalog, Hitchcock writes of the "impossibility of assigning fixed values" to Wright's "sonorous vocabulary." *Modern Architecture: International Exhibition* (New York: MoMA, 1932), 29.

99   "We all feel very proud": Abby Aldrich Rockefeller, telegram to Johnson, 9 February 1932. CUR, Exh. #15. MoMA Archives, NY.

100   "Here we have": Edward Alden Jewell, "Modern Architecture Shown," *New York Times,* 9 February 1932; H. I. Brock, "Architecture Styled International," *New York Times Magazine,* 7 February 1932.

100   "I can safely say": Johnson to Oud, 17 March 1932. CUR, Exh. #15. MoMA Archives, NY.

100   "Every trace of his name": Frank Lloyd Wright to Johnson, 11 February 1932. CUR, Exh. #15. MoMA Archives, NY.

100   "One of the great architects": *Modern Architecture, International Exhibition* (New York: MoMA, 1932), 29–37.

101   "Why, I ask you": Wright to Johnson, 11 February 1932. CUR, Exh. #15. MoMA Archives, NY.

101   "I regret very much": Johnson to Wright, 16 February 1932. CUR, Exh. #15. MoMA Archives, NY.

101   "Good God, my boy": Wright to Johnson, 19 February 1932. CUR, Exh. #15. MoMA Archives, NY.

101   "Of Thee I Sing": Frank Lloyd Wright, "Of Thee I Sing," in Bruce Brooks Pfeiffer, ed., *Frank Lloyd Wright: Collected Writings, vol. 3, 1931–1939* (New York: Rizzoli, 1993), 113–115.

102   "To have an experience": See *Shelter,* vol. 2, no. 3 (April 1932), *passim*.

102   "Philip, my King": Wright, quoted in Schulze, *Johnson,* 83.

102   "I have appreciated your efforts": Johnson to Wright, 25 April 1932. CUR, Exh. #15. MoMA Archives, NY.

103   "I regret now": Hitchcock to Wright, 22 April 1932. CUR, Exh. #15. MoMA Archives, NY.

103   Given it a name: Just who came up the term, and when, has been something of a debating point within academic circles for decades. See Terrence Riley and

Stephen Perrella, *The International Style: Exhibition 15 and the Museum of Modern Art* (New York: Rizzoli, 1992), 89–93 for a reasonable chronology.

103 "Brilliant young authority": Edward Alden Jewell, "The Museum of Modern Art to Install a Department of Architecture as a Regular Feature," *New York Times,* 3 July 1932.

Chapter 5: The Maestro

105 "We must learn": "Hitler Addresses Huge Youth Rally," *New York Times,* 2 October 1932.

105 "The only salon in New York": Watson, *Prepare for Saints,* 176.

105 "At-homes": The principal source on the Askews' parties is Virgil Thomson, *Virgil Thomson* (New York: Knopf, 1974), 214–217. See also Anthony Tommasini, *Virgil Thomson: Composer on the Aisle* (New York: Norton, 1997); Eugene Gaddis, *Magician of the Modern: Chick Austin and the Transformation of the Arts in America* (New York: Knopf, 2000); Watson, *Prepare for Saints*; Fox Weber, *Patron Saints.*

105 "He collected people": Watson, *Prepare for Saints,* 176.

106 "Smiling, relentless": Houseman, quoted in Tommasini, *Virgil Thomson,* 220.

107 "New York is the greatest": The repeal of Prohibition would make matters worse by placing so much more of the city's social life out in the open where it could be policed. On gay life in New York in the Jazz Age, see, among others, George Chauncey, *Gay New York* (New York: Basic Books, 1994).

109 "In a pet": Kirstein, unpublished diaries, 1931–32, 267. New York Public Library for the Performing Arts, Lincoln Kirstein Papers.

109 "I tried to have him": Johnson, quoted in Charles Kaiser, *Gay Metropolis: The Landmark History of Gay Life in America* (New York: Grove Press, 1997), 41.

109 "Sleep on it": Thomson, *Virgil Thomson,* 217. See also Tommasini, *Virgil Thomson,* 226.

109 Cage cut it off: Schulze, *Johnson,* 97. Daniels, it should be noted, became a beloved New York institution, opening a nightclub under his own name on Lenox Avenue in Harlem. When he died, in 1984, Leontyne Price sang at his memorial service.

109 One sexual experience a day: Robert Melik Finkle, interview with the author, 10 August 2010.

110 "His specialty": Kirstein, unpublished diaries, 1931–32, 248. New York Public Library for the Performing Arts, Lincoln Kirstein Papers.

110 "Dull and disagreeable": Johnson to Oud, 17 March 1932. CUR, Exh. #15. MoMA Archives, NY.

111 "We don't want people": Draft catalog statement written by Johnson. MoMA, CUR, Exh. #23. MoMA Archives, NY.

112 "A fancy camera": Quoted in Schulze, *Johnson,* 89.

113 "I had thoroughly convinced myself": Johnson to Louise Pope Johnson, 14 February 1926. GRI, box 25.

113 His first taste of the man: Schulze places Johnson at the Potsdam youth rally, based on his interviews with Johnson. Johnson often inaccurately claimed his first experience of Hitler was at a Nuremberg *Parteitag* rally.

114 Hitler Youth leader: On Baldur von Schirach and the Potsdam youth day, see Schirach, *Ich glaubte an Hitler* (Hamburg: Mosaic Verlag, 1967), 157–166; Michael H. Kater, *Hitler Youth* (Cambridge: Harvard University Press, 2004), 17–18.

114 "We must learn": "Hitler Addresses Huge Youth Rally," *New York Times,* 2 October 1932.

114 "A spellbinder": Johnson, taped interview with Peter Eisenman, 19 October 1982. Glass House Archive (GHA).

116 Blood-red gate: See Terry Kirk, *The Architecture of Modern Italy,* vol. II (New York: Princeton Architectural Press, 2005), 84–102.

117 They didn't speak: Tommasini, *Virgil Thomson,* 315.

117 His only client: On the Slater Blakeman apartment, see Schulze, *Johnson,* 105.

118 Bauhaus originals: Most of the Barrs' furniture was by Donald Deskey. I am especially grateful to Martin Eidelberg for his knowledge of the apartment and furnishing programs of Barr, Johnson, and their cohort.

118 "Satisfy the new craving": Johnson, "Architecture of the Third Reich," in *Writings,* 54.

119 Trouble getting them published: An exception was his piece for *Hound & Horn* on the German film industry under the Nazis, which was not nearly so sanguine as Johnson's architectural analysis of the Third Reich. Mostly, however, publishers were uninterested in the cultural ramifications of Nazi policy. Barr, "Nationalism in German Films," *Hound & Horn,* March 1934, 278–83.

119 "Left on the junk heap": On the Nazis and Schlemmer, see Lillian Tone, *Bauhaus: A Conceptual Model* (Ostfildern: Hatje Cantz, 2009), 312–14.

119 "Just to spite": Alfred H. Barr, undated note. Museum of Modern Art, Paintings & Sculpture departmental files, Schlemmer file.

120 "The first important modern German painting": Museum of Modern Art, press release, 17 September 1932. Shortly thereafter Mayer-Hermann, a prominent Jewish doctor who catered to the stars of the Berlin stage, followed his portrait to New York, a refugee from the Nazis. Though you wouldn't think it from the portrait, he was in fact a handsome man with a sly wit, and he took to visiting the museum and stationing himself near his portrait to eavesdrop on the smart remarks of passers-by. Dix did not fare so well. The Nazis deemed his work degenerate, burned what they could, and removed him from his teaching post.

120 The Schlemmer did not: Johnson did not give the painting to the museum until the 1940s, by which time he was so besmirched by his own fascist history that the museum accepted it anonymously.

120 Merely a typo: In a letter to Josef Albers of 23 January 1934, Johnson acknowledged receiving a dunning letter from Schlemmer, forwarded by Albers. In the letter he claimed he would forward Schlemmer 400 reichsmarks, and also that he was trying to find a buyer (presumably Austin) "so that I might be able to send him more money." The Josef and Anni Albers Foundation Archives, Bethany, Conn., Johnson files.

121 The grand premiere: On the opening of *Four Saints,* see especially Fox Weber, *Patron Saints,* 217–30, and Watson, *Prepare for Saints,* 267, as well as Tommasini, *Virgil Thomson* and Gaddis, *Magician of the Modern.*

121 "I wanted that job badly": Johnson to Alfred H. Barr, August 1933. MoMA Archives, Alfred H. Barr Jr. Papers [AAA 2164 1279].

123 "That's what I like": The chair was one of Mies's MR chairs. They had a tendency to slip before Knoll took on their manufacture. On the Warburg commission, and Warburg generally, see Fox Weber, *Patron Saints,* 238–43, passim.

123 "Restful simplicity and bright airiness": "Simplicity in the House of an Art Lover," *House & Garden,* January 1935, 22–3.

123 All parties agreed: *Summer Exhibition: Project for a House in North Carolina by William T. Priestley* ran at the Museum of Modern Art from 10 July to 30 September, 1933.

123 "I am not sure": Johnson to Oud, 23 November 1933. CUR, Exh. #34. MoMA Archives, NY.

124 Whoever was responsible: The circumstances regarding the authorship of the house are unclear. The Chapin family maintains that the house was designed by Johnson, though he never formally took credit for it. Ruhtenberg did. Priestley also washed his hands of it. Today, it has been renovated and its original qualities lost.

124 "Carefully selected show": Nelson A. Rockefeller to Johnson, 13 January 1933. CUR, Exh. #34. MoMA Archives, NY.

125 "The craft spirit": Johnson, in *Machine Art* (New York: Museum of Modern Art, 1934; reprint 1994), np.

125 "By beauty of shapes": Plato, quoted in *Machine Art,* np.

126 "For the first time": Museum of Modern Art, press release, 1 March 1934.

127 To design the catalog: Johnson's role in Albers's emigration wasn't exactly heroic: called in for his opinion, he enthusiastically recommended Albers for a teaching position at Black Mountain College in North Carolina. He had come to know Albers and his wife—Anni Albers, a textile designer who also taught at the Bauhaus—on his trips to Germany. He admired them both and would later give Anni a show at the Museum of Modern Art. Their position was precarious because Anni, though she had converted, was born Jewish. Johnson, however, was little interested in their fate beyond the prestige in having his advice solicited and the convenience of having a talented designer at his disposal. "I wish no responsibility for him," he wrote Barr in an undated letter of 1933, though he acknowledged there "was not a better person could be got from the lot of ex Bauhauesler[s]." Johnson to Alfred H. Barr, 1933. Museum of Modern Art, Alfred H. Barr Jr. Papers.

127 "His assistance in designing": *Machine Art,* np.

128 "All those who are skeptical": Museum of Modern Art, press release, 5 March 1934. For an extensive discussion of the "beauty contest," and of the show generally, see Jennifer Jane Marshall, *Machine Art, 1934* (Chicago: University of Chicago Press, 2012), passim.

128 "Recognition at last!": The cartoons appeared, respectively, in the April 7 and April 14, 1934 issues of *The New Yorker.*

128 "A practical guide": Museum of Modern Art, press release, 5 March 1934.

128 "Exhibition maestro": On the show's reception, see Marshall, *Machine Art, 1934*, passim.

129 "I do not think": Nelson A. Rockefeller to Johnson, 9 March 1934. Rockefeller Archive Center, Sleepy Hollow, NY, collection III, record group 2E, box 20, folder 198.

Chapter 6: The Gold Dust Twins

131 "The tragedy of youth": "Youth Benefit Stressed Here," *Sandusky Register*, 5 December 1935.

131 "Two Quit Modern Art Museum": Joseph Alsop [uncredited], "Two Quit Modern Art Museum for Sur-Realist Political Venture," *New York Herald Tribune*, 18 December 1934.

132 "As soon as a thing's": Alsop [uncredited], "Two Quit Modern Art Museum."

132 "We're adventurers": Alsop [uncredited], "Two Quit Modern Art Museum."

133 Sixteen people came: Johnson decorated in much the same fashion as his previous apartments, and with the same furnishings. The design was published in the January 1934 issue of the tony shelter magazine *Arts & Decoration*.

133 "Cross-section of the people": "Two Forsake Art to Found a Party," *New York Times*, 18 December 1934.

133 She was there: Merrill was interviewed by the FBI in 1942. See Federal Bureau of Investigation Headquarters Files 161-2482 and 100-32734.

133 According to testimony: See Federal Bureau of Investigation Headquarters Files 161-2482 and 100-32734.

135 "Business needs to receive orders": Dennis advocated a massive ($10 billion) tax hike spread evenly across the population, with that new revenue devoted to an energetic program of government stimulus. Lawrence Dennis, *Is Capitalism Doomed?* (New York: Harper & Bros., 1932).

135 Followed up that success: On Dennis's passing, and his personal history, see Gerald Horne, *The Color of Fascism: Lawrence Dennis, Racial Passing, and the Rise of Right-Wing Extremism in the United States* (New York: New York University Press, 2006).

136 Resigned in a flurry: "Charges Renewed by Dennis Against State Department," *Washington Post*, 11 March 1927.

136 Looked like a prophet: Horne, *Color of Fascism*.

136 "The international bankers": Dennis, *Is Capitalism Doomed?*

136 "Could not leave the kitchen": Dennis, *The Coming American Fascism: The Crisis of Capitalism* (New York: Harper & Bros., 1936), 258.

137 Intellectual elite caste: "A powerful State guided by a capable elite loyal to some scheme of the national interest is far more expressive of the popular will than a weak liberal State," Dennis wrote. Dennis, *American Fascism*, 241.

137 "Cooperation to keep the peace": Dennis, *Is Capitalism Doomed?, 301.

137 "I felt like immediate assassination": Kirstein, unpublished diaries, 6 May 1934. New York Public Library for the Performing Arts.

137 "No great fear of Phil Johnson": Kirstein, unpublished diaries, 6 May 1934. New York Public Library for the Performing Arts.

138 "This outrageous development": Henry-Russell Hitchcock to Lewis Mumford, 19 December 1934. University of Pennsylvania Archive, Lewis Mumford Papers, MS collection 2, folder 2215.

138 Curatorial savvy: I am grateful to Jennifer Tobias for her insight in suggesting *Objects* as a source for this show's curatorial strategy.

139 "Extraordinary gift": Draft of Museum of Modern Art staff memo (with edits by Nelson Rockefeller), 28 December 1934. Rockefeller Foundation Archive, collection III, record group 2E, box 20, folder 198.

139 "It will take a man like Long": Dennis, quoted in Arthur Schlesinger, *The Politics of Upheaval* (Boston: Houghton Mifflin, 1960), 77.

139 "The fate of the country": Report, 1942. Federal Bureau of Investigation Headquarters Files 161-2482 and 100-32734.

141 To go "scalping": "Quit Art to Knife Huey Long," *Circleville* [Ohio] *Herald,* 22 December 1934.

141 The week the two: "Long Announces Plans for Drive to State Capitol," *New Orleans Times-Picayune,* 28 December 1934.

142 An already volatile situation: Long's travails were front-page national news. See, for example, "Tried to Kill Long, Ex-Deputy Admits," *New York Times,* 3 February 1935.

142 Flanked by phalanxes: "Huey Long Departs from the War Zone," *New York Times,* 4 February 1935.

143 "The appeal is tremendous": "Two Huey Long Admirers Are Unpaid 'Tutors,'" *Washington Post,* 11 April 1935.

143 "How many votes have you got?": GHA, Johnson-Eisenman taped interview, 1982. The Long deputy is identified by Schulze as Earle Christenberry.

144 With nothing waiting: Schulze, *Johnson,* 115–18. Note there are some discrepancies between the chronology Johnson remembered in his respective interviews with Schulze and Eisenman.

144 "The largest piece of glass": GHA, Johnson-Eisenman taped interview, 1982.

144 Here was a premonition: On Johnson's renovation of the house, see Geoffrey Blodgett, "Philip Johnson's Great Depression," *Timeline,* June-July 1987, 2–17.

146 "The tragedy of youth today": "Youth Benefit Stressed Here," *Sandusky Register,* 5 December 1935.

146 An enormous sum: This was the estimate of the FBI in 1940.

146 "Guilt for being rich": GHA, Johnson-Eisenman taped interview, 1982.

146 "I demand a peaceful settlement": Quoted in Blodgett, "Philip Johnson's Great Depression," 8.

147 Cheating...procrastinating: "Airs Milk Fight," *Mansfield News Journal,* 6 January 1936.

147 "If you want to hurt your father": GHA, Johnson-Eisenman taped interview, 1982.

147 Anson Gear: See Federal Bureau of Investigation Headquarters Files 161-2482 and 100-32734.

149 "Bankers of the nation": Notice in the *Hamilton Daily News Journal,* 20 January 1936. See also Schulze, *Johnson,* 124–5.

150 Johnson donated $5,000: The contribution is detailed in an extensive report on Johnson's activities prepared by the FBI in 1945, when Johnson was being considered for hire as architect of an American embassy building in Bogota, Colombia. He did not get the job.

151 Modeled on the Hitler Youth rally: Johnson was also aware of the elaborately staged Nuremberg rallies that had taken place in the 1930s, even if he had not seen them in person. In interviews, he often confused those rallies with the Potsdam event he attended.

151 It opened in April: In fact, Keck helped Johnson arrange for the show to travel to the Century of Progress exposition, where it was exhibited following its run in New York.

152 "We were never introduced": Betty J. Blum, Interview with Robert Bruce Tague, Chicago Architects Oral History Project, Art Institute of Chicago, 1995, 14–16.

152 Conscripted into fascist service: On Johnson's architecture and fascism, and in particular on the Coughlin platform and the Keck office participation in making it, see Joan Ockman, "The Figurehead: On Monumentality and Nihilism in Philip Johnson's Life and Work," in Emmanuel Petit, ed., *Philip Johnson: The Constancy of Change* (New Haven: Yale University Press, 2009), 82–109.

153 "Form your battalions": Parke Brown, "Coughlin Slams President: Vast Crowd Cheers," *Chicago Tribune,* 7 September 1936. Brown's account was rewritten as "Coughlin Declares Rome Report a Lie," *New York Times,* 7 September 1936. Video clips of Coughlin's speech are widely available online.

154 Coughlin was unrepentant: Before his speech, he delivered a radio address to the nation from a facsimile of his office in the Shrine of the Little Flower erected adjacent to the platform.

154 "Resembled the Nazi salute": John M. Cummings, "Crowds Cheer Fr. Coughlin at Big Rally Here," *Philadelphia Inquirer,* 27 September 1936. The observation was repeated verbatim in "Coughlin Repeats Roosevelt Attack," *New York Times,* 27 September 1936.

154 "We didn't want to be associated": GHA, Johnson-Eisenman taped interview, 1982.

Chapter 7: An American Führer

156 "Instead of politics": "Message of Youth to Nation Given in New Radio Program," *Social Justice,* 16 November 1936.

156 "America cannot exist": "Youth, Impatient with Excuses, Demands Action and Leadership," *Social Justice,* 14 December 1936.

157 Johnson led the motorcade: On the Young Nationalists, see Schulze, *Johnson,* 128. Schulze interviewed Richard Bowers, a member of Johnson's group.

157 Cutting the radio station's power line: "Youths Unite after Air Talk, Crave Action," *Social Justice,* 22 March 1937.

158 Published in America: Werner Sombart, *A New Social Philosophy,* Karl Frederick Geiser, trans. (Princeton: Princeton University Press, 1937).

158 Johnson met Sombart: Schulze, *Johnson,* 130.

159 These trips: Schulze, *Johnson,* 129-30. See also Johnson's interview with Ludwig Glaeser in Johnson, *Mies Van Der Rohe* (1947; reprinted New York: MoMA, 1978). In this interview, Johnson gives an earlier date (1931, which seems unlikely) for the trips to Lübeck and Stettin, and mentions the dinners at Schlichter's. His memory of driving past Sachsenhausen seems plausible, however, and certainly could have taken place during trips with Mies closer to Berlin.

159 "Wealthy, liberal clients": Schulze, *Mies van der Rohe: A Critical Biography* (Chicago: University of Chicago Press, 1985).

161 A brand-new 1937 Chevrolet: The estimated value of the car was $500.

161 "One thinker to another": O. John Rogge, *The Official German Report: Nazi Penetration 1924–42, Pan-Arabism 1939–Today* (New York: Yoseloff, 1961), 177.

162 A personal guest: Rogge, *The Official German Report,* 174–86.

162 Which he would self-publish: Technically, the book was published under the imprint of the Weekly Foreign Letter, which Dennis had purchased in 1939 to use as his personal mouthpiece.

163 "The philosophy of individualism": Philip Johnson, "A Dying People," *The Examiner,* Summer 1938, 305–20.

163 "Carried away": GHA, Johnson-Eisenman taped interview, 1982.

164 "Purely social": Johnson, FBI interview, 18 June 1942. Classified Subject Files, General Records of the Department of Justice (Classification 146-6). National Archives and Record Administration, College Park, Md.

165 "All generalities": Johnson, FBI interview, 18 June 1942.

165 A more plausible scenario: Rogge, *The Official German Report.*

165 "What interests me": Johnson to Viola Heise Bodenschatz, 23 April 1939. Federal Bureau of Investigation Headquarters Files 161-2482 and 100-32734.

165 "Do you look for war?": Johnson to Bodenschatz, 23 April 1939.

166 "A new spirit of cooperation": Friedrich Auhagen, "The American Fellowship Forum," *Today's Challenge,* June-July 1939, 3.

167 George Sylvester Viereck: Rogge, *The Official German Report.*

168 "Writing for a small influential public": Rogge, *The Official German Report,* 346.

168 Lindbergh returned in 1937: On Lindbergh, Ford, and the Nazi movement in America, see Max Wallace, *The American Axis: Henry Ford, Charles Lindbergh, and the Rise of the Third Reich* (New York: St. Martin's Press, 2003).

169 "Jew deal": McWilliams was the organization's "National Commander." Dale Kramer, "The American Fascists," *Harper's,* September 1940, 380–93.

169 Violence was not uncommon: Kramer, "The American Fascists."

169 Stabbed on the subway platform: "Youth Is Stabbed in Subway Dispute," *New York Times,* 23 February 1939.

169 Among their targets: Kramer, "The American Fascists."

170 "The Jews bought the paper": Johnson to Bodenschatz, 23 April 1939.

170 "To preserve anonymity": Rogge, *The Official German Report,* 346.

171 "A long tradition": Johnson, "*Mein Kampf* and the Business Man," *The Examiner,* Summer 1939, 291–296.

171 "Doctrinal purity": Johnson, "*Mein Kampf* and the Business Man," 291–296.

172 "The present policy": Johnson, "London and Paris — Midsummer 1939," *Today's Challenge,* August-September 1939, 19–26.

172 "Such an influx": Johnson, "Aliens Reduce France to an 'English Colony,'" *Social Justice,* 24 July 1939.

173 "Today the Germans": Johnson, "Inside War-Time Germany," *Today's Challenge,* November-December 1939, 17–25.

173 A sharp confidential warning: Ned Hoopes, "Viola Bodenschatz: America & Germany," unpublished ms., 544-556. Hoopes Collection, Columbia University Library, box 3.

174 "Any fool knows": William L. Shirer, *Berlin Diary* (Boston: Little, Brown, 1940), 173.

174 "Well, Philip": Hoopes, "Viola Bodenschatz," 544-556.

174 "The longer I am here": Johnson, "Poland's Choice Between War and Bolshevism Is a 'Deal' with Germany," *Social Justice,* 11 September 1939.

174 A 1935 booklet: Viola Bodenschatz, *Mournful Memel* (Self-published, 1935).

175 "Some awful plague": Johnson, "Poland's Choice."

175 "A subhuman Slavic racial type": Hoopes, "Viola Bodenschatz," 544-556.

175 "A slum without a city": Johnson, "Poland's Choice."

176 An ill omen: Hoopes, "Viola Bodenschatz," 544-556.

176 "All the Polish officials": Johnson, "Poland's Choice."

176 "Time to receive your stamps": Hoopes, "Viola Bodenschatz," 544-556.

176 "The Poles are brave": Hoopes, "Viola Bodenschatz," 544-556.

177 "What do you want?": GHA, Johnson-Eisenman taped interview, 1982.

177 He was now required: *Otto Eisler: 1893–1968* (Brno: Obecni dum, 1998), 23.

177 "One of the worst moments": GHA, Johnson-Eisenman taped interview, 1982.

177 "In all cases": Karl Bodenschatz, testimony at Nuremberg Trial. Nuremberg Trial Proceedings vol. 9, day 77, 8 March 1946. Morning session.

177 Eisler's harrowing story: *Otto Eisler: 1893–1968,* 23.

178 "I just felt excitement": GHA, Johnson-Eisenman taped interview, 1982.

178 "She added nothing": Tommasini, *Virgil Thomson,* 315. Thomson was rather cavalier about the effects of the war in its early days. "Paris has never been sweeter and quieter and pleasanter and kinder and more sensibly reasonable about everything," he wrote to a friend in January 1940.

178 "None of us can stand the fellow": Shirer, *Berlin Diary,* 213.

179 "Grotesque the spectacle": Shirer, *Berlin Diary,* 215.

179 "Do you remember Markow?": Johnson to Bodenschatz, undated. Federal Bureau of Investigation Headquarters Files 161-2482 and 100-32734.

180 "America knows too much": Johnson, "War and the Press: Propagandists Who Fight with Lies Always Lose when Truth Attacks," *Social Justice,* 6 November 1940.

180 "Corruption of sources": Homer Johnson's remarks as reproduced in the *Pinehurst Outlook,* 17 March 1920.

Chapter 8: Pops

181 "It is an unusual": *The Forum Observer,* vol. 1, no. 1, 29 February 1940.

182 Bruce Simmons: What exactly Simmons did is unclear. Johnson, in interviews, spoke about an informant who helped him design a lamp. Simmons indicated greater responsibilities in his interviews with the FBI.

182 "ESPIONAGE": J. Edgar Hoover to Special Agent in Charge, Cleveland, Ohio, 24 June 1940. Federal Bureau of Investigation Headquarters Files 161-2482 and 100-32734.

182 "It sounds as if": *The Philip Johnson Tapes: Interviews by Robert A. M. Stern* (New York: The Monacelli Press, 2008), 76.

182 "Twiddling my thumbs": *Johnson Tapes,* 77.

183 "The bunk": Johnson to Ernestine Fantl, 15 August 1935. CUR, Exh. #43. MoMA Archives, NY.

183 Placed under the direction: In fact the seat was not entirely vacant, having been occupied first by Ernestine Fantl and then by Betty Mock. Neither woman was seriously considered as a department chair.

186 "I don't see anything wrong": *Johnson Tapes,* 78.

187 "Copy to": Commandant, Third Naval District to Philip Johnson, 24 September 1940. GRI, box 25.

187 "Thoroughly kindred spirits": Landis Gores, "Seven Houses in Search of a Principle." Unpublished ms. (1989), 45.

187 "Eccentric bird": Schulze, *Johnson,* 149.

188 "With assurance": Gores, "Seven Houses," 50.

189 Two days later: Carter Manny, interview with the author, 16 April 2010.

190 "On the whole delighted": Gores, "Seven Houses," 62.

192 "It is a good house": Johnson to Louise Pope Johnson, 2 May 1943. WRHS.

192 A furious Johnson: Ulrich Franzen, interview with the author, 10 August 2010.

193 The only sour note: Quotes in Johnson Projects Clippings File. MoMA Archives, Philip Johnson Papers, II.19.

193 "When ve do this": *Johnson Tapes,* 92.

194 A year-in-architecture essay: "Architecture in 1941" in Johnson, *Writings,* 56–61.

194 "The Warren G. Harding": *Johnson Tapes,* 86.

195 "My age makes it harder": Johnson to Johnson family, 26 April 1943. WRHS.

195 "Candy, Candy, CANDY!": Johnson to Johnson family, 2 May 1943. WRHS.

195 "A constant example": Johnson to Alfred Barr, AAA.

196 "My interpretation": Johnson to Johnson family, 13 June 1943. WRHS.

197 "Of course the army": Johnson to Johnson family, July 1943. WRHS.

197 "Fascist tendencies": Department of Justice memo, 11 October 1944. Federal Bureau of Investigation Headquarters Files 161-2482 and 100-32734.

198 "The situation there": Johnson to Johnson family, 18 October 1943. WRHS.

199 "My testimony is crisp": Johnson to Johnson family, 14 November 1943. WRHS.

199 "His character": Federal Bureau of Investigation Headquarters Files 161-2482 and 100-32734.

Notes

200 "On the whole": Johnson to Johnson family, 21 November 1943. WRHS.

200 "It may even get built!": Johnson to Louise Pope Johnson, 28 September 1944. WRHS.

201 "I am afraid": Johnson to Johnson family, 13 July 1944. WRHS.

201 "The feeling of being": Johnson to Louise Pope Johnson, 28 September 1944. WRHS.

Chapter 9: A New New Beginning

204 Live-in lover: On Stroup, see Schulze, *Johnson,* 185–88.

205 "Instead of being regarded as toys.": MoMA Archives, press release, 25 May 1945.

205 "A new high": "As Simple as That," *Ladies' Home Journal,* July 1945.

206 "High degree of taste": "A House for a Millionaire with No Servants," *Ladies' Home Journal,* April 1946.

206 Contacted Gores's wife: Pamela Gores, interview with the author, 22 April 2010.

207 The Booth site: On Johnson's early commissions, see Gores, "Seven Houses."

207 The design of the house: On design development of the Glass House, see Stover Jenkins and David Mohney, *The Houses of Philip Johnson* (New York: Abbeville, 2001), 60–91 and Gores, "Seven Houses."

208 Barr simply refused: On Barr, see Lynes, *Good Old Modern,* 240–84.

208 "She was more interested": Museum of Modern Art Oral History Project.

209 "The people who commission monuments": Johnson to Mies van der Rohe, 16 October 1945. MoMA Archives, Philip Johnson Papers, IV.8.

209 "Man needs concrete symbols": Johnson, "What Aesthetic Price Glory?," *Art-News,* September 1945, 8–10, 24–5.

210 "This country may now": MoMA Archives, press release, 15 September 1947.

211 "Breathtaking": Edward Alden Jewell, "A Van der Rohe Survey," *New York Times,* 28 September 1947.

212 "Satisfactory": On the Barcelona buttons, see Johnson to Mies van der Rohe, 26 November 1947, and the reply from Mies's office, Felix C. Bonnet to Johnson, 1 December 1947. MoMA Archives, registrar files, Exh. 356.

212 "Holy Roman Empire": Johnson, *Mies van der Rohe* (New York: Museum of Modern Art, 1947), 9.

213 "The idea of a glass house": Joseph Giovannini, "Johnson and His Glass House: Reflections," *New York Times,* 16 July 1987.

214 "Build it?": *Johnson Tapes,* 112.

215 Construction took a year: The contractor, John C. Smith, was recommended by Eliot Noyes, who had recently completed his own house in New Canaan.

215 Dissolving the walls: "Romantic Lighting for a Glass House," *Flair,* February 1950. See also Dietrich Neumann and Robert A. M. Stern, *The Structure of Light: Richard Kelly and the Illumination of Modern Architecture* (New Haven: Yale University Press, 2011).

215 Alone in a dark room: Gores, "Seven Houses."

217 News to Gores: Gores, "Seven Houses."

217 The anti-Semitic feelings: On Johnson's postwar anti-Semitism and fascism, see especially Ockman, "The Figurehead," 82–109.

218 Sharp rap with his cane: Interview with Paul Rudolph by Robert Breugman, Chicago Architects Oral History Project, Department of Architecture, Art Institute of Chicago.

218 "The Frontiersman": Johnson, "The Frontiersman," *Architectural Review*, 1 April 1949.

219 A natural fit for the Tremaines: On Meteor Crater and the Tremaines, see Gores, "Seven Houses"; Kathleen L. Housley, *Emily Hall Tremaine: Collector on the Cusp* (Meriden, Conn.: Emily Hall Tremaine Foundation, 2001); and William Earls, *The Harvard Five in New Canaan* (New York: W. W. Norton & Company, 2006).

222 "I don't think she knows anything": *Johnson Tapes*, 125.

222 That was news: On the Rockefeller Guest House, see Gores, "Seven Houses" and Robert A. M. Stern, Thomas Mellins, and David Fishman, *New York 1960: Architecture and Urbanism between the Second World War and the Bicentennial* (New York: The Monacelli Press, 1997), 305–6.

224 Grace Rainey Rogers Memorial: Stern et al., *New York 1960*, 476–7 and Peter Reed, "The Space and the Frame: Philip Johnson as the Museum's Architect" in *Philip Johnson and the Museum of Modern Art* (New York: Museum of Modern Art, 1998), 70–103.

224 He installed Peter Blake: See Peter Blake, *No Place Like Utopia: Modern Architecture and the Company We Kept* (New York: W. W. Norton & Company, 1993), 130–135.

225 "I feel I can tell you": Nelson A. Rockefeller to Robert J. Ullman, 29 December 1948. Rockefeller Archive Center, Sleepy Hollow, NY, collection III, record group 4, series L, box 144, folder 1419.

225 "All executive authority": René d'Harnoncourt to Johnson, 1 March 1949. MoMA Archives, René d'Harnoncourt Papers, IV.117.

226 Found Blake ensconced: Blake, *No Place Like Utopia*, 130.

227 "He could be arrogant": Blake, *No Place Like Utopia*, 149.

228 A petri dish: Earls, *The Harvard Five*, 19–20.

229 They chose the latter: Gores, "Seven Houses."

229 His first Texas commission: On Johnson and the Menils, see Frank Welch, *Philip Johnson and Texas* (Austin: University of Texas Press, 2000), 36–58.

233 "A small, contained temple": Vincent Scully, "Archetype and Order in Recent American Architecture," reprinted in Scully, *Modern Architecture and Other Essays*, Neil Levine, ed. (Princeton: Princeton University Press, 2003), 64–73.

234 Speculated that the selection: Blake, *No Place Like Utopia*, 137.

234 "The museum will present": MoMA Archives, press release, 8 April 1949.

237 "You have achieved": Nelson A. Rockefeller to Johnson, 21 September 1953. Rockefeller Archive, collection III, record group 4, series L, box 141, folder 1379.

Chapter 10: An Apostate at Worship

239 "I have been called Mies": Johnson, "Retreat from the International Style to the Present Scene," in *Writings*, 89.

240 I notice you: GHA, Johnson-Eisenman taped interview, 1982.

240 You are either: *Johnson Tapes,* 123.

241 That his Prohibition-era dealings: Bronfman could be his own worst enemy; when asked by Abby Aldrich Rockefeller for a substantial gift to the Museum of Modern Art, his response (undelivered) was "You tell that Mrs. Rockefeller to go fuck herself."

242 "NO NO NO NO NO": The letter is reprinted in Phyllis Lambert, *Building Seagram* (New Haven: Yale University Press, 2013), 240–46.

243 Three categories: Lambert, *Building Seagram,* 33. Lambert also visited with Ralph Walker, a gray eminence known for his Art Deco–era commercial buildings.

244 "Shall we make it": *Building Seagram,* 35.

245 White fiberglass screens: John Manley, interview with the author, 19 May 2010.

245 Johnson would never have become: Robert A. M. Stern, interview with the author, 13 April 2010.

246 Like a puppy: Manley, interview with the author, 19 May 2010.

246 Embezzling his money: *Johnson Tapes,* 145.

246 "Mies's approach": Manley, interview with the author, 19 May 2010.

247 The split allowed Johnson: On Johnson's role, see Manley, interviews with the author, 19 & 25 May 2010 and Lambert, *Building Seagram,* chaps. 2–5.

247 The "burping fountain." As part of the agreement to avoid the circular driveway, Johnson had also designed stepped canopies from the lobby to the side street; Mies ordered those redesigned without the step. See Lambert, *Building Seagram,* chap. 3.

248 A tour of the building: Manley, interview with the author, 19 May 2010.

249 "All I want": Lambert, *Building Seagram,* 137.

249 The Four Seasons: On the restaurant, see Lambert, *Building Seagram,* chaps. 4 & 5; John F. Mariani and Alex Von Bidder, *The Four Seasons: A History of America's Premier Restaurant* (New York: Smithmark, 1999).

249 The "power lunch" was born: Lee Eisenberg, "America's Most Powerful Lunch," *Esquire,* October 1979.

250 "It was done for obvious reasons": *Johnson Tapes,* 145.

251 "Strictly malicious intent": On the Rothko affair, see Lambert, *Building Seagram,* 161–5.

251 A gay bar: Manley, interview with the author, 25 May 2010.

252 Critics immediately understood: Lewis Mumford, "The Lessons of the Master," *The New Yorker,* 13 September 1956.

253 "More to our liking": Homer Johnson, open letter to friends. GRI, box 23.

253 For years he had stalled: Memo of 1 July 1949. Oberlin College Archive, Donald M. Love Papers.

254 A luxury hotel in Havana: On the Monaco, see Lambert, "Philip Johnson: Breaking with Modernism—The 'Whence & Whither' of It" in *Philip Johnson: The Constancy of Change,* 194; Manley, interview with the author, 25 May 2010.

254 "What does it cost you?": *Johnson Tapes,* 125–6.

255 Cribbed from the earlier project: The relationship between pavilion and sanctuary is more fluid in the original scheme. See Ockman, "The Figurehead," 88.

255 A wavy ceiling: On the details of Johnson's commissions for Temple Sholom and Kneses Tifereth Israel, see Gavriel D. Rosenfeld, *Building After Auschwitz: Jewish Architecture and the Memory of the Holocaust* (Yale University Press, 2011), 68–73. Whether the origin of the project was originally a church, a temple, or an office is unclear.

256 "The difficulty comes": Johnson, quoted in *Recent American Synagogue Architecture* (New York: Jewish Museum, 1963).

256 "Lou Kahn, especially": Johnson, "Retreat from the International Style to the Present Scene," in *Writings*, 89.

259 Pei recalled the evening: I. M. Pei, speech at New York Preservation Award Ceremony in honor of Johnson, 20 October 1994. GRI, box 34.

Chapter 11: Crutches

261 "I do not believe": Johnson, "The Seven Crutches of Modern Architecture," in *Writings*, 140.

261 "Don't go to college": *The New Yorker*, 31 October 1953, 23–27.

262 "This is almost good": Robert Melik Finkle, interview with the author, 10 August 2010.

263 Not one of these: A Studebaker, a Ford, and a Volkswagen appeared only tangentially, in a gallery of photographs alongside a Maserati, a Porsche, another Bentley, and a Muntz Jet (a bubbly American sports car).

264 "I am not being funny": Johnson, opening remarks at Symposium on the Esthetics [sic] of Auto Design, 12 April 1950. MoMA Archives, Philip Johnson Papers, I.20. In the ad, the car was retouched onto the lawn.

264 "The automobile is the greatest catastrophe": Johnson, "The Town and the Automobile," in *Writings*, 81–3.

265 "I'm an architect, too": Robert Melik Finkle, interview with the author, 16 October 2010.

265 "I was in love with the girl": Robert Melik Finkle, interview with the author, 16 October 2010.

265 Johnson's longtime friend Curt Valentin: Valentin, a protégé of the legendary German-Jewish dealer Alfred Flechtheim, was one of Barr's trusted sources.

265 Seeing other people: On Johnson and the Stroup-Hohnsbeen triangle, see Schulze, *Johnson*, 216–9, 264–6.

266 Together for nearly a decade: Schulze, *Johnson*, 265–6.

266 "Philip used people": Robert Melik Finkle, interview with the author, 16 October 2010.

266 "The Seven Crutches": Johnson, "The Seven Crutches of Modern Architecture," in *Writings*, 136–40.

267 "I'm a traditionalist": "The Seven Crutches," 140.

267 A 1958 study: On the MacKinnon study, see Pierluigi Serraino's excellent *The Creative Architect: Inside the Great Midcentury Personality Study* (New York: The Monacelli Press, 2016).

268 "He showed many classic features": Serraino, *Creative Architect*, 172–9.

268 Where Johnson placed himself: Serraino, *Creative Architect*, 72.

268 "The battle of modern architecture": *Built in USA* (New York: Museum of Modern Art, 1952).

268 "A style is not a set of rules": Johnson, "Style and the International Style," in *Writings*, 72–9.

269 With irreverent cattiness: Johnson, "Retreat from the International Style," in *Writings*, 84–97. Rudolph's estimation came in the introduction to Johnson at the opening of his solo exhibition at Yale in February of 1959. MoMA Archives, Philip Johnson Papers, I.42b.

269 "My stand today": Johnson, "Whither Away—Non-Miesian Directions," in *Writings*, 227–40.

270 Scully's 1954 essay: Vincent Scully, "Archetype and Order in Recent American Architecture," in Scully, *Modern Architecture and Other Essays* (Princeton University Press, 2003), 64–73.

270 At Harry's Bar in Venice: Vincent Scully, interview with the author, 27 July 2010.

270 A problem resolved: Manley, interview with the author, 2 June 2010.

272 "The Israelis are the greatest clients": Johnson, "Informal Talk, Architectural Association," in *Writings*, 106–16.

272 "It is a temple": MoMA Archives, Clippings file, Philip Johnson Papers, II.65.

272 American technical training: On the political implications of Rehovot, see Ockman, "The Figurehead," 94–6.

273 "I immediately felt": Welch, *Johnson and Texas*, 69.

273 "Her interest in me was physical": *Johnson Tapes*, 168.

275 History of mankind: In his 1973 survey, *Modern Movements in Architecture*, critic Charles Jencks derided Johnson's work as "camp" architecture—a brand of unserious, knowing formalism devoid of principles—and suggested the Roofless Church, with its ostentatiously monumental and historicist entry, was a reference to Nazi villas of the 1930s.

275 Apparently eluded her: Johnson's staff was convinced Blaffer Owen did not understand that he was gay.

275 "When I heard you speak": Jane Blaffer Owen to Johnson, 19 January 1980. GRI, box 26.

276 Whitney fit the type: On Whitney, see Irene Mei Zhi Shum, "David Grainger Whitney: A Curated Life and Extraordinary Eye," unpublished ms., May 2011.

276 Burned in the past: On Johnson and *Flag*, see Kirk Varnedoe, "Philip Johnson as Donor to the Museum Collections: An Overview" in *Philip Johnson and the Museum of Modern Art* (New York: MoMA, 1998), 12-33; Annie Cohen-Solal, *Leo and His Circle: The Life of Leo Castelli* (New York: Knopf, 2010), 346; and Jodi Hauptman, "Philip Johnson, MoMA's Form Giver," *Magazine of the Museum of Modern Art* 22 (1996).

278 Also of Miesian origin: A similar stair was designed by Mies for his Bacardi Building.

279 "Today we do not build": Johnson, introduction to a booklet celebrating the opening of the Amon Carter Museum. MoMA Archives, Philip Johnson Papers, I.52.

283 "He was perfectly generous": Denise Scott Brown and Robert Venturi, joint interview with the author, 22 August 2010.

284 "Gentle manifesto": Robert Venturi, *Complexity and Contradiction in Architecture* (New York: Museum of Modern Art, 1966).

Chapter 12: Cocktails on the Terrace

285 "We're having a fire today": On the fire, see Lynes, *Good Old Modern*, 359–76.

286 "I don't care about the people": Manley, interview with the author, 9 June 2010.

286 The perfect occasion: On the expansion plan, see "Towards the New Museum of
Modern Art" brochure, CUR, Exh. #654. MoMA Archives; "The Museum of
Modern Art Builds," MoMA Archives, September 1962, René d'Harnoncourt
Papers, IV.89; and Stern et al., *New York 1960*, 480–3.

289 "If steel can be said to be subtle": On the expansion and reception, see Stern et al.,
New York 1960, 482–5.

291 "In regard to the attitude": Johnson to Lincoln Kirstein, 23 August 1949. New
York Public Library for the Performing Arts, Lincoln Kirstein Papers, box 8,
folder 125.

293 Robert Moses's insistence: Stern et al., *New York 1960*, 677–717.

293 "We just sat there": *Johnson Tapes*, 157.

296 The only real sour note: On the reception of the State Theater, see Stern et al.,
New York 1960, 690–5.

297 "A small, sophisticated jewel": Ada Louise Huxtable, "A Jewel of a Museum,"
New York Times, 15 December 1963.

299 "The aim is to make giants": "Philip Johnson," *Perspecta* 7 (1961), 3–8.

299 "One step further along the road": "Full Scale, False Scale," *Show* (June 1963),
72–5.

299 "It is the most important art movement": Johnson, quoted in "Pop Art: Cult of the
Commonplace," *Time*, 3 May 1963, 69–72.

300 "Philip made his own judgment": Ivan Karp, interview with the author, 15 May
2010.

301 Within the Johnson office: Manley, interview with the author, 2 June 2010.

304 A "sophisticated folly": On the New York State Pavilion, its controversies, and
receptions, see "Young Artists at the Fair and at Lincoln Center," *Art in America*
(MoMA Archives, Philip Johnson Papers, I.82); Stern et al., *New York 1960*,
1034–9; Editorial Board of *Art in America* to Robert Moses (open letter), 26
December 1961 (Rockefeller Archive, collection III.4, box 86, folder 1875); and
Johnson to Nelson A. Rockefeller, 27 April 1964 (Rockefeller Archive, collection
II.4L, box 144, folder 1419). Art International was the tchotchke company founded
with Lincoln Kirstein to exploit Rockefeller Center.

305 "That is not considered stealing": Johnson, address to Yale University architecture
students, 19 April 1965. MoMA Archives, Philip Johnson Papers, I.82a.

306 "What dream cities we could build": Johnson, "If I Were President for a Day," speech to the Women's National Democratic Club, 27 April 1961. MoMA Archives, Philip Johnson Papers, I.53b.

306 "A cocktails-on-the-terrace architect": Rick Brettell, interview with the author, 9 May 2017.

308 "If Omaha allows": On Omaha and the Glessner House, see MoMA Archives, Philip Johnson Papers, III.10.

308 "No one now entering": Mumford, "The Disappearance of Pennsylvania Station." See Stern et al., *New York 1960*, 1114.

309 AGBANY: See Stern et al., *New York 1960*, 1117–9.

Chapter 13: Third City

311 "There was no fear": "2 Area Men Escape Injury, 2 Are Hurt as Plane Crashes," *Stamford Advocate*, 20 August 1966; "Philip C. Johnson in a Plane Crash," *Times Sunday*, 21 August 1966.

312 "Our Ugly Cities": Johnson, "Our Ugly Cities," in *Writings*, 156-61.

312 "He has repented": Staff memorandum, Dan H. Fenn Jr., John F. Kennedy Presidential Library, Boston, Papers of John F. Kennedy, President's Office Files.

313 "We believe": Johnson, Summary Report on the Governor's Conference on Natural Beauty, 25 February 1966. MoMA Archives, Philip Johnson Papers, I.88.

314 Neighbors saw the proposed scheme: On Johnson and his plans for the Village, see Stern et al., *New York 1960*, 236–41.

315 "I mean it is very boring": *Johnson Tapes*, 172–3.

318 A return to Dallas: On the JFK Memorial, see Welch, *Philip Johnson & Texas*, 123–31.

320 "It is always good": Johnson, "Review of *Philip Johnson: Architecture, 1949–65*," in *Writings*, 254-7.

321 "My task is to honor": MoMA Archives, Philip Johnson Papers, II.17.

321 "The library is outstanding": Ada Louise Huxtable, "A Sensitive Succession," *New York Times*, 24 September 1973.

321 "I was very tired": *Johnson Tapes*, 175.

323 The plan was preposterous: On the Ellis Island plan, see Stern et al., *New York 1960*, 234–48.

324 "You won't mind if I don't believe you": On the Johnson office culture of the time, see Manley, interview with the author, 9 June 2010.

325 His campaign was animated: Jaquelin Robertson, interview with the author, 19 October 2010; Alexander Garvin, interview with the author, 26 August 2010; Robert A. M. Stern, interviews with the author, 13 April and 6 October 2010; and Stern et al., *New York 1960*, 92–5.

325 "When he speaks": MoMA Archives, Philip Johnson Papers, III.17.

326 His campaign strategy: Jaquelin Robertson, interview with the author, 19 October 2010.

326 "He made himself indispensable": Vincent Scully, interview with the author, 27 July 2010.

327 What the group produced: *The Threatened City: A Report on the Design of the City* (New York: Mayor's Task Force on Urban Design, 1967).

329 Most stinging was a rebuke: On the reception of *The Threatened City*, see Stern et al., *New York 1960*, 93.

330 *The New City*: CUR, Exh. #818. MoMA Archives, NY; Manley, interview with the author, 9 June 2010.

331 "Who cares?": John Wesley Cook and Heinrich Klotz, *Interviews with Architects* (New York: Praeger, 1973).

332 What Breuer proposed for Grand central: see Stern et al., *New York 1960*, 1138–43.

333 *The Island Nobody Knows*: On Johnson's Roosevelt Island plan, see *The Island Nobody Knows* (New York: Metropolitan Museum, 1969). Also Stern et al., *New York 1960*, 641–59.

Chapter 14: Towers and Power

338 Put Burgee in charge: Carter Manny, interview with the author, 4 April, 2010; John Burgee, interview with the author, 28 January 2011.

339 "Without John Burgee": Gerald Hines, interview with the author, 11 January 2011.

340 Sculpture interests me: Francine du Plessix, "Philip Johnson Goes Underground." *Art in America*, July-August 1966, 86–93. MoMA Archives, Philip Johnson Papers, I.93.

340 "Statement of aesthetic withdrawal": Jodi Hauptman, "Philip Johnson, MoMA's Form Giver." *Magazine of the Museum of Modern Art* 22, 1996.

343 Excitement was largely confined to Corpus: On the Museum of South Texas and the Rothko Chapel, see Welch, *Philip Johnson & Texas*, 66–8, 138–48.

344 The New York Five: Peter Eisenman, interviews with the author, 12 July and 3 August 2011; Michael Graves, interview with the author, 11 November 2010; and Richard Meier, interview with the author, 19 October 2010. See also *Five Architects* (New York: Wittenborn, 1972; the second edition, with Johnson's postscript, was published by Oxford University Press in 1975).

344 "Five on Five": "Five on Five," *Architectural Forum*, May 1973.

346 "I'll do whatever": Burgee, interview with the author, 28 January 2011. On IDS see also *Johnson Tapes*, 176–7.

348 Jumble of ice cubes: Manley, interview with the author, 15 June 2010.

349 "Minus ten percent": Manley, interview with the author, 15 June 2010.

350 Hines's first impulse: On Hines, Liedtke, Brochstein, Post Oak, and Pennzoil, see Welch, *Philip Johnson & Texas*, 161–77.

352 "Yeah, *that's* it": Denise Scott Brown was convinced Johnson stole the profile from her partner Bob Venturi's landmark Mother's House, which also had a roofline of angled planes broken by a gap. There is no evidence to confirm that suspicion, though from certain angles they are reminiscent.

353 Attia told Johnson: Eli Attia, interview with the author, 11 March 2011.

353 "Synthesis of structure and style": Ada Louise Huxtable, "Pennzoil: Houston's Towering Achievement," *New York Times*, 22 February 1976.

354 A bottle of scotch: Paul Goldberger, interview with the author, 26 October 2011.

354 Goldberger's feature: Paul Goldberger, "Form and Procession," *Architectural Forum,* January/February 1973, 33–50.

354 Three-person exhibition: "Work in Progress: Architecture of Philip Johnson, Kevin Roche, Paul Rudolph" (exhibition brochure). CUR, Exh. #940. MoMA Archives, NY.

355 Johnson worked through: On the museum-expansion plans, see Reed, "The Space and the Frame," in *Philip Johnson and the Museum of Modern Art,* 70–103.

357 "What did they expect?": Johnson, Museum of Modern Art Oral History, 108.

359 The story of how: On the making of AT&T, see the indispensable Craig Unger, "Tower of Power," *New York Magazine,* 15 November 1982.

360 Doubling down: Burgee, interview with the author, 28 January 2011.

360 Irritated Johnson: Manley, interview with the author, 30 June 2010.

361 "First major monument": On the history and reception of AT&T, see Robert A. M. Stern, David Fishman, and Jacob Tilove, *New York 2000: Architecture and Urbanism Between the Bicentennial and the Millennium* (New York: The Monacelli Press, 2006), 493–502.

364 Went in together: They were initially joined by a third team member, Gianfranco Franchini.

364 "Sex, food, and art": Mary Blume, "Philip Johnson and Les Halles," *International Herald Tribune,* 10 May 1980.

365 "Monumental demonstration": Ada Louise Huxtable, "Philip Johnson: Clever Tricks or True Art," *New York Times,* 16 April 1978.

365 "The blameless dead": Michael Sorkin, "Philip Johnson: The Master Builder as a Self-Made Man," *Village Voice,* 20 October 1978.

366 "A straight cash arrangement": The letter is reprinted in *Johnson Tapes,* 186–7.

367 "Johnson did not create": Robert Hughes, "Doing Their Own Thing," *Time,* 8 January 1979. Johnson appeared on the cover.

368 "See that building there": Ian Volner, *Michael Graves: Design for Life* (Hudson, NY: Princeton Architectural Press, 2018); Graves, interview with the author, 11 November 2010.

Chapter 15: The Head of the Circle

369 "I do not believe": Jaquelin Robertson, *The Charlottesville Tapes* (New York: Rizzoli, 1985), 15.

370 "Sense of pressure": Myron Wright to Michael DeBakey, 24 January 1975. GRI, box 26.

370 "Let's not get rushed": Burgee, interview with the author, 28 January 2011.

370 Successful double-bypass: Schulze, *Johnson,* 335–6.

371 "It was always a toe dance": Burgee, interview with the author, 28 January 2011.

372 Invited him to stay: Attia, interview with the author, 11 March 2011.

372 As Attia would have it: Johnson, letter to whom it may concern regarding Eli Attia, 4 February 1993; Eli Attia to Philip Johnson, 1 March 1993; Johnson, open letter regarding Eli Attia, 1 March 1993. GRI, box 21.

373 "I have only one question": Burgee, interview with the author, 28 January 2011.

374 "An imaginary museum": On the reception of the Crystal Cathedral, see MoMA Archives, Philip Johnson Papers II.4.

374 "If this is not": Paul Goldberger, "Architecture: Johnson's Church," *New York Times,* 16 September 1980.

376 "Not innocent": *Philip Johnson/John Burgee: Architecture 1979–1985* (New York: Rizzoli, 1985).

376 Burgee was furious: Burgee, interview with the author, 28 January 2011. Attia explained it thus: "Kalikow invited me to participate in a competition that they were having for a building on Park Avenue, and I did and I won the competition. And I called Philip and at that moment he stopped talking to me." Attia, interview with the author, 11 March 2011.

377 "It was the first time": Pat Hackett, ed., *The Andy Warhol Diaries* (New York: Twelve, 1989), 305 (3 July 1980).

377 "As soon as Philip": *Warhol Diaries,* 551 (4 December 1983).

377 "Pops pops off": *Warhol Diaries,* 706 (24 November 1985).

377 "I wish you to be": Johnson to Burgee, 1 October 1985. GHA, Whitney files, Johnson folder.

383 "It was all very male": Jaquelin Robertson, introduction to *The Charlottesville Tapes,* 6–11.

383 The inquisition that followed: *Charlottesville Tapes,* 14–19.

385 "Philip: Here's a building": Michael Sorkin, "A Bunch of White Guys (And Three Japanese) Sitting Around Talking or The Three PPP," *Design Book Review,* Spring 1986. Reprinted in Sorkin, *Exquisite Corpse: Writings on Buildings* (New York: Verso, 1991), 166–70.

385 Attempted to blackball him: Century Association Archives, New York, Johnson file.

386 Over a lunch: Meier, interview with the author, 10 October 2010. See also Richard Meier Office Archives, New York, Century Club and Johnson files.

386 "The head of the circle": Graves, interview with the author, 11 November 2010. See also interviews with Meier, 10 October 2010 and Stern, 25 April 2009 and 6 August 2010.

389 David Dillon wrote: "The Crescent: Dallas' Newest, Glitziest High-Rise Promises Us a Great Building, But Does It Deliver the Goods?," *Dallas Morning News,* 30 March 1986.

389 The faculty was opposed: Welch, *Philip Johnson & Texas,* 206–17.

390 "He never really meant it": Burgee, interview with the author, 28 January 2011.

391 Born in Lahore: Raj Ahuja, interview with the author, 12 August 2010.

391 "You talk and I draw": Ahuja, interview with the author, 12 August 2010.

392 "The Iran disease": Robertson, interview with the author, 19 October 2010.

393 A man out of place: Ahuja, interview with the author, 12 August 2010; Vidya Preya, interview with the author, 25 August 2010; Manley, interviews with the author, 15 and 30 June 2010.

395 885 Third Avenue: On the Lipstick Building, see Stern et al., *New York 2000,* 530–2.

396 "The idea is not merely": Carter Wiseman, "Brave New Times Square," *New York Magazine,* 2 April 1984, 28–39.

397 It was a demonstration: On the reception of the Johnson Times Square proposals, see Lynne B. Sagalyn, *Times Square Roulette: Remaking the City Icon* (Cambridge, Mass.: MIT Press, 2001) and Stern, et al., *New York 2000,* 94–8, 683–90.

Chapter 16: Things Fall Apart

399 That party went on: Schulze, *Johnson,* 3.

400 "I'm tired": Burgee, interview with the author, 28 January 2011.

401 "Everything about this": "Architect's Retreat," *Architectural Forum,* July 1983.

403 A lot of weed: Frank Gehry, interview with the author, 15 June 2011.

403 "I don't know why": Lincoln Kirstein to Johnson, 12 September 1982. GRI, box 21.

406 "First it has become clear": Memorandum from John Burgee to Johnson, 15 April 1988. GRI, box 21.

407 "His contribution": Drexler, quoted in MoMA Archives, press release, 3 April 1984.

407 "The Museum is the most": Johnson, Museum of Modern Art Oral History, 95.

408 "However delicious": Johnson, introduction to *Deconstructivist Architecture* (New York: Museum of Modern Art, 1988), 7.

409 The theme was in the air: Johnson, *Deconstructivist Architecture,* 9; CUR, Exh. #1813. MoMA Archives, NY; Johnson, Museum of Modern Art Oral History, 92–5; Michael Sorkin, "Canon Fodder," 1 December 1987 and "Decon Job," 5 July 1988, both in *The Village Voice*; and Joseph Giovannini, "A Note on the Genesis of Architecture Unbound" (unpublished ms.).

410 "It is the ability to disturb": *Deconstructivist Architecture,* 10.

410 "What is truly challenging": Herbert Muschamp, "The Leaning Tower of Theory," *New Republic,* 29 August 1988.

411 "Not an application": *Deconstructivist Architecture,* 11.

412 What the two drummed up: Sagalyn, *Times Square Roulette* and Stern et al., *New York 2000,* 694–8.

413 "Abysmal": Herbert Muschamp, "For Times Square, a Reprieve and a Hope for a Livelier Day," *New York Times,* 6 August 1992.

414 "We should have let him": Mitchell Pacelle, "Noted Architect's Firm Falls Apart in Fight Over Control, Clients," *Wall Street Journal,* 2 September 1992; Ahuja, interview with the author, 12 August 2010.

414 "This was a real double cross": Burgee, interview with the author, 28 January 2011.

415 The Judgment: Pacelle, "Firm Falls Apart." Ahuja's lawyer, Donald L. Kreindler, claimed the sum was closer to $16.5 million, including interest. See "Two Gentleman Part, Was It Really Hubris?," *Wall Street Journal,* 5 October 1992 (letters to the editor from Herbert L. Curtis Jr., and Donald L. Kreindler).

417 "As a foreigner": Johnson, "Berlin's Last Chance—Schinkel, Mies van der Rohe—Now What?" MoMA Archives, Philip Johnson Papers, I.123 (13 June 1993).

417 According to Burgee: Burgee, interview with the author, 28 January 2011; Peter Eisenman, interview with the author, 3 August 2011.

418 "As you know": Johnson to Peter Eisenman, 22 February 1983. GHA, Whitney files, Eisenman folder.

419 "Where Was Philip?": Michael Sorkin, "Where Was Philip?," *Spy*, October 1988.

419 "Jerusalem awaits": Johnson, "An Open Letter to Teddy Kollek," *New York Times,* 26 February 1971.

420 "Personally I think": The letter was discovered by architectural historian Rosemarie Haag Bletter. See Martin Filler, "Philip Johnson," in *Makers of Modern Architecture,* vol. I: *From Frank Lloyd Wright to Frank Gehry* (New York: New York Review Books, 2007), 147.

420 "Brother-sister act": Rosamond Bernier, interview with the author, 12 November 2010.

421 "With no word of warning": Bernier to David Whitney, 17 November 1993. GHA, Whitney files, Johnson folder.

421 "The world's dullest man": Kurt Andersen, "Philip the Great," *Vanity Fair,* June 1993; Gerald Hines, interview with the author, 12 January 2011.

422 "I'm not in there": Johnson, Museum of Modern Art Oral History, 119–21.

422 "In the biography": Paul Goldberger, "The Man in the Glass House," *New York Times Book Review,* 27 November 1994.

Chapter 17: The Irresistible Allure of the Fantastic

425 "Johnson's faults": Herbert Muschamp, "A Man Who Lives in Two Glass Houses," *New York Times,* 17 October 1993.

425 "From your standpoint": Donald J. Trump to Johnson, 2 September 1992. GRI, box 21.

426 "Very Trumpish": William Geist, "The Expanding Empire of Donald Trump," *New York Times,* 8 April 1984; Manley, interview with the author, 14 July 2010.

426 Trump offered his philosophy: Julie Baumgold, "Fighting Back: Trump Scrambles off the Canvas," *New York Magazine,* 9 November 1992.

426 "Does everyone know Philip Johnson?": Baumgold, "Fighting Back."

427 Television City: On the saga of Riverside South, see Stern et al., *New York 2000,* 826–38.

427 On that trip: Manley, interview with the author, 14 July 2010.

427 "Refinement was never": Herbert Muschamp, "Going for Gold on Columbus Circle," *New York Times,* 19 November 1995.

428 "Ladies and gentlemen": Donald J. Trump, Toast to Philip Johnson, New York Preservation Award Ceremony, 20 October 1994. GRI, box 34.

428 Johnson was flabbergasted: Manley, interview with the author, 14 July 2010.

428 "After thinking for some time": Johnson, fax to Donald J. Trump, 25 July 1995. Trump's reply was handwritten on Johnson's missive and faxed back in return. GRI, box 2.

429 "Glitz packaged as class": Muschamp, "Going for Gold."

430 "Johnson long ago perfected": Muschamp, "Two Glass Houses."

431 "Radically novel": Muschamp, "A 'Monster' of a Masterpiece in Connecticut," *New York Times,* 17 September 1995.

432 "Bold International Style": Song by Christopher Mason in honor of Johnson's ninetieth birthday. MoMA Archives, Philip Johnson Papers, VI.4.

432 "There is something I want to say": There are alternate versions of Whitney's toast that are more lewd.

434 "Sense of inertia": These cavils are rehashed in Robin Pogrebin, "Leaving His Mark on Design as He Leaves MoMA," *New York Times,* 5 November 2005.

435 Johnson had a harder time: On the dynamics of the late Johnson office, I am especially indebted to John Manley.

439 "It seems only fitting": Brad Gooch, "Mr. Johnson's Opus," *Out,* May 1996.

439 "I was attracted to him originally": Gehry, interview with the author, 15 June 2011.

440 "They resented the fact": Manley, interview with the author, 14 July 2010.

445 "During his recent hospitalization": Frank Gehry, birthday toast (nd). GHA, Whitney files, Gehry folder.

Index

Note: The abbreviation PJ refers to Philip Johnson. Italic page numbers refer to illustrations.

About the Author

MARK LAMSTER is the architecture critic of the the *Dallas Morning News* and a professor in the architecture school at the University of Texas at Arlington. He has won numerous awards for his work, and in 2017 was a Loeb Fellow at the Harvard Graduate School of Design. His writing has appeared in the *New York Times*, the *Los Angeles Times*, and the *Wall Street Journal*, among many publications. He is a native of New York City and now lives with his family in Dallas.